URBANISM AS WARFARE

EXPERTISE

CULTURES AND
TECHNOLOGIES
OF KNOWLEDGE

EDITED BY DOMINIC BOYER

A list of titles in this series is available at cornellpress.cornell.edu

URBANISM AS WARFARE

Planning, Insecurity, and the Remaking of Downtown Bogotá

Federico Pérez Fernández

CORNELL UNIVERSITY PRESS

ITHACA AND LONDON

First published 2025 by Cornell University Press

Librarians: A CIP catalog record for this book is available from the Library of Congress.

ISBN 9781501784767 (hardcover)
ISBN 9781501784774 (paperback)
ISBN 9781501784798 (pdf)
ISBN 9781501784781 (epub)

GPSR EU contact: Sam Thornton, Mare Nostrum Group B.V., Mauritskade 21D, 1091 GC, Amsterdam, NL, gpsr@mare-nostrum.co.uk.

Contents

URBANISM AS WARFARE

INTRODUCTION

In February 2012, commuters woke up to an unusual scene in downtown Bogotá. The city administration had closed off several blocks of the Carrera Séptima (Seventh Avenue) to create a makeshift boulevard for pedestrians and cyclists. The historic avenue, once a colonial icon known as the Calle Real (Royal Road), had been for decades a focal point of anxieties over urban decay. Lined with a mix of republican structures repurposed as cheap cafeterias, small casinos, and artisan markets, as well as modernist buildings housing state offices and financial institutions, the Séptima had been the central stage of downtown's unbridled vitality and deep-seated fractiousness. On a regular day, buses roared down the avenue spouting smoke and scooping up passengers, while street vendors and pedestrians navigated the clogged street amid a chorus of honking cars. But that February morning, a row of planter pots with stunted trees ran through the middle of the road, separating foot traffic from bikers. Pedestrians reclaimed the thoroughfare, somewhat disoriented, strolling along the temporary signs and plastic barricades. Street vendors, previously accustomed to fierce competition on congested sidewalks, suddenly found ample room for their dealings while making themselves increasingly visible for surveillance and control. The Séptima's newfound spaciousness and eerie calm showcased the city center's mounting transformations. It signaled downtown's long-awaited "revitalization," as was announced on a street-wide banner hanging at the end of the fifteen-block stretch, where the avenue met the city's main plaza, the emblematic Plaza de Bolívar.

Yet for many city officials involved in the project, much more was at stake than urban beautification. According to Félix, an urban designer working for the city administration, the conversion of the Séptima into an apparently innocuous pedestrian boulevard was ultimately a form of warfare. "We are at war," he confided to me as we talked in a small government office overlooking the northern edge of the city center, "and the war is about gaining territory." A public university lecturer, practicing architect, and longtime city consultant, Félix was far from being a security hard-liner. With his untrimmed gray hair and wool scarf, he was more of an urban intellectual, an urbanist, as his business card read. His career had revolved around public-space policies and regional planning, and he was now advising the leftist administration of Mayor Gustavo Petro (2012–15), a former member of the demobilized M-19 insurgency and four-time congressman since the 1990s. Despite his progressive leanings, Félix rendered a crime-inflected account of the spatial conflicts installed in downtown: "The issue with El Centro is that it's the city's most conflict-ridden space. Many interests converge here . . . criminal interests. The city's urban mafias are in El Centro. These are mafias that manage prostitution, gun trafficking, street vending, the homeless. They handle all that and they are embedded [*incrustadas*] in El Centro."

For Félix, criminality was at the core of local conflicts, a pervasive force that lurked behind even the most fragile spaces carved out by the urban poor. Mafias were materially embedded in the fabric of downtown, *incrustadas*, so that any attempt to rid the city of their presence required reconstruction. "The administration comes in," he continued in a matter-of-fact, almost professorial tone, "as just another actor struggling to recover territory." Even though the avenue had never been a criminal hotspot, the revitalization of the Séptima appeared as a highly symbolic and strategic action that cemented the gradual takeover of the city center. Félix recalled how the mayor himself had recently given him and a group of advisers marching orders: "Look, the only thing that I want with the plan to pedestrianize the Séptima is that we take over and secure the Séptima. This is a question of fighting, fighting for territory. As soon as we capture [*tomemos*] the Séptima we will move down to Eighth and Ninth Avenues, but we have to continue securing the area."

As striking as these words were for a leftist administration whose government program was called Bogotá Humana (Humane Bogotá), they also revealed the reach of security as a paradigm of urban intervention across the political spectrum. They offered a glimpse into the connection between the country's history of warfare and ordinary invocations of security in planning circles and on the street. As I listened to Félix, I wondered about the past insurgent militancy of the mayor and his ex-M-19 collaborators, and how it shaped their views of urban governance and their new roles as state officials. As if guessing my thoughts, and in a surprising gesture for an adviser to a demobilized *guerrillero*, Félix drew a comparison between the revitalization of the Séptima and counterinsurgency tactics. He recalled a planning workshop between local and regional functionaries, citing an official report that mapped the corridors used by guerrilla fronts in rural areas surrounding the city: "Previously, that [kind of knowledge] wasn't available, everyone used to simply say, 'The guerrilla is around' [*por ahí anda la guerrilla*]. [With the new study] we identified the corridors that connected Los Llanos [the eastern plains region] to other places, the areas in which they operated." Tapping on the table as if to refocus my attention, and then using his finger to draw invisible lines on the surface, he concluded his proposition about the metonymic relationship between Andean mountain passes and downtown streets: "These are territories, it's always an issue of territories, either at the macro, national, or regional level, or at the micro, urban level. It's always a problem of territories."

This was not the first time I heard narratives of violence and military control surface in descriptions of downtown Bogotá's transformations. As my research for this book progressed, I became attuned to the ways in which people invoked the language of security to make sense of and orient their actions within a changing urban landscape. Such speech acts revealed an underlying grammar of security that structured urban politics, planning practices, and the materiality of urban space.[1] In his remarks above, Félix conceptualized urban reconstruction as a matter of securing territory. He conjured a battleground, an urban terrain in which opposing factions struggled over state sovereignty. Planning literally emerged as the "continuation of war by other means."[2] Other experts went further in their tactical conceptions of urban design, focusing more deliberately on the form and material properties of the built environment—from the layout of streets to architectural appearance. They evoked what French cultural theorist Paul Virilio calls "military space" and its central problem of the "reduction of obstacles and distances."[3]

In following this thread of downtown renewal, I discovered the breadth and lability of security idioms, as well as their varied enactments in everyday urban life.[4] While planners mobilized affects and ideologies linked to national sovereignty and public order to articulate redevelopment projects, residents experienced and critiqued such interventions as forms of institutionalized violence. Many of them confronted the threat of eviction as a direct reflection of the country's entrenched conflicts over rural land and the widespread displacements these had caused. One owner who was facing eminent domain in a neighborhood slated for renewal put it best: "In the countryside they displace with guns; here in the city they do it with decrees." She had redeployed the language insecurity against the state, locating violence not in decaying street corners but at the core of bureaucratic logics. A community leader living in another downtown neighborhood elaborated further on these forms of bureaucratic violence. She called the use of zoning regulations and their gradual production of decline over the years "a dirty war." According to her, the prohibition of commercial and building activities had "finished off" the neighborhood, opening it to reconstruction and real estate speculation. Urban property also emerged in residents' accounts as a battlefield resembling the country's land-grabbing violence. For residents who had themselves experienced forced expulsion from the countryside and moved into dilapidated tenements and small shacks (*ranchos*) in the margins of the city center, urban renewal often appeared as just another, more sophisticated strategy of dispossession.[5]

This book is both about the remaking of downtown Bogotá and about the urban epistemologies through which the city is reimagined and rebuilt. It examines the ways in which broader social currents associated with struggles over sovereignty and belonging shape planning expertise and urban forms—from city spaces and bureaucratic artifacts to housing arrangements. I am concerned with how the imagery and lived experiences of insecurity make their way into the constitution of expert and non-expert knowledges about the city. If security and its criminal obsessions have become key organizing frameworks in the current era, then this book illuminates the long-standing and shifting entanglements between insecurity, urban knowledges, and the city's material form.[6]

The rise of contemporary counterterrorism and the fear-ridden and surveillance-infused spaces it has engendered in the North and South, East and West, are by now well established in the global urban imagination. This is what Stephen Graham calls the "new military urbanism": the city reenvisioned as a site of boundless warfare through an expanding array of technologies of control, defense, and disruption.[7] Although these portrayals usefully call attention to the insidious operations of security apparatuses in everyday urban life, they are primarily modeled after the cities of the global North and projected through the lens of the global war on terror.[8] Post-9/11 sensibilities take precedence here. They have structured a global common sense about planetary urban securitization and suffused the design and governance of urban space with the language of defensibility and resilience.[9]

In Bogotá, narratives of terrorism are undoubtedly relevant to securitized urbanism, yet they predate such global milestones and have been filtered through a range of understandings of danger associated with contests over sovereignty, military warfare, criminal violence, bureaucratic force, and economic dispossession.[10] This book explores this historically layered and differentially experienced landscape of urban (in)security. My analysis centers on the multiple and emergent meanings of security and their situated influences on individuals' knowledge practices as they seek to understand, transform, and inhabit urban space. In doing so, I show how the security-inflected composition of such epistemic forms is inextricably connected to deeper conflicts over the material fabric of urban governance and belonging.

In Colombia, the ideological effects of security discourses are wide-ranging and kaleidoscopic. Throughout the nation's string of post-Independence wars, decades of guerrilla and paramilitary warfare, and contemporary drug wars, security has proven to be a fundamental register in which national identities are forged and contested. Views of Colombian society as inherently insecure and inevitably prone to violent conflict have saturated public imagination through tropes of an essentialized and ahistorical "culture of violence."[11] Most revealing of the reach of security within national representations was the emergence in the late twentieth century of a distinctively Colombian intellectual tradition known as "violentology."[12] Although this tradition comprises a vast and heterogeneous body of social science scholarship, which produced nuanced accounts of the historical, political, and geographic dimensions of violent conflict, violentologists largely approached insecurity as an objective reality in need of expert diagnostics. Political violence and the country's armed conflict of the twentieth century were central to their work, overshadowing the intimate and quotidian cartographies of individual and collective insecurities.[13]

Moreover, as violentologists produced some of their key works under commissions created and funded by the state, their reifications of security became integral to projects of nation building and, ultimately, to the formation of a "nationalist epistemology" rooted in the violent conflict.[14] Such forms of knowledge not only exacerbated the conceptualization of violence as "an ontological reality of Colombian culture," as Myriam Jimeno puts it, but also reified processes of state formation and their spatial coordinates.[15] National identities were shaped by an enduring sense that insecurity originated primarily in the countryside as a result of the incomplete radiation of state power from the administrative center.[16] The imagery of guerrilla-infested jungles, isolated towns terrorized by paramilitary forces, and crime-ridden shantytowns dominated this geography of insecurity and reverberated with colonial echoes of a civilizing urban core and an unruly rural periphery. The city appeared as a bastion of order imperiled by the invasion of outside forces: of peasant migrations and forced displacements, rural warfare, drug violence, and criminality.

This book unsettles such spatial praxes of security by attending to the ways in which "security talk" has permeated planning expertise and citizenship practices in downtown Bogotá.[17] Security emerges in this context as a malleable and shifting vernacular through which urban actors stake claims on space and contest the meanings and everyday politics of urban governance.[18] Vernacularization here does not simply indicate the vertical flow of global ideas to local settings, but rather the dialectical constitution of epistemic frameworks.[19] It points to the urban habitus and material environments that mediate and are in turn produced by understandings of insecurity. Etymological variants of vernacular associated with domesticity, as in vernacular architecture, are particularly apt in this context. In this sense, residents' and planners' allusions to the imagery of warfare, crime, and territorial control are best viewed as integral to their modes of inhabiting the city. If building is already a form of dwelling, then the making of urban worlds in Colombia proves inseparable from the sedimentation of repertoires of insecurity.[20] Experiential and affective dispositions toward the country's securitized institutions and social spaces are inseparable from the knowledge and organization of urban space. This book tracks these modes of practical awareness as they are transposed into seemingly abstract and fixed epistemic forms. Furthermore, it shows how they are reified in the material qualities of city life, rendering buildings into battlefields, legal documents into artifacts of destruction, and property regimes into sources of danger.

Security, Planning, and Knowledge

From the medieval citadel to the geometric spaces of modernist cities, scholars have long recognized the security and defense underpinnings of city building. In his monumental treatise on the history of cities, Lewis Mumford went so far as to argue that "war and domination, rather than peace and cooperation, were ingrained in the original structure of the ancient city."[21] The figure of the military engineer, Mumford noted, was instrumental to the development of the destructive and ordering capabilities of baroque town planning. The invention of radiating streets from a central point meant "that artillery could command every approach"—it embodied a "military aesthetics . . . for the parade of power."[22] And perhaps nowhere was the technology of the grid more visible than in colonial Spanish America, where the fetishization of spatial form—the symmetrical organization of streets and elaborate design of facades—became integral to authoritative conceptions of urban order and security.[23]

Most famously, Baron Haussmann's emblematic renovation of nineteenth-century Paris became widely recognized as much for paving the way for modern capitalism and bourgeois aesthetics as for expanding military surveillance and control.[24] The ample boulevards built on the ruins of the rebellious Parisian slums facilitated both the flaneur's stroll and the circulation of police troops. Such spatial techniques, as further scholarship demonstrates, grew out of earlier experiments of pacification and control in colonial settings from Algeria and Morocco to Indochina and Madagascar.[25] Critics have followed the reverberations of securitized planning across imperial geographies and into the present.

Twentieth-century slum clearance schemes in New York and London, modernist utopias from Brasilia to Chandigarh, and contemporary mass evictions in Mumbai and Rio de Janeiro have all borne the imprints of this history. In his characteristically climactic tone, Mike Davis writes about the rapidly expanding cities of the global South as the "distinctive battlespace of the twenty-first century," with the "counterinsurgency-driven strategy of slum removal" reemerging as "Haussmann in the tropics."[26]

Far from presupposing an ontological link between security and the city, these accounts pose fundamental questions about knowledge-making practices: How is the urban realm made into a security issue? How do urbanites come to think about urban phenomena as security problems? What are the experiential bases and material implications of such epistemological orientations? Anthropological critiques of city planning offer a useful point of departure to consider these questions. In his ambitious study of French planning in the nineteenth and early twentieth centuries, Paul Rabinow examines the emergence of the "practices of reason" that constituted what came to be known as "social modernity."[27] He follows a loose network of colonial administrators and planners, "technicians of general ideas," to illuminate the construction of "society" as an object of knowledge and intervention.[28] Significantly, security emerges in his account as an essential component of what early French technocrats envisioned as a modern, regulated urban society. "Pacification policy," Rabinow argues, encompassed both discipline and welfare: military force, health, education, sanitation, roads, and markets. It "rested on the artful combination of politics and force" and was ultimately geared toward the "transformation of the socio-natural milieu into a healthy and peaceful environment."[29]

While Rabinow offers an illuminating genealogy of modernist planning and its relationship to security discourses, his main concern is with knowledge as a detached and abstract field. Insofar as urban knowledges appear primarily as "norms and forms," their situated enactments and on-the-ground modulations remain out of sight.[30] In the larger body of scholarship on modernist rationalities, similar issues come to the fore through the analysis of technocratic epistemology as vision.[31] Take for example James Scott's influential study of "high modernism" and its portrayal of state classificatory and planning schemes as constituting a unique mode of "seeing."[32] Epistemological optics emerge here as a tool of wide-ranging simplification and control whose power resides in its alleged transparency and transcendence. But taking at face value this "gaze from nowhere," to borrow Donna Haraway's famous phrase, occludes the material and pragmatic foundations of knowledge practices.[33] It overshadows other ways of knowing that are constitutive of urban experience, including the experiences of planners and experts.[34] Put differently, social science research on planning can easily mistake technocratic *claims* of visual mastery for actual practices. This results in portrayals that reinforce dichotomies between state and nonstate actors, expert and nonexpert knowledge. Technocrats are portrayed as disembodied agents removed from the everyday traffic of social life, while ordinary citizens are viewed as radically removed from expert practice.[35]

This book is partly aimed at dissolving this binary by shedding light on both experts' social praxis and non-experts' intellectual labor—that is, by showing that planning expertise is crafted as much in offices and boardrooms as it is in urban neighborhoods, and that everyday urban knowledge is produced both in homes and on the street and through quotidian engagements with technical documents and instruments. Adopting this perspective has direct implications for questions about security and urbanism. It entails tracing how experiences and understandings of security are enacted and distributed in the construction of urban worlds. The main issue in this regard is how security ideologies circulate and how they are *materialized* in the things and forms of everyday city life.[36]

Literature on urban neoliberalism and the rise of insecurity has emphasized these ideological mediations. From the securitized "rescue" of downtown Mexico City and the "pacification" of Rio de Janeiro's favelas to the policing of Cape Town townships and the criminalization of poverty in US cities, scholars have stressed the increasing confluence of urban development policies and security agendas.[37] This is what geographer Neil Smith famously termed "urban revanchism" in his analysis of gentrification and class and racial violence in the New York of the late 1980s and early 1990s.[38] But exactly what role do security frameworks perform in these urban processes? How do they refract modes of urban transformation? In his critique of public security and contemporary capitalism in Mexico and Brazil, John Gledhill offers a compelling account of the ways in which the "securitization of poverty" is central to strategies of urban governance and accumulation. According to Gledhill, the rendering of certain populations and spaces as threats to public safety has come to define neoliberal development in the region. The war on drug trafficking and criminality, Gledhill shows, slips easily into a war on the poor. Brazil's favela pacification policies since 2008 have made life for residents more insecure both in terms of greater vulnerability to criminal networks and racialized police violence and in terms of land speculation and market-driven displacement. In one revealing example from his work in Salvador da Bahia, Gledhill recounts how private security agents and off-duty police perversely stretched the meaning of favela pacification, forcefully evicting shantytown dwellers on behalf of real estate developers. Most significantly, he argues, the logic of securitization "distorted understandings of social life in favelas," portraying them as inherently disorderly and as requiring militarized control and an entrepreneurial makeover.[39]

Gledhill moves beyond analyses that conceive security only as a discursive formation integral to urbanism and state policy. Instead, he examines "how social situations shape the way that different kinds of social actors think about questions of security" and how they in turn shape their "behavior and subjectivities."[40] This approach illuminates the contradictory processes through which ideologies of security get woven into the urban fabric and entangled in everyday practice. At the same time, however, and despite his attention to how diverse actors shape and deploy security knowledges, Gledhill views contemporary security paradigms as essentially concealing the operations of global capital. He writes about the need to "peer through the smoke created by the securitization of poverty" to shed light on its "hidden agendas."[41] In this context, as in other critiques of neoliberal urbanism, security ideologies take on a rather narrow meaning as class-based sources of mystification. But conceiving security primarily as a smokescreen for real estate speculation and urban displacement leaves little space for considerations of the diverse historical and institutional settings in which security knowledges are forged and the different political agendas to which they are linked. Most problematically, it precludes fine-grained analyses of individual praxis— that is, of the experiential, affective, and semiotic dimensions of security ideologies as they are put into practice and materialized into built forms. Additionally, such views ignore the fact that residents themselves often critique certain uses of security as tactics of obfuscation geared toward displacement and speculation. This is precisely what Keisha-Khan Perry shows in her fine-grained ethnography of "black women's collective resistance against the violence of land evictions and displacement" in Salvador da Bahia.[42]

Rather than adopting a narrow view of security as a tool of misrepresentation used by planners and real estate developers, I am interested in the various ways in which security becomes constitutive of understandings of and interventions in urban space. A dialectic between actors' social locations and their epistemological commitments is certainly at work here, but it is not one that is based only on suppression and concealment. Instead the main issue is how contingent and situated experiences of (in)security are objectified and transposed into forms of knowledge about urban reality and its material embodiments. How are they reified into ideas about city life and, more tangibly, into things and forms? How and to whom do certain urban spaces emerge as inherently insecure, while others appear to create order and safety? Addressing these questions requires a study of security frameworks in all their plurality, within and beyond the confines of state institutions. More importantly, it involves a subtler tracking of the idioms, practices, and embodied experiences through which security knowledges are formed and projected back onto the urban world. At stake here is what Teresa Caldeira describes as the productive qualities of security narratives. In her pathbreaking work on urban insecurity in São Paulo, Caldeira carefully follows the circulation of the "everyday talk of crime," making a powerful argument about security narratives as epistemological forms that not only "produce certain types of interpretations and explanations" but also "organize the urban landscape and public space, shaping the scenario for social interactions."[43] In the São Paulo of the 1990s, discourses about crime constituted a critical medium for individuals to make sense of wide-ranging social realities such as poverty, inflation, police authority, citizenship, and urban transformation. They produced a "symbolic order," Caldeira argues, that had sociopolitical and material repercussions: most notably, the reproduction and legitimation of urban violence and spatial segregation.[44]

This book expands on these critical insights to explore the multiple and contradictory ways in which experiences and narratives of (in)security mediate urban plans, practices, and materialities. Rather than focusing on urban policing and crime, I adopt an oblique perspective through the lens of planning expertise, urban law and bureaucracy, and property.[45] In this regard, this book contributes to a growing anthropological literature that takes as its central objects of inquiry the various forms, practices, and effects of security.[46] Moreover, it builds on ethnographic work that explores the variegated urban realms that are shaped by securitization processes—from development and mobility to the environment—and follows recent calls to explicitly address the spatial dynamics of security at the urban scale.[47]

This shift in outlook is important for several reasons. First, looking beyond traditional security sites illuminates the scope and malleability of security thinking. Rather than presupposing the circulation and reproduction of a culture of (in)security, the main question here is how security ideas are assembled and recontextualized across multiple sites. In Bogotá, urban actors are constantly recalibrating repertoires of (in)security to make sense of and intervene in redevelopment processes. They stretch narratives tied to the historical and geographical registers of Colombia's armed conflict and its trials of nation building and anchor them to the interactional contexts of urban planning and renewal. Far from a coherent cultural formation, security appears as an unfinished category that individuals continually mobilize, resignify, and reenact. Adopting this vantage point thus allows for a more fine-tuned account of the ways in which security is brought into the composition of urban knowledges.

Second, focusing on planning practices and urban materialities allows for closer scrutiny of the relationship between security frameworks and sociospatial realities. While scholarly literature has emphasized the connection between urban insecurity and segregation, security frameworks can become entangled with a wide variety of spatial formations, from high-rise development and infrastructural networks to technologically infused spaces of surveillance.[48] Instead of presupposing an immanent relationship between security narratives and built forms, it is necessary to interrogate the mechanisms and practices through which social actors materialize repertoires of (in)security in different ways and contexts. Of critical importance, in this regard, is an analytical approach that, according to Lucy Suchman, Karolina Follis, and Jutta Weber, can account for both "the material and discursive infrastructures that hold the logics of (in)security in place, as well as the practices through which these logics realize their effects."[49] This requires attending to what Keith Murphy, writing about the anthropology of design, calls the "form-giving" practices through which people shape their sociomaterial worlds.[50] Rather than privileging urban materiality and its securitized effects and then assuming a correspondence with cultural forms or retroactively imputing agency to social actors or things, this perspective foregrounds the dynamic interactions between intentional human action, ideological mediation, and material forms.[51] It illuminates more clearly how planners, designers, developers, and residents mobilize security knowledges in their city-making projects, and, importantly, it brings into sharper relief the politics of urban securitization, in particular what Murphy describes as "the structures of accountability and responsibility that undergird social relations."[52]

Finally, this book is inspired by what Laura Nader famously called "studying up, down, and sideways" in her 1969 essay "Up the Anthropologist."[53] Although her intervention has been typically interpreted as a call to study the powerful, Nader was pointing to a more complex and integrated understanding of power relations across social realms—what she described as a "vertical slice."[54] For her this brought up both ethical and methodological questions about how, why, and from what locations a researcher studied what they studied. Building on these insights, I move vertically, but also horizontally, across social domains to grasp the power and epistemic relations and frictions that surround urban transformation. This entails the recognition of social actors' critical and self-aware knowledge-making practices and their overlapping affinities with scholarly critique. My aim is thus not to subordinate local understandings of urban life to the analytical lens of social theory and anthropology, or to carry out an exercise in demystification aimed at lifting the veils of misrecognition.[55] The following pages recount instead the uneasy yet generative encounters between ethnographic research and the parallel "epistemic jurisdictions" of urban experts and non-experts alike.[56] My research was directly informed by planners' analytical orientations toward urban space, policy implementation, and local socialities, including their frequent use of ethnographic methods in their professional work. Developers, property owners, and residents also developed their own theories and collected data, articulating sophisticated critiques of urban governance, insecurity, and material transformations. In this context, I became directly enrolled in contradictory knowledge-making projects ranging from community leaders' drafting of bureaucratic complaints and their documentation of neighborhood conditions to planners' organization of academic and policy conferences and the design and analysis of field research protocols. These tentative collaborations not only exposed the divergent locations and sociopolitical circumstances of urban knowledge production but also made apparent the "epistemic contingency" of my own project.[57]

Reflexive awareness—a central feature of the anthropology of expertise, as Dominic Boyer argues—is particularly relevant in the study of (in)security and its intersections with urban knowledges and practices.[58] Looking up, down, and sideways compels the recognition of the shifting nature of security ideologies, their situatedness, and their interactions with other logics of urban sociality. In short, it helps avoid the reification of security as a totalizing narrative and an overly coherent semiotic and material order. Capturing the conceptual slipperiness of security through lateral epistemic engagements is therefore important not only for analytical purposes but also for ethical and political reasons.[59] Representations of insecurity—scholarly and otherwise—ripple through social worlds, creating fear, criminalizing populations and places, and creating the conditions for more violence. They reproduce the "finer weave of terror," as Michael Taussig writes.[60] An approach guided by reflexivity and collaboration highlights instead the contingent and contextualized links between security, knowledge making, and sociomaterial life, allowing for more nuanced accounts and new political imaginaries to take shape.

Topographies of Urban Knowledge

This book is based on research conducted in the offices of city officials and developers, ruined and semiabandoned construction sites, and the living rooms and neighborhood stores of residents caught up in urban renewal struggles. My entrance into these circuits of urban knowledge and transformation was guided by my previous experience working in Bogotá's city administration in the early 2000s. This was a period in which Bogotá was making headlines for its innovations in urban governance under the leadership of Mayors Antanas Mockus (1995–97, 2001–3) and Enrique Peñalosa (1998–2000). Policymakers during these years focused on the so-called "construction" of urban citizenship and public space.[61] Social practices and interactions—what the city government named "culture of citizenship [*cultura ciudadana*]" with distinctly class-related and civilizatory overtones—became key objects of expert knowledge. The Mockus administration developed a range of communication strategies—from street mimes to artistic interventions—designed to interpellate city dwellers and compel their transformation into law-abiding, democratic citizens. Equally central to these experiments in "pedagogical urbanism" was the rebuilding of public space.[62] City parks, plazas, and sidewalks—the "environs in which one is a citizen," as a policy document put it—emerged as critical sites for the forging of "good citizen behavior."[63] As public-space policies gained more visibility during the Peñalosa administration, they also became more directly associated with policing tactics and spatial control. Crucially, the remaking of culture and spaces of citizenship emerged as both the inversion of and the alleged antidote to the country's purported culture of violence. Most striking to me, as a recent college graduate working closely with senior officials in city hall, was how the crafting of urban policy became intimately tied to broader understandings of national security and sovereignty.

Drawing on this background, I conceived this book as an ethnography of the constitution and materialization of urban knowledges and their wide-ranging political meanings. Upon my return to Bogotá in 2009 to launch the project, I initially focused on the site most directly associated with the production of urban expertise: Bogotá's Secretaría Distrital de Planeación (City Planning Department). As a technocratic space ostensibly shielded from the politics of everyday urban life, the Secretaría provided a unique opportunity to bring into sharper relief the opaque intersections between planning expertise and security ideologies. I gained full access to the institution in July 2011 and became embedded within a team of mid-level and senior functionaries responsible for revising the city's master plan, the Plan de Ordenamiento Territorial (Territorial Ordering Plan), or POT. For seven months, I followed experts in their quotidian activities and interactions. Part of my time was spent in the team's office, an open layout of modules where I was furnished with my own desk, chair, and landline. As planners became more comfortable with the idea of having an anthropologist in their midst, I became privy to everyday office routines, off-the-record debriefings, and casual exchanges. I also became a regular participant in the team's coffee breaks and lunches outside the office. Cafeterias and neighborhood restaurants proved key sites in which my "coworkers" shared some of their most critical perspectives about planning knowledge and institutions.

A significant portion of my time was devoted to attending official meetings between members of my adopted unit, senior planning officials, and other dependencies within the Secretaría. Meetings were typically held in the planning director's boardroom around a long, polished wooden table with leather-upholstered chairs, next to a large window overlooking the city. Introduced sometimes as a visiting researcher, other times as part of the planning team, I sat in the corner, notebook in hand, documenting the scripts and choreographies of technical meetings. Planners also dedicated considerable time to presentations in town hall meetings and policy conferences. This circuit of public exchanges constituted a critical site in which experts not only crafted but, more importantly, performed planning knowledge and its broader significance. Finally, as my research progressed, I conducted in-depth interviews with my immediate collaborators and with other planning officials and consultants, allowing for more reflexive commentary on the politics and practice of their professional work.

Carrying out ethnographic research at the core and interstices of Bogotá's Secretaría Distrital de Planeación evinced the subtle ways in which repertoires of security shaped bureaucratic routines and technical discussions. This was apparent in one of the focal areas of planners' efforts (and of my own research): the restructuring of the city's Plan de Ordenamiento Territorial. As much as the POT consisted of technical regulations to guide real estate and infrastructure development, it was also a critical site to reimagine state power and urban order. Making territory knowable and manageable was paramount to planners' designs and was intimately tied to their understandings of security. Far from representing a static backdrop for state intervention, territorial qualities and potentialities appeared as objects of intense scrutiny and debate within planning and policy circles. At the core of the revision of the POT was the creation of legal and technical frameworks to reenvision territory as a collection of building and population densities—what planners called urban densification (*densificación urbana*). Urban governance appeared as a matter of stimulating and harnessing the distribution of people, activities, and structures in space. If the planning frameworks of the late 1990s had focused on the creation of open spaces and corridors, experts redrafting the city's plan conceived of territory as dynamic and relational—a "volumetric terrain."[64] Following Stuart Elden, *territory* emerged as a "political technology" central to projects aimed at making the city governable and secure, and *terrain* as the material expression of such territorial practices.[65] Significantly, such calculative techniques were permeated with planners' situated knowledge of the country's histories of contested territorial sovereignty and sociopolitical conflict.

Tracking the production and materialization of densification policies and their entanglements with repertoires of (in)security led me to explore circuits of knowledge and practice beyond planning institutions. Downtown Bogotá became the focus of my study in 2012. Given the city center's position as a seat of official bureaucracy, a hub for cultural institutions and businesses, and a haven for working-class residents and popular commerce, downtown's social topography has been one of extreme proximity and friction. Its entrenched conflicts and symbolic weight as a stage of nation building and citizenship have made it a recurring target of state intervention and reconstruction. Since at least the 1940s, planners and designers have repeatedly called for the "renewal," "recovery," "revitalization," and "redensification" of downtown districts. Such plans were originally motivated by the rapid influx of rural migrants escaping violence in the countryside and the steady flight of middle- and upper-class residents to new affluent neighborhoods in north Bogotá. A downtown of overflowing commerce, bustling crowds, dilapidated tenements, and clandestine operations gradually encroached on the downtown of museums, stately buildings, and official heritage.[66] Renewal and densification plans—large-scale demolitions, displacements, and projects to attract middle-class residents—emerged as a siege on these insurgent geographies and forms of sociality.[67] Significantly, shifting repertoires of (in)security mediated planners' expert practices and residents' critical interpretations of urban transformation and shaped the material and aesthetic qualities of city spaces.

During 2012 and over the course of research trips in the following years, I explored how wide-ranging repertoires—from militarized warfare and land grabbing to bureaucratic violence and postconflict security—had been discursively and materially sedimented in downtown spaces. I followed city planners, project promoters, consultants, residents, and community leaders who had been involved or were actively engaged in some of the city center's emblematic renewal plans. It was in the performances and materiality of these encounters that security emerged as a crucial vehicle for the enactment and contestation of urban transformation: both a rationale for intervention and a medium for critique and dissent. Urban securitization appeared here not as a detached and technocratic affair, but rather as a process grounded in everyday experience, local knowledge, and the materiality of urban environments.

I moved primarily through three downtown districts—Las Aguas, La Alameda, and Santa Inés—and excavated local histories of reconstruction reaching back to the mid-twentieth century. Far from telling a story of singular events and representative places, I explored the spatially and temporally interconnected production and materialization of urban knowledges. Geological and archaeological metaphors seemed particularly apt in this context—in some cases quite literally, as when the ruins of an early twentieth-century bridge resurfaced in the 2000s during the construction of a pedestrian boulevard and as an adjacent block of houses and small apartment buildings were being expropriated and demolished for the development of high-rises. Sitting in disrepair behind a chain-link fence, next to an emblematic public space, and under the shadow of the new residential towers, the early twentieth-century remnant revealed a textured palimpsest of built forms and discursive layers.[68] At the core of this urban topography was the juxtaposition of fragments of urban security linked to visions of hygienist reform, sociospatial order, bureaucratic force, and property development.

From this perspective, downtown emerged not as a collection of discrete spaces but as the sedimentation of epistemic and material traces (chapter 1), and its transformations resembled tectonic shifts in which movements in one area had durable impacts on others. To parse these ruptures and continuities, I focused on the logics behind four renewal projects: the militarized planning and design of an emblematic city park in the late 1990s and early 2000s (chapter 2), the use of bureaucratic force and expropriation in two mixed-use developments launched in 2006 and 2010 (chapters 3 and 4), and the rise of models of inclusionary and participatory densification crystallized in an inner-city revitalization project put into motion in 2012 (chapters 5 and 6). I followed planners, designers, and experts who had crafted and negotiated these plans, from officials and developers staking claims in specific localities to investors and consultants shaping downtown imaginaries from the upscale neighborhoods of north Bogotá. Many experts had worked in several of these or related downtown projects, and they often moved fluidly between public and private institutions. Ultimately, urban professionals contributed to the creation and circulation of techniques and conceptual frameworks, shaping a distinct, if changing and contested, "ecology of expertise."[69]

In addition to analyzing policy documents, conducting in-depth interviews with key officials and consultants, and attending public meetings, during most of 2012 I became embedded within the planning team in charge of designing the city's first inclusionary renewal project. The official promoter of the plan was an elite, private university, the Universidad de los Andes, and the team comprised faculty and researchers from a range of disciplines. Here again, as in the Secretaría Distrital de Planeación, I became privy to official and informal planning practices. In contrast to city officials' fairly contained professional milieus, university experts moved between citywide regulations, neighborhood specificities, and the concrete aims and demands of the project. They produced multiple forms of knowledge about the area—financial, legal, ethnographic—and engaged in sustained negotiations and communications with residents.

In addition to inhabiting the worlds of these planners and experts, I also created lasting relationships with community leaders, property owners, and renters.[70] My research followed residents closely as they, too, engaged in the production and materialization of urban knowledge. This included attempts to contest and reinterpret opaque regulations and authoritative planning frameworks, as well as the production of alternative modes of knowing and city-making. Knowledge practices were thus far from homogenous, and they often reflected neighborhood fissures and conflicts. Some residents articulated forms of dissent that questioned the assumptions of planning expertise, others pragmatically pursued advantageous positions of negotiation, while others exploited renewal struggles to further their own political and economic agendas.

Taken together, however, Bogotá's waves of downtown renewal reveal changing security logics, from overtly militarized projects of spatial control, to the insidious operations of urban bureaucracy and law, to mixed-income housing and participatory development. Such transformations parallel Colombia's embattled transition from counterinsurgent warfare to the postconflict era. More broadly, they mirror global shifts from policing and militarism to "human security" paradigms that, as Paul Amar puts it, seek to "expand the notion of politics to reintegrate social justice and economic development."[71] But the emergence of new security frameworks, as Amar argues, constitutes not a linear progression but unstable amalgamations that are "intensely dynamic" and "contradictory."[72] Crucially, while militaristic and criminal narratives seem to have receded in the official scripts of Bogotá's downtown renewal plans, the specters of warfare have continued to reemerge as residents fight urban transformations and call attention to their underlying violences. This book's three main parts follow this contested submergence and reemergence of urbanism as warfare and its translation into the city's materialities. Urban knowledges mediate the constitution of material forms so that city spaces emerge as terrains of military control (part I), paperwork as a site of (para)state violence and opposition (part II), and housing as a landscape of progressive promises and covert displacement (part III).

A final note on my position within these topographies of urban knowledge: My research was marked by the sense of familiarity and discomfort afforded by my place within Bogotá's stark social stratification. As I am a white middle-class Colombian from north Bogotá, it was inevitable for my field counterparts to either assume my work carried a certain class politics or suspect where my true sympathies lay.[73] From the perspective of many policymakers and experts, ethnography and social critique were directly at odds with the technical and pragmatic exigencies of their work. Planners often assumed that I shared their technocratic ethos—particularly when they identified me with the many consultants working in the city government. At other moments, when my interest in power relations and the contingency of planning practices became apparent, our exchanges became somewhat strained. In my work with downtown residents and community leaders, the risk was to appear insufficiently critical of the alleged intentions and agendas behind urban renewal. Given my close ethnographic work with planners, developers, and experts—of which residents were aware—locals often pressed me to disclose my affinities. They worried that I might be too close to city managers and urban promoters, whom they viewed as irredeemable neoliberals (as they themselves often put it), elitists, or dishonest opportunists.

There was no obvious solution to these issues. Instead of limiting my study to any faction in Bogotá's renewal battles, I provided different people with nuanced portrayals of each other and of the processes in which we were all involved. To do this I relied on urban actors' knowledge and followed as closely as possible their critical engagements with and reflexive understandings of the city's circuits of expertise and material transformation. This was central to my work with urban planners, where their research and critical insights blurred into my own analysis. Yet there is no monopoly over urban expertise, and urban renewal is instructive of the ways in which local populations craft themselves into epistemic communities to articulate critiques of power arrangements and advance political claims. Many of my interlocutors in downtown neighborhoods had become specialists in planning law and surveyors of their own districts to engage in a politics of counterexpertise.[74] I followed closely these everyday practices of dissent as they recast the meaning of urban insecurity and rearticulated planning and city building practices. In every case, performances of knowledge materialized conflicting urban visions and forms. This book is thus also about ambivalent ethnographic collaborations and their critical place in the contemporary research of emerging urban worlds.

Throughout the book's six chapters, I excavate the city's epistemic and material layers from the mid-twentieth century into the present. Rather than being a rigid chronology, the narrative seeks to show the recursive nature of city making: the gradual and fractured processes of destruction and reconstruction on which actors ground their knowledges and political claims and which in turn feed back into projects of urban transformation.[75] This is what Alberto Corsín Jiménez describes as "the city as a problem of method . . . of designs, problematizations, and theories—in constant auto-construction."[76] In this regard, scholars have shown how urban informality and peripheral urbanism constitute modes of inhabiting and envisioning urban space that unsettle dominant urban epistemologies: the "slum as theory," in the words of Vyjayanthi Rao.[77] In downtown Bogotá, center and periphery comingle, and the lines that separate them are contested through disputes over the texture, aesthetics, and experience of urban space. In this sense, this book follows the shifting lines, traces, and voids left by processes aimed at peripheralizing the center and recentering the periphery. What emerges is an unruly repository of urban practices, knowledges, and materials—of epistemic spaces shot through with the country's pervasive registers of security. This is "a very messy kind of archive," as Rao argues, and one that is deeply processual and emergent. "As an evident, material archive," she perceptively notes, "the built environment of the city reveals as much as it conceals about the political and historical processes to which cities are subjected through time."[78] It is the contested production, destruction, and materialization of urban archives that is at the core of this book.

Chapter 1 begins by showing how urbanization in twentieth-century Bogotá became entangled with counterinsurgency and national security agendas. I revisit an emblematic event of downtown destruction in the late 1940s and its aftermath as the city center was becoming a key object of planning expertise and intervention. Reading this history against the grain reveals the critical ways in which security knowledges linked to militarism and territorial control were encoded in the recurring dialectics of destruction and reconstruction that have shaped modern Bogotá. In chapter 2, I follow these trajectories as they made their way into one of the city center's most momentous contemporary transformations: a project of large-scale demolition launched in the late 1990s for the construction of an expansive park known as Parque Tercer Milenio (Third Millennium Park). Drawing on research with planners and experts and engaging with scholarship on the affective and material qualities of space, I show how repertoires of militarized policing, risk management, and humanitarianism came together to render urban space into a terrain to be cleared and conquered.

Chapter 3 focuses on the shift from overt securitization and "spatial cleansing" to plans centered on bureaucratic operations and real estate development.[79] Based on fieldwork on one of Bogotá's first renewal projects of the twenty-first century, Manzana Cinco (Block Five), I turn to residents' experiences as they were being evicted in the name of the downtown recovery and development. In close conversation with work on bureaucratic materiality and legal geography, I examine emergent knowledge practices centered on juridical insecurities and materialized in official paperwork. The chapter shows how neighbors carved out an epistemic space to articulate critiques of renewal, recasting urban policy and property development as oblique manifestations of state violence and land grabbing. In chapter 4, I expand my analysis of local strategies of dissent, drawing on fieldwork with community leaders and city officials in a neighborhood targeted for infrastructural and real estate development through a plan known as Estación Central (Central Station). Contests over the aesthetics and value of urban property were at the core of local renewal conflicts, as neighbors questioned official representations of the area's history of decay. Drawing on their intimate knowledge of neighborhood dynamics, residents unearthed a very different story of decline and ruination. For them, government action—from zoning regulations to building codes—had been integral to the gradual erosion of built forms and land uses and to the expansion of property insecurities linked to criminal organizations and the violent misappropriation of land.

The last two chapters explore the apparent move away from securitized interventions through policies of urban densification and inclusionary revitalization. Chapter 5 takes the reader into the offices and boardrooms of city planners and developers and tracks the discourses and practices surrounding the revision of the city's Plan de Ordenamiento Territorial. It examines the rise of "densification" as a paradigmatic category of urban expertise, a political tool, and a framework to reenvision urban space. The chapter builds on the growing anthropological interest in design and what Lucy Suchman calls its "cultural imaginaries and micro-politics,"[80] and it draws inspiration from the "volumetric turn in political geography," as Franck Billé puts it.[81] Far beyond the two-dimensional surfaces of maps and blueprints, at stake here are urban epistemologies centered on the management of spaces and populations as three-dimensional assemblages. Tracing such forms of knowledge and their textured material projections reveals shifting regulatory and territorial practices, as well as the implicit reworking of notions of security and sovereignty through techniques of "territorial ordering."

In chapter 6, I return to downtown Bogotá to explore the on-the-ground practices and conflicts associated with inner-city densification. I draw on fieldwork with experts and residents who became involved in an ambitious participatory revitalization plan, Progresa Fenicia (Fenicia Progresses). In contrast to previous interventions that "emptied out" urban areas for spatial control and real estate speculation, the plan set out to reassemble local populations and structures to attract new residents while ensuring the permanence of existing inhabitants. Far from flattening urban space, the project aimed at harnessing—in an allegedly more inclusionary manner—the potentialities of a multidimensional urban terrain composed of heterogenous actors, uses, and material structures. Critical to these designs were modes of knowledge production aimed at making urban dwellers and their homes amenable to the physics and metrics of a particular conception of urban density—as a collection of entrepreneurial partners, floor areas, and land uses. Residents, for their part, controverted such epistemologies, drawing on the long-standing insecurities and conflicts that had permeated regimes of property and belonging.

This book ultimately calls attention to the politics entailed by the recursive nature of urban knowledge and material transformation. Social actors' epistemic engagements are inextricably bound to the unfinished and sedimentary character of cities—to their recurring processes of accumulation, accretion, and destruction. City making is always already a form of knowledge, and knowledge takes shape in the materiality of urban life. And because cities are the outcome of continual overlaying, erasure, and recomposition, epistemic frames resurface and get reencoded in new urban forms. These are not mere iterations, as Ann Stoler argues, but "partial reinscriptions, modified displacements, and amplified recuperations."[82] In Colombia's uncertain transition to a postconflict era, urban fragments and shards of knowledge are recomposed to create new openings.[83] But these new urban worlds, even in their most progressive incarnations as ruptures with the past, are still partially constructed with the materials and ideas of yesterday.[84] Similar processes are also at work, although often less visibly, in urban landscapes across the globe, where the echoes of older violences—racial, economic, ethnonationalist—reverberate in the sleek and glitzy spaces of rapidly gentrifying cities.[85] This book invites more encompassing reflections on the afterlife of (in)securities across historical trajectories and social contexts, and on their enduring cultural and material legacies in contemporary urban life.[86]

Part I

PLANNING
BATTLEGROUNDS

DOWNTOWN GROUND ZERO

In March 2009, excavations for the construction of Bogotá's Centro de Memoria, Paz y Reconciliación (Center of Memory, Peace, and Reconciliation) uncovered a vast burial site on the western edge of the city's historic Cementerio Central (Central Cemetery). The Centro de Memoria had been planned as a memorial, museum, and activist space dedicated to struggles for the historical memory of violence, accountability, and peace.[1] As construction work came to a halt and forensic archaeologists descended on the cemetery, the scale and significance of the mass grave became clear: It held the remains of more than three thousand anonymous bodies spanning a period between the 1820s and the 1970s. The discovery came at a time when the unearthing of mass graves (*fosas comunes*) across the country had become a powerful symbol of both the viciousness of Colombia's armed conflict and the elusiveness of a postconflict transition. But unlike the thousands of mass graves unearthed in remote towns terrorized by paramilitary, guerrilla, and state forces, this was a historic *fosa común* in the heart of the capital, linked to the very origins of Colombia's civil war.

The area where the burial site emerged—two large lots (Globo B and Globo C) to the west of the cemetery's stately mausoleums and tombstones—had been informally known as the Cementerio de los Pobres (Cemetery of the Poor). The overflowing bodies that did not make it to the main graveyard had been for years interred in six neoclassical columbaria, built in the mid-twentieth century, and their surrounding grounds. Importantly, the site had been the improvised grave for hundreds killed during one of Colombia's most emblematic events of political violence, El Bogotazo: an urban uprising in 1948 after the assassination of leftist Liberal leader Jorge Eliécer Gaitán that left parts of downtown Bogotá in ruins and marked the intensification of a period of widespread violence across the country—a period known as La Violencia (1948–58). By the end of the twentieth century, the entire area had been closed off, and bodily remains from the columbaria had been moved to the working-class Cementerio del Sur (Cemetery of the South). As a security guard told me in 2017, "They finally took the bones of the poor away."

The cemetery's recent history illuminates the difficulties of coming to terms not only with the afterlives of Colombia's armed conflict but also with its haunting presence in Bogotá's history of urbanism. In the late 1990s, then-mayor Enrique Peñalosa set out to demolish the two lots (Globo B and Globo C), including the columbaria, for the construction of a metropolitan park. By the end of the decade, the city government had razed the westernmost lot (Globo C), swiftly removing another vast collection of forgotten remains and creating a park tellingly named Parque del Renacimiento (Renaissance Park). The lack of any effort to identify the anonymous bodies and the absence of any acknowledgment of the history of violence that surrounded the mass grave—except for a small commemorative monument to Jorge Eliécer Gaitán hidden away at the very end of the park—epitomized a form of intervention that effaced the deep ties between contemporary urbanism and the country's long-running history of violence.

The other lot, Globo B, continued to fall into disrepair until the Mockus administration took the first steps to reverse its fate. In 2001, the city government painted large signs on the empty columbaria's facades that read "La vida es sagrada" (Life is sacred). The intervention was one of the many symbolic acts through which the administration enacted its calls—characteristically top-down and with civilizing overtones—for a citizen culture of nonviolence. Most significantly, it was a first move to "patrimonialize" the area and insert it into emerging discourses of memory and reconciliation.[2] In response to the mobilization of human rights and victims' organizations, the area was rezoned in 2005 as the Parque de la Reconciliación (Park of Reconciliation), a site for "the recovery of historical memory in the city of Bogotá."[3] In 2007, the city administration of Luis Eduardo Garzón (2004–7) commissioned renowned artist Beatriz González to carry out an art intervention on the crumbling columbaria. González created *Auras anónimas* (Anonymous Auras), a public artwork that involved the creation of nine thousand new gravestones displaying variations on an iconic figure of the armed conflict: carriers (*cargueros*) who transport the dead using plastic tarps, hammocks, and poles across war-torn villages and towns. The city administration would go on to back the creation of the Centro de Memoria, Paz y Reconciliación as well as the large-scale archaeological exhumation of the mass grave discovered at the construction site. The Centro de Memoria was finally inaugurated in 2012 during the Petro administration, just weeks after the start of peace negotiations between the Colombian government and the guerrilla organization Fuerzas Armadas Revolucionarias de Colombia (Revolutionary Armed Forces of Colombia), or FARC, in Cuba. The contrast with the neighboring Parque del Renacimiento—erected atop a mass grave and through the physical obliteration of historical traces—could not be starker.[4] The columbaria and its surroundings—which now included the Centro de Memoria and a landscaped park dedicated to historical memory and repair—emerged as a critical component of a larger official plan of urban memorialization named Bogotá, Ciudad Memoria (Bogotá, Memory City).[5]

But the opaque connections between trajectories of urban development and histories of warfare were far from resolved, as was made apparent by the latest conflict surrounding the columbaria turned art installation. With the reelection of Peñalosa as mayor in 2016, the four funeral pavilions became once again visibly abandoned. Overgrown with weeds, gravestones missing, and enveloped by yellow caution tape, the site now looked more like a ruin waiting to be demolished. And that was precisely what the administration was hoping to accomplish as it revived Peñalosa's old plan to build a second park on this remaining lot,

FIGURE 1.1.   Centro de Memoria, Paz y Reconciliación (right) and the abandoned columbaria (left). Photo by the author.

Globo B. But as city officials worked to bypass regulations limiting interventions in the area, in February 2019 the national government declared the columbaria and González's art intervention national heritage, mandating their restoration and preservation.

A debate ensued in major media outlets, with cultural critics and intellectuals celebrating the official decision to protect the "memory of all the people who were buried there from the very moment the Cementerio Central was built in the nineteenth century, including the anonymous victims of April 9, 1948 [El Bogotazo]."[6] González herself stressed the importance of the columbaria as "a place of mourning."[7] As she explained in an interview, "Colombia just went through a period of a very long war and practically every family in Colombia is mourning because of that conflict. We need to recognize that experience to give the country some peace and tranquility."[8] Peñalosa in turn questioned the value of both the structure and the art installation and accused "intellectual elites" of depriving residents of nearby working-class neighborhoods of a "sports park." Ironically, he also invoked the specter of violence in his response to the national government's pronouncement. In a vitriolic flurry of tweets, the mayor mocked artists and intellectuals who, he imagined, "will explain at cocktail parties in London and Paris how their work . . . expresses the horror of violence . . . [but who] will not say that leaving thousands of children and youth without a park causes drug addiction and violence."[9]

The Urban Residues of Warfare

While the dispute over parks and graves became a visible media spectacle through tweetstorms and news stories, the event pointed to a longer and deeper urban history: the ensconced entanglements between urban planning and warfare. Downtown Bogotá bears the marks of Colombia's history of political violence. Its streets and buildings, parks and plazas, have been materialized in the crucible of war. Far from being merely a stage on which conflict occasionally erupted, the city center has been forged out of knowledges, practices, and materialities intimately tethered to the country's long-running trajectories of violence and (in)security.

During the colonial era, cities in Latin America were held up as centers for the cultivation of order and advancement opposed to the allegedly unruly hinterlands. This is what Ángel Rama famously called the "lettered city": an urban ideal fashioned after baroque sensibilities and principles of rational and systematic knowledge.[10] After independence, nation-making projects, according to Rama, continued to portray "cities as civilizing nodes in a countryside capable of engendering only barbarism."[11] Yet the dream of modern civility and order was itself built on the logics of colonial and postcolonial violence. In Colombia, as Cristina Rojas argues, "the civilizing power of the nation's capital" not only reproduced extant social and racial hierarchies but also entrenched a geographical imagination in which the enlightened Andean highlands dominated the savage lowlands.[12] Urbanization was inextricably connected to the nation's violent and exclusionary projects of capitalist modernity.

Yet as with the forgotten graves of the Cementerio de los Pobres, the violence of urbanism has been continually submerged, displaced, and effaced in downtown Bogotá's transformations. As a layered accretion of fragments, this urban history has been "silenced" through power-laden narratives of urban civility and modernization, and literally paved over, demolished, and rebuilt.[13] Such processes, however, have never been smooth. They are "urban palimpsests," to use Andreas Huyssen's term, that are shot through with fractures and crevices.[14] They are catalysts of epistemic struggles and their attendant materialities: from planning expertise and its visions of territorial authority to grounded urban knowledges and their critiques of everyday insecurities and dispossession. In what follows, I illuminate two central aspects of this sociopolitical and material stratigraphy.[15]

First, far from scholarly and popular depictions that separate the urban from the rural and focus on violent struggles at the edges of sovereignty, I draw attention to how the logics of warfare have shaped the very heart of the capital city. While rural migration and violent displacement have long been recognized as critical forces in Colombia's history of urbanization, cities have been typically conceptualized as preformed spheres—havens of urbanity—at the receiving end of such processes. In this view, the city has only partially been molded by such trajectories, at best, or deformed and tainted by outside dynamics, at worst. Such is the case of well-worn narratives of cities besieged and occasionally invaded by criminal gangs, cartel violence, and armed groups. Excavating the making and remaking of contemporary downtown Bogotá reverses this line of thinking and blurs the boundaries between the city and the country. It reveals how the conflicts over sovereignty and land at the core of Colombia's rural war have been woven into the urban fabric. From this perspective, urban planning and development cannot be severed from the political economy of property in countryside, nor can urban governance and citizenship be disassociated from violent contestations over authority and belonging on the frontier. The city emerges here as a sign—inscrutable at times and manifest at others—of the violence of law, civility, and order integral to nation-making projects in Colombia and beyond.

This oscillation between the absence and presence of violence leads to my second main point: Downtown Bogotá is an urban landscape littered with the residues of war.[16] At stake here is what Yael Navaro, Zerrin Özlem Biner, Alice von Bieberstein, and Seda Altuğ have theorized as the "residuality of violence, its afterlife and spillover effects, its material and immaterial traces, and its ability to be inflicted in social and political relations."[17] This perspective calls for an analysis of the "reverberations of violence" across time and space that recognizes the critical mediation of both human action and imagination as well as stubborn materialities and sedimented traces.[18] Political violence and its "lingering effects" and shifting forms emerge in this sense from the interplay between knowledges, practices, and things.[19] The trajectories of downtown renewal in Bogotá show how urban planning and design have been imbricated with the country's histories of violence. As urban scholars have argued, cities are not merely the background on which human actors and collectives exercise violence. Rather, architecture, infrastructures, and the very things that make up urban worlds can themselves become privileged media for the articulation and propagation of violence and (in)security.[20]

As a form of expertise centered on physical space, planning has performed a key role in this context, and not only in terms of instrumentalizing the built environment in contests over territorial control. In Bogotá, I argue below, planners have regularly reified urban materiality as both the cause of and the solution to sociopolitical conflict and insecurity. In doing so, they have both obfuscated political accountability and partially erased the sociomaterial contours of entrenched warfare. In this sense, planning has at once enabled and occluded what anthropologist Manuel Delgado calls "urbanistic violence": the interconnected violence of urban planning, real estate, and finance.[21] At the same time, the contentious remains left behind have continually resurfaced in urban dwellers' daily experience, shaping critical urban knowledges and modes of political engagement. This chapter explores some of the fault lines of downtown Bogotá's transformations since the mid-twentieth century. I aim to bring together histories that are often kept apart: the trajectories of city planning and its projects of urban reconstruction, on the one hand, and broader patterns of political violence and social mobilization, on the other. Putting these narratives in the same frame and locating them in the materiality of urban space sheds light on the elusive yet enduring force of violence and insecurity in the making and remaking of the city center.

I begin with El Bogotazo, that critical event of urban destruction in the 1940s that became a foundational myth in modern Bogotá and a milestone in the history of political violence in Colombia. While much has been written about the episode—primarily as an explosive fracture of the body politic and of the city's sociospatial structure—I explore El Bogotazo as part of an ongoing struggle over urban sovereignty shaped by national and global security currents, from Colombian class and land warfare to Cold War imperialism. The chapter then follows the lasting yet submerged aftereffects of such urban battles through an analysis of planning policy and insurgent urbanisms between the 1960s and 1970s. I turn here to urban development and inner-city densification plans and their clash with a landscape of housing activism and struggles. My aim is to draw attention to the entanglements between progressive planning and counterinsurgency tactics supported by the US Alliance for Progress program during those decades. Finally, I conclude with an exploration of Colombia's rising security state in the late 1970s and 1980s and its close links to a downtown shaped by military repression, urban protest, and violent destruction. I focus on an unfinished renewal plan and the ruined landscape it left behind. The razed area, which has remained barren for decades, mirrored the state, insurgent, and criminal violence that erupted in Bogotá during these years and would continue to haunt residents' imaginations and officials' interventions for the years to come. At stake here, as in the other plans detailed in this chapter, was the materialization of state security anxieties and the ongoing efforts to cement officialdom in the space of downtown Bogotá.

Counterrevolutionary Urbanism

The traces of the urban destruction of April 9, 1948—a date that is fixed in Bogotá's memory perhaps like no other—can be adumbrated in the streets and walls of the city center. In addition to the thousands that were killed that day, one of the casualties of the violence following the assassination of Jorge Eliécer Gaitán was the city's old streetcar (*tranvía*). The streetcar had been constructed in the late nineteenth century and became a vital connection between the city center and Bogotá's expanding working-class neighborhoods. As the multitude took to the streets during El Bogotazo, lynching Gaitán's alleged murderer and unleashing their fury on official buildings and commercial establishments, several streetcars were also burned and damaged. Almost immediately after the events, newspapers and officials rushed to declare the death of the streetcar with alarmist reports about the extent of the damage. Yet as historian Jacques Aprile-Gniset documented in his essential work on the urban impacts of El Bogotazo, the number of streetcars destroyed was modest by most counts. Most importantly, the streetcar had already been the target of a concerted "offensive" led by politicians, local media, and the private sector since at least 1947.[22] As a municipal transit system that provided a relatively efficient and affordable service, it had become a roadblock for the profitable and rapidly growing business of private urban buses. According to Aprile-Gniset, there is evidence to suggest not only that some of the attacks may have been carried out by employees of private bus companies but, most importantly, that the demise of the streetcar actually gained momentum after El Bogotazo.[23] Through disinvestment and the removal of key transit nodes in the city center, along with the stimulation of bus imports from the United States and the creation of new bus routes, authorities and politically connected operators effectively dismantled the streetcar in the years that followed.

Parts of this history can be pieced together going back to the Séptima, downtown's main artery. Although the city moved quickly to pave over the streetcar infrastructure in 1950, some rails remained visible at the intersection where Gaitán was shot. With the 2012 transformation of the avenue into a pedestrian walkway, other stretches of the railway emerged. The revitalization project itself was mired in delays, cost overruns, and difficulties associated with the protection of archaeological remains—in addition to the streetcar rails, other colonial and republican vestiges such as old piping, wells, and cobblestone surfaced during the process.[24]

As the project dragged on, anxieties mounted. By 2017 the improvised planter pots that the administration had used to close the avenue were gone, and construction work was in full swing. One afternoon that year, I took pictures of recently uncovered rails to the north of the Avenida Jiménez, only to be turned away by a site manager, who, visibly uncomfortable, pulled up a green tarp and declined to comment on the project's progress or the fate of the rails. It was only in 2021 that the roughly fifteen blocks of the pedestrianized Séptima were completed. Significantly, the final design included an "open air museum" in the first section of the walkway. Through thick and opaque windows on the sidewalk, passersby could now see the shadowy remnants of the railway. A slab in between contained a map etched in stone of the tranvía system in 1933 and a description of its importance for working-class neighborhoods (*barrios obreros*). All this stood only two blocks away from an older memorial to Gaitán on the wall next to which he had been murdered; the memorial featured his image above stone plaques commemorating his death and a lengthy passage from one of his momentous speeches.

The juxtaposition of these residues—the memorial of the political martyr next to the obliterated infrastructure—gestured to the deeper currents of violence before, during, and after El Bogotazo. The popular insurrection, on the one hand, was about more than the death of Gaitán. It pointed to the sustained onslaught of working-class spaces in the city center and growing partisan violence under the Conservative national government. The urban transformations that preceded and followed El Bogotazo, on the other hand, were not simply about modernizing and reconstructing downtown. They constituted counterrevolutionary plans, with distinct class and racial overtones, aimed at purging the city center of its unruly crowds at a time of rising US imperialism in Latin America. Like the demise of the streetcar, large-scale demolition and reconstruction in downtown

FIGURE 1.2.   Ruins of El Bogotazo in downtown Bogotá, a few blocks from where Jorge Eliécer Gaitán was assassinated. April 10–11, 1948. Photograph by Sady González. Archivo Fotográfico 1938–1949. Colección de Archivos Especiales. Sala de Libros Raros y Manuscritos. Biblioteca Luis Ángel Arango.

Bogotá from the 1940s through the 1960s tell a story about planning violence deployed against the urban poor and aimed at expanding elite control over urban land and capital.

These broader conflicts have been typically occluded in historical narratives about El Bogotazo. Accounts of the uprising are rife with images of maddened masses and indiscriminate destruction. Yet the multitude's actions that day were far from arbitrary. The multitude was a "political crowd [*muchedumbre política*]," as Medófilo Medina puts it, that blurred the boundaries between mob violence and revolutionary action.[25] The destruction of bureaucratic and luxury artifacts took on particular significance from the beginning of the upheaval. Downtown streets became littered with mounds of official documents and typewriters, office desks and chairs, and burning merchandise.[26] As one protester screamed, "We have come here to destroy, to end everything, not to steal!"[27] The uprising would then besiege the city's official architecture. It targeted the presidential palace, Congress, national ministries, and the palace of the archbishop, among other buildings. Ultimately, the crowds had aimed to overturn the city's social and political order by "systematically destroying the symbols of power, inequality, and exclusion that had once been so easily accepted," as historian Herbert Braun writes.[28]

Yet perhaps nothing illustrates the deeper significance and reverberations of El Bogotazo than the presence that day in downtown Bogotá of two central figures in Latin America's revolutionary and counterrevolutionary history: Fidel Castro and George Marshall. A young Castro traveled to Bogotá that April, eleven years before the Cuban Revolution, as the organizer of a Latin American student conference against imperialism. Castro and student representatives met with Gaitán days before his murder, and they were supposed to meet with him again on the fateful afternoon of April 9. While Castro was walking to the appointment, El Bogotazo erupted, and he swiftly joined the multitude as protesters stormed a police division to seize weapons.[29] Now armed and on the front line of a nascent urban insurgency, Castro took part in the urban combat that followed until a truce was reached by the Liberal and Conservative Parties the next day. Recounting his experience during El Bogotazo decades later, Castro recalled the hours he spent as the only foreigner barricaded with insurgents in a police division waiting for an assault by the army that never happened. At some point he questioned his place in the uprising, but then he had an "internationalist thought," as he put it, and decided to stay in the struggle, realizing that "the pueblo here is the same as the pueblo in Cuba, the pueblo is the same everywhere, this is an oppressed people, an exploited people."[30] Witnessing firsthand "the spectacle of a popular revolution," Castro reflected, had a definitive impact on his political consciousness.[31] "Revolutionary sentiments" had gained material and historical concreteness during El Bogotazo. Significantly, this was a battle waged both in the geopolitical register of hemispheric imperialism and in terms of control and conflict over the city itself.

This dual nature of urban warfare was further evinced with the visit of US Secretary of State Marshall to Bogotá that same week of April. A few blocks from where Gaitán was shot, Marshall was presiding over the ninth International Conference of American States, or Pan-American Conference, an event that led to the creation of the Organization of American States and the expansion of anti-Communist military doctrine in the region. Here again, imperialist designs took form in the space of downtown Bogotá and would continue to shape the social and material contours of the city center in the decades to come.

The positioning of Colombia as a leader of hemispheric cooperation under the aegis of the United States was already visible by the mid-1940s, when authorities launched urban beautification projects in Bogotá in preparation for the conference. Large-scale restoration, demolition, and infrastructure projects, according to Aprile-Gniset, generated "durable speculation and the aggravation of the living conditions" of downtown residents, and particularly of its working-class inhabitants.[32] In some respects, this was the continuation of plans launched in the early 1930s, some of them with hygienist overtones, such as the "cleaning" (*saneamiento*) of the Paseo Bolívar, which led to the displacement of hundreds of residents from impoverished settlements on the eastern hills of the city center.[33]

By the late 1940s, the wide-ranging urban interventions for the Pan-American Conference were more firmly grounded in the tenets of modernist planning.[34] They included the expansion of avenues, the removal of traditional markets, and the construction of mid- and high-rise buildings. These reforms made deeper inroads into downtown's working-class neighborhoods (*barrios populares*), ravaging the areas where many of Gaitán's followers lived and worked. Displacement and rising costs of living provoked unrest and catalyzed vigorous opposition well before the Pan-American Conference and El Bogotazo took place. Residents filed lawsuits against the city administration to counter evictions and increased taxes associated with beautification projects. In some cases, protests turned violent, as in one episode in 1947 recounted by historian Micah Oelze, where people rioted in front of the presidential palace after the government demolished several downtown houses. At least one man fired a shotgun at the state building.[35]

Most famously, Gaitán summoned a march on February 7, 1948, to protest increasing state violence in the countryside under the Conservative government of Mariano Ospina Pérez. Known as the Marcha del Silencio (March of Silence), the mobilization brought nearly one hundred thousand people to the streets of downtown Bogotá. In absolute silence and holding black flags, the crowd streamed into the Plaza de Bolívar for Gaitán's speech and then returned solemnly to their homes.[36] It was a demonstration of the power of the political mass and of the grievances simmering under the city's recently embellished surface. As a grassroots leader explained years later, this was the kind of "silence that could later transform into a storm."[37] Arguably, the protest had been directed against both state violence in the countryside and urban deprivation and expulsion. In this sense, the years leading up to El Bogotazo illuminated the layered nature of the city's conflicts. Thousands of migrants arrived in Bogotá fleeing rural violence only to encounter renewed displacement under urban modernization plans linked to the rise of Cold War imperialism. Not surprisingly, Marshall was quick to blame the events of El Bogotazo on a Communist conspiracy, an accusation that was picked up by President Ospina Pérez and disseminated in the media.[38]

Counterinsurgency and post-Bogotazo plans melded in the following years. The uprising had invigorated ongoing infrastructure and property-development projects as matters of national security. Experts and officials seized on the episode of ruination to accelerate their aggressive plans of reconstruction and expulsion. Media and authorities magnified the extent of the destruction to justify the need for the radical reconstruction of the city center.[39] Architects who had long decried the backwardness of peasant markets and downtown tenements went so far as to celebrate the riots, declaring that "Bogotá's urban problem . . . had been frankly cleared and partially resolved."[40] With the ashes of El Bogotazo still settling, one columnist applauded the administration's ambitious reconstruction plans, calling for the creation of a city that would be "more beautiful, more welcoming, and more secure and protected against the possibility of horrors such as those of the black Friday [of April 9]."[41] The built environment became the central target and medium for the expansion of state power and for a full-scale "business offensive."[42]

One of the most significant projects of urban control and speculation was the construction of the Carrera Décima, a forty-meter-wide and eight-kilometer-long avenue. The avenue cut through the heart of the city, displacing thousands of residents and severing the west side of the city center from the administrative and cultural districts of the east side. The Carrera Décima became Bogotá's "road to modernity," concentrating most of the city's new developments and architectural innovations.[43] At the same time, it proved to be a strategic space for the deployment of security forces. Mirroring the nation's larger efforts to develop

FIGURE 1.3. Military groups march along the partially inaugurated Carrera Décima. 1953. Photograph by Saúl Orduz. Fondo Saúl Orduz/Colección Museo de Bogotá.

transportation infrastructure and conquer what Marco Palacios describes as the country's deep "social and regional fragmentation," the downtown road project constituted a spectacle of state building and of territorial control.[44]

On the legal front, a battery of ordinances opened the terrain for counterrevolutionary urban operations. Immediately after the uprising, President Ospina Pérez decreed a state of siege, advancing a series of controversial measures to quell the insurrection and initiate the reconstruction. One early governmental measure ordered the expropriation of several houses near the presidential palace to install emergency state offices and army troops. It invoked a "state of abnormality" and called for the centralization of military power.[45] Through extraordinary legislation, Ospina Pérez created commissions for the assessment of the damage and the emergency planning of a new civic center. Other decrees authorized an urban reconstruction credit line with the United States as well as the issuance of reconstruction bonds and higher property taxes.

Most significant was the creation of Colombia's first condominium law by presidential decree only twelve days after the riots. This legal framework was presented as a definitive step toward urban reconstruction and one that would "solve in satisfactory fashion the problem of middle-class housing."[46] The promotion of modern real estate—particularly apartment buildings—was an attack on the fractioned, small-scale ownership arrangements that had characterized inner-city districts and that elites had associated with moral decay and revolutionary dispositions. According to Aprile-Gniset, the securitization of property regimes ultimately laid the groundwork for the displacement of urban smallholdings (*minifundios urbanos*) by urban estates (*latifundios urbanos*) with increased rents and firmer control over land. High-rise rental buildings (*edificios de renta*) replaced subdivided houses and tenements (*inquilinatos*), both concentrating ownership and eliminating overlapping property claims.[47]

Urban destruction and reconstruction during El Bogotazo can be viewed as the tentative materialization of an urban "securityscape."[48] The technocratic war over downtown Bogotá was an irregular and incomplete process that took material form in the city's bureaucratic and physical infrastructure. Most visibly, this brand of counterrevolutionary urbanism was materialized in the modernist high-rises and avenues built in the years following the uprising and reached new heights under the military dictatorship of General Gustavo Rojas Pinilla (1953–57).[49] As the US expanded the commercialization of military technology in the region, it also increased the export of construction materials and expertise. A new urban landscape of steel, glass, aluminum, and concrete emerged in close connection with this nascent military-industrial order. Modernist planning blurred into a mode of "strategic-military urbanism" that continued to reverberate in downtown's sociomaterial transformations for decades.[50]

Counterinsurgent Housing

Although later visions for a renewed city center were apparently not as belligerent as the Bogotazo reconstruction plans, in the 1960s and 1970s downtown planning became more firmly embedded in Cold War renderings of development as counterinsurgency. The promotion and management of urban densities emerged as a central strategy to absorb rural migrants, quell their potential rebelliousness, and transform them into middle-class citizens bound to the promises of capitalist development. In his work as mayor between 1961 and 1966, for instance, architect Jorge Gaitán Cortés stressed the need to respond to the city's explosive demographic growth—now intensified due to increasing violence in the countryside—through plans "to stimulate the densification of the main commercial sectors and adjacent residential areas."[51] In contrast to the real estate reconquest of the city center that was launched in the early post-Bogotazo years, he called attention to the importance of rehabilitating working-class neighborhoods (*rehabilitación de barrios obreros*) and building social housing (*vivienda social*). For Gaitán Cortés, the key issue was devising mechanisms to insert rural migrants into the modernizing city. "The fundamental problem that our cities confront," he declared, "resides in the need to receive, absorb, and incorporate into the monetary economy those 2,400,000 inhabitants that come from an agrarian economy."[52] The crowd—in the form of dispossessed rural masses—emerged as a potentially insurgent force, a destabilizing urban density. For Gaitán Cortés, however, the main challenge was to create technical instruments that would address the shortage of housing, services, and jobs in order to enable the urban integration of the "wretched conglomerate of displaced persons."[53]

A longtime adviser for the national government, the Canadian development economist Lauchlin Currie, became a central figure within these emergent planning frameworks. Working alongside Gaitán Cortés, under succeeding mayor Virgilio Barco in the 1960s, and later as presidential adviser in the 1970s and 1980s, Currie spearheaded studies aimed at the planned densification of Bogotá and other urban centers in Colombia. He firmly defended the idea that intensive urbanization, along with large-scale agricultural production, was the route to accelerated economic growth.[54] His views tacitly aligned with the country's US-backed counterinsurgency strategies, which held up socioeconomic progress as a critical measure to defeat Communist insurgencies.[55] Yet instead of addressing entrenched inequalities and the concentration of rural land—which was the government's initial yet ultimately failed reformist path—Currie proposed to draw peasants away from the countryside and transform them into productive urban residents through wide-ranging housing development policies.[56] In a broader sense, the redesign of urban densities and property regimes was aimed at promoting a "mode of urban life," as Currie put it in one study, and its far-reaching social and cultural effects, including family planning and education, ultimately "breaking . . . the vicious circle of underdevelopment."[57]

Here again, urban planning mirrored broader political junctures as Colombia entered a period known as the Frente Nacional (National Front) from 1958 to 1974. This was a power-sharing agreement struck by the Liberal and Conservative Parties to usher Colombia into the allegedly peaceful path of democratic reform. Rather than overt demolition and expulsion, as in previous years, urban interventions would be directly tied to agendas of socioeconomic development. As A. Ricardo López-Pedreros explains, the Frente Nacional pivoted on a "hierarchical vision of democracy" and its ideals of middle-class citizenship. With the ascendancy of John F. Kennedy's Alliance for Progress in Colombia and its tenets of development and anti-Communism, this "classed and gendered definition of democracy" ultimately "legitimized imperial rule on a transnational terrain."[58]

Yet planners' technocratic ethos, coupled with their class- and race-inflected assumptions about urban living, inevitably clashed with the city's politicized landscape of urban housing. Since the late 1950s, radical leftist housing organizations—most notably the Communist-founded Central Nacional Provivienda—had successfully coordinated land invasions in both central and peripheral urban areas, becoming the frequent target of police repression. The history of Policarpa Salavarrieta, a neighborhood located only a few blocks from the presidential palace and named after the iconic nineteenth-century independence revolutionary, became a forceful demonstration of the violent undersides of the city's reformist plans.[59]

In 1961, Communist militants and downtown tenement dwellers, many of whom had been violently displaced from the countryside, took over vacant land owned by the Instituto de Crédito Territorial (ICT).[60] The ICT was a national housing lender that had been created as part of an agrarian reform initiative in the 1930s. It had been charged with financing campesino housing, and as peasant migration to the city accelerated, it became a centerpiece institution within urban housing and formalization policies from the 1940s onward. In the very same year that Policarpa founders set up the first wood, tin, and asphalt fabric houses, the ICT was launching Ciudad Kennedy, one of its most ambitious housing programs on the western periphery of Bogotá. The massive housing project was based on state-backed mortgages and wide-ranging plans for auto- and progressive construction. Supported by the Alliance for Progress and visited by Kennedy himself in its first year, the growing suburb became a symbol of anti-Communist development. Importantly, as historian Amy Offner argues, it was primarily middle-class bureaucrats and workers who were able to access property ownership through the plan. Provivienda and other critics, Offner writes, "denounced

ICT developments as manifestations of the National Front's clientelism and dis-regard for the poor."[61] Not only had Ciudad Kennedy failed to include the most marginalized residents in its designs, but as the district grew and new residents became wary of newcomers and nearby squatters, it also reproduced "the very inequalities, social animosities, and political conflicts" that reformist housing policies had intended to address.[62]

It was thus meaningful that those who did not fit into the ICT's plans would take over a piece of land owned by the agency. Moreover, unlike most of the ICT's developments in urban peripheries, Policarpa would carve out a space for hundreds of families in the city's core. The ICT's and local authorities' response to the invasion was no less telling—it offered a glimpse into the enduring vio-lence of urban housing plans. In what would become a protracted battle over the following years, the ICT stationed police to halt construction and harass locals, and it eventually constructed walls sealing off the neighborhood's entrances. Authorities intimidated residents, threatening to exclude them from future hous-ing applications if they did not vacate the zone and, at one point, hiring agents who allegedly set a community toilet on fire. Military authorities surveilled and detained Provivienda leaders, some of whom now lived in Policarpa. One police commander made explicit the government's anti-Communist sentiments: "Invaders are directed by professional agitators and with people from the coun-tryside foreign to Bogotá."[63]

In his detailed reconstruction of Policarpa's foundation, Alfonso Torres Car-rillo describes how residents gained ground every year by skirting official control and repression. Drawing on their tight-knit organization and leadership, Poli-carpa residents issued public demands and mobilized political support for access to utilities and services. They smuggled construction materials through check-points and devised stealthy building techniques. Most famously, they deployed "walking houses"—light structures that could be carried by a few people—which "ran" across fields and populated blocks in a matter of minutes.[64] Authorities were at pains to respond to the rapid and covert mode of urbanization of these moving houses, which acted as extensions of the bodies routinely expelled from downtown. By 1965, residents had strengthened their position. They had resisted several evictions and eventually took over a police station that had been installed by the ICT and transformed it into the barrio's first school. Tensions came to a head in April 1966 on what became known as Viernes Santo Sangriento (Bloody Good Friday). After a round of unsuccessful Provivienda invasions to the south of the city center, several families took refuge from the police in Policarpa. Within a month, residents had decided to house the newcomers in one of the remaining vacant areas within the neighborhood—the soccer fields. Aware of this new plan, the police responded in full force with cavalry and the riot squad, while locals repelled the attack with gasoline, sticks, rocks, and other homemade weapons. By the end of the day, the urban battle left one resident dead, hundreds injured, and more than seventy detained. Police retreated, and "although the barrio was destroyed and they put many compañeros in jail," one longtime resident recalled, "we kept the land. After the Viernes Santo Sangriento the police did not come back to Policarpa."[65]

The battle for Policarpa was a conflict between models of middle-class proper-tied ownership and collectivist working-class housing. Reformist urban policies would thus reveal their anti-Communist undercurrents and, most importantly, their tacit contribution to the forceful displacement of downtown's poorest inhabitants. At a public seminar on urbanization and marginality in 1968, one of the country's leading military counterinsurgency experts, then–army colonel Alvaro Valencia Tovar, made these connections explicit when he called for the "eradication of urban shantytowns [*tugurios*]" as a matter of national security.[66] Valencia Tovar had participated in key operations against insurgent groups, served as military commander in the city of Bucaramanga in the 1960s, and was later chief of the armed forces in the 1970s. Describing a plan spearheaded by the military in Bucaramanga, he called tugurios "black zones" and decried how they "precariously harbor[ed] an unstable promiscuity of beings predisposed to swell the criminal ranks or currents of social perturbation."[67] For Valencia Tovar, housing policy was closely connected to the destruction of shantytowns and their "demagogic, rebellious, and resentful" sociality.[68] Backed by the ICT and implemented by the army, the Bucaramanga plan became the militarized ver-sion of self-help development models. It was also a harbinger of the increasingly securitized atmosphere that would shape urban development in the following years.

Security State Spaces

Calls for the densification of the city center continued apace during the 1970s and 1980s. In a national climate marked by the end of the Frente Nacional (at least nominally, as bipartisan power sharing continued) and calls for market liberaliza-tion and state privatization, urban planning in Bogotá shifted decisively toward what Alberto Saldarriaga Roa calls the "real estate city."[69] Echoing only minimally the principles of Currie's "new design of urban growth"—which included the pro-motion of class integration, diverse land uses, and the "capture [of increasing values] for social purposes" in denser urban cores—new developments in central Bogotá emerged as stripped-down versions that facilitated real estate speculation and privileged middle-class property and values.[70]

In one sense, urban boosterism during these decades deepened existing patterns of expulsion and segregation and catalyzed forms of social mobilization. An oft-cited case in this regard was the so-called Avenida de los Cerros (Avenue of the Hills), a road planned in the early 1970s that would cut through the eastern hills of downtown Bogotá and displace thousands of working-class families that had lived there for decades. Fierce opposition from residents, however, along with financial and management issues, ultimately led to the demise of the Avenida project.[71] Importantly, the organized mobilization became a milestone in the history of urban protest in Bogotá and laid the groundwork for the contentious years ahead.

More broadly, behind the official veneer of progress embodied by new high-rises, avenues, and malls was the militarization of everyday urban life and the intensification of violent conflict. Emblematic of the ties between capitalist development, reformist agendas, and an emergent security state was the first post–Frente Nacional administration, that of Alfonso López Michelsen (1974–78). While López Michelsen had been elected as a progressive left-leaning Liberal candidate—he had cofounded the dissident Movimiento Revolucionario Liberal (Liberal Revolutionary Party)—his administration not only favored the elite sectors that he came from but also expanded the state-of-siege powers of the government, attacked union and labor rights, and criminalized protest across the country.[72] This period marked the intensification of Colombia's late twentieth-century regimes of violent capital accumulation as well as the state and paramilitary assault on working-class political organizing.[73]

By the end of the 1970s, the Liberal government of Julio César Turbay Ayala (1978–82) decreed the Estatuto de Seguridad (Statute of Security), which further institutionalized the state's exceptional powers to police everyday life as well as wide-ranging measures to criminalize and repress social mobilization. With the pretext of combating threats to the state and reestablishing the public order (*orden público*), while continually invoking the specter of leftist guerrillas, the statute ushered in a "constitutional dictatorship" that had lasting effects.[74] In 1979, human rights lawyer Gustavo Gallón Giraldo mordantly portrayed a bleak future in his study of the state of siege in Colombia. "The military apparatus will continue to consolidate positions as a branch of public power," he predicted, adding that, as large-scale capital and illegal economies thrive, "popular sectors will continue to bear the brunt of this flourishing paradise with the disposal of their primary liberties and the product of their labor and at the expense of the progressive degradation of their conditions of survival."[75]

During this period, downtown renewal plans centered more decisively on the notion of "decay" (*deterioro*), an official discourse that mapped closely onto elite anxieties about the loss of control over central spaces. As Samuel Jaramillo has noted, the talk of decay was integral to a class-inflected attack on the "cen-tro popular"—the working-class downtown of tenements, rural migrants, and street commerce.[76] Critiques of urban reconstruction and displacement such as Jaramillo's, however, have focused primarily on the political-economic agen-das behind redevelopment initiatives, selective historic conservation, and the so-called "recovery" of the city center.[77] Yet the destruction and emptiness left behind by urban development was both the result of the fight for the control of downtown and a manifestation of the ravages of warfare. In looking back at the contemporary struggles over the city center, it is thus imperative to uncover the ways in which the broader currents of militarism and security ran through the remaking of downtown Bogotá. The bluntness of urban reconstruction speaks little of such residues of violence, leaving them instead buried under the immediacy of real estate battles and projects of sociospatial control. At stake here, ultimately, is the recovery of the everyday knowledges and materialities that have punctuated urban conflicts and that are often muted in the dominant narratives about urban transformation in Colombia.

Take, for instance, an apparently banal incident reported in *Alternativa*, an avant-garde political magazine led by leftist intellectuals, including writer Gabriel García Márquez, and closely aligned with the nascent M-19 urban insurgency.[78] In its distinctly irreverent tone and exemplifying its aims to "divulge popular struggles" and "counterinform [*contrainformar*]," the magazine published a short note in 1974 titled, "How to Discover Letters from the ELN Inside a Mattress."[79] The story was a powerful indictment of the opaque links between heightened political persecution and urban development. The author recounted how city officials and the police had attempted to frame Carmen de Rodríguez during an eviction process. Not only was de Rodríguez a well-known human rights activist, but she had also become a visible leader in the movement against the Avenida de los Cerros on the east side of the city center.[80] Two police officers, a judge, and functionaries from the Instituto de Desarrollo Urbano (Institute of Urban Development) showed up at her house two weeks after she had left. "The unusual police deployment" was even odder as the house was vacant, yet the "move [*jugada*]" that authorities had "staged" soon became apparent.[81] Police entered and "opened a mattress with some papers attached to it."[82] When the judge saw the postscript "ELN"—the initials of the leftist guerrilla organization Ejército de Liberación Nacional (National Freedom Army)—he quickly concluded that it was "subversive material."[83] Yet "the provocateurs who so grossly attempted to fabricate evidence of the crime of rebellion," the *Alternativa* journalist continued, "had left behind a saw which they had apparently used to open a hole and enter the abandoned house."[84] According to several neighbors, the saw belonged to the Instituto de Desarrollo Urbano, whose workers moved quickly to demolish the house, even before the judicial expropriation order had been signed. In this man-ner, police stratagems to "repress the people's fighters [*luchadores del pueblo*]" converged with state-backed displacement—in this case for the construction of a parking lot for new real estate development.[85] The case of the letters in a mat-tress was thus both about militarizing social life and about "crushing the right to housing of the urban poor."[86]

Far from exceptional, this incident can help bring new light to downtown interventions during those decades and to their tacit entanglements with expanding security agendas. Such is the case of Nueva Santa Fe, an emblematic downtown renovation project that started to take shape in the 1970s. The plan, which was partially implemented by the late 1980s and early 1990s, involved the state-led demolition of nine blocks of the historic Santa Bárbara neighborhood on the south side of the city center. Only three lots were developed as commercial and apartment buildings, leaving several other spaces vacant and abandoned to this day. Nueva Santa Fe has come to embody many of the contradictions and conflicts of downtown renewal. Not only did it lead to the expulsion of hun-dreds of families, but it also created a middle-class enclave severed from its sur-roundings. More broadly, Nueva Santa Fe exemplified the contested politics of official discourses of decay and historic preservation. While the neighboring La Candelaria was protected as architectural and historic patrimony, the less afflu-ent Santa Bárbara was slated for demolition despite its equally significant colo-nial and republican past. In this sense, and as scholars have noted, Nueva Santa Fe is representative of the power-laden deployments of urban value, historical worth, and deterioration at the core of downtown renewal in Bogotá.[87] Less often acknowledged, however, are the security and military roots of the plan.

Critically, one of the first moves to target the area was directly tied to the security of the presidency. During the administration of López Michelsen, the office and residence of the president moved from the Palacio San Carlos to the nearby Casa de Nariño on the south side of the Plaza de Bolívar. According to economist Rodrigo Botero Montoya, a government minister involved in the restoration of the new presidential palace, the project was quickly reframed as an "integral intervention in the area."[88] "As we toured the Casa de Nariño we found a depressing situation," Botero Montoya recalled years later, "not only because the building was in ruins, but also because . . . the surrounding blocks had become a slum [*tugurio*]."[89] While Nueva Santa Fe would be remembered mainly as a housing project, its original impetus had been "national security," as renowned architectural historian Germán Téllez noted years later.[90] "The worst thing that can happen to a neighborhood in Bogotá is to be located close to power," a jour-nalist in *El Tiempo* commented after Santa Bárbara had been demolished and Nueva Santa Fe was under construction. "Conservation and preservation," the author continued, "gave way to the thesis of constructing modern buildings to elevate the socioeconomic level of the area and thereby create a security cordon [*cinturón de seguridad*] to protect the Palacio de Nariño, the Ministry of Finance, and other buildings of the central power."[91]

Most tellingly, buried in a piece of legislation leading up to the renewal of the zone was one of the plan's key objectives: the "construction of the barracks of the Presidential Guard Battalion."[92] The date when this law was signed was particularly meaningful: December 15, 1977, just three months after a historic urban protest had erupted throughout the city and successfully confronted the government and its increasingly authoritarian leanings. Since El Bogotazo, a popular mobilization had not shaken the official establishment as much as the Paro Cívico Nacional (National Civic Strike) of September 14, 1977. The Paro Cívico was the culmination of years of labor and urban activism, and it resulted from the wide-ranging coordination of leftist movements and neighborhood organizations. What started as a general labor strike, historian Frank Molano Camargo explains, led to a "gigantic explosion of urban popular sectors."[93] The ongoing struggle against capitalist exploitation, government repression, and worsening labor and living conditions had taken its distinct shape in the space of the city. "The shared interests of homeowners, tenants, small store owners, high school students, informal workers and, of course, blue-collar workers," Molano Camargo argues, "became interwoven in the urban space of the capital."[94] During the protest, thousands of working-class residents flooded city streets, blocked main avenues, and shut down factories. Cars were destroyed, company filing cabinets were burned on the street, and large stores were looted.[95] Authorities issued a citywide curfew, and police and military intensified attacks on protesters. By the end of the day, state forces had killed at least twenty-five people, injured more than five hundred, and detained more than three thousand. According to reports, several of the dead had been executed.[96]

Urban renewal in the vicinity of the presidential palace and in Santa Bárbara was thus integral to the conflicts made visible during the Paro Cívico. In one sense, and following Molano Camargo once again, Nueva Santa Fe—with its displacements and its favoring of financial and class interests—represented the "hegemonic urban model" that had driven sociospatial segregation and galvanized working-class mobilization.[97] In another sense, and as the plans to build a military garrison and enforce security around state buildings illustrated, downtown renewal was closely imbricated with the expansion of the militarization of everyday urban life. Prior to the Paro Cívico, the administration of López Michelsen had refused to respond to the demands of labor organizations, deploying instead "counterinsurgent prose" and calling the strike a "subversive paro."[98]

The day before the Paro Cívico, the government implemented the so-called Plan Tricolor, which involved the militarization of barrios such as Policarpa, the prohibition of public gatherings, and the arrest of organizers.[99] It is not surprising, given this context, that Nueva Santa Fe had been launched with the construction of a security cordon around downtown's governmental district, which included the acquisition and demolition of nearby working-class neighborhoods for the creation of the Presidential Guard barracks.

The militarized undersides of the demolition of Santa Bárbara, the renovation of the presidential palace, and the creation of the middle-class enclave of Nueva Santa Fe reverberated once again in one of Colombia's most spectacular scenes of urban warfare. On November 6, 1985, an M-19 guerrilla command captured the Palacio de Justicia (Palace of Justice), a modernist building that housed the country's main courts and that sat across from Congress and the presidential palace on the north side of the Plaza de Bolívar. Following its media-savvy style of urban sabotage—which had included stealing independence leader Simón Bolívar's sword from a museum in 1974—the M-19 insurgency had planned the takeover as an armed demand before Supreme Court magistrates to carry out a "public trial [*juicio público*]" of President Belisario Betancourt for the violation of a recent ceasefire agreement.[100] Significantly, the guerrilla unit organized and deployed from a nearby house in the Calvo Sur neighborhood to the south of the Plaza de Bolívar and a few blocks from Santa Bárbara—which at the time was an active demolition site for Nueva Santa Fe.[101]

If the guerrilla operation had literally sprung from the rubble of urban renewal, the state's overwhelming response had also been materially anchored in the remaking and securing of downtown spaces. The recapture (*retoma*) of the Palacio de Justicia, remembered by some as a state massacre and temporary coup d'état by the military forces, was launched from the barracks of the Presidential Guard built during the first phase of the Santa Bárbara project.[102] Any prospect of negotiating with the insurgent group or rescuing the more than two hundred hostages vanished as military tanks, helicopters, and thousands of soldiers stormed the palace. Within hours the structure was engulfed in fire, and by the end of the siege, more than a hundred people had died, eleven had disappeared, and seventy-five had been injured.[103] A new ruin had been created by state forces deployed from what had recently been itself a demolition site—the new barracks behind the presidential palace—and as displacements and construction for urban renewal in Santa Bárbara unfolded just blocks away. The devastated structure was a forceful embodiment of the state violence that would consume Colombia in the following decades. It was the tangible materialization of the rising security state that had also led to the razing of Santa Bárbara and the creation of Nueva Santa Fe.

The afterlife of the renewal site and the ruined building further illuminate the threads tying them together. At stake here is something similar to what Hiba Bou Akar, in her study of urban warfare and development in Beirut, calls the "doubleness of ruins."[104] In Bogotá, both the razed lots left behind by the partially constructed Nueva Santa Fe and the burned remains of the state building were "the product of overlapping conflicts" around urban space and (in)security.[105] Both of these urban residues, however, gradually dissolved, ultimately submerging the undercurrents of violence that had shaped them.[106] The years following the destruction of the Palacio de Justicia were revealing in this regard. The ruined structure stood in the Plaza de Bolívar for three years while experts and officials produced and debated designs for the reconstruction. The plaza took on the "appearance of tragedy, ruin, and void," architecture critic Tania Maya Sierra argues.[107] The wreckage, moreover, was a stark reminder of how state violence had obliterated justice and legality both figuratively and materially. For decades the fate of the disappeared persons remained unknown, and military and government officials evaded responsibility for the atrocities committed during the recapture.

As an artifact of state violence, the burned palace channeled impulses to "repress memory" and "forget history," Maya Sierra explains.[108] During the visits of Pope John Paul II and President François Mitterand in 1986, for instance, the government covered the scorched structure with an enormous flag.[109] The ruined building had become a tangible reminder of the so-called Holocausto del Palacio, the brutal violence orchestrated by the military against civilians, and the rising persecution of leftist movements across the country. This was brought to light forcefully in 1987 during the funeral procession of Jaime Pardo Leal, leftist presidential candidate for the Unión Patriótica party. Pardo Leal was among the thousands of the party's militants killed during the 1980s by state and paramilitary forces in what is often described as a political genocide. When a multitude descended on the Plaza de Bolívar after his death, a group of students broke into the palace's ruins as riot police responded with tear gas. "From the ruins of the Palacio de Justicia, monument to ignominy," Arturo Alape would later write, "from all its floors came a vertical rain of stones, the students had taken over its smoky ruins in conscience."[110]

Finally, in 1988, the government removed the "unbearable vision" of the palace.[111] Rather than using explosives or heavy machinery to demolish it, which might have stirred memories of the siege, "the building was taken apart, piece by piece, as through an act of sorcery [una operación de sortilegio]," according to one reporter.[112] Far from any commemoration of the victims or gesture to the violent destruction, an entirely new, monumental building was raised on the site between 1993 and 1999.[113] The new Palacio de Justicia—a neoclassical-inspired monolith wrapped in yellow limestone—projected, according to Maya Sierra, a sense of "accessibility and transparency" with its columns, ample portico, and walkways.[114] Yet as Maya Sierra argues, this apparent openness ultimately "masked" a radically securitized design integral to its construction materials and surveillance technologies, as well as to the "separation of the building's interior spaces from its facade, the management of circulations and fixed points, and the disposition of accesses and separation from public space."[115] The new palace not only embodied the erasure of downtown's overlapping histories of warfare and urban transformation but also epitomized the materialization of ideals of state sovereignty and territorial control under the semblance of democratic public space. Such an approach would be amplified in the following years, as I show in the next chapter, with the construction of a monumental park in the vicinity of the Plaza de Bolívar.

Urban Traces of Violence

Michel-Rolph Trouillot argues that the material traces of events—from buildings to graves—"embody the ambiguities of history."[116] "Their concreteness," he notes, "hides secrets so deep that no revelation may fully dissipate their silences."[117] In downtown Bogotá, the concrete and tangible immediacy of built forms has partially hidden an ongoing story about security, warfare, and popular struggles. Tracking the city's submerged historical processes thus challenges taken-for-granted narratives about urban planning and renewal. In Bogotá, demolition and reconstruction were as much about the unfolding of capitalist development as about counterinsurgent violence, territorial control, and the consolidation of a security state. A central question here, one that I take up in the following chapters, is how the logics of warfare infuse everyday knowledge practices, urban materialities, and experiences of city life. More broadly, I ask how security becomes a key lever in conflicts over the remaking of urban space.

The trajectories sketched out in this chapter reveal both how state violence underpinned twentieth-century urban plans and how it was gradually paved over and obfuscated. Counterinsurgent ideologies seemingly faded away in what would simply become the construction of an avenue, the creation of affordable housing, or the remodeling of a presidential palace. At the same time, however, urban dwellers and activists opposed such material transformations, making apparent their continuities with the broader violent conflicts engulfing the country. As I argue in the remainder of this book, such struggles left traces in people's epistemological and experiential orientations toward the very materiality of the city.

Furthermore, as the horizon of a postconflict era started to become visible in the first decades of the twenty-first century, a retracing of Bogotá's violent undersides gained renewed urgency. An apparently minor yet telling episode around the historical narrative of the takeover of the Palacio de Justicia illustrates such battles for urban memory. In November 2012, a group of relatives of the victims of the siege and recapture of the palace gained the support of the Petro administration to install a granite plaque on one of the exterior walls of city hall, the Palacio Liévano, on the west side of the Plaza de Bolívar. The names of the eleven disappeared persons, along with the 2010 convictions that found former military officers Alfonso Plazas Vega and Armando Arias Cabrales responsible for the crimes, were etched on the stone. After the Supreme Court absolved Plazas Vega in 2015 due to insufficient evidence, however, city council members from the right-wing Centro Democrático party called for the removal of the plaque.[118] Here again, as with the controversy over the urban cemetery that opened this chapter, the dispute over history and urban space echoed through mayoral politics. Soon after being elected for a new term as mayor, Enrique Peñalosa granted the request and ordered the removal of the plaque in 2016. As with other inscrutable remnants of the violence of urbanism, all that was left were the marks of its absence—a faint rectangular contour where the memorial had been attached to the wall.

The plaque was just one attempt at making visible the ties between urban space and the country's history of warfare. The Centro de Memoria, Paz y Reconciliación—the new hub for memory work inaugurated in 2012 next to the restored columbaria and the exhumed mass grave—had led a more ambitious project that followed the "traces of memory [*huellas de memoria*] in the streets, plazas, and constructions in Bogotá which rememorate the history of political violence and struggles for democracy and peace."[119] Drawing on the work of human rights activists, historians and journalists, and victims' organizations, the aim was to "piece together a sort of puzzle of the fragmented maps of our violence," as writer and poet Juan Manuel Roca put it in the government-published book *Bogotá, ciudad memoria*, which showcased the project.[120] Very much a reflection of the country's moves toward truth, justice, and reparation programs, at stake here was the uncovering of silenced pasts, or what Roca described as a "collective memory that is always in rough construction [*obra negra*]."[121] While *Bogotá, ciudad memoria* centered on emblematic events and political figures, it also called attention to ordinary people's experiences of violence and insecurity and how they are mapped onto the "streets, roads, and avenues that make up the city's urban fabric [*entramado urbano*]."[122] It is these everyday mappings of Bogotá as a terrain of warfare—figurative and literal, epistemic and material—that I explore in the following pages.

THE CITY AS TERRAIN

One weekday morning in October 2012, I trailed behind a group of commuters as they hurried across Parque Tercer Milenio (Third Millenium Park). Coming from the west side, we passed by the only two buildings still standing from the more than six hundred structures that had been demolished for the creation of the expansive downtown park. One was the old Santa Inés school, a once elegant brick and plaster republican building that had been closed and was now crumbling away. The other was the Instituto Nacional de Medicina Legal y Ciencias Forenses (National Coroner's Office), for decades surrounded by what were widely considered to be the deadliest streets in Colombia. My accidental walking companions continued their hasty march as I stood in the park's central boulevard. The ample brick esplanade was deserted. Except for the occasional military band rehearsal, the most use it had seen in its short history was when it became the impromptu site for a tent city set up by hundreds of internally displaced persons during a four-month occupation in 2009.[1]

As I searched for people other than commuters, Isidoro, a private security guard, was pulled toward me by his heaving Rottweiler. Seemingly accustomed to the lone tourist or researcher, he offered to take me along on his morning round. Originally from the coastal city of Barranquilla, he had worked in the park since its opening in 2006. With the characteristically approachable demeanor of *costeños*, as people from the coast are known, he talked about his first years on the job, including how drug addicts and old dealers from the area would sometimes threaten him and his partners, and how they would have to call the police for backup. "Now things are better," he noted; the job mostly consisted of waking up

FIGURE 2.1. Parque Tercer Milenio. Photo by the author.

the street dwellers (*habitantes de calle*) to prevent "their enemies"—other addicts or drug dealers—from attacking them in their sleep. As we walked behind the panting guard dog, Isidoro caught sight of a young man drifting along one of the grass hills near the northwest corner of the park. He told me I should talk to the Engineer, as people called him, to get a better sense of what life in the area was like.

The Engineer, a man possibly in his thirties, had short dark hair and a stubby moustache; his appearance did not immediately reveal that he had been living on the streets for several years. "The world's largest *olla* [open air drug market], we're standing on what used to be the world's largest olla! Did you know that?" the Engineer said, chuckling to himself, after Isidoro asked him if he could tell me what life in the park and its surroundings was like. He was talking about El Cartucho, the twenty-block neighborhood that had come to be known as Bogotá's most dangerous place in the 1980s and 1990s. For years, the area had functioned as the city's main hub for the drug trade and other illicit dealings, as well as a haven for impoverished migrants, street vendors, and small businesses. "Underneath this park is one of Latin America's longest tunnels," the Engineer continued, with the hurried speech and fidgeting common to bazuco smokers.[2] He turned to Isidoro to assure me that he was not exaggerating: "The parking garage down there is huge, right?" Isidoro's approval encouraged him to say more. "You see, that's why El Cartucho was here. When it existed [gang leaders] put everything below, the bombs, drugs, weapons . . . that's where they moved everything. That's why the olla was here, because of those tunnels down there. That's where the parking garage is now, but the only thing they did was plaster the walls. When they built the park, they didn't even dig out a hole, they just used the old tunnels that were there . . ."

The Engineer went on to talk about his descent into addiction—his journey between two Bronxes. The son of a police officer, he had studied environmental engineering and worked in natural gas plants in the city's southern periphery. During a trip to visit family in New York, he tried cocaine in the Bronx. When he returned to Bogotá, he smoked bazuco and was hooked. After a few months he was living on the streets of a nearby olla known also as El Bronx: an outgrowth of El Cartucho to the west that became the destination of many of the former dealers and clientele after the neighborhood's demolition. And even as he described the park as a "change of 360 degrees that benefited all the community," he also painted a landscape of danger and violence. "We call [the olla] the Temple of Shaolin," he confided, "all darkness and death."[3] The Engineer talked about the risk of running into "enemies" in the park, people willing to "roast you, put you to sleep" if they found out you had money or drugs. Isidoro interjected, recalling how not long before, "people came in an SUV, killed a couple of people, and drove away." Other times, "they came by throwing leaflets saying they were the [paramilitary squad] Águilas Negras." But things had improved, he said again. The Engineer agreed, although he cut himself off, noticeably uncomfortable with the turn the conversation had taken. "I only know that I know nothing," he said. He returned to the subject of the tunnels and spoke about how, as a student of environmental engineering and sanitation, he was brought to the old Cartucho "with blueprints" to study the networks of "tunnels and narrow underground passages" that went all the way up to the Plaza de Bolívar and underneath the colonial La Candelaria. Some of these, he noted, were still used by people from the olla as stashes (*caletas*). Enthralled by the image of an underground city, his voice trailed off as he asked for a cigarette and told us he had to leave.

As we continued our round, Isidoro decided to show me the subterranean world conjured by the Engineer. We walked toward the south side of the park and descended into the parking garage. With the city noise now muffled and the large, empty concrete vault before us, Isidoro looked around with unease. "You see those sewage gratings there," he said, "those are the tunnels the Engineer was telling you about, and those tunnels go all the way across, underneath the garage." He paused as if trying to take in the place's eeriness and concluded with an unexpected image: "I always say this park and garage are like Iraq, you know in Iraq where the [insurgents] are holed up, you don't see or feel anything because you're inside something that feels like a shelter."

Excavating Urban Terrain

In talking about the monumental park and the disappearance of El Cartucho, Isidoro and the Engineer had turned their gaze downward. Their fixation on the underground world of tunnels, itself part of local lore, pointed to the enduring traces of what had existed there before. The urban substratum emerged as a testimony to the obduracy of the area's physical and social topography—the submerged remnants of violence and power that had defined El Cartucho, marked its dissolution, and continued to echo through the empty park and its vicinity. In one sense, then, the plastered tunnels, now turned into an unused underground garage, exemplified the "rubble" of urban development—what Gastón Gordillo suggestively describes as the "void that haunts modernity."[4] Above ground, the few residues of the demolition, such as the old Santa Inés school, emerged as ruins from another time, fenced off and left behind by the city's transformations. Below ground, as Isidoro and the Engineer intimated, the garage/tunnels told a different story, one of still active and unwieldy vectors of violence that had been concealed by the concrete facade of the expansive park. These traces "reveal[ed] the material sedimentation of destruction," as Gordillo observes in his study of state and capitalist expansion in the Argentine Andes.[5] They were not "inert remains," as Ann Stoler argues, but "sites that condense[d] alternative senses of history," spaces of "vital refiguration."[6]

Isidoro's mention of Iraqi battlefields was thus particularly meaningful. It evoked a warscape that extended into the core of downtown and flowed under the monumental park.[7] By likening the empty garage and its hidden tunnels to a bunker, he recast the landscaped park as a terrain of violence. In his ruminations on postwar Europe, Paul Virilio finds in the bunkers littered across the Atlantic littoral the "landmarks of contemporary military space."[8] For him, the architectural monoliths announced the momentous expansion of warfare beyond the battlefield into cities and across the skies. They foreshadowed "total war, risk everywhere, instantaneity of danger, the great mix of the military and the civilian, the homogenization of conflict."[9] Similarly, Isidoro's bunker-park hinted at the violent underside of urban transformation. He imbued the materiality of Tercer Milenio and the fading traces of El Cartucho with an intimate knowledge and experience of insecurity.

Inspired by Virilio's "bunker archeology" and its phenomenological orientations, in this chapter I excavate the layers of knowledge sedimented in Parque

Tercer Milenio. In its reified physicality, the park not only obscured the social and material transformations of El Cartucho but also occluded the knowledges, practices, and affective dispositions that went into the destruction of the old neighborhood and the refashioning of a new sociomaterial environment. Among critics and scholars, Tercer Milenio has epitomized contemporary paradigms of urban security.[10] Its hard surfaces and premature obsolescence, along with the spillover of the unruly populations it was supposed to erase, have emerged as tangible embodiments of the contradictions of securitization. And yet the precise manner in which ideas and experiences of security became entangled with urban epistemologies and materialized in the creation and undoing of urban forms has remained out of sight.

In the following pages I mine the park's flattened topography to unearth these knowledge practices and to examine how they shaped the making and unmaking of El Cartucho. By interpreting the neighborhood's material transformations through repertoires of warfare, local residents and former inhabitants pointed to the deep-seated struggles that had come to define the area. Planners, architects, real estate consultants, and social workers, in turn, articulated forms of knowledge aimed at taming El Cartucho's unwieldy geography by making legible and disentangling its dense sociomaterialities. At its core, Tercer Milenio was a project of planned destruction. Although the expectation of future real estate development was integral to the construction of the park, it was secondary to the objective of total removal. As one critic noted, the uniqueness of the plan resided "not necessarily in the structures created . . . but in the 'anarchic' spaces erased."[11] Rather than pointing to yet another instance of capitalist "creative destruction,"[12] Tercer Milenio made apparent the significance of techniques of spatial obliteration and epistemologies of destruction.[13]

During the planning and demolition process, experts became intensely involved in producing knowledges about the material complexities of the urban environment and how they shaped social practices. Such knowledges were then deployed to unbuild physical and social infrastructures. Ideas about the materiality of urban space and the socialities attached to it were infused with security frameworks. Experts and planners' experiential registers—from their sense of everyday insecurity to their practical awareness of the country's broader history of violence—permeated the composition of urban knowledges. The crafting of such knowledges was a material process: ideologies anchored in tangible realities and geared toward the reconstitution of objects, people, and the relations among them. But unlike locals' attunement to the complex history of territorial struggles in the area—which they viewed as a continuation of the country's wide-ranging conflicts over land—planners' situational, pragmatic, and affective knowledges centered on state security and control. Crucially, epistemologies of urban reconstruction were shaped by and gave form to the idea of urban terrain.

Bogotá planners and officials often talked about the city as terrain. Common expressions such as "visiting the terrain" (*salida al terreno*) and "understanding the conditions on the terrain" (*entender las condiciones en el terreno*) highlighted their interest in gathering knowledge about local urban circumstances through fieldwork. At the same time, the notion of terrain pointed to the enduring influence of field sciences and the study of physical space—from geology and topography to cadastral surveys and mapping—in the urban planning and design professions. From this perspective, social practices appeared subordinated to the physical attributes of space. At their most extreme, they positioned space as a key site for the strategic reengineering and control of social milieus. Taken a step further, such conceptualizations evoked long-standing connections between terrain and militarism. From Sun Tzu and Carl von Clausewitz to Ernesto Che Guevara and Mao Tse-tung, natural topography has been central to ideologies and practices of warfare. As Clausewitz put it, "The relationship between warfare and terrain determines the peculiar character of military action."[14] Commanding high ground and taking advantage of hostile terrain are the very stuff of military strategy and guerrilla tactics.[15] This is no less true in cities, where theaters of war take the form of urban grids, infrastructure, and buildings. And here is where planning, as a technology aimed at organizing and refashioning urban forms, takes on strategic value.

In his analysis of the Israeli military occupation of Palestinian territories, Eyal Weizman shows how urban space emerged "not just [as] the site, but as the very *medium* of warfare."[16] He traces the ways in which city planning and architectural practices became "tactical tools" within militarized forms of territorial control and dispossession.[17] According to Weizman, the layout of settlements and the design of roads and overpasses "embodied aggressive intent" against Palestinians, supporting the overarching logic of military occupation.[18] In this context, scholars have further argued that the urbanization of warfare so emblematic of the global war on terror has become a dominant paradigm under widely varying sociopolitical and economic agendas.[19] From postdisaster New Orleans and Olympic Rio de Janeiro to Gaza and the occupied West Bank, cities are now increasingly the target of security strategies and military intervention.[20] They appear as battle spaces in which the lines between urban environments and tactical terrains, civilians and enemies, are blurred—places in which, as Stephen Graham puts it, "life itself is war."[21]

My analysis of Tercer Milenio extends these debates by looking more closely at the knowledge practices through which the city is reconstituted as urban terrain. I am interested in the expert labor that rendered El Cartucho and the park—epistemically, affectively, and materially—battlegrounds to be conquered and secured. Terrain, in this sense, is far from a preexisting backdrop on which political actions, such as the militarized spatial interventions described by Weizman, take place. Instead, projects of state sovereignty and social control are brought to life through the intimate knowledge and active shaping of terrain— whether it be rivers and mountain passes or the circuitous streets and layered infrastructures of downtown districts. "Terrain," as Stuart Elden argues, "makes possible, or constrains, political, military, and strategic projects, even as it is shaped by them."[22] In Tercer Milenio, city officials sought to materialize ideas of spatial order and state sovereignty by clearing, leveling, and smoothing urban ground.[23] The process, however, was incomplete and contradictory. The new park was anything but a disciplined environment, and surrounding neighborhoods remained impervious to the intervention. The terrain partly recrafted by planners proved to be more obdurate than anticipated—a fact astutely noted by Isidoro and the Engineer in their own portrayals of an enduring landscape of war and its underground world of tunnels. The sociomateriality of urban space was never fully domesticated by planners and architects—only partially reassembled through their expert engagements.

From this perspective, urban terrain emerges neither as the exclusive outcome of human action nor as a fully autonomous material substrate, but rather as a dynamic ideological and material process. It encompasses people's experiences and practices as well as the tangible qualities of urban things. This is what Yael Navaro-Yashin, in her ethnography of postwar Northern Cyprus, aptly calls "make-believe space": a process that "refers not singularly to the work of the imagination or simply to the materiality of crafting but to both at the same time."[24] I follow a similar direction below, focusing on both the knowledge of urban materiality and the materiality of urban knowledge. Exploring the epistemic crafting of urban terrain illuminates planning expertise not simply as a form of mystification or technocratic "camouflage" for securitized control and violent dispossession.[25] Instead it calls attention to the material and experiential conditions under which urban space itself becomes knowable as a terrain of warfare.

From Santa Inés to El Cartucho

El Cartucho was a long time in the making. Originally known as Santa Inés, it had been a stately residential district at the beginning of the twentieth century and a strategic node of commerce and transportation since colonial times. The site of the city's peasant market and train station, Santa Inés and neighboring

San Victorino formed a crossroads for the movement of all variety of people and things during most of the city's history. By the mid-twentieth century it housed the city's intercity bus terminal and numerous hostels and was still largely considered Bogotá's gateway and dry port. Topographic features proved central to the area's development as a liminal space at odds with the aspired order of the urban grid. The course of two rivers, the San Francisco and the San Agustín, had shaped the organization of Bogotá in profound ways since the colonial era.[26] These unwieldy geophysical elements both mediated and stubbornly obstructed colonial and republican planning and its idealized visions of the urban fabric as regular geometrical latticework. For decades, officials engaged in attempts to manage and mold this fractured topography through the construction of bridges, the canalization of streams, and the construction of roads.

Flowing from the eastern mountains to the west, the streams defined the limits of the city's four foundational parishes. The first to be established, between the two rivers, was the main parish of La Catedral, home to the cathedral and the Plaza Mayor (renamed the Plaza de Bolívar in the nineteenth century). Later on, and expanding to the north and south, were the less eminent Las Nieves and Santa Bárbara. And the last to be founded, in 1598, was San Victorino, a more peripheral location where Santa Inés would eventually be located and where the strictures of urban order and social status were more tenuous. Critically, as the San Francisco River reached San Victorino its course turned sharply to the south, where it met the San Agustín River. In contrast to the symmetric quadrangular plazas of the other parishes, the San Victorino Plaza had a curved triangular shape, and the urban gridiron gave way to sinuous streets. "The ideal of the renaissance city," as historian Carlos Carbonell Higuera puts it, "succumbed to the imminence of geography."[27]

For many years, the irregular topography of San Victorino and El Cartucho became inextricably bound to ideas and practices of encounter, transgression, and difference. Subaltern lifeworlds appeared closely juxtaposed to the urbane aspirations of the rapidly growing metropolis: first as the meeting ground for Spanish and Indigenous inhabitants and, later on, as a zone of exchange between urbanites and peasants, elites and popular classes. With migration from the countryside exploding at the end of the nineteenth century and continuing to run apace during most the twentieth century, thousands of rural migrants and violently displaced peasants found a place to live and work in the precarious tenements and busy streets of San Victorino and Santa Inés. In the process, the area became more firmly tied to imaginaries of rurality, of the largely unknown and purportedly unruly world beyond the capital. In the mid-twentieth century, such urban epistemologies—now articulated in the language of illicitness and informality—further solidified after the Bogotazo uprising and construction of the Carrera Décima. These momentous events deepened the material and symbolic fissure between the city center's western districts and the east side.

Since at least the 1940s, city officials and elites had become intent on reshaping the area's physical contours, starting with the San Victorino Plaza and what Carbonell Higuera calls "its irregular, rhomboid form."[28] While many commentators framed their calls to regulate and expand the plaza as a matter of improving the city center's worsening traffic, the class politics of such demands were not difficult to see. A downtown lawyer, for instance, argued in a newspaper article in 1948, not long after El Bogotazo, that such reforms would "also be useful for large popular assemblies [*grandes reuniones del pueblo*], so that protests and political meetings, which are common in Bogotá, do not obstruct transit in main avenues and roads so frequently."[29] The new material environment was thus imagined as a space to which contentious politics and popular movements could be evacuated. The Bogotazo's ruins appeared as the perfect starting point for such reconstruction plans and their visions of sociospatial control and segregation. In conjunction with interventions across downtown, the city carried out public works in 1949 "to level several areas [in San Victorino] for the planning of a large parking garage," according to Carbonell Higuera.[30] The plaza-garage was intended as a kind of outlet for excessive traffic, disorderly vending, and working-class culture.

But officials' ambitions to reorganize the urban environment—which included paving over the San Francisco River upstream to the east—soon proved profoundly contradictory as San Victorino, Carbonell Higuera notes, became prone to constant and "violent flooding."[31] Additionally, the newly opened Carrera Décima had expanded the Bogotazo's trail of destruction and virtually severed the area from downtown's institutional and business core. With land values plummeting and middle and upper classes fleeing to new upscale neighborhoods in north Bogotá, San Victorino and Santa Inés took on a more overtly marginal character. Further cementing west downtown's reputation as an enclave of poverty, abandonment, and insecurity, in the 1960s the city government relocated street vendors to the plaza-garage and installed hundreds of stalls in what became a makeshift commercial arcade, the Galerías Antonio Nariño, for three decades. By this point, the division between a historic center and a popular one had been more firmly established: a "high downtown" of middle classes and elites in the east, and a "low downtown" associated with Indigenous and peasant populations, informal commerce, and clandestine operations to the west of the Carrera Décima.[32] What was once a liminal space of social friction was materially and symbolically reconstituted as a terrain to be tamed and contained. Tellingly, a news headline in 1963 described the area as a "red zone"[33]—a term not only linked to danger and immorality but also charged with ideas of insecurity and militarism central to Colombia's geography of political violence.

El Cartucho's name itself indexed such militaristic sensibilities. Records suggest that in the nineteenth century, a street in Santa Inés was unofficially known as El Cartucho due to the existence of a clandestine gunpowder factory and the paper packages (*cartuchos*) it used. According to historical accounts, the factory provided ammunition to early revolutionary fighters, and its owners were eventually executed along with other republican insurgents in the years preceding Colombia's independence from Spain in 1819.[34] The name El Cartucho would continue to circulate informally for decades, ultimately becoming the de facto label of the entire neighborhood by the twentieth century. By this point the term had a more direct connection to violence: *Cartucho*, in its contemporary usage, means "bullet" or "firearm cartridge."[35]

The entanglements between this epistemic and affective terrain and the country's history of warfare crystallized during the late twentieth century.[36] The transformation of Santa Inés into El Cartucho, of urban space into urban terrain, became increasingly linked to the intensification of armed territorial struggles and criminal violence in Colombia from the 1980s to the 2000s. Not only did such conflicts continue to forcefully displace people from the countryside to Santa Inés's crowded residences, but also, crucially, they provided the repertoires through which the area was further resignified and rematerialized as a battleground. In neighboring San Victorino, for instance, a business owner who arrived in the 1980s talked about El Cartucho as a "small Caguán, a zone of distension in Bogotá."[37] He was referring to a demilitarized zone that the government of President Andrés Pastrana Arango had created in southern Colombia between 1999 and 2000 for peace negotiations with the FARC guerillas. The zone had epitomized the idea of a parallel sovereign, "a state within the state." After alleged human rights violations and accusations that the FARC continued to launch military operations from the area, El Caguán was largely portrayed as a space of lawlessness and violence. In 2015, one of San Victorino's oldest and wealthiest business owners also hinted at these militaristic undercurrents when he spoke to me about the district's history as a "dangerous, hot" spot. He recounted how he and other local leaders had created an organization known as the Corporación de Comerciantes Mayoristas Asociados (Corporation of Associated Wholesalers), or COMAS, for security and self-defense. "It's basically a CONVIVIR," his son, next to him, whispered to me as we sat in a modest office hidden in the back of one of their warehouses. The CONVIVIR, or Cooperativas de Vigilancia y Seguridad Privada (Cooperatives for Surveillance and Private Security), were created in 1994 by the national government to promote rural self-defense organizations across Colombia. In the following years the cooperatives would become a key legal vehicle for the expansion of paramilitary control in the countryside. In San Victorino, these veteran *comerciantes* suggested, paramilitary logics had been reenacted in the form of unofficial underground detention rooms, private security patrols, and guarded borders.

While many of El Cartucho's residents experienced the neighborhood's downfall as a contested and contradictory affair—calling attention, for example, to the many legitimate businesses and livelihoods that subsisted in the area until its demise—they also evoked the distinctly material process through which Santa Inés–El Cartucho slowly turned into a battlefield. Former residents' memories of life in the neighborhood were often permeated with the imagery and sensorial experience of violence. In 2013, Sandy, a longtime resident now living on the city's outskirts, told me about her life in the area since she was a child. Talking over coffee and *almojábanas* in a small downtown cafeteria, Sandy constantly came back to the physical and affective signs through which she became increasingly aware that the "normal neighborhood" she had once known was no longer there. She began her account with a poignant remembrance of the M-19 guerrilla siege and military takeover of the Palacio de Justicia, a few blocks east of her home, in 1985—one of modern Colombia's most emblematic events of urban warfare: "When the tanks came in it sounded really loud; it shook the ground. I was only six or seven years old and imagined we were at war. You could hear the shots, the bombs, the ambulances, everything under siege. And because we were only a few blocks away they could have launched a bomb at us at any time."

Sandy went on to narrate how Santa Inés had "degenerated" and El Cartucho had formed from a rapidly growing drug economy closely tied to the area's informal waste recycling business. Paralleling this account was a story about family decline. Both her stepbrother and father had been murdered, another brother had been running from the police after a bar brawl turned deadly, and her mother's cafeteria had closed when the landlord rented the space to a waste-picking business with possible ties to the bazuco trade under the control of a local leader known as Ernesto "El Loco" Calderón. Closely woven into her recollections was the intimate knowledge of a changing material landscape. Far from the "clean streets" of her childhood, she now found "trash everywhere, street dwellers burning trash in front of [her] house every day to get copper from cable wiring." She saw "houses crumbling down" as drug gangs, known as *ganchos* (hooks), drew lines across the neighborhood in their bid for power.[38] At some point, her mother's modest restaurant became "a strategic point to stash weapons" and "for undercover police to gather intelligence." In the end, Sandy explained, with unmistakable military overtones, "we were mined with drugs, homelessness, even paramilitaries and guerrillas."

Before she and her family were finally displaced, Sandy was brought more directly into the fractious terrain created by the demolition of El Cartucho. By the 1990s, she was living between a small shack in one of the city's poorest peripheries and a dingy mezzanine above a restaurant her mother now ran in El Cartucho. She also sold lottery tickets on the street and frequently managed recycling warehouses, coming into closer contact with local strongmen and their street enforcers. In this precarious situation, and already pregnant with her first child, Sandy heard that the city government was looking for people from the area to conduct a socioeconomic census for the Tercer Milenio plan. She applied and was immediately hired for the job. As a broker between city officials and residents, in particular gancho leaders, she was now thrown directly onto the front lines of the struggle to unbuild El Cartucho. "There were places where [functionaries] couldn't go and I would talk so they would let them enter," Sandy recalled. "One day they went in without letting locals know, and they were chased off with bullets [*a plomo*]." But the job also extended to persuading residents about the inevitability of the demolitions and reconstruction. In response to the often-threatening questions about how she, a local, could work for the city enabling her own displacement, Sandy would tell people that the plan would happen "even if [they] opposed it." Or, as she quipped, "A donkey going downhill had more chances of going in reverse."

By the early 2000s, Sandy had been twice displaced from El Cartucho: first by the bazuco and recycling business and, finally, by a renewal plan in which she herself had participated. In the process she had become a census taker for government programs, the job that would keep her afloat for the next few years. But the ironies of her story were not lost on her. "It was kind of unfair, don't you think?" Sandy asked me pensively the last time we met. Reflecting on the disintegration of the neighborhood, the expulsion of residents, the spillover of violence, and the mostly empty park, she stressed how all along she had "always felt the abandonment of the state." Ideologies and affects linked to Colombia's embattled sovereignty had permeated her intimate and now professional knowledge of the place where she had grown up, so that it appeared as an unruly terrain abandoned and only partially reconquered by the state. Mirroring her contradictory position as both longtime resident and official contractor, her security-infused vision of urban terrain became the grounds for a critique of state intervention and urban reconstruction.

The complex entanglements between the destruction of El Cartucho and struggles over sovereignty were made tangible in a spectacular way in 2002. The expansion of military operations and the escalation of guerrilla and paramilitary violence throughout Colombia that year culminated with the election of security hard-liner Álvaro Uribe Vélez to the presidency. Authorities in Bogotá were on high alert as insurgent attacks rattled the country, and police raided houses in central neighborhoods in search of weapons caches. In July, the country's leading newspaper, *El Tiempo*, featured a special report that presented the partially demolished El Cartucho as a key link in the country's illegal arms trade: "Among the houses in ruins that still remain in El Cartucho, after two years of demolitions to build the park Tercer Milenio, there are still enough weapons and ammunition to create a FARC front."[39] And on August 7, 2002, Sandy's childhood fears that Santa Inés would be bombed were realized. That day mortar shells aimed at Uribe Vélez's swearing-in ceremony at the presidential palace missed their target, landing instead a few blocks to the west on a partially demolished El Cartucho. The bombing, presumably launched by the FARC, resulted in the death of several people who were clinging to the ruins left by the city's bulldozers. Significantly, the rockets hit a house whose demolition had been ordered in the very first stages of the renewal plan. Gancho Amarillo (Yellow Hook), as the building was known, was one of the area's largest tenements and bazuco houses.[40] Along with several *cambuches* (shacks) made of plastic tarp and sticks, it was among El Cartucho's last holdouts in a sea of rubble. The accidental bombing was the coup de grâce in the long process that had naturalized El Cartucho as a terrain of warfare.

Crisis Planning: Expertise as Strategy

Nonetheless, the epistemological and material destruction of Santa Inés–El Cartucho had largely unfolded at the drafting tables and in the offices and boardrooms of planning professionals whose urban sensibilities had been shaped by the country's explosive armed conflict and cartel violence. During the 1980s and 1990s, a sense of being under siege permeated the residents of major Colombian cities. Kidnapping had peaked as armed groups' weapon of choice, and representations of Colombia as "a country held hostage" circulated widely.[41] Middle- and upper-class urban residents feared the world beyond the city limits—those "mountains of Colombia" from where guerrilla and paramilitary groups typically signed off their official communications. In Bogotá, it was not only that well-off residents lived enclaved lives, a common trend in Latin American cities,[42] but rather that they conceived of the city itself as an enclave within a dangerous and unruly territory. If displaced peasants and rural migrants had for years arrived in the capital carrying their visceral histories of violence,[43] more affluent residents perceived only the impending threats of a war raging outside. Urban bombings, kidnappings, and rising crime appeared as signs of external forces making inroads into the urban world.[44]

At stake here was the deep divide between the city and the country that has marked Colombian history and shaped its geography of warfare: the imagery of a fractured territory and of state sovereignty radiating from the center to fill the alleged void of the hinterland.[45] Such ideas shaped urban intellectuals' views of rural peripheries as "no man's land," "red zones," and "internal frontiers."[46] This is what anthropologist Margarita Serje aptly terms "the reverse of the nation."[47] But as much as this geographic ideology became the backbone of nation-state projects across remote peripheries and its enclaves of extraction and exploitation, it was also directed inward and mapped onto the metropolis. By the late twentieth century, El Cartucho epitomized such an internal frontier, the urban counterpart to rural Colombia's zones of conflict and emergency. Much as simplistic accounts portrayed the war-torn countryside as the reflection of an absent state, experts materialized El Cartucho as a radically ungoverned and insecure urban terrain.

The transformation of downtown Bogotá was thus fundamentally guided by what we might call a metonymic epistemology: the idea, as one city planner told me, that the city center was a "microcosm" of national and global territorial conflicts. The particular ways in which people braided their experiences and knowledges of the city with geographic ideologies of insecurity varied considerably, as did the political ramifications of such epistemic practices. For locals like Sandy, viewing downtown transformation through the lens of armed conflict and land violence shed light on intractable struggles over sociopolitical and economic power. It brought into focus the injustices of state intervention, ultimately shaping a politics of dissent. For the officials and experts behind Tercer Milenio, whose lives mostly unfolded in the wealthy districts of north Bogotá and who had typically experienced the war from afar, El Cartucho embodied anxieties about the nation's unruly topographies. Echoing long-standing views about how dense jungles and steep mountains constituted an "intrinsically opaque" and ungovernable geography,[48] planners portrayed the people, things, and spaces of El Cartucho as constituting an inherently perilous terrain that could be secured only through total destruction. As the project manager of Tercer Milenio told me years later in her upscale development firm, "It was a black hole, a cancer, right next to the city's main institutional buildings; it was the most dangerous place in the city, a place in front of which people walked every day and no one dared look inside."

In this way, Tercer Milenio became central to planners' fantasies of territorial order and security. It was the target of a form of crisis planning that precluded alternative urban imaginaries and compelled a particular course of action: demolition and radical reconstruction. Crisis, as Janet Roitman argues, is an epistemological a priori starting point, an unquestioned "transcendental placeholder . . . for the production of knowledge."[49] In El Cartucho, planners' claim to an urban crisis led to militarized and strategic conceptions of urban renewal. It reaffirmed ideas about the city as terrain and conjured a future of order and security. Most importantly, crisis planning became linked to technocratic efficacy and managerialism, ideals that would come to define the administration of Mayor Enrique

Peñalosa (1998–2000) and its implementation of the Tecer Milenio plan. In an op-ed in *El Tiempo* in December 2000, diplomat and policy scholar Fernando Cepeda Ulloa celebrated the Peñalosa administration's "recovery of downtown," particularly of El Cartucho and San Victorino, stressing the "overwhelming power" of the administration's "leadership-planning-execution formula."[50] For him, Mayor Peñalosa and his Empresa de Renovación Urbana (Company of Urban Renewal) exemplified a distinctive style of planning and governance that was strategic, was geared toward execution, and decisively targeted the spatial manifestations of Colombia's crisis of governance (*crisis de gobernabilidad*).

Among city officials and colleagues, Peñalosa was known for his resolve and managerialism. Stories circulated about how, in his daily commute to the Alcaldía, he would take note of potholes in the streets and place calls to city agencies to demand that they be immediately repaired. He would leave voicemails for functionaries of all ranks congratulating or reprimanding them on their regular duties. And, as several planners and architects who worked with him in the late 1990s recalled, Peñalosa, who was not a designer, had single-handedly drawn the plan for Parque Tercer Milenio on a paper napkin. His disposition for action and leadership—what some would describe as his authoritarian inclinations—were on display when I met him in 2012, by which time he was a globe-trotting urban expert. In contrast to the many demure bureaucrats or rehearsed politicians I had encountered in government agencies, Peñalosa moved energetically around his consulting office as if it were the stage of a TED Talk auditorium.[51] With a picture of Tercer Milenio hanging behind his desk, the former mayor drew schemes and jotted notes on a large paper board as he avidly recalled the key stages of the plan. Significantly, Peñalosa described the crisis of El Cartucho not as a moment of rupture in the turbulent years of the late twentieth century but rather as part of a longer history of disorder and modernization—a history that for him was personal and went back to the work of his father, Enrique Peñalosa Camargo.

"It was my father who came up with the idea of [demolishing] El Cartucho," Peñalosa explained in his distinctively categorical tone. "He would always tell me, 'Look, there is a unique opportunity here to tear down that dump [*porquería*], which is in the center of the city, and develop a project there," he recalled, standing in front of a window overlooking the tree-lined streets of the upscale district of La Cabrera in north Bogotá. He traced the idea back to his father's work as a city councilor in the 1950s as well as Peñalosa Camargo's close friendships and professional collaborations with Jorge Gaitán Cortés, a respected city councilor (1958–61) and one of the most "technical" mayors in the city's contemporary history (1961–66),[52] and with Virgilio Barco Vargas, also a former Bogotá mayor (1966–69) and later president (1986–90), widely recognized for his technocratic approach to government. As a public functionary in the National Ministry of

Public Works in the late 1940s, Gaitán Cortés had proposed an unrealized plan known as the Ciudad del Empleado (City of the Employee), which would have razed the Santa Inés district for the construction of "hygienic and comfortable" housing.[53] For Peñalosa, his father, like Gaitán Cortés and Barco Vargas, epitomized an elite generation of mid-century urban technocrats. "[He and his colleagues] worked without pay in the city council . . . and they worked every day until two in the morning and wrote books and studies, and carried out projects," Peñalosa stressed. This was "the group of people I grew up with, people captivated by Bogotá and by urban issues."

Such forms of expertise became intimately tied to an emergent international technocratic apparatus directed at global urban problems—domains of policy and expertise that would be increasingly identified with the terms "habitat" and "human settlements." And here again, Peñalosa traced his own lineage and connection to this history through the figure of his father, who played a key role in global circuits of expertise in the 1970s. Peñalosa Camargo had been secretary general of the first United Nations Conference on Human Settlements (also known as Habitat), held in Vancouver in 1976. Habitat was a watershed moment for the consolidation of a transnational framework of urban governance, and it ultimately led to the creation of UN Habitat (the United Nations Human Settlements Program), which Eugene McCann describes as a "key global informational infrastructure" for the circulation and legitimation of expert urban knowledge.[54] Drawn by a sense of urgency, hundreds of official delegates, NGOs, and journalists convened to confront "the extremely serious condition of human settlements" across the globe and especially in "developing countries."[55] As Felicity Scott argues in her history of modern architecture and global environmental governance, the Vancouver conference ultimately "sought to garner support, particularly among industrialized countries, for new policies and forms of governance by mobilizing fear of population growth in the Third World and with it the specters of scarcity, insecurity, and war."[56]

Urban habitat emerged as a distinctly technical and strategic issue, one whose adequate redesign would serve as a critical source for nation building, social pacification, and the expansion of global capitalism. The appointment of Peñalosa Camargo as secretary general of the conference was thus appropriate. His trajectory as an expert in Colombia was closely aligned with Habitat's reframing of urban development as a critical component of strategies of governance and security. Furthermore, he embodied the action-oriented, technocratic ethos showcased at the conference. This, according to Scott, was the idea that "human settlement problems . . . were technical, not political in nature, and the conference was an occasion for the exchange of information."[57] As Peñalosa Camargo remarked during the Vancouver conference, "We will be coming together for a global exchange of ideas, techniques and systems for solving specific problems."[58] Questions about whom development and security agendas served were obscured. Instead, planning appeared primarily as a logistical question dependent on technical resources, strategies, and execution.

Peñalosa Camargo's role within this emergent milieu of expertise had a lasting impact on his son's own trajectory as an urban expert. It partly explained the contradictions that would come to characterize Peñalosa's vision as mayor in the late twentieth century: on the one hand, his alleged emphasis on progressive values of equality and inclusion through a new breed of technocratic knowledge directed at public spaces (of which Tercer Milenio was a culminating project), and on the other, his strategic views of urban space as an ideal medium to cement security, governance, and development. But most of all, his father's legacy lived on in Peñalosa's aspiration to a form of urban expertise that was radically action oriented and based on principles of efficacy and transformative outcomes. In describing to me previous "socioeconomic studies" of El Cartucho and San Victorino and failed interventions in the area, Peñalosa called attention to the fundamental gap between rhetoric and action: "This world is divided into two kinds of people: those who talk and those who do [*hacen*]." The suggestion was that he, like the technocrats he admired before him, were *doers*. For Peñalosa, the imperative of "doing" was the only real response to Colombia's lasting crisis of sovereignty and order.

Critical scholarship on technocracy has typically called attention to how expert knowledge is mobilized to create a simplified and depoliticized social reality subject to intervention and management.[59] In Peñalosa's account, the drive to intervene, to *do*, emerged as both the ruling ideology and the central aim of urban technocracy. Strategic and logistical thinking mediated the production of urban knowledge and its corresponding forms of intervention. This outlook, as Peñalosa made clear in his personal recollections, was not simply the function of a particular body of knowledge or institutional matrix but had been anchored in his experience and location in a particular social milieu. As an elite urban professional who, like his father, saw the country's alleged crisis of sovereignty manifested in the material and social forms of the city, he assumed that urban expertise had to be strategic. Appeals to scientific expertise—to the calculations and designs integral to modernist urban planning—were subordinated to wideranging visions of sovereignty and governance. The invocation of strategic action and logistics, furthermore, pointed to what theorists from Carl von Clausewitz to Michel Foucault and Paul Virilio have argued is the mutually informing connection between war and politics, militarism and everyday life.[60] Strategy, in this context, is primarily concerned not with tactical maneuvers on the battlefield or the political stage but with the terms themselves in which theaters of engagement are organized. It is in this sense—as a structuring logic—that military-strategic thinking has been viewed as a blueprint for the operations of power across myriad fields of knowledge and political practice, in times of both war and peace.[61]

Significantly, Peñalosa's technocratic sensibility pointed to the performative and material dimensions of expert strategy and its securitized overtones. At stake here was not only the emergence of an epistemological space known as urban habitat but also a practical and phenomenological approach that envisioned the urban realm as a field of military-strategic intervention. In *On War*, Clausewitz himself had already noted that strategizing is aimed at "persuading others" with "clear ideas."[62] It is a framing device that "provides the script and the props for a convincing performance of the future in the here-and-now," as Martin Kornberger puts it.[63] Strategy, Kornberger adds, is "an aesthetic phenomenon. . . . [It] favors images over plans, evangelism over analysis, and the poetry of the possible over the prose of the present. The pathos of the strategist replaces the bureaucratic ethos of the planner."[64]

Far from suggesting a strategy without a strategist,[65] Tercer Milenio called attention to the ways in which ideas of crisis and strategy became incorporated into expert knowledge and ingrained in a terrain of intervention. This not only made apparent the lines of continuity between urban warfare and planning, military logistics and development, but also posed critical questions about what form of war was meant by strategists, who their imagined enemies were, and what kind of battlefield was materialized in the process. In Bogotá, such questions were directly shaped by geographic ideologies of insecurity linked to Colombia's armed conflict and informed by global paradigms of securitization ranging from Cold War geopolitics to counterterrorist discourses to risk management and humanitarian frameworks. Planners drew on these repertoires, which were in turn mediated by their experiences as middle-class urban professionals, to render urban space into a tangible object of expertise and intervention: a terrain of knowledge.

In his recollections of the early stages of the plan, Peñalosa rehearsed the main coordinates through which El Cartucho and San Victorino emerged as battlefields and in which nothing less than national sovereignty was at stake. As he explained it to me, "The struggle to remove San Victorino was monumental. [Clearing] San Victorino was something that no one would have dared, it was almost like the FARC, no one dared touch it. . . . It's unimaginable what it was, it was the symbol of the impotence of the state: the center of Bogotá totally occupied, it was complete chaos." Peñalosa portrayed the public plaza and its street vendors as comparable to Colombia's insurgent enclaves. The image of the "absent state" was transposed to the core of the country's capital, and the operation became a matter of state sovereignty. The politics of informality and poverty were assimilated to the politics of warfare, making impoverished vendors "legitimate" targets of governmental force. Back in his office, channeling the "pathos of the strategist," Peñalosa elaborated on the logistics of this military takeover as he got up from his desk and drew my attention to a map hanging on the wall:

> [San Victorino] was taken over by thousands of mafia organizations with political and military power. . . . So how was I able to get them out? Basically, because I had a police chief, a tough guy, who was later killed, and we carried out a military operation. When we launched the final operation, we brought in everything: fifteen hundred police officers, helicopters, armored vehicles, everything! Why? Because when you're going to carry out one of these operations you always have to have overwhelming force, so the guys can clearly see they have no chance. [Back then] no one dared even to say that San Victorino was going to be cleared, everyone panicked! Much less that El Cartucho was going to be torn down!

Military thinking and strategic force were woven into urban knowledge, producing a mode of crisis planning that recrafted San Victorino and El Cartucho into a terrain of warfare. As chief strategist, Peñalosa had enacted the urban theater of operations in which planners and experts would perform.[66] They were the ones, however, who would be confronted with the task of making the complex realities of El Cartucho—its people and things—knowable as a terrain of danger awaiting radical transformation.

A Materialist Phenomenology of Insecurity

Ideas about the materiality of urban space were central to the plan to demolish El Cartucho and build a metropolitan park. Planners and experts shared an orientation toward the urban environment that linked its sensorial and affective qualities to understandings of violence and insecurity. The materiality of insecurity was integral to planning and design knowledges, so that securing the neighborhood appeared as a matter of disassembling its forms and erasing its physical attributes. The expert attention to urban materiality reflected political imaginaries that juxtaposed the allegedly orderly spaces of the city with the rugged, unruly topographies of the countryside. Such aesthetic criteria were mapped onto the city's geography, making visible the rifts between affluent, modern districts and impoverished, disinvested neighborhoods such as El Cartucho. Professionals' urban lifeworlds, their daily experience at home and in their offices, embodied this aesthetic order, which was reproduced in their expert engagements and embedded in their understandings of territorial (in)security.[67]

Take for example a senior official by the name of Lucía who oversaw the implementation of Tercer Milenio from 1998 to 2003. I met her at her architecture design firm in April 2012. A business administrator by training, Lucía had spent most of her career managing and promoting high-end real estate developments. Her firm was located in the upscale El Nogal neighborhood, not far from Peñalosa's consulting office, in one of the countless orange brick buildings that roll down the green eastern hills into the sprawling Sabana de Bogotá. Her office's surroundings embodied local ideals of cleanliness, safety, and beauty: wide concrete and brick sidewalks (one of the legacies of the Peñalosa administration), tree-lined parks, and a handful of Victorian-style houses that were once the defining characteristic of the area when it was an affluent suburb in the 1940s.

Sitting at her desk next to the frosted glass partition of the sleek office space, Lucía was the personification of an elite Bogotana. She wore a tailored cream suit that matched her light complexion and talked with the casual politeness, slightly pursed lips, and elongated *s* common among the upper class. Addressing me with the informal *tú*—sensing our overlapping social backgrounds—Lucía candidly shared some of her most memorable experiences working in the Tercer Milenio project. "I had never been to El Cartucho and I was left with my mouth open for three days because it was such a horrible thing," she said with a mix of disdain and fascination. The sensorial and aesthetic qualities of that first visit left a strong impression on her, one that she was at a loss to describe: "If I could paint or write, I'd try to write about that first impression when I entered [the place]." The "images" that came back to Lucía were revealing of the social and cultural sensibilities that had shaped her perception of El Cartucho. One that stuck with her was an apparently banal observation about the doorways used by *jíbaros* (drug dealers): "Their houses' doors were . . . how are those things called? Those things that they use in hot lowlands [*tierra caliente*] that you can move to the side, like rattan blinds [*bambulitas*]. They would peer outside [through them]." Implicit in her recollection was the long-standing imaginary of Indigenous and Black lowlands and coastal regions as uncivilized and disorderly,[68] which carried echoes of the same apprehension toward rural migrants that had infused representations of downtown Bogotá since the late nineteenth century.

Further compounding these geographic assumptions and their manifestation in El Cartucho's decaying materiality was Lucía's depiction of an idealized urban past that had been all but completely lost: "First I saw houses and the prettiest things in the world; they still remained even though they had smoked up [almost] all of them, because they smoked up [even] the houses. I saw a family, a lady that had never gone out of there, who said she had afternoon refreshments [*onces*] in the home of Indalecio Liévano and that she raised her family in that place. We took her out of there and put her in a refuge when we started the renewal process." In sharp contrast to her misgivings about the material aesthetics of *costeños* and *calentanos*—people from warm tropical climates—she waxed nostalgic about a traditional Bogotá culture epitomized in the city's republican architecture and in eminent gentlemen (*cachacos*) like Indalecio Liévano—a respected twentieth-century historian, politician, and diplomat. For her, such historical relics had been besieged by the materiality of violence and disorder, eventually disappearing or becoming "refugees" in an allegedly inevitable process of destruction. Although initially troubled by the "horrible poverty" she had seen, Lucía was soon persuaded in her conversations with Peñalosa that, at its core, the problem of El Cartucho was one of "degeneration" and "illegality" crucially mediated by the materiality of things and people. "Because what one found in El Cartucho," Lucía explained, "was a very strong form of illegality that defended itself with disorder, filth, and chaos. [Illegality] attracted vulnerable populations, made them drug addicts . . . and human shields."

The idea that urban insecurity and disorder were aesthetically and materially ingrained in El Cartucho became central to the reenvisioning of the area as a terrain of warfare, one in which urban planning and military-strategic intervention merged into each other. This was something already apparent in officials' seemingly innocuous and common description of Tercer Milenio as a "detonating project" that would ripple through downtown and remake its urban fabric. Such militarized framings pervaded planners' everyday work so that conflicts with local actors were scaled up and recast as signs of a looming battle. As Lucía put it, "At some point we were worried, concerned about the process, so I went to speak to the army, because there were tensions [in the area], and they told me, 'Look, we're not going in, because if we do, there'll be a civil war and *they* will probably win because they're too strong. We, as soldiers, can only fire bullets [*echar bala*]." The implication was that overt military action had to take new forms, transmute into other techniques and modes of political action, that would more effectively reconquer the physical and social terrain of El Cartucho. For Lucía, the conjunction of militarism and politics was most apparent in the work of the police: "The police helped us a lot; there was a commander who was very political. In reality, the police are more political than anything else." During the project, policing was underpinned by other, more covert forms of intervention—from negotiation to co-optation—aimed at diffusing local leaders' control over the area. But as other experts made clear, the logics of warfare had also extended and merged into the politics of demolition, land acquisition, and urban design.

Cristina, one of the lead designers on the project, talked with me about these entanglements as she clicked through one of her old PowerPoint presentations on Tercer Milenio. We discussed the plan in her home office in late 2011 in Santa Bárbara, one of north Bogotá's most exclusive neighborhoods. The elite enclave is known for its ample houses, lush greenery, and twenty-four-hour private security force. It has also been characterized by its homeowners' opposition to high-rise construction and mixed-use development. Cristina lived in one of two three-story townhouses that formed a boxy brick-and-stone structure enclosed by a heavy steel gate. It faced a hilly park shaded by eucalyptus, pine, and cypress trees—three common species imported by the Spanish and a living remnant of the time when the area was a large hacienda. Although the building bore little resemblance to the Spanish-inspired architecture of white stucco walls, wood window frames, and red tile roofs visible around the neighborhood, it was still closely aligned with ideals of residential living that harked back to the Spanish country home and its bucolic relationship to a domesticated landscape—something akin to what Raymond Williams famously described as a pastoral "structure of feeling."[69]

Cristina's views on the military-strategic nature of the intervention and the material decadence of El Cartucho illuminated the ways in which geographic ideologies "are actively lived and felt," as Williams puts it.[70] Sitting in her dimly lit and soberly decorated studio, soft jazz music playing in the background, she articulated a vision of the city through the familiar spaces of her home and office. "If you have [a place] in a house, like the space I have there under the stairs," Cristina said, pointing outside her office door, "and there is the possibility of leaving a piece of cardboard or something else, then you start to put more little cardboards and other things in there." Evoking El Cartucho, she called this "the human tendency to clutter [encartuchar]," something she had experienced not only in the intimacy of her home but also, ironically, when she directed a city office in charge of overseeing the construction and maintenance of public space: "People started leaving files [carpetas] somewhere in the office and then everyone thought that was the spot where files had to go before they would be taken down to the archive. After three months there was a Cartucho there, full of files!"

From this perspective, El Cartucho emerged as the ultimate manifestation of threats haunting the very core of urbane life—the alleged tranquility of the bourgeois home and orderly routines of state bureaucracy. For Cristina, the neighborhood's decay posed a fundamentally logistical issue not unlike the one entailed by home organizing and state restructuring. And in the absence of the knowledge and mechanisms to relocate, compensate, and expropriate residents, Cristina noted, the military-strategic nature of the logistical challenge was laid bare. The "logic of the private sector," the real estate world from which most experts came, fused into the logic of warfare. "The strategy to purchase land was almost a military strategy," Cristina explained bluntly. "[The strategy] was to buy entire blocks" instead of individual properties, in order to gain territory and create a secure perimeter. That is why land acquisition was carried out "along the edge [of the neighborhood]," she continued, "because we knew that the most complex issues of drugs and weapons were in the core. That's why we had to acquire land in the periphery."

Turning to her computer screen and pointing to an aerial photograph of El Cartucho, Cristina remarked on the importance of "working from above" during the process. What Eyal Weizman calls a "politics of verticality" proved central to the city's bid for territorial control.[71] Such planning optics not only contributed to representations of El Cartucho as a theater of operations but also made visible its contours as a terrain of insecurity. Planners often called attention to the irregular and rough spatiality of the neighborhood, to its "zigzagging" and "crooked" streets. As one expert put it to me, "Morphologically El Cartucho was like a triangle with a very particular urban form, so people *se encartuchaban*, they got into a space into which authorities could not easily penetrate." She had indexed key meanings of *cartucho*—which in addition to gun cartridges also refers to paper packages, cones, and rolls—and mapped them onto the neighborhood, suggesting a "morphological" homology between words and material forms. El Cartucho thus emerged as an opaque and striated terrain impervious to the gaze of the state. But more than pointing to the city's immanent material qualities and how they admittedly overwhelmed human action, these expert discourses called attention to the ways in which enactments of materiality themselves became a critical medium of politics. Planners' obsession with the rugged physicality of El Cartucho, and their tacit references to the country's terrains of warfare, proved integral to militarized strategies of demolition and reconstruction. As one architect told me, the plan ultimately aimed to "desencartuchar El Cartucho": to unroll the unroll, as it were, and smooth out the area's convoluted material geography.

At work here was an understanding of the materiality of insecurity shaped by experts' everyday knowledge and experience of the city. Many planners and designers held the conviction that urban space did indeed have immanent material features and that it had the power to dictate social and political realities: from the civilizing environments of middle- and upper-class living to the inherently dangerous and unruly spatialities of the urban and rural margins.[72] As Lucía noted with almost absolute certainty, "Physical space defines the behavior of people, of humans, even animals." In El Cartucho this meant that the disposition and qualities of things and people inevitably led to violence, insecurity, and disorder. By materializing the neighborhood as a tangibly unwieldy and dangerous terrain, experts reasserted the need to fully disassemble it. This was perhaps most apparent in officials' reluctance to preserve any trace of the neighborhood's architecture or topography. Leaving any structures standing was seen as inherently risky, one functionary explained to me. Unbuilding had to be complete, and transformation had to reach, as another senior planner put it, "a point of no return."

Mapping Human Terrain, Unbuilding Social Infrastructures

The strategic acquisition and demolition of physical structures was the most visible dimension of the rematerialization of El Cartucho as a terrain of warfare. According to Cristina, however, Tercer Milenio had been a complex process of knowledge building (*construcción de conocimiento*) in which softer techniques targeting social relations underpinned the plan's harder military-strategic logics. Behind the physical dismantling of the neighborhood, experts had deployed modalities of intervention aimed at disassembling "social infrastructures": local forms of sociality, ownership, and organization.[73] Significantly, such modes of governmental knowledge were framed in the language of humanitarianism and development. Property relations and everyday livelihoods emerged as key battlefronts, illuminating the multiple security logics that converged in Tercer Milenio. Echoing Colombia's long history of armed conflict and the state's embattled sovereignty over an unruly social and physical topography, the downtown neighborhood was recrafted into something akin to a zone of disaster and vulnerability, with thousands of alleged victims waiting for humanitarian assistance and the promise of development. Ironically, experts' enactments of a social emergency became an increasingly tangible reality amid an enveloping atmosphere of destruction and ruination put into motion by the same state actors in charge of rescuing its supposed casualties.

These other facets of the militarized intervention surfaced most clearly in the accounts of officials and experts working closer to the ground. These were the functionaries directly charged with carrying out the plan, or what is known in Colombia as the *gestión* of a project. While the term is close to the English "management" or "governance" (e.g., *gestión pública*), gestión refers more directly to the practical demands of bearing out a project—that is, of dealing with real-world contingencies and working through the mechanics of implementation. Néstor, for example, was an architect who had worked in the city's Instituto de Desarrollo Urbano (Institute of Urban Development), or IDU, the city agency responsible for executing the Tercer Milenio project, and who described his work as being neither strictly planning nor policymaking but rather *gestión urbana*. I met Néstor in 2012 in his consulting office near the city center. In contrast to Lucía and Cristina, he had spent most of his career in the public sector. Far from the glossy real estate companies and design studios of north Bogotá, his firm looked more like a modest bureaucratic office: a shared space of four desks in an older building in the traditional La Soledad neighborhood. As a result of his proximity to the city government's day-to-day official business in Tercer Milenio, Néstor's experience revealed the continuities between the strategic-securitized dimensions of the intervention and the prosaic, seemingly technical aspects of providing social assistance.

Unlike other officials involved in the operation, Néstor was wary of describing Tercer Milenio as a security intervention. As he explained hesitantly, "I think our objective was not to end the illegal drug trade of the city; that was not the objective of the plan . . . although that's still debatable." As an IDU functionary with experience in public works, Néstor saw the park primarily as public infrastructure that, like roads or dams, had inevitably displaced residents. "So our main problem wasn't getting rid of crime," he stressed, "like in that favela in the movie *Elite Squad*. No, our objective was to do urban renewal, and a key component was to carry out a plan of *gestión social*." Instead of characterizing the plan as a form of urban warfare, epitomized in the popular 2007 Brazilian film about a violent special operations police unit in Rio de Janeiro, Néstor called attention to its resettlement schemes.[74] The planning team searched for existing models and finally adopted "the World Bank's methodology to deal with resettlement, to deal with displacement," he told me. The main challenge in El Cartucho was the widespread absence of property owners, making it impossible for the state to follow eminent domain protocols. So "experts turned to other experiences," Néstor explained, "and the closest one was resettlement in vulnerable areas, where people did not hold property titles." Drawing on the World Bank's framework to "reestablish initial conditions" and the city's own experience in "zones of risk and vulnerability," Néstor continued, experts created a "baseline" and a system of compensation.[75] Crucially, technologies aimed at governing insecure peripheries had been transposed to the city core. "Parque Tercer Milenio was really interesting," Néstor said, "because it was the first lesson in how to manage vulnerability in nonmarginal zones. We have an urban pattern where we typically think that poverty is located in the periphery and the city knows how to handle those situations well, zones of risk, zones of informal urbanization. So that was the referent but transferred to a central area."[76]

In talking about "vulnerable" populations that had to be "rescued and resettled," Néstor conjured the imagery of humanitarianism and its complex ties to military and police intervention—a familiar script in Colombia's theater of warfare. As a central periphery defined by vulnerability, El Cartucho was made to resemble a zone of emergency, one in which the causes of urban crisis were obscured and the moral imperative to intervene took precedence. As Didier Fassin and Mariella Pandolfi argue regarding contemporary military-humanitarianism, the intervention brought together "a logic of security and a logic of protection."[77] Such affective and epistemological sensibilities rendered visible the "social" dimension of the battlefield. If planners' vertical optics made tangible the material contours of terrain, social and real estate *gestores* (individuals who perform gestión) recrafted

El Cartucho into something akin to the "human terrain" of contemporary counterinsurgency.[78] Aimed at making the intervention more humane, to "socialize" (*socializar*) the plan, as the expression goes in Bogotá's policy circles, officials produced knowledge about local communities in an attempt to distinguish law-abiding residents from alleged criminals and to better direct social assistance and relocation programs. The process, however, was riddled with contradictions, not only exacerbating conflicts and criminalizing entire swaths of the population but also serving as a strategic technique of persuasion and intelligence gathering that prepared the ground for territorial control and displacement.

Consuelo, a senior sociologist with a long career as a consultant in the public sector and one of the experts in the Tercer Milenio operation with the most field experience, elaborated on the stakes of the plan's "social component." Soberly dressed and restrained in her manner, Consuelo met me for coffee at a busy street café in a boutique hotel next to the ritzy Parque del Virrey, a park she described as "an oasis in the chaos of Bogotá." During our conversation it became apparent that her long-running engagement with downtown conflicts and exclusions had reached a breaking point. She confessed feeling "moral fatigue" and being often "fearful and tired of Bogotá." Her already strained relationship with the city had been exacerbated by a recent break-in at her north Bogotá apartment, and she now spent most of her time in a small house she rented in the countryside. Consuelo's urban disenchantment also pointed to the conservative social reformism that shaped the professional practices of many gestores sociales. She seemed genuinely concerned for her "street friends [*ñeros*]"—something resembling motherly care—and intimately attuned to their lifeworlds. "I spend all day doing this, I can't stop doing activism," Consuelo said as she gave some change to an old woman who had been weaving around the espresso- and pastry-filled tables asking for money. And yet her approach to urban poverty had a moralizing undercurrent, favoring ideas of social betterment over an acknowledgment of the contentious politics of urban renewal.

Consuelo's moral conviction about the necessity of implementing a "strategy of social intervention" gave the city's social schemes an aura of technicality, one that, as Fassin and Pandolfi put it, "neutraliz[ed] political choices by reducing them to simple operational measures."[79] In a distinctly procedural tone, she listed some of the initial actions carried out in the neighborhood: "Psychosocial attention for families, comprehensive support in their condition of unemployment, their health condition, their educational condition, et cetera." As she elaborated further, Consuelo offered a more unvarnished account that made apparent the political underside of gestión social. She presented socio-humanitarian intervention as a tactical resource that had been deployed to support the larger strategy of territorial control. Not unlike the counterinsurgent war for "hearts and minds," social assistance programs emerged as a means of persuasion—what Consuelo called "a strategy of seduction"—and as a source of information, which she in turn described as a matter of "identifying and recognizing" the social reality of the area. On the one hand, officials set out to create a sense of "proximity" and "build trust" among local residents. On the other hand, they gathered data that would be indispensable in later stages of the plan. The central tool in this regard was a socioeconomic census that was carried out "behind closed doors," Consuelo admitted. "We closed El Cartucho so no one could enter or exit," she explained, "and then there was a zero hour [*hora cero*] for the census." Cordoned off and surveyed, people were counted, classified, and mapped. "We had so many maps; the cartography was so impressive," Néstor recalled, talking about the same process.

Ultimately, Consuelo said, the operation had aimed to "support families so they could start preparing to exit the zone [*la salida de la zona*]." Her phrasing was reminiscent of the language used in Colombia to describe militarized enclaves and zones of conflict, amplifying the sense that the plan was an emergency evacuation to rescue vulnerable subjects from a zone of danger. Further uncovering the politics of Tercer Milenio's urban humanitarianism, she more openly stressed its strategic value as a technique of both legitimation and logistical expediency: "First came in the strategy of social and humanitarian intervention, and then behind it the real estate intervention of urban renewal for the purchase of the properties. So that was what was smart about Peñalosa's idea. He said, 'Let the humanitarian issue pass first, let it take care of whatever it needs to take care of, and when it's guaranteed that even the very last of all the human beings there is sheltered or protected or at least intervened or accompanied, then we come in with the purchases and the bulldozer.'" By intervening in the very bodies and livelihoods of people, gestión social was supposed to accomplish what militarized planning alone could not. Although government assistance allowed some families to eventually access permanent housing, an indeterminate number were relocated transitorily and then left to their own devices. Far from a long-term resettlement policy, the scheme was more directly aimed at allowing officials to "peacefully" unbuild El Cartucho's social infrastructures and launch demolition and reconstruction plans. Temporary resettlement, initially for one year and later on only for three months, was a "truce [*tregua*]," as Consuelo put it, "a truce while all real estate matters were taken care of."

In one sense, gestores sociales had recast "people as a geographic space to be conquered—human beings as territory to be captured," as Roberto González argues in his critique of counterinsurgent "human terrain."[80] Mapping and managing this terrain, however, proved to be a much more contradictory and conflict-ridden affair than Consuelo's techno-humanitarianism implied. The census, for instance, was actively opposed from the start of the operation. "You want to get us out and on top of that you want us to open our doors so you can see what you are getting rid of?" Néstor recalled residents telling him. Inevitably, he admitted, the census became a source of intense negotiations and, more problematically, of tensions and eventually outright violence: "The census implied a negotiation, reaching agreements with local actors; otherwise, it would have been impossible to do it." City officials identified specific "groups" ranging from tenement dwellers and street vendors to owners of typography stores and recycling businesses. In the process, Néstor pointed out, "forms of leadership emerged, some of which were terrible, some among them even died, there were several threats and deaths." Here he was confronted with the realities of the intervention. As a gestor social, he had done work that had overlapped with matters of security and policing. "It's a complicated issue," he said about meeting with local jíbaros, "because as a functionary you can't meet with criminals." With some hesitation, he hinted at the threats he had received from rivaling local factions and how he had finally decided to resign.

If Consuelo had presented the official version of gestión social as a technical-strategic operation, experts like Néstor were more forthcoming about the complex terrain of conflicts and insecurities that gestores sociales had had to navigate. What emerged here was something akin to a "public secret": the partially disclosed truth that social programs relied on stealthy maneuvers and tactical compromises.[81] "There was a tacit agreement," Néstor explained cautiously, "and one has to be careful about saying this. What one presumed was that while the project's chronogram was established, during the months of the census, the other stages of the plan, et cetera, some of the groups that had illegal economic interests would have time to leave. The groups that had some fear, and again you have to say this carefully because it wasn't an official agreement, those groups would start withdrawing." In different ways, officials involved in the process admitted knowing that some of the main jíbaros in the area and their ganchos promptly relocated their business to nearby areas. As Néstor put it guardedly, "It seems some of the criminal groups moved immediately to neighboring San Bernardo, and we didn't prepare some form of resistance, we didn't carry out any police or social action."

Relocation of "vulnerable families and individuals" was also plagued with conflicts and uncertainties. The city had scarce institutional resources to permanently resettle local inhabitants, especially the hundreds living in the streets, and residents in other city districts, including very impoverished and marginalized neighborhoods, were actively opposed to receiving El Cartucho's stigmatized inhabitants. "So very painful things occurred; some were frustrating, some had to be hidden," Néstor continued. "We had to do things secretly. For example, in

Antonio Nariño, people organized a protest because we were bringing children from El Cartucho, and in another neighborhood in Usme, too, they even built barricades because we were taking some people from El Cartucho. So we had to do things individually, we had to take families out and accompany them covertly."

These tensions intensified during the property acquisition and demolition process, the so-called *gestión inmobiliaria*. The real estate operation had been led by Felipe, a successful real estate agent, who met me in his expanding firm, not far from where I had talked with Consuelo in the upscale El Virrey neighborhood. Tercer Milenio had been his first job after graduating from an elite university in downtown Bogotá. At the time, he had never set foot anywhere near El Cartucho, and other officials joked about the unlikely scene of a "rich kid" negotiating with homeless addicts and hoodlums. At the end of the demolition, he was known by locals as "El Gucci del Cartucho." Like Consuelo and Néstor, Felipe stressed the "social" dimension of his work. Looking back on his experience with some nostalgia, he explained that his role in the project had been "more as a social worker than a real estate agent." Felipe had become passionate about relocating commercial clusters without dispersing them, while lamenting the fact that the city had not compensated businesses more fairly. He had found the work most rewarding when he felt he had "improved" people's lives: "More than a real estate satisfaction it was a social satisfaction, helping those people to move on to something better, helping an elderly woman find the apartment she wanted." In Felipe's account, humanitarian sensibilities emerged under the guise of a caring form of socioeconomic development. And yet, as with other experts, his ethical and moral convictions aligned closely with the practical and operational demands of the project. "You have to understand the social situation of each one of those persons to be able to give them a solution," he clarified, "[rather than] simply tell[ing] them, 'I'm going to give you money so you can leave,' because [in that case] you will probably lose the money, the house, and end up worse off."

Felipe recounted a flamboyant scene that captured the tensions between his personal-affective investment in the project and his commitment to strategic pragmatism. During one of the early field visits, some of his team's topographers had been met with threats while attempting to take measurements on an inner block. Ernesto "El Loco" Calderón, a local leader and recycling business owner—the same man who had outbid Sandy's family and taken over their restaurant—had confronted the city functionaries, allegedly threatening them with a gun and a grenade. Under intense pressure from his superiors and with a trip to Miami with his girlfriend coming up, Felipe went into the very core of El Cartucho, donning his suit and tie, to resolve the issue. He retraced his steps with me, almost in disbelief of what he had been capable of at the time: "I started walking, I passed in front of the city morgue, things were a bit strange, strong, ugly, but I kept going and then reached Ninth Street and I asked, 'Hey, where's the man they call El Loco Calderón, I'm looking for him.'" Amid perplexed looks, someone told him to go to a nearby bakery. He went in and asked again if anyone had seen El Loco. "The only crazy person here is you!" a tall, corpulent man with curly hair, dress shirt, and graying stubble beard shouted, standing up from the crowd of scraggly men. "What do you think you're doing here?" El Loco himself had asked, genuinely surprised.

Felipe explained that he came on behalf of the office of urban renewal to get El Loco's permission to measure the block. "This guy is crazy," Felipe recalled him saying. "I don't even know how you managed to get to Tenth Street alive dressed like that." But El Loco laughed it off, appreciating Felipe's boldness, or perhaps his utter obliviousness. He told him to come back the following week, but Felipe explained that he had to do it that same day or the next at the latest. El Loco asked him why, and the exchange that followed, Felipe recalled, "marked the beginning of their relationship": "I just told him, 'Look, the truth is I'm going to Miami with my girlfriend and I don't want to cancel the trip.' The guy burst into laughter, saying, 'OK, I'll let you take your measurements if you bring me a leather jacket from Miami.' And that's how I ended up buying a leather jacket for El Loco Calderón in Miami!" In one sense, the gift—a leather jacket—was emblematic of the moral-humanitarian impulse that shaped experts' understanding of urban intervention: it was a gesture of goodwill and empathy, much like Consuelo's tacit equation of alms giving to activism when we spoke at the outdoor café.[82] As an exchange, however, Felipe's gift was the opposite of what scholars have described as the unreciprocated gift of development aid—it was a hollow token, a coat for a neighborhood.[83] It enacted a social bond between the men, one of respect and reciprocity, that would ultimately prove a thin veneer for the plan's underlying territorial violence.

The tensions between social assistance and militarized displacement, cooperation and co-optation, played out more prominently in later stages of the plan. Confrontations with jíbaros and their ganchos became more frequent, and police increasingly escorted demolition crews into the neighborhood. City workers were often attacked and machinery sabotaged. "Someone even threw a grenade at us in a camp where we had trucks and machinery," Felipe recalled. And here again, military logics melded with ideals of socioeconomic development. Local leaders, including some of the very same jíbaros who were orchestrating the attacks, were offered job opportunities and contracts with the city. Ironically, many of them were hired to protect the city's machinery and to accompany real estate appraisers in their daily work. Crucially, experts saw these initiatives both as an extension of frameworks for social assistance and economic compensations and as a strategy to co-opt and defuse criminal networks. As Felipe put it, "It was an interesting move in the sense that you generated jobs, you paid them salaries for their assistance, and you divided them. It was an interesting strategy that worked well; it was recruiting people from the zone. [This strategy] also created many problems, because it generated complex internal wars among them."

The remaking of El Cartucho into a human terrain—a double-sided ground of morality and strategy—ultimately proved much more volatile and unwieldy than experts had expected. In March 2000, around four hundred people organized a protest in El Cartucho; according to local press reports, that protest soon became a full-blown "rebellion." Police intervened and violence escalated, leaving two dead and many more injured. Protesters blocked major streets, burned cars, and threatened to set a gas station on fire. According to journalistic coverage, the area had transformed into "a combat zone into which not even ambulances could enter."[84] During the event, El Loco Calderón gained visibility as the leader of the uprising. For several officials who were involved in the project, this was typical of Calderón's ambivalent shifts between incendiary opposition and pragmatic agreements. Almost exactly a year after these events, Calderón was shot dead by a rival gancho gunman. For Felipe, the assassination had been directly related to Calderón's many contracts with the administration: "They said he had contracts with the city's welfare department, with demolition companies, with everyone, so they started accusing him of being a sellout and he started having serious rivalries."

In 2005, demolitions had reached an end, and Parque Tercer Milenio would soon be inaugurated. In April the city administration carried out the last incursion to remove the people who had stayed behind and were still living in the neighborhood's ruins. Initial reports spoke of hundreds of former inhabitants wandering through downtown neighborhoods as residents in their path took to the streets to oppose their presence.[85] These last inhabitants epitomized the recalcitrance of the human terrain that planners had charted and sought to manage. While a combination of assistance and negotiation had enabled officials to identify, sort out, and move a considerable part of the population, these remaining ruin dwellers—the "floating population," in technical jargon—revealed the extent to which the plan had made people into tactical objects to be either removed or strategically exploited. Literally stripping them down to bodies in circulation, and in a cynical enactment of their disposability,[86] city officials decided to shelter almost two thousand people in the city's former Matadero Distrital (slaughterhouse).[87] But in yet another demonstration of the obduracy of the terrain conjured and allegedly conquered by experts, during the following months, and as the park opened, drug dealers, street vendors, waste pickers, and bazuco smokers slowly trickled back and resettled along the margins of the now paved-over, landscaped terrain from which they had been displaced.

An Urban Prototype in Ruins

In December 2003, several years before I began the research for this book and while I was working as an assistant in the mayor's office in Bogotá, I was invited to an unlikely event: a city-funded art performance created by the art collective Mapa Teatro and former inhabitants of El Cartucho on the rubble of the partially demolished neighborhood. A motley audience of city functionaries, local intelligentsia, and former residents, we watched the ruined neighborhood come back to life in the cold downtown night. An assortment of longtime residents emerged from a field of debris in which grass and plants had started to grow. Like the weeds sprouting in an abandoned demolition site, these individuals would enact something that exceeded ruination, showing the "heterogenous and unexpected life amid rubble," to borrow Bettina Stoetzer's phrase.[88] The "stage" was loosely configured by lines of candles marking former walls and streets, two large screens at the back, and recovered furniture: an antique wardrobe, a radio cabinet, old wooden chairs, and bed frames. The "actors" included street dwellers, street vendors, impoverished migrants, circus performers, and tenement dwellers, all of whom had made a life for themselves in El Cartucho. As they recounted their experiences and memories of the place that was no longer there—some of them guiding the public through imaginary structures and roads—a video of the demolition process was projected in the background. The uncanny installation-performance dissolved the lines between performers and audience, ruined landscape and new infrastructure, memory and reality. At some point a disheveled man still living on the site came from behind, launching into an unintelligible tirade, only to be removed by the police. At the end, in an improbable scene of rebirth and regeneration, the residents-performers came together and danced slowly to a melancholic bolero as Christmas fireworks lit up the wasteland around them.[89]

In sharp contrast to the strategic terrain crafted throughout the planning process, the theatrical installation rendered visible the people, knowledges, and things that urban renewal had set out to erase. In a conversation years later with Rolf Abderhalden Cortés, one of the cofounders of Mapa Teatro, he described the performance to me as a "counterdiscourse," one that questioned the "official narratives" and "mythologies" that had been inscribed on El Cartucho. The project had interrogated preconceived notions of urban decay and "problematized the figure of the victim by situating [residents] in a new terrain in which their agency was acknowledged." It shook the foundations of the modes of crisis planning that had recrafted the neighborhood into a battleground. To illuminate such narratives and stories, it put materiality at the center of performance: the texture and sensorial qualities of the world that had been inhabited by displaced residents.

FIGURE 2.2. *Prometeo*. Mapa Teatro, 2002. Photo by Fernando Cruz.

The ruin emerged as a site of possibility and critique. "The community's stories," Abderhalden Cortés states elsewhere, "were a substantive part of the architecture of the neighborhood's memory. A form of resistance in the face of oblivion, a potential footprint among the ruins."[90] At its core, the performance illuminated a particular configuration of knowledge and materiality that unsettled the epistemologies of destruction that had been mobilized for the creation of Tercer Milenio.

Mapa Teatro's artistic intervention in El Cartucho had various iterations. In addition to the two performances in the semidemolished neighborhood, the collective staged installations and video performances in its own exhibition space—a downtown republican house very much like the ones that had been razed in Santa Inés—and in galleries across the globe. Their final act, *Witness to the Ruins*, which was inaugurated in 2005 (the same year the park opened), brought one of the last residents of El Cartucho and a close collaborator of Mapa Teatro to the stage. Juana Ramírez stood in front of screens that showed images of the demolition and testimonies of former inhabitants, as she performed what had been her daily activity in El Cartucho: working at her small stand making hot chocolate and *arepas* (corn cakes) on a wood charcoal grill. It was a "live archive," Abderhalden Cortés explained to me, one that "reintroduced vital elements of her practice." The installation homed in on the materiality of local knowledge and the local knowledge of materiality—"the smell, materials, and bodies," he stressed.

Mapa Teatro's documentary, ethnographic, and artistic installations constituted an urban prototype, not only in its status as a provisional model of urban engagement reassembled over time, but more centrally as what Alberto Corsín Jiménez describes as "an emerging sociomaterial design . . . whose social and material components retrofit each other as being in mutual suspension."[91] Operating as what Abderhalden Cortés called a "laboratory of social imagination," Mapa Teatro's recrafting of material and social relations not only called attention to the "lost material and immaterial patrimony of El Cartucho" but also crucially destabilized planning epistemologies and pointed to alternative urban futures.

Conversely, Tercer Milenio itself appeared not as monumentalized space but rather as an unfinished and fraught prototype of urban renewal. Despite all the efforts to leave no trace of what had been there before, the park was haunted by the sociomaterial worlds it obliterated, its surroundings falling into disrepair and suffused with the memories of El Cartucho and its destruction. "For old residents," as Abderhalden Cortés put it bluntly, "the park you see today is a cemetery." Soon after its inauguration, the park emerged as an obsolescent infrastructure. Three blocks on the north side were left undeveloped. Originally slated for commercial developments, the barren plots became a de facto garage for police cars, including armored riot-control vehicles like the ones used to "clear" the area not long before. Between 2015 and 2017, the development of a shipping container mall for popular commerce and an affordable housing complex on the remaining plots added new layers of meaning to the urban terrain. And yet the park continued to be a solitary space burdened by its history. By the end of 2018, Peñalosa returned to his theater of operations after being reelected as mayor and almost two decades after his first term. In an eerie scene, excavators and bulldozers rolled onto the grassy esplanade of Tercer Milenio to "renew and completely transform" the fourteen-year-old urban renewal project. Alongside intensifying police operations in the area, the administration now aimed to revitalize the park through new sports-and-recreation amenities.[92] This was the reworking of a prototype, but one troublingly familiar and closely entangled with the vestiges of militarized displacement and territorial control. It was a prototype in ruins, one that foreclosed rather than enabled new paths. It signaled the shifting yet enduring violence of epistemic terrains in the remaking of downtown Bogotá.

Part II

THE COUNTER-EPISTEMICS OF INSECURITY

3

THE VIOLENCE OF BUREAUCRACY

"We're the displaced [*los desplazados*] of Manzana Cinco!" Hernando declared with indignation as he stood in front of his crumbling home. The stocky man pressed his hands down into his pockets and stretched his jacket desperately over his bulging shirt. Hernando was a traditional downtown Bogotano. He had the coarseness and street smarts of a man familiar with day-to-day hustling—what Colombians call *rebusque*—as well as the dignity of a propertied working-class *vecino* (neighbor). I met him on one of my many visits to the demolition site in which he now lived in the neighborhood of Las Aguas on the east side of downtown Bogotá. The Empresa de Renovación Urbana (Company of Urban Renewal), or the ERU, as it became more commonly known to residents, had slated the area for redevelopment in 2006 with a plan known as Manzana Cinco (Block Five). In contrast to the *barrios populares* of the western and southern edges of the historic center, this was a city block located at the intersection of three busy commercial and cultural corridors, in the close vicinity of several prestigious universities and museums and at the foot of the emblematic hill known as Monserrate. By 2012, the block's aging houses, low-rise apartment buildings, and crowded parking lots had been expropriated and demolished, except for three houses on the northeast corner. One of them was Hernando's family home, a rustic house with a tile roof and crimson walls, where he and his elderly mother still lived.

During my fieldwork, Manzana Cinco became a vivid illustration of the layered and unstable processes of ruination operating at the core of urban renewal. An earlier state encroachment in the area had occurred in the late 1990s and early 2000s when the city administration created a pedestrian boulevard, the

FIGURE 3.1. The last houses standing in Manzana Cinco, with the Las Aguas neighborhood and the Universidad de los Andes campus in the background. Photo by the author.

Eje Ambiental (Environmental Axis), along the winding course of the old San Francisco River and the historic Avenida Jiménez. Some properties on the east side of the block had been expropriated for the expanded corridor and its new public spaces. Unexpectedly, the construction had uncovered an early twentieth-century brick-and-stone bridge, one of the many bridges built since the nineteenth century to overcome the city's broken topography and later buried under downtown's modern road infrastructure. The weed- and grass-covered republican-style remnant now stood, partially visible, alongside the debris and lonely columns and walls of the new project's active demolition site.

As I took pictures of this "piling [of] wreckage upon wreckage," to use Walter Benjamin's felicitous phrase, I sensed someone looking intently in my direction.[1] It was Hernando and his friend Ismael, a middle-aged man who owned a historic preservation house on a nearby street. They interrupted their street corner conversation to ask if I was a journalist. After becoming visibly disappointed when I explained I was not, the two launched into a passionate diatribe. "Those sons of bitches from the ERU simply robbed us!" Hernando shouted indignantly. "The ERU shields itself with laws, it uses, modifies, and knocks them down to its benefit."

Ismael interjected, pointing to the area's new buildings and their "aggressive architecture . . . the glass facades, the metallic, machine-like structures." Urban legalism, design, and the very materiality of property regimes, they suggested, had come together in officials and developers' bid to "take over and appropriate [*apropriarse*] downtown." Hernando described the judicial battles in which he had become embroiled, the multiple lawsuits he had filed and many courts he had visited. "This has really been an odyssey," he concluded, distraught, "and I'm so angry, those assholes came in and stole from us." Before we parted ways, Hernando gave me his telephone number, unprompted, and offered to tell me more about the Manzana Cinco ordeal and show me documents in a future meeting. As he walked back into his house, its peeling and cracked walls looking even more fragile in the sea of rubble, he turned back and said once again, as if to make sure I understood the significance of his predicament, "We're the displaced of Manzana Cinco!"

Counterepistemologies of Insecurity and Renewal

Hernando had gestured to Colombia's prolonged history of violent displacement, a history intimately tied to the country's tumultuous and rapid urbanization during the twentieth century. With guerrilla and paramilitary violence reaching new heights by the turn of the century, the *desplazado* (internally displaced person) had become a ubiquitous urban figure, one that populated everyday spaces and the public imagination. The phrase "the displaced of Manzana Cinco" reappeared many times in conversations with local residents and in their communications with government agencies. By calling on the imagery of rural warfare and dispossession, property owners reframed the ostensibly technical processes of expropriation and redevelopment as forms of violence. They mobilized long-standing repertoires of insecurity and directed them back at the state and its instruments of governance. If official epistemologies had previously rendered city spaces and populations into battlefields to be pacified and reconquered, residents now construed bureaucratic artifacts and legal instruments as themselves constituting a terrain of danger and insecurity. In this way, they condemned one of the most central aspects of Colombia's history of warfare: what Francisco Gutiérrez Sanín calls the "interweaving of armed extortion and juridical technique."[2]

In one sense, the Manzana Cinco project was emblematic of a form of "structural violence . . . enacted through everyday practices of bureaucracy," to borrow Akhil Gupta's terms.[3] In this vein, one local scholar described the plan as a form of "quotidian . . . silent and slow violence."[4] Bureaucratic violence appears in this context as an arbitrary, indirect effect of the dispersed and contradictory operations of the state. This is a form of violence defined by the lack of discernible intentions and identifiable perpetrators. But in Manzana Cinco, far from unaware, passive targets, residents proved to be acutely attuned to the violence of bureaucratic paperwork and procedures. They actively traced and rendered visible the specific contexts, means, and actors responsible for those otherwise diffuse modes of structural violence.[5] Ultimately, they unsettled reified visions of the state as they aimed to tease apart the various governmental arms, agents, and things involved in their dispossession.[6]

The materiality and aesthetics of bureaucracy—what Julie Chu calls the "atmospherics of law"—became central to locals' critical elaboration of and response to urban renewal.[7] Property owners did not merely recognize the extent to which the things and forms of bureaucracy crucially mediated processes of destruction and displacement.[8] They also conceptualized official documents and notices as perilous bureaucratic artifacts and, in so doing, denounced institutional injustices and assigned political accountability. Through the production of knowledge about urban bureaucracy and law, residents "performatively materialize[d]" official artifacts and spaces into sources of insecurity and transformed them into a medium for sociopolitical dissent.[9] This chapter seeks to illuminate such modes of street expertise and reveal their significance and limits as counterepistemologies of urban planning and renewal.

The displaced of Manzana Cinco were ultimately unsuccessful in their battle to block the project or obtain greater compensation, but their legal engagements rendered visible the lopsided negotiations surrounding downtown renewal. Moreover, they proved to be powerful enactments of dissent with lasting effects on the city's circuits of urban expertise and policymaking. At the same time, such modes of opposition were predicated on and constrained by an epistemics and affectivity grounded on liberal conceptions of property and the state. In this sense, residents' knowledge of insecurity and its materialization in the things and spaces of urban governance emerged as a platform for the praxis of urban politics, albeit one constrained by the grammar of warfare and victimhood.

In the following pages I attend to the ways in which the epistemic engagements of the displaced of Manzana Cinco were mediated by the forms and materiality of social hierarchies, property regimes, and state sovereignty. The crucial question here is how people composed and materialized knowledges out of the fabric of everyday urban life and what kind of politics such knowledges shaped. How did the residents of Manzana Cinco come to think of their neighborhood as violently razed land? Why did bureaucratic documents and officials appear to them as agents of terror? How did they come to view themselves as victims of violent displacement, and with what political implications?

In one sense, these are phenomenological questions about the lived experience of inhabiting the city and, more specifically, about how dwelling shapes ways of knowing the urban world.[10] It was through their everyday, practical orientations that residents encountered bureaucratic and urban things as materializations of violence and insecurity. "Orientations," as Sara Ahmed argues, "shape not only how we inhabit space, but how we apprehend this world of shared inhabitance, as well as 'who' or 'what' we direct our energy and attention toward."[11] Individuals' locations vis-à-vis Colombia's sedimented histories of violence fundamentally shaped residents' knowledges and those knowledges' materialization in a landscape of urban things and bureaucratic artifacts. Social and political relations mediated the constitution of spaces and objects as particular sites and instruments of warfare.[12]

In Manzana Cinco, residents' pursuit of middle-class urbanity—a sense of respectability and industriousness—was closely entangled with regimes of individual private property, racialized and class-inflected notions of social propriety and progress, and ideals of state legitimacy and authority. The "warscape" that emerged was thus not unlike renderings of Colombia's armed conflict centered on ideas of state absence and the weakness of law.[13] In this manner, property owners directed their critique of institutional violence primarily at indolent bureaucrats, corrupt functionaries and judges, and inept officials, and not at the juridico-political and technical logics behind downtown renewal. The implication was that displacement would have been avoided had the law been enacted in more technically sound and legitimate ways. Locals' grievances were thus less about the violence of renewal and more about not having been spared by the city's bureaucracy given their aspirational status as lawful, propertied citizens.

Significantly, many of the block's residents had arrived in the area in recent decades to achieve their own investment and development ambitions. "My neighbors were also to blame," Hernando once told me reluctantly, explaining that they had demolished "many beautiful homes" long before planners set their sights on the area. So even though residents experienced the materialities of bureaucracy and renewal as forms of warfare, theirs was not a critique of the insidious links between state power, property regimes, and long-standing violence and injustice. Instead they denounced an allegedly rogue institution, the ERU, and appealed to the state as victims of "illegal" and "irregular" operations that had imperiled their entitlement to property and development. Local critiques of bureaucratic and juridical insecurities were thus more about securing existing visions of urban order, legality, and progress than about directly challenging planning epistemologies and structures of dispossession. A central question I explore here, then, is what it means for urban political horizons when renewal is confronted as bureaucratic violence and the defense of property rights is mediated by the class and racial politics of liberal citizenship.

Waiting for the State

The story of Francisco, one of Manzana Cinco's largest property owners, brought into focus the paradoxes of local epistemic practices. Francisco was a savvy businessman in his eighties, an "old fox," as a city planner once told me, who had been buying property on the block for decades, ultimately becoming the owner of one-sixth of its total area. Although his business had seemingly seen better days, Francisco's social and economic standing set him apart from his neighbors. Educated as a chemist, he had worked for years in pharmaceutical and textile firms in Medellín, Colombia's second-largest city and the capital of Antioquia. He had moved to Bogotá in the 1970s and decided to "put [his savings] into something that would not lose value." This was the beginning of his career as a downtown real estate investor and independent business owner. He ran a plastics manufacturing company in a middle-class residential neighborhood to the west of the city center and lived in an affluent, leafy district in north Bogotá.

We met in the two-story, modest concrete house in west Bogotá that he had converted into his small factory. The living and dining rooms and kitchen were now the shop floor, and the second-floor bedrooms and den had been turned into offices. Francisco recounted his long history in Manzana Cinco in a small meeting room that looked out into a larger office in which two aging secretaries counted wads of bills surrounded by mid-century metal desks, overflowing file cabinets, and typewriters. Dressed in a slightly worn, classic suit, he sat back and talked slowly in a deep, throaty voice. The formality of his speech and the way he dragged out the ends of his sentences evoked the figure of the downtown *cachaco*—an early twentieth-century archetype of the cultivated and cosmopolitan Bogotano. As our conversation unfolded and Francisco poured glasses of whiskey, his Antioqueño origins became more palpable in his frequent shift to the melodic accent of *paisas*, as Antioqueños are known, and, more significantly, in his enactment of paisa ideals of self-reliance and pragmatic industriousness.

"It was a heist," Francisco stated. "[The city] violated the law at each step along the way." He drew on detailed knowledge of urban law, fiduciary trusts, and real estate development to describe a string of bureaucratic manipulations and abuses. If his neighbors had channeled their middle-class aspirations into their denunciations of bureaucratic violence, Francisco's critique of urban renewal was colored by his experience as a real estate investor and his ambitions as a developer. In his account, he gave full expression to the liberal ideals of property and citizenship that residents had tacitly upheld in their construal of renewal as bureaucratic insecurity. Crucially, his outlook on urban life brought him tangibly close to the epistemic space inhabited by city planners and real estate promoters. In a narrative tinged with longing for both a bygone past and an unfulfilled future, the city center emerged for him as a malleable medium for the materialization of ideals of nationhood, progress, and sociopolitical belonging.

Much like urban experts, in his navigations of the urban world Francisco rendered the city into an ensemble of legal and sociopolitical forms ready to be reimagined and reassembled.[14] After arriving from Medellín, he had initially considered real estate investments in the downtown neighborhood of La Perseverancia. This was a *barrio obrero* that had been built over decades by workers at the Bavaria beer-brewing factory, one of Colombia's oldest and largest companies, and had eventually become a working-class enclave surrounded by museums, financial institutions, and up-and-coming residential neighborhoods. In a manner resembling planning fieldwork techniques, or what some experts framed in security terms as intelligence gathering (see chapter 2), Francisco had carried out "detective work," he told me, spending time in bakeries and shops to get a sense of local sociospatial dynamics. What he saw in his stints as a neighborhood ethnographer—following the gossip and quarrels on the street, as he put it—turned him away. Noting that I, as an anthropologist, would appreciate his forensic reasoning, he explained: "So what was the problem? That La Perseverancia, and here comes the anthropological part, does not work [for real estate development]. It is subdivided into very small lots with all kinds of family disputes, possessions [*posesiones*], and property tenure issues. In other words, the only way to do it is with a very firm official intervention; it is the only way to transform that neighborhood."

This led him to Las Aguas, where he purchased his first property from a "broke intellectual" who lived in an aging republican-style house. Francisco allowed the man to stay as his tenant, as he continued to buy adjoining properties during the next fifteen years. During this period, he crafted a vision for the block in which investment agendas became indistinguishable from a larger political project. At that point, Francisco said to himself, "I'm going to take care of this block, because this is a truly tremendous block for Bogotá to shine globally." Ironically, what he envisioned then was not far from what the ERU would seek to implement more than twenty years later at his and his neighbors' expense.

In 1983, Francisco drew on his personal connections with a member of the city council from the Liberal Party to propose a redevelopment plan for the block. He drafted a study on the neighborhood's socioeconomic conditions and its potential as a cultural and tourism hub. The eighty-page proposal, which included statistical appendices, urban plans, and relevant legislation, was titled

"Guidelines for the Project of a Metropolitan Cultural, Recreational, and Tourism Center in Las Aguas Neighborhood." The typed manuscript—which Francisco located in his overflowing file cabinets after a few days of searching and shared with me—followed the conventions of a governmental report, as well as well-established planning narratives about urban decay and renewal. According to the study, renovating the area would restore "national dignity and pride" to what had become downtown's "chaotic environment of abandonment, filth, and misery." Las Aguas was ideally suited to these purposes, the document continued, because it concentrated "touristic, landscape, recreational, economic, and social values" that would "come to light in all their splendor" through an adequate legal and spatial intervention. The proposal went nowhere, and Francisco was left sitting on several properties for decades as he waited for a new opportunity to come along.

While Francisco had come to understand Manzana Cinco as a "government heist" and a form of "legal theft," his critiques of the plan and visions for the block ultimately obscured the constitutive violences and inequalities of Colombia's liberal sociopolitical order. In contrast to the ERU's mainly speculative project, he argued, his project would materialize "the coexistence [*convivencia*] of social classes and political ideas" and help "erase the image of Colombia as a violent country." His use of the term *convivencia* was revealing. It recalled a policy trend, inaugurated in Bogotá by Mayor Antanas Mockus in the late 1990s and taken up by city administrations around the country, that focused on the creation of a so-called *convivencia ciudadana* (citizen coexistence) and *cultura ciudadana* (citizen culture). Aimed at fostering civism and law-abiding behavior through pedagogical interventions, such initiatives elided questions about entrenched structures of inequality and violence.[15] Convivencia also had an earlier history from when political elites of the Liberal and Conversative Parties formed the Frente Nacional in the late 1950s to share power for almost two decades. Also known as convivencia, this period embodied a "politics of civility" that rested on long-standing and violent hierarchies and geographies of class and racial difference.[16]

Tellingly, one of my last conversations with Francisco took an unexpected turn as we talked about the failures of the city's bureaucracy and the difficulties of meaningful political engagement. "We have to recover our Hispanidad!" he exclaimed, looking at me intently with his small gray-blue eyes as he described Colombia's troubled national identity, where "'Indio' is an insult and 'Spaniard' is shameful." His yearning for Iberian culture bore the marks of what Aníbal Quijano calls the "coloniality of power": the Eurocentric systems of differentiation and domination that have defined knowledge production, state making, and capitalist development in Latin America from the conquest to the present.[17] Within such long-standing elite regimes of *mestizaje*—where racial mixing allegedly held the promise of whitening—Antioqueños like Francisco had been portrayed "as intrepid white pioneers who civilized a wild frontier" through a vibrant coffee-growing economy, and as forerunners of a brand of industrial capitalism based on moralistic paternalism.[18] Francisco channeled this entrepreneurial spirit of civism and progress when he told me that "the best way to optimize the utility of any [real estate] operation [was by] making it useful not only for oneself but also for the community."

In saying this, he reached back to a conception of the public good that perpetuated exclusions under ideals of civic pride and economic efficiency. Here again, Antioquia's history of urbanization was instructive. As a successful industrial center and national model of technocratic governance, the regional capital of Medellín had been built on "the careful balance of elite hegemony and economic access," in the words of historian Mary Roldán.[19] Investments in public services, education, and homeownership were very effective at keeping popular mobilization and contentious class politics at bay.[20] At the same time, Medellín's elitist and moralistic establishment proved incapable of absorbing the growing numbers of urban poor within this regime of control and conformity. Mounting exclusion along with a rising drug trade created the conditions for explosive urban violence in the city's *tugurios* (shantytowns) by the 1980s and 1990s and for an increasingly distrusted and coercive state apparatus. These trajectories of power and exclusion came to mind not only as Francisco talked about his vision of convivencia and a profitable "common good" but also in his decrying of the neighborhood's "slumification [*tugurialización*]," as he put it in his 1983 plan, and what he described as the "unfortunate necessity of displacing a certain number of inhabitants from the area" in order to fulfill its civic and economic potential. His critique of Manzana Cinco as bureaucratic theft was, therefore, far from an indictment of state authority and existing property regimes. Instead, Francisco seemingly invoked the restoration of statehood and its attendant ideals of property and citizenship. For him, the block took the form of a beleaguered and abandoned territory in need of state presence and intervention. As he put it, "I saved those lots for the state for over thirty years!"

In a sense, then, he framed his role in downtown as a proxy of the state, an agent of sovereignty working toward the future materialization of ideals of governance, property, and belonging. Such views resonated with the violent contestations over territorial control that have been integral to state making in Colombia from urban shantytowns to rural areas. Within this history of fragmented sovereignty, the state has emerged as an always tentative proposition, a claim to rule taken up and disputed by a host of actors—from guerrilla and paramilitary forces to criminal organizations and business syndicates.[21] In critiquing the ERU, Francisco was thus opposing what he construed as a competing, illegitimate actor seeking to exercise some form of sovereignty: "The ERU, as an institution, can offer public-sector jobs, construction licenses, administrative privileges. And what can we property owners offer? Nothing!" In questioning Manzana Cinco as a political project, as well as the motives of the ERU, he nonetheless evoked the image of an idealized state modeled after his conceptions of convivencia and the common good, with the exclusions they implied. He had been waiting for the state—as he put it, "taking care of those lots"—only to become the victim of an illegitimate bureaucratic takeover orchestrated by the ERU.

The Apple of Discord

Such histories of conflict and sovereignty were mediated by the block's material and cultural transformations. Its sensorial and semiotic qualities had become closely entangled with local understandings of state and property and had ultimately shaped residents' critiques of bureaucratic insecurity. After Manzana Cinco was launched in 2006, the block remained under construction for more than a decade, its gradual ruination embodying the conflicts and contradictions of the plan. Hernando and one of his neighbors had managed to keep their houses standing for several years, eluding demolition through tactics of evasion and making visible the intense legal confrontation that residents and the city had been embroiled in. For an even longer period of time, half the block had remained empty as the administration scrambled to create a project for a public amenity. This void was significant, as Manzana Cinco had been originally launched and partly justified with a plan to construct a cultural center funded through Spanish international cooperation. After six years, and as a result of Spain's 2008 financial crisis, the Spanish government had ultimately canceled the project. For the next few years, the only visible development on the expropriated land was the construction of the upscale residential and commercial complex. The half-demolished block was the crystallization of the brand of entrepreneurial urbanism epitomized by the ERU:[22] an opaque assemblage of public and private partners that invoked "social interest" (*interés social*) and mobilized urban laws to create new land for real estate speculation.[23]

By 2018, there was almost no trace of the old Las Aguas block. Thirty properties had been demolished, two towers for high-end student housing had been inaugurated, and the construction of a public cinema and media library (*cinemateca distrital*) was almost complete. The housing complex stood on three levels of commercial space, including brand-new Starbucks and Juan Valdez coffee shops with outdoor seating. Signs advertising the new development, known as CityU, were visible around the area, and private security with dogs guarded the "permeable public spaces"—a term employed by designers—at the base of the structures. One afternoon I walked along the storefronts with Camilo, an expert in urban law and redevelopment who had followed the Manzana Cinco plan closely. As we talked about the uneasy juxtaposition of private and public spaces—itself a clear embodiment of the character of the plan and its implementation—Camilo shared his sense of discomfort. "It feels strange to be here," he said. He hinted at the erasure of the former neighborhood and its social and material histories. Only the early twentieth-century stone-and-brick bridge uncovered during previous rounds of construction remained under overgrown grass and on the edge of the glistening new complex. It was an uncomfortable ruin that pointed to the block's history and to the disappearance of almost all traces of the people and things that had been there before.

For the residents of Manzana Cinco, the material and symbolic resignification of their neighborhood—the layering over and reinscribing that it became subject to—was from the start a contentious affair. For many locals, the official nomenclature employed in the plan—"Manzana Cinco"—had itself constituted an affront, a stripping down of the local histories and sociocultural practices tied to Las Aguas. Property owners responded to official categorizations by talking about the block as the city center's "apple/block of discord."[24] Beyond its religious and mythological symbolism and its tacit critique of the conflicts unleashed by the block's reconstruction, the expression was connected to local history. Residents were referring to *Don Chinche*, one of the most popular shows on Colombian television, which aired from 1982 to 1989 and was set in one of the neighborhood's old houses and in several locations on the block. The original and less-known title of the series had been *Manzana de la Concordia* (The apple/block of Concord), a reference to the nearby historic downtown neighborhood of La Concordia but also, according to the show's director Pepe Sánchez, a celebration of local forms of solidarity among unemployed and impoverished urban residents, most of them rural migrants from across the country.[25]

The sitcom followed a construction worker and jack of all trades, nicknamed Don Chinche, in his daily exploits to makes ends meet in the bustling city: a paradigmatic urban *rebuscador*. In contrast to most telenovelas, the show was unique in its neorealist style; it was filmed with a single movie camera in local interiors and exteriors and it documented everyday life in a working-class barrio. It was not only a rare primetime TV portrayal of working-class urban culture but also a hopeful depiction of rural migration and ordinary life in the midst of the ravages of war and urban violence.[26] The show, as Sánchez explained in an interview, reflected the "great exodus toward the capital . . . that had started in the 1950s," subtly weaving social critique into humorous, everyday urban scenes.[27] An example of this was the story of the recurring character Doña Berthica, the owner of a small neighborhood restaurant who had come from the department of Huila with her son Eutimio, Don Chinche's sidekick. Over the course of the series, it emerged that Doña Berthica's first husband had been killed by the police in her rural village. Eutimio, in turn, seemed constantly out of place, with his pet pig and provincial naiveté, in his daily adventures in the big city.[28] Without making it obvious, the comedy exposed, arguably for the first time in primetime television, the everyday trials of displaced populations in the capital. In 1983, one year after the show aired, an edition of *Semana* magazine illustrated the underlying relationship between the series and the country's deepening violence. The issue featured *Don Chinche* on its cover, calling it a "TV phenomenon," while also publishing the magazine's first article on the rise of the infamous drug cartel leader Pablo Escobar, the "Robin Hood Paisa."[29] Don Pablo, as people called him, would become an emblematic antihero in Colombia's popular imagination: a "pariah capitalist" who amassed extraordinary wealth and became both the benefactor of the urban poor and a ruthless criminal with a penchant for excessive violence.[30] Don Chinche, in contrast, emerged as an ordinary hero who responded to the injustices of Colombian society with the humility of manual labor, the solidarity of rural life, and the cunning of the urban hustle.[31]

In referring to the "apple of discord" and remembering *Don Chinche*, residents were doing more than simply recalling the neighborhood's quaint history. They indexed an urban ethos, a lived experience and atmosphere linked to working-class urban culture and its enduring rural sensibilities. According to one of the few scholarly analyses of *Don Chinche*, the series presented an "urban sensorium," a form of affective knowledge that resonated with audiences precisely because of how it evoked viewers' everyday life and engaged their aesthetic and sensorial dispositions.[32] These sensibilities constituted an epistemological, performative, and aesthetic medium that became integral to Manzana Cinco residents' political outlook and opposition to the plan. Hernando and his neighbors' tactics of deferral, the way they shrewdly avoided eviction proceedings over several months, could very well have been the plot of a *Don Chinche* episode. The deployment of street knowledge and the idea of outsmarting authorities and developers, a key trait of the urban rebuscador, became integral to how residents confronted the threat of renewal and navigated bureaucratic and juridical insecurities.[33] On one occasion, for instance, Hernando was telling me about his frustrating encounters with ERU officials when he called me to the side and lowered his voice as he pulled a small recording device from the front pocket of his shirt. He whispered that he was on to city officials and had been recording meetings to gather evidence of their inconsistencies and deceits.

Residents became attuned to the power differentials encoded in bureaucratic performances, and they embodied the middle-class aspirations at the core of

Don Chinche's humorous caricatures. Another scene recounted to me by various residents was their first public audience with senior officials from the ERU, who informed them about the urban project and their inevitable fate. One elderly property owner told me with indignation how the agency's director had talked down to her and her neighbors, how the woman had "scolded them" and boasted about her familiarity with cities across the world. The condescending official had implied that residents did not know enough about contemporary urbanism to understand the significance of the plan. The elderly woman then recalled with satisfaction how the son of one of the block's oldest and most well-to-do property owners responded to the functionary, telling her that although he had just returned from graduate studies in England, he, unlike her, did not "humiliate people or raise his voice." The anecdote, which I heard several times, pointed to residents' vindications of the dignity of working-class propertied citizenship and their willingness to question official expertise and its classist overtones.[34]

These performances were intimately connected to a distinctly working-class and bucolic urban sensorium of sights, smells, and textures. Most residents opposed the new sensory regimes of urban renewal and longed for the neighborhood's disappearing stores, restaurants, community spaces, and distinctive architectural forms. Miguel, a longtime baker and one of the first residents to be evicted from Manzana Cinco, dwelled on the neighborhood's "traditional [*típica*]" atmosphere. I met him on an April morning in 2012 in his busy cafeteria: an old terra-cotta plaster-and-tile house similar to his now-demolished home across the street. Amid the loud clatter of coffee cups and plates, and with the smell of fresh bread and empanadas wafting from the ovens and deep fryers in the back, Miguel recounted his arrival in Las Aguas in the late 1950s. Like many others, he had come from the countryside to reunite with relatives who lived in the area. He settled into a large house in which he and his family ran a successful *tejo* court for decades (tejo is a popular sport with pre-Columbian roots in which a metal disc is thrown from a distance into a box with clay and gunpowder packets that explode upon impact). Lining the streets, he recalled, were stores, cafeterias, and *piqueteaderos*—barbecue restaurants typically associated with the countryside and rustic settings. While some piqueteaderos continued to operate in the area, the more common practice among local residents in recent years was to pull out grills onto the sidewalks in the afternoon and sell food to university students and passersby. Hernando, for instance, had described this as one of the activities he engaged in to earn income until his very last days in his family house.

Also close by, Miguel noted, had been the "famous *chichería* El Gallo." This reminiscence was evocative, as chicha, a traditional fermented maize beverage that was consumed widely in Bogotá, was associated with rural habits, backwardness, and disorder. Its production had been banned in the late 1940s as part of the government's modernizing reforms. The "battle against chicha" was also an important step for the expansion of the beer industry and other "hygienic" alcoholic beverages—a history particularly meaningful in Las Aguas as the home of one of the city's main beer factories.[35] By the twenty-first century, the legacy of chicha halls was still visible, though it was rapidly fading in downtown's dwindling beer parlors and pool halls. These aesthetic and sensorial qualities were integral to what Miguel described as Las Aguas's "traditional" and "authentic" character. Like many of his neighbors, he invoked *Don Chinche* to make this point: "This neighborhood was so traditional that *Don Chinche* was filmed here. My house, the historic house that was taken away from me, was the restaurant of Doña Berthica [in the show]. It had a huge courtyard and the entrance was one and a half meters wide. They filmed inside and around the block, in the stores and cafeterias." Calling attention to the material textures of these urban atmospheres, Miguel remembered with sadness how the very matter out of which the neighborhood had been built had painfully disintegrated during the demolition: "When they knocked down my house you could see the eighty-centimeter walls were all made of pure stone!"

Most residents, however, recognized that the dissolution of these affective and material ensembles had started long before the Manzana Cinco plan. Small apartment buildings had been built in the 1970s and 1980s, and many owners had willingly demolished their own properties to create parking lots. Gustavo, a former carpenter and restaurant owner, described the many defunct businesses that had dotted the area: a hat factory, a beer and bottling company, butcher shops, traditional cheese makers, and bakeries. "Eventually," he lamented, "all that beautiful commerce had died and would never come back." Yet locals were intent on recovering and making visible the traces of this urban sensorium during their property battle with the city. Critically, such sociomaterial and affective experiences framed their juridical and political opposition to the plan. The neighborhood would be materialized as an urban village, one in which, as in *Don Chinche*, rural identities and working-class sensibilities harmoniously converged and implicitly supported the figure of a socially ascendant urban dweller. Most importantly, this rendering of the neighborhood brought to life an idealization of individual ownership closely tied to the rural smallholding (*minifundio*), a form of property that had been central in the Andean coffee-growing areas—from where many residents like Francisco and Miguel had migrated—and within the country's political economy of capitalist expansion. In Colombia, the ideal of small-scale property became integral to the fashioning of a modern middle-class subject and the rooting of an ethos of individual entrepreneurialism, both of which closely aligned with the country's violent history of sociopolitical fragmentation.[36] In Manzana Cinco, such notions formed the trappings of a shared epistemological and affective framework through which residents reconceptualized renewal as a form of state violence akin to land dispossession and bureaucratic misappropriation. This was the backdrop against which the urban intervention's new sensory regimes would be rendered visible and contested and an idealized understanding of propertied citizenship and state authority would be reinscribed and defended.

Cursed Terrain

A host of signs, things, and people started to invade residents' everyday routines soon after the ERU launched the Manzana Cinco plan. The urban worlds that people had inhabited unraveled before their eyes as new landscapes of bureaucracy and real estate took hold of their lives. It was the dissipation of what Kathleen Stewart calls "little worlds" and their "rhythms and labors of living," and the irruption of the new materialities and sensibilities of urban renewal.[37] Inherent to such shifting "atmospheric attunements" were residents' lived, practical epistemologies—"textures of knowledge" ingrained in the aesthetics and affectivity of everyday urban life.[38] Crucially, as inhabitants became attuned to these world-making things and practices, they assimilated them to the contentious history and cultural politics of Colombia's armed conflict. Far from becoming simply absorbed or burdened by the creeping aesthetics and unsettling moods of renewal, they actively rendered them meaningful as part of the political atmospherics of juridical insecurity and property violence. For them, the city's plan constituted a siege on modes of urban dwelling tied to rightful ownership and contested territorial sovereignties.[39]

Residents' intimate and politically inflected knowledge of sociomaterial environments was made apparent to me a few weeks after my first conversation with Hernando. We met once again in front of his house, at the time still spared from demolition, so he could recount in more detail some of the key events that had sent shock waves through the neighborhood. Hernando recalled how one day, without warning, people had come "to measure the land [*tierra*]." His choice of words and inflection were revealing. His intonation dropped when he uttered the word "land," and he also smirked and paused. He didn't talk of functionaries or topographers but rather of an "old guy who came to threaten us, to trample on us, [saying], 'You have to go because they are going to demolish all of this, they're going to knock it down.'" The scene of misappropriation and displacement resonated closely with Colombia's history of land violence. It was a portrayal of intimidation at the hands of anonymous men, stand-in officials, who had ignored property rights, treating people's homes and lots as open land (*tierra*) and terrain (*terreno*). Hernando's emphasis on the measurement of land was haunting given the centrality of boundaries (*linderos*)—of their manipulation and enforcement—to the country's long history of violent land grabs.[40] He thus conjured an atmosphere of dispossession intimately tied to what scholars have described as Colombia's enduring modalities of "primitive accumulation" in the countryside—the amassing of land and resources through a combination of overt violence and legal force.[41] In this sense, the theatrics and materiality of eviction in Manzana Cinco constituted a reenactment of modes of violent expulsion and accumulation integral to the country's civil war. They illuminated a continuum of legal and property violence, from the rural frontier—from which many downtown residents had migrated or been violently displaced, and whose sensibilities had been woven into their everyday lives—to the center of the modernizing urban core.[42]

During those first months of 2006 when the plan was launched, residents had received repeated phone calls from "alleged social workers," as one local inhabitant put it, who "threatened" and "harassed" them. The calls and unannounced visits made them feel enveloped by an increasingly "oppressive atmosphere [*un ambiente pesado*]," a sensation that would only get worse. One day, Hernando and his neighbors woke up to discover that signs had been posted on their doors and front walls. In large black and red letters, the white placards proclaimed, "This lot is property of the Empresa de Renovación Urbana de Bogotá D.C. Entry without permission is forbidden under penalty of incurring the corrective measures established in Article 164 of District Agreement 79 of 2003 'Police Code.'" The announcement was a display of official legalese; it included names and seals of government institutions and the citation of relevant regulations. For residents, it was one of the ERU's most "abusive" actions. Not only had the government not yet acquired all the lots, but a handful of lawsuits were still being considered in court. Most unsettling, however, was the fact that the ERU had declared the ban even as owners were still using and residing in their properties. According to locals, the signs' graphic elements were an eloquent demonstration of the legal statement's threatening qualities: the word "forbidden" written in large red letters in the middle of the sign, and the mention of the "Police Code" at the bottom. The specter of legal force soon became all too real for residents. "Officials started coming at midnight to get us out," Hernando recalled, "and they came with the police and patrols."

The notices were the first of several inscriptions through which the ERU laid claim to the land and enacted a vision of the new urban world to come. At its core, and as residents were quick to recognize, the announcements emerged as a dubious performance of urban sovereignty, one that invoked a muddled amalgam of public and private institutions and emblems. It constituted, along with the signage that cropped up on the block in the following years, what Joe Hermer and

FIGURE 3.2.   Manzana Cinco residents find a city notice on their door. October 22, 2008. Photo from the personal archive of Amelia Sanabria de Suárez and Saúl Suárez.

Alan Hunt call "official graffiti": the standardized and impersonal signs that dot streetscapes with a visual order of imperatives, instructions, and prohibitions.[43] At work here was an economy of material signs that operated through appropriation and that involved the "assertion of an implied authority."[44] In Manzana Cinco, official inscriptions not only indexed the distant and inchoate authority of the newly formed ERU but also served as crucial enactments of property.[45] Together with the workings of legal instruments and courts, the deployment of placards, notices, and enclosures gradually eroded existing property forms and relations and rematerialized them as open parcels of land ready for occupation.

As evictions and demolitions moved forward, the ERU encircled the site with a fence and billboard promoting the project. Architectural renderings and new signage adorned the temporary tin walls with phrases such as "the renewal of downtown Bogotá," "two projects that will transform the center of Bogotá," "housing," "public space," "entertainment," and "culture." The official graffiti further indexed the implied authority of urban renewal, as it attempted to legitimize the plan by conjuring an imaginary audience of citizens centered on abstract sociopolitical ideals. At some point, the private development company that won the public tender installed a sales office and new billboard on the south side of the block. Facing toward the city to the west, with the Monserrate mountain and the historic Las Aguas neighborhood behind it, the sign announced, "The rebirth of the center of Bogotá starts here." The emblems of the city administration and the

ERU now appeared next to the logo of the private development company QBO. The urban inscription was an amalgamation of public and private entities, real estate interests and civic ideals. This problematic juxtaposition was not lost on residents. Commenting on the withdrawal of the Spanish government from the project and the cancelation of the cultural center, Hernando pointed to the billboard and said, "They already changed the project's facade, the Spaniards don't have money so now they came up with another story, now apparently there's a consortium in our lot."

When half the land was officially turned over to the private developer, a new wave of unofficial inscriptions began to appear on the lot's temporary walls, superimposed over the city's slogans. The phrase "public space," for instance, which had been stamped by the ERU all over the fence, was repainted to read "pribate space [sic] [espacio pribado]": a critique of the plan's unfounded expropriations and its profit-seeking, privatizing agendas.[46] In 2013, after months of legal pressure, Hernando's and his next-door neighbor's houses were finally demolished. The corner, which for years had symbolized the last bastion of resistance, was gone. But it was exactly there, where their houses had stood, that some of the most damning graffiti emerged. On top of the city's official catchphrases, now papered over with peeling posters of all sorts and indecipherable tagging, a final round of inscriptions condemned Manzana Cinco as a form of urban land grabbing and enclosure. One of these was a drawing of a skull and crossbones next to the phrase "ERU thieves!" Further along the fence another graffiti read, "Rotten ERU, the new urban guerrillas."

With the block in ruins, locals increasingly drew parallels to war zones and to the countless armed takeovers of Colombian rural towns. Margarita, a longtime property owner, described the plan as an armed incursion: an act of pilfering and violence. On one occasion she told me, distraught, "This has been savage, they stole the block from us so savagely." Echoing the long history of colonialism and racial violence, Margarita decried the city's treatment of residents as "if we were little Indians in loincloths [indiecitos con taparrabos]." Her remarks were a forceful accusation of the ERU's schemes to "steal our land," as she put it. Her evocation of the racialized imagery of colonial dispossession of Indigenous land was also a jab at the early role of the government of Spain and its planned donation of a cultural center—echoes of colonial conquest in the form of global capital and so-called international cooperation. At the same time, Margarita's indignation and choice of words indexed her own class and racial aspirations. She and Hernando, like others on the block, were lighter-skinned, propertied urbanites who had struggled to rise from their working-class, provincial backgrounds to something that resembled an urban middle class. By sharply distinguishing themselves from the indiecitos con taparrabos, they asserted their status as dignified, deserving property owners. The implication was that it would be their aspirational status as middle-class property owners, not their trajectory as marginalized urban dwellers or racialized subjects, that would legitimize their rights claims and their status as victims of the bureaucratic takeover.[47]

Manzana Cinco's changing atmosphere became a fundamental medium for the articulation of critical knowledges about urban renewal. Far from an abstract or mystified construct, this was a lived and textured ideology emanating from the very stuff of everyday existence. It was thus that the old neighborhood materialized class aspirations, property ideologies, and the national communities so memorably depicted in the *Don Chinche* series. The arrival of the signs and things of urban renewal appeared as forceful incursions into this idealized urban village, brutal events of violence and dispossession. Such imagery of territorial violence—from colonial conquest to modern civil war—was most vividly captured in one last graffiti that simply read, "cursed terrain [*terreno maldito*]." In one sense, the scrawl called attention to the unsettling qualities of the neighborhood's material textures now that homes and businesses were in ruins. It epitomized what Yael Navaro-Yashin describes in her work on postwar environments as the "eeriness discharged by a territorial space and material objects left behind by a displaced community."[48] In another sense, the material resignification of the razed block as "cursed terrain" pointed to what residents viewed as the gradual corrosion of urban property and its transfiguration into barren, "irritable" terrain.[49] Although residents articulated a forceful critique of the urban operation, putting their eviction into the epistemic frame of territorial warfare, they ultimately experienced the materiality of dispossession as urban homeowners and, primarily, as an assault on their rightful ownership, not as a process integral to unequal property regimes and state violence. Something similar would be at work in residents' composition of counterbureaucratic knowledge.

The Counterforensics of Bureaucratic Knowledge

Margarita and Humberto were an elderly couple of retirees who had for years owned a parking garage on the block. They also became the neighborhood's leading legal activists. Hernando, Francisco, and other neighbors urged me to get in touch with them if I wanted to truly understand their juridical battle. After being evicted from their property and losing their main source of income, the couple had moved into their son's modest apartment a few blocks from the Manzana Cinco site. Surrounded by kitschy porcelain figurines and crystal decorations, they welcomed me with a glass of juice and the formal hospitality of a rising middle-class family. The couple mentioned with great pride how their grand-daughter, whose portrait stood on a living room mantelpiece, was about to enroll as a medical student at the elite Universidad de los Andes—Colombia's premier private university and Las Aguas's most powerful neighbor since the 1950s. Making clear the significance of this milestone for the family and the depth of their loss when the city government approached them with the expropriation notification, Margarita noted that "all we had, we built from nothing."

As our conversation shifted to the Manzana Cinco project and the ensuing legal processes, the couple became agitated. They moved and talked hurriedly, as if they had incorporated the frenzied rhythm of their bureaucratic ordeal into their ordinary routine. Then, as I pulled out my voice recorder, Humberto told me he preferred "to display the facts on their own terms" so I could judge for myself what had happened on the block. His reluctance to be recorded seemed to be both a reflection of the wariness resulting from his involvement in protracted juridical proceedings and an indication of his newfound legal expertise. For Humberto the burden of proof was so conclusive that explanations were superfluous. Margarita, on the other hand, was more than willing to share her experience and interpretation of the events. In particular, she was keen on elaborating on the violence encoded in the materiality and aesthetics of bureaucratic artifacts. Like others on the block, she had become finely attuned to the ERU's legalistic attacks. Margarita recognized that the law was being wielded as a weapon by state actors, even as she herself mobilized legal instruments to pursue some measure of justice and accountability. Hers were not simply metaphorical allusions to the technical battlegrounds of lawfare or abstract invocations of the force of law.[50] Rather, in her engagements with the materiality of bureaucracy, Margarita continually reenacted the intimate relationship between law and violence, or what she conceptualized as the continuum between legality and warfare.

While Margarita recalled many of the scenes that others in the block had recounted, she trained her attention on the aesthetics and affectivity of official paperwork. Setting the tone for our conversation, she started by narrating how she and her neighbors had first learned about the redevelopment plan when they received "pamphlets without a signature or anything" in their homes. "Can you believe it?" she repeated. "Just pamphlets there [on our doorstep], not even signed." In Colombia, pamphlets (*panfletos*) are one of the central "mimetic performances" of state power through which armed groups and criminal organizations have intimidated and extorted populations for decades,[51] primarily in urban peripheries and rural towns. In talking about the documents' pamphlet-like appearance and missing signatures, Margarita invoked a genre of bureaucratic materiality associated with violence and usurpation to question the ERU's authority and legitimacy. By attending to the performative and tangible qualities of bureaucracy, she and her neighbors composed critical local knowledges about the illegibility and injustice of state action, which in turn informed their counterdocumentary practices.

Anthropological work has shown that the appropriation of the language and aesthetics of bureaucracy—through imitation and forgery, for instance—can become an integral part of people's attempts to overcome projects of state domination.[52] In the case of Manzana Cinco, however, more than simply mimicking documentary forms, locals became fixated on the materiality and form of bureaucratic artifacts with the hope of disentangling the plan's contradictions and deceptions.[53] In their own paperwork, furthermore, they recharged bureaucratic forms affectively and politically with ideals of state justice. This involved what Winifred Tate calls the "aspirational state."[54] In her analysis of state formation in the contested Colombian frontier region of Putumayo, Tate argues that inhabitants developed an "aspirational critique of present politics focused on the qualities of the state, its affective ties to its citizens, and the state as an ideal form: caring, responsive, generous, and abundant, rather than distant, repressive, and extortive."[55] Such visions have not been restricted to war-torn peripheries. The displaced of Manzana Cinco and their struggles against legally enforced dispossession show a similar kind of political imagination at work. As self-formed bureaucratic and juridical experts, residents developed an oppositional and materially attuned knowledge of urban law. Crucially, these critiques were both enabled and limited by ideologies of statehood and victimhood intimately tied to Colombia's history of warfare.

Margarita and Humberto's emergent bureaucratic knowledge was further evinced once we moved from the living room to a small study where they had a computer and a large file cabinet. Drawing on Margarita's past experience as an administrative secretary, the couple had assembled a voluminous archive documenting the Manzana Cinco project. They had carefully collected hundreds of official letters and documents, newspaper clippings, copies of decrees and laws, and videos of local reports and hearings. Margarita leafed through the files, muttering names of functionaries and technical jargon, visibly distressed. "Receive a warm greeting," she read to me from one letter derisively, and then she sighed, saying, "They're phonier than a leather coin." As she continued sorting through the documents and rehearsing the timeline of events that she had meticulously reconstructed, it seemed that the couple had increasingly latched on to the cumulative materiality of paperwork as their property physically disintegrated. The archive had become the last recourse in their struggle, a politically and affectively charged embodiment of their counterepistemic practices.

In one sense, Margarita and Humberto had been carefully reading state documents "along the grain," as Ann Stoler describes the combing of archives' "unexplored fault lines, ragged edges, and unremarked disruptions to the seam-less and smooth surface."[56] They had rearranged records and facts, searched for gaps and inconsistencies, and reflected on the conditions of documentary pro-duction. By scouring official and unofficial records, the couple had directly ques-tioned the state's archival power.[57] At the same time, Margarita and Humberto's work as amateur archivists proved to be a form of intense emotional labor. They were driven by what seemed like an imperative, almost a compulsion to follow the paper trail left by Manzana Cinco.[58] Such urgency was the reflection of the desire to unearth the political motivations behind the project and to counter, in some measure, the physical disappearance of their neighborhood: to ward off amnesia. Although the homemade archive bore the promises of memory and justice, its material excesses also proved burdensome, a tactile presence that over-whelmed residents' sense of loss.[59] As Margarita lamented, still ruffling through the files, "Oh, I have so many papers . . . I'm fed up!"

The couple's counterarchive was punctuated by the sensibilities and anxieties of knowledge production amid political violence and, increasingly, under the sign of the postconflict. Their struggle to reassemble and destabilize state nar-ratives about urban renewal had unfolded as the country was becoming fully immersed in public debates about transitional justice, memory, and peace. In 2005, just around the time when property owners in Las Aguas were receiving eviction notices, the national government had created the Comisión Nacional de Reparación y Reconciliación (National Commission for Reparation and Reconciliation) through a law known as the Ley de Justicia y Paz (Justice and Peace Law).[60] The commission was established by the administration of right-wing President Álvaro Uribe Vélez, who repeatedly denied the existence of an armed conflict, characterized guerrilla warfare as terrorism, and was primarily interested in the demobilization of paramilitary organizations. Most problem-atically, although the initiative aligned with discourses of solidarity, it eschewed accountability and, more specifically, any admission of state crimes—issues that have plagued transitional justice mechanisms in Colombia ever since.[61] And yet the commission opened spaces that became important sites of social critique and political dissent. The Grupo de Memoria Histórica (Historical Memory Group), for instance, which was launched as part of the commission, became a vital "agent of knowledge production about a violent past," according to scholars and activists Pilar Riaño Alcalá and María Victoria Uribe.[62] The group's man-date included the promotion of the "right to truth" and the "duty of memory" through the "preservation of" and "access to archives."[63] Crucially, according to Riaño Alcalá and Uribe, it became the platform for "comprehensive and plural narratives about violence" centered, for the first time in Colombia, on "victims' voices and perspectives."[64] This focus was deepened in the following years with the creation of the Ley de Víctimas y Restitución de Tierras (Law of Victims and Land Restitution) and the Centro Nacional de Memoria Histórica (National Center of Historical Memory).[65] Victimhood became a potent lens, a critical affective epistemology at the core of expanding and increasingly visible modes of memory work in the country's troubled transition to the postwar era.

Margarita and Humberto's archival project bore the imprint of this historical juncture. In collecting and reinterpreting the documentary traces left behind by the urban intervention, they engaged in something akin to what Eyal Weizman calls "counterforensics": an investigative practice that "turns the state's own means against the violence it commits."[66] Margarita and Humberto viewed their work as a process of evidence gathering aimed at uncovering the crimes committed by the state. During their investigation the couple had carefully documented the unfairly low appraisal of their properties as well as how the ERU had mistakenly processed and consigned their expropriation funds, leaving the money frozen for years in the wrong account. Their meticulous recording of the demolition and construction process, which included dozens of photographs, supported one of their main legal arguments against the project: the fact that the delayed start of the development warranted, according to existing laws, a reversal of the expropriations and a restitution of property. Finally, Manzana Cinco residents and their lawyer had carefully tracked the actors behind stalled rulings and unfavorable juridical decisions, finding troubling connections between at least one judge and a functionary involved in a highly publicized and large-scale infrastructure corruption scandal known as the "contracting carousel [*carrusel de la contratación*]."

Residents' efforts to demonstrate the government's "thievery" and "forceful takeover" ultimately pointed to the broader universe of activism integral to postwar and postdictatorship politics in Latin America. For Margarita and Humberto, their struggle was essentially of the same nature as the search for *desaparecidos* (disappeared persons) or the investigation and denunciation of human rights violations and state violence.[67] Crucially, as urban archives became key sites of "postconflict empowerment," to use Kirsten Weld's term, property owners also emerged as victims pursuing reparation and restitution.[68] In this sense, residents' legal and political claims were mediated by their adoption of the subject position of victim. Practices of citizenship and ownership became, in this manner, closely entangled with repertoires of trauma and injury.[69] What Kimberly Theidon calls a "contentious politics of victimhood,"[70] linked to understandings of property and class, became central to how residents came to embody urban victimhood through juridical performances and paperwork practices.

The Mise-en-Scène of Urban Victimhood

The entanglements between practices of counterexpertise, ideologies of property and citizenship, and repertories of victimhood became apparent in the sociomaterial contours of residents' juridical dispute. Carlos, a young attorney who represented several of the block's owners, articulated these connections and made them an integral part of residents' legal strategy. As I waited for Carlos in one of the city's expansive new malls to the west of the city center, I expected to meet a traditional downtown lawyer. These are typically unscrupulous attorneys, pejoratively known as *tinterillos* (ink spillers), who hover over social disputes and legal troubles in their well-worn suits and ties, looking for opportunities to profit. Instead I was greeted by a young man draped in denim, with close-cropped hair and a backpack, who looked more like an activist. Contrary to the typical loquaciousness of litigants, Carlos's demeanor was understated and grave. As we talked over coffee, he described himself as a "lawyer of the poor" and confessed his personal obsession with the Manzana Cinco lawsuit. Significantly, before taking on the case, he had worked for years investigating forceful disappearances as an attorney for victims of the armed conflict. The experience still weighed on him, Carlos hinted, as he recalled the many difficult hours spent "reading those files."

Most importantly, the epistemics of legal activism in the midst of war became ingrained into his approach to the Manzana Cinco case. For Carlos, the property dispute mirrored Colombia's armed conflict and was structured by the same logics of state and land violence. The "administrative irregularities" that had permeated the process, and which he was contesting in court, were for Carlos essentially maneuvers to "displace people." The violence of such administrative displacements, he noted, had wide-ranging significance. "Colombia," he stated, "is a country of *desarraigados* [uprooted persons]." With the term *desarraigado*, he conjured the imagery of banishment and expulsion, giving urban displacement a shade of meaning directly linked to rural warfare. The implication became clearer as he elaborated: "Here in the urban sector we are doing the same thing [as in the rest of the country]; the difference is that we don't use rifles, but rather laws, which are being twisted and manipulated, so that what isn't done with a rifle is done with paper, by force. Because after issuing the expropriation resolution and registering the property in the office of public instruments and register, the administration can go with the police and evict people. And that, in any case, is displacement." This critique of urban renewal as a form of juridical insecurity—of warfare by legal means—was materialized through aesthetic and affective enactments. Carlos led his clients through judicial itineraries that included news reports and interviews, a congressional hearing, and appeals to local and international human rights organizations. It was a mise-en-scène of legal activism that aligned closely with the trappings of justice and victimhood that, according to Theidon, characterize Colombia's perpetual "prepostconflict" moment.[71]

Back in their home office, Humberto and Margarita played several videos they had filed in their counterarchive as key pieces of evidence in this regard. The first was a news report about the Manzana Cinco project that had aired on a local TV station in 2010. The video's editing, its visual rhetoric and linguistic turns, shaped a distinctly victim-centered testimony. The segment started with images of the semidemolished block and a camera pan across Hernando's rustic tile-and-plaster housing as a melancholic guitar played in the background. The camera then trailed behind Margarita as she strolled, holding Carlos's arm, in front of the fenced site and along the street where her property used to stand. A narrator, in voice-over, introduced the story: "A dream for Bogotá became a nightmare for several families. This is the other side of Manzana Cinco."

Next, Margarita appeared in her son's apartment, her face shown in close-up as she stated firmly, "I want to make a public denunciation of the arbitrary acts, the robberies, that the ERU is carrying out." Carlos was then shown explaining the legal irregularities that plagued the project since its inception, followed again by an interview with Margarita and her account of the abuses and manipulations that residents underwent during the process. These testimonies were accompanied by scenes of Margarita and Humberto inspecting sheaves of documents in their son's dining room and standing at the edge of the demolition site looking over the rubble. The narrator then summed up the injustices of the project, stressing the social and emotional damage it caused: "The project was imposed without the participation of the owners of more than thirty lots and it quickly led to a distressing expropriation process that razed [*arrasó*] the future of many." The imagery of devastation, of violent *arrasamiento*, was followed by more pointed remarks about the government's crimes against residents. "[Margarita], along with her husband," the journalist continued, "was a victim of abuse that in the blink of an eye finished what she had built to reach old age with dignity. The harm that was done to these families is irreparable."

The report ended with Margarita saying, "We worked all our lives, so we could have something," to which the journalist, out of frame, casually asked, "And how are you doing now?" Margarita covered her eyes, breaking into tears, as the camera moved toward her face in slow motion, capturing a grimace of pain she was trying to hide. Back in the studio, the show's host expressed surprised at how "land was being taken [*la manera cómo se están tomando los terrenos*]." Hinting at violent land grabbing, he wondered whether urban displacement would "entail the savage expulsion [*salida salvaje*] of many people who have historically lived in the city center" or if the law would prevail. As we watched these final scenes on the old computer monitor, Margarita turned to me, scoffing at such pretenses of bureaucratic judiciousness and legal politesse.

Margarita and Humberto turned back to the computer and played a second clip. It was a hearing at the Congress's Chamber of Representatives in which both Margarita and Carlos had testified. The chamber's First Commission, whose legislative and oversight functions included issues of territorial ordering (*ordenamiento territorial*), had invited former residents and city officials to a public meeting about the Manzana Cinco renewal plan. The grainy video had been aired on the Congress Channel. With its national-flag-inspired logo at the bottom of the screen and characteristically uncinematic, still camera shots of talking heads, at first glance the clip contrasted sharply with the overtly narrativized and dramatic depiction of the news report. It seemed to epitomize the official gaze of the state and to display a performance of legal rationality and accountability. First on the screen were the commission's congressional members, sitting at a central desk in the back of the room, on an elevated platform, under a large Colombian coat of arms on the wall. Former residents, lawyers, and families were positioned in front of them and slightly below their gaze, behind a large elliptical table enveloping the room, a layout that reinforced their status as subjects of the state pleading for justice.

The congressional hearing room was an aesthetic and material ensemble through which ideals of justice and legality were enacted in particular ways. Similar to courtrooms, the commission room emerged as a spatiotemporal enactment of law. It was a "chronotope," as Mariana Valverde argues, drawing on Mikhail Bakhtin, "in which a specific temporality . . . shapes and helps define the space" and "space is constitutive of judicial time, official legal time."[72] So even though the hearing was supposed to be simply an informative meeting designed to give citizens a chance to voice their complaints, its rhythmic textures and architectural forms gave it a distinctly juridical quality. The representative who was chairing the meeting was emphatic about the timing of the interventions. Holding his wristwatch in his hand, he moderated the proceedings, moving back and forth between officials and citizens, central desk and general seating. As the meeting unfolded, such enactments of official business gave way to more emotionally charged testimonies and exhortations. Participants' embodied performances lent force to and materialized a particular rendering of justice centered on state accountability, reparation, and victimhood. This is what Kamari Clarke calls "affective justice": "[complex assemblages] materialized through expressions, representations, discourses, and feeling regimes that shape the way that justice is embodied and expressed by people."[73] What was supposed to be a routine congressional hearing quickly became a more complex legal and political performance through which residents resignified urban eviction as a crime and staked their claims as victims.

Carlos was the first to speak. After greeting everyone and saying he would read quickly to stay within the allotted time, he started to "narrate [*relatar*] . . . [Manzana Cinco's] current decay, represented in great filthiness, breeding grounds for vectors [of disease] and rodents, drug trade, among other things, which stimulate the increase of theft and mugging every day in the area." He went on to stress that "all of this resulted from the displacement of the original owners [*raizales*]." His use of the latter term, an inflection of *raíz* (root), was significant. It recast the residents of Manzana Cinco, many of whom had bought property as recently as the 1980s and 1990s, as original inhabitants, rooted in place. Furthermore, the use of *raizal* had distinct connotations linked to ethnic identity and geographic belonging. *Raizales* is the name for the Afro-Caribbean communities indigenous to the San Andrés archipelago, a Colombian territory with a long history of colonial and postcolonial sovereignty disputes. Although officially one of the country's thirty-two departments, with their 2002 declaration of self-determination (*autodeterminación*), raizales epitomized a form of local struggle against cultural, economic, and sociopolitical pressures from the Colombian mainland. While Carlos was not directly referencing this history, his gestures to rootedness, along with his assertion that insecurity was the result, not the cause, of state action, mirrored class- and race-inflected narratives of violent dispossession and Indigenous resistance.

He had also framed his intervention as a *relato*, a testimony. A rich body of scholarship has followed "the globalization of the testimony" in postconflict settings,[74] showing how the testimonial narrative is integral to struggles over memory, justice, and the construction of victimhood.[75] While cohesive "national narratives" about the country's recent history of violence are still arguably lacking in Colombia, Myriam Jimeno notes, there has been a "proliferation of testimonial narratives that register the most terrifying and varied experiences of the violence of the past decades."[76] Significantly, the production and circulation of the testimonies of survivors of state, guerrilla, and paramilitary violence have shaped collective imaginaries and repertoires of injustice and victimhood. They are at the core of an emergent yet deeply contested politics of accountability, reparation, and memorialization. Carlos indexed these cultural and political repertoires in his narrative performance at the congressional hearing. His intonation and use of words were telling, as he gravely called on the representatives to understand the "merciless delay" that residents had been subjected to after being "forcefully expelled from their land." He stressed residents' suffering at the hands of city officials and mentioned how the ERU had sent "emissaries specialized in the psychological abuse of the owners and dwellers of Manzana Cinco." To conclude his statement, Carlos returned to his preferred metaphor about state violence and urban renewal, by now a frequent trope among Manzana Cinco residents. "All this to simply conclude," he said, raising his voice as he grasped a sheet of paper, "that in the countryside the population is displaced by armed actors, and here in the capital district, displacements are caused by the ERU. There it is with the use of force and weapons, and here with the tortious [*torticera*] and crooked [*amañada*] application of norms under an apparent cloak of legality."

Along with the sociopolitical coordinates outlined in Carlos's narrative, residents' testimonies channeled distinctive affective and experiential force. They called forth what Jimeno describes as *relatos*'s capacity to create an "emotional community."[77] This became apparent when Margarita took the microphone. Dressed in a gray suit and blue silk shirt—probably one of her outfits from her days working as a secretary—she addressed the men at the main table with both humbleness and resolve. In sharp contrast to the city official who had spoken immediately before her using bureaucratic generalities and making vague promises, Margarita's remarks were decidedly personal as she interpellated the individuals and motives behind the city's machinery of bureaucratic dispossession. With her voice slightly quivering, she turned directly to the invited city functionary and said, "Dr. Jiménez, in relation to Manzana Cinco you haven't said anything. So, I ask: If the Alcaldía Mayor is the boss of Renovación Urbana [ERU], I have to think they are not informed of all the abuses they have committed against us, the displaced of Manzana Cinco." Margarita framed her intervention in distinctly moral terms, appealing to the city official's goodwill while subtly holding authorities accountable: "I don't understand how it is possible for the Alcaldía Mayor de Bogotá to not have realized all these abuses were happening with all the reports and the audits that the Concejo [City Council] and the Contraloría [City Government Accountability Office] carried out. [To not have seen] how they trampled on our fundamental rights. So I ask, Dr. Jiménez, please, if you are not aware of this, if you need documents, we have countless documents of all the mistakes committed by Renovación Urbana."

Her account of bearing witness to and documenting the ERU's misdeeds became increasingly emotional. No longer simply a respectful citizen pleading with a representative of an indolent state, she turned to her suffering as a victim of theft and displacement by evoking the imagery of warfare. "This is where all our lives we worked to have our shack [*rancho*] and our business," Margarita continued, "and then Renovación Urbana came like a guerrilla force, worse than the guerrillas, and kicked us out without rhyme or reason [*sin ton ni son*]." While many downtown residents talked about eviction as a militaristic takeover of their "shacks" and "lands," they often drew parallels to paramilitary groups. They thereby called attention to the violence of the state and to the continuities between paramilitary land grabbing and exclusionary urban property regimes. Comparing the ERU with guerrillas, as Margarita had done, had different socio-political connotations. In the context of the capital city, it hinted at the typi-cally middle-class, urban fear of Colombia's Marxist peasant guerrilla group, the FARC. Furthermore, it implied that the ERU was something like an "illegitimate," rogue institution that had merely deviated from the city's legitimate governmen-tal apparatus. At stake here was a reinstating of the boundaries between legality and illegality, peace and war, as well as the reaffirmation of residents' status as respectable citizens governed by a lawful state and legitimate property relations.

Further asserting the dignity of propertied belonging as the basis for her understanding of bureaucratic violence and her own sense of victimhood, Mar-garita concluded her testimony with a note about her family's social decline: "Look, we're living in my son's apartment; if we didn't have that apartment we'd be living under a bridge. We would be living like any street dweller [*habitante de calle*]. Look, the fact that a state agency did this is incredible, for God's sake; that thieves do it is all right, but that a state agency because it had a building permit kicked us out and stole everything from us is impossible." Then, sitting up slightly to straighten her suit in a gesture of dignified propriety and looking politely again at the city functionary, she said softly, "Forgive me for what I said and thank you."

Affective *Oficios* and Performing Bureaucratic Dispossession

The Chamber of Representatives had served as a critical medium for residents' enactments of legality and justice in the affective registers of victimhood. Margar-ita and her neighbors drew on what Kimberly Theidon, in the context of postwar Peru, describes as a "collective narrative . . . that proves systematic violations of human rights and tends to foreground suffering."[78] Former residents of Manzana Cinco materialized this "sense of traumatic citizenship,"[79] with all its ambiguities and contradictions, not only through the legal space and performative aesthetics of TV news reports and congressional hearings but also through paperwork and documentary forms. In their many *oficios* (official letters) to local, national, and even global institutions, they combined legal parlance with personal testimonies of distress and abuse at the hands of city officials. In all our meetings, Hernando would pull out at least one of these oficios and read fragments hurriedly, some-times trailing off and mumbling to himself as if reliving one of the many injuri-ous moments in the long-running dispute with the city. Limited literacy and the stylistic features of Colombian legalese hampered residents' ability "to master the conventions of bureaucratic documentation," as Matthew Hull argues in his study of urban bureaucracy in Pakistan.[80] And yet, to borrow again from Hull, it was precisely by "contravening the conventions" of bureaucracy—its allegedly "context-free, abstract language" and emotionless formulas[81]—that residents' oficios gained affective force. The typically stale and formulaic instruments of urban bureaucracy reemerged as critical materializations of suffering and dispossession. At stake in such oficios was what Francis Cody, writing about literacy and bureaucratic activism in India, calls the "performativity of the signed petition."[82] If paperwork is the "material infrastructure of citizenship,"[83] as Cody suggestively puts it, then residents' letters reworked such material media to embody the affective and contradictory modalities of citizenship shaped by the country's histories of violence and insecurity.

One of Hernando's oficios, which he and his family had addressed to the city's Contraloría Distrital (Accountability Office), reproduced in semibureaucratic fashion the sequence of events since the ERU had first notified them about the Manzana Cinco project. This was a citizen audit that at first glance unsettled the genre of the oficio through its irregular grammar and punctuation and its variable use of numbering and bold and uppercase fonts. Most importantly, Hernando and his family had woven into the list of procedures (*trámites*) and complaints (*quejas*) a narrative of state absence, injustice, and pain. The informational tone of the letter was punctuated by the irruption of expressive clauses and notes, informal language, and tacit references to places and moments, giving the communication a distinct experiential and affective quality. The opening page started, without introduction or context, with a list of the ERU's communications with residents and relevant decrees. A few lines down, a note appeared, inserted between two items: "Note: under pressure from the ERU's lawyers and SANDRA GÓMEZ social Worker $46.000.000 A ROBBERY." The oficio continued with a bullet point for every letter the "familia Casas" had filed (*radicados*) with embassies, national and local institutions, and politicians:

a) **EMBASSY OF SPAIN:** November 7 of 2006 (they didn't respond to the complaint)

b) **EMBASSY OF FRANCE:** November 23 of 2006 (they didn't respond to the radicado and complaint)

. . .

g) **COUNCIL OF STATE:** 8 of November of 2006 (we were told that it couldn't do anything and that the ERU or the Alcaldía would solve the problem).

h) **CONSTITUTIONAL COURT:** 6 of November of 2006 (there was no solution at all)

Each parenthetical comment on the list—"they didn't respond," "there was no solution"—revealed the family's mounting frustration. The letter's narrative features, its "emplotment," to use Paul Ricoeur's term,[84] mediated Hernando and his family's practical experiences of state violence and displacement. If the initial annotated list indexed the indolence of governmental agencies and agents across scales and jurisdictions—a sense of state abandonment—the rest of the letter brought to life the family's plight. This was apparent in a longer bullet-pointed list that followed the letter's telegraphic list of bureaucratic events and communications. With scarce punctuation and a distinctly conversational tone, the paragraph unraveled the linear temporality of officialdom and rendered a phenomenological elaboration of abuse and distress at the hands of the agents of the state:

> On June 21 there was a negotiation with the ERU there was a phone call the previous day that is on June 20 we were threatened on the telephone in a call at 11:00 a.m. by **ESTELA MORENO** and the Dra. Attorney **SOLEDAD** who called us under threats and abuses that no; that we would face the consequences if we didn't sign that they would remove us with the police and psychological pressure and in several calls ordered by the acting Manager of the ERU with pressures in that negotiation in Notary 21 with the social worker **ESTELA MORENO** and the Attorney **ESPERANZA**, the day 21 of June at 5:00 p.m. with tears my mother the señora **MARIA TERESA MARTINEZ** with the Doctor from the Veeduría [city's Oversight Office] and I notified the personería [the municipal agency charged with defending human rights] which didn't come. My brother **WILSON** recorded with a small voice recorder the entire cassette remains as forceful proof that we signed under threats and pressure of the ERU and especially of **ESTELA MORENO** Social Worker. . . .

Rather than an example of limited bureaucratic literacy, the text, with its ellipses and grammatical blunders, vividly embodied Hernando's harried retelling of the events. It was a linguistic performance that captured his family's distress and disorientation, seeking to elicit some measure of sympathy and conjuring affective affinities around the injustice of dispossession. But the oficio was not simply about state abuse and negligence. As its plot unfurled, it culminated with a more insidious form of bureaucratic violence. Two final notes, inserted before the six family members' signatures, gave the letter a fateful ending, one in which the Manzana Cinco project appeared to be a matter of life and death:

> **NOTE:** one time the architect **DIANA MOSQUERA** came with the attorney from the office of HABITAT when my father was still alive they made him **cry and from there my father's health deteriorated and my mother's a couple of elders deserving of respect and that their**

fundamental rights and human rights were not respected and other mistreatments to them.

NOTE: Until the day 21 of July my father passed away due to all these problems.

Margarita and Humberto had also subtly embedded the language of institutional violence, humanitarian law, and death in their many complaints and testimonies before local, national, and international organizations. In one of their oficios, which Margarita read to me at her home archive, the couple combined their intimate knowledge of the bureaucratic intricacies with an affectively charged portrayal of urban renewal as a crime against humanity. The letter had been addressed to the national government's director of human rights with the subject line, "Displacement and violation [*quebranto*] of Fundamental Rights." Like Hernando's, it was a narrative replete with expressions of indignation and suffering explicitly framed as state violations of human rights. In one passage, Margarita and Humberto asked the human rights official, "What is happening, where is the compliance with the law, the respect of HUMAN AND FUNDAMENTAL RIGHTS?" After narrating dragging negotiations and the final unexpected notification of their expropriation, the oficio arrived at its tragic denouement:

> NOTE: Such was the psychological pressure and mortification from the functionaries of the ERU . . . that some have already literally died from the grief [*de pura pena moral*], seeing that Renovación Urbana robbed them of all they had financially and had acquired with years of work. These people are: HERNANDO CASAS [Hernando's father], JAIRO ANIBAL NIÑO, famous children's book writer, who due to this problem was ill for a long time and was unable to recover. Other inhabitants of the manzana 5 are also in poor health, [with illnesses] such as diabetes, a condition that with these pressures is killing them day by day, because they stole their land, demolished the buildings and businesses that sustained them.

"The displaced of Manzana Cinco," as residents signed this and many other letters, had effectively subverted local forms of legal and bureaucratic violence and remade them into a medium of opposition and critique. Through their affective performances in court, in front of the camera, and on paper, they had reconstituted themselves into victims of dispossession and transformed their urban block into violently razed land. In doing so, however, they had reinscribed the materiality and aesthetics of state governance and law. This irony was not lost on Margarita. As she pulled back from her computer during one of our conversations and dropped the letters she had been reading to me, she asked, waving toward the burdensome archive behind her, "Whom can we talk to, *padrecito*, if what they call justice is really injustice?" And yet she and many of her neighbors had continued to evoke an idealized state that would recognize their status as deserving victims. Residents had enacted their claims as a matter of human rights, appealing to the moral and ethical sentiments of humanitarian logics that have shaped political engagement in Colombia since the 1980s.[85] The rise of liberal conceptions of individual human rights, as Lesley Gill has argued, coincided with the violent repression of social movements and class politics, ultimately forming a "narrower political horizon" unable to account for "the economic marginalization and social fragmentation" at the core of the country's enduring conflict.[86] The residents of Manzana Cinco embodied these sensibilities in their materialization of urban victimhood and in their claims for more humane treatment at the hands of the ERU. Far from a critique of the structures of inequality and social hierarchies pervading urban renewal and underpinning Colombia's history of violent displacement, it was more a pursuit of recognition and redress based on the prerogatives of middle-class, propertied citizenship. Rather than a critique of the violence inherent to state bureaucracies, it was ultimately a call for law and order.

The Counterepistemics of Insecurity and Its Limits as a Political Horizon

The rendering of Manzana Cinco as a settlement under attack, of bureaucratic artifacts as sources of insecurity, and of residents themselves as displaced victims, left intact existing structures of urban governance, inequality, and accumulation. Local critiques of urbanism as a form of warfare brought to the fore the injustices and contradictions of the Manzana Cinco plan, in particular the arbitrary evictions and speculative operations carried out under the masquerade of an intervention for the public good. They also served to directly confront the ERU as a state institution, challenging its legitimacy and even putting into motion the destitution of mid-level officials. But in the end, these were epistemic maneuvers limited by the grammar of insecurity and aligned with hegemonic understandings of state authority, property regimes, and citizenship.[87] The fight for their recognition as victims of the ERU was aimed at obtaining better compensation or a restitution of their property rights, but it did not question urban renewal as a political project or galvanize collective mobilization around a more just urban order. As Hernando himself admitted, worn down by his indignation, "We were also to blame, each one taking care of their own." Like him, other residents had lamented the lack of union and solidarity among property owners.

In Manzana Cinco, the performative materialization of victimhood and displacement revealed the contradictions of citizenship and belonging in the midst of war. At stake here were the limits of the epistemics and materiality of insecurity as a horizon of urban politics. Local understandings of warfare and their projections onto urban environs and urban selves had been shaped by class- and race-inflected regimes of progress, property, and propriety. This became apparent to me the first time I spoke with Hernando, when he was still living in his family home, surrounded by the demolition rubble. After detailing his violent displacement at the hands of the city's bureaucracy, he launched into a racist tirade against the Indigenous street vendors who worked nearby: "They took over this shit. All the investments in this area and now so ugly, invaded. Haven't you seen the vendors are now all Indians?" His contempt for Indigenous vendors who had made their way to the capital after being violently displaced from their land was a piercing reminder of the paradoxes of race, class, and citizenship in Colombia. Hernando had condemned his bureaucratic expulsion only to rearticulate the deep inequalities and violences of Colombia's land and property regimes.

This does not mean, however, that residents were victims of a form of ideological mystification or that they merely instrumentalized repertoires of violence and insecurity. Their understandings of urban renewal as bureaucratic violence were grounded in their urban experiences and aspirations and gave form to and were shaped by the material and affective environments they inhabited.[88] Far from the seamless reproduction of dominant discourses about authority and belonging, local epistemological orientations embodied people's contradictory experiences of sociomaterial worlds. Such modes of street expertise would be best understood as forms of "practical consciousness," to use Raymond Williams's term.[89] They constitute what William Roseberry calls, in an oft-quoted elaboration of Gramscian thought, "a common material and meaningful framework for living through, talking about, and acting upon social orders characterized by domination."[90]

In downtown Bogotá, insecurity emerged in this way as an epistemic and material medium through which residents both challenged and reaffirmed the violence of bureaucratic power and unequal regimes of citizenship. An exchange in 2019 with one of the first property owners to be expropriated from the block became a forceful illustration of the ironies of such processes. Jorge was a tailor who had run a successful business and lived in the neighborhood for more than thirty years. Like Francisco, he had migrated to the city from Colombia's coffee-growing region, from the department of El Quindío, bringing with him a similar entrepreneurial ethos. Unlike Francisco and others on the block, Jorge had accepted the ERU's meager offer without putting up a fight. True to his pragmatic outlook and serene temperament, Jorge explained in his soft-spoken voice and with distinct forbearance that the prospect of a legal battle had seemed futile. He had relocated to a building across the street from his old property, so that now, from a sixteenth-floor apartment, his shop floor looked over the recently inaugurated cinematheque and two apartment towers. "Of all those people who lived on the block only three or four are still alive," he said wistfully. We talked about Francisco's, Humberto's, and Miguel's recent deaths and how he had recently seen Margarita, who lived nearby, in a wheelchair and visibly ill. That same month, October 2019, the Consejo de Estado (Council of State) had dismissed a lawsuit filed jointly by Francisco and Humberto years earlier, the only remaining case under consideration. The posthumous ruling, a material conjunction of death and law, had marked the end of a thirteen-year juridical battle.

"It was very hard [what happened to us], many of us had depression, it was traumatic for many people," Jorge said with a mix of calm and dejection. After he had so vividly brought together his understanding of the bureaucracy's "methodic, premeditated deception" and the pain of trauma, victimhood, and

FIGURE 3.3.   The view from Jorge's tailor shop in 2019. Photo by the author.

death, we looked out the window of his shop and I asked what he thought about the new development. "It's quite beautiful, I think it came out well," he replied. "I think transformation is good, it's part of the cycle of cities." The seemingly stable, finished architectural forms had congealed the same encompassing visions of urbanity and citizenship that residents had left unchallenged in their struggle.[91] Yet, as we will see, these epistemic and material formations are inherently unstable, their cracks and fissures opening new spaces for the composition of urban knowledges and political critiques.

RUINOUS KNOWLEDGE

"Nothing is being hidden here [*aquí no se está ocultando nada*]," the city func-tionary said, raising his voice, rather shaken, as the number of people and the grumbling grew in the audience. Below him, Paulina, a local activist and owner of a billiard hall in the downtown neighborhood of La Alameda, hurried through the auditorium distributing a small strip of paper with the following warning:

> ATTENTION
> **WE INVITE THE COMMUNITY TO AVOID SIGNING** THE ASSIS-TANCE [SHEET] OF THE INVITATION TO THE PRESENTATION OF THE PROPOSAL OF THE ESTACIÓN CENTRAL PARTIAL PLAN, BECAUSE YOUR SIGNATURE ENDORSES THE APPROVAL OF SAID PARTIAL PLAN. WE NEED FIRST TO UNDERSTAND IT FULLY AND OBTAIN THE INCLUSION OF OUR PROPOSALS, DIS-AGREEMENTS, AND CONCERNS. THIS PLAN MUST BE INCLU-SIONARY FOR **ALL, NOT LIKE IT WAS FOR THE PEOPLE THEY ALREADY REMOVED FROM LA ALAMEDA AND THAT ARE TODAY DISPLACED AND WITHOUT A ROOF OR OPPORTUNI-TIES BECAUSE WHAT THEY GAVE THEM WAS NOT ENOUGH.**

The event was an informational meeting organized by the Secretaría Distrital de Planeación (City Planning Department) at the Jorge Eliécer Gaitán Theater in late June 2012. The art deco building—one of the city's main cultural venues—faced a busy pedestrianized section of the historic Carrera Séptima, only a few blocks from the site of the ongoing renewal plan Estación Central (Central Station). As we waited for the doors to open, a planning official I had met at several town hall meetings told me she was concerned that the morning paper had publicized the event as a general session on downtown renewal. Instead, planners had hoped to gather only property owners and residents within the area of the Estación Central plan. "Now everyone is going to show up," she said nervously. And she was right. Behind me on the sidewalk were Hernando and Humberto from Manzana Cinco, as other downtown community leaders and residents ambled around the entrance.

Distrust of the administration had deepened since the first round of evictions and demolitions swept through La Alameda in 2009 when Estación Central was launched. A new cohort of progressive planners in the recently elected administration of Gustavo Petro was now reframing Estación Central as an "associational plan [*plan asociativo*]" for "urban revitalization [*revitalización urbana*]." It was thus that the senior planner leading the event reassured the crowd that this was not simply a "socialization [*socialización*]" of the plan, as such meetings were typically called, but rather a "participatory process." Yet Paulina's slips of paper, now in the hands of many attendees, were a reminder of locals' wariness of the language of participation. The term itself, *socialización*, had long been a blatant, almost ironic display of the top-down, ex post facto nature of planning in Bogotá. Participation, for most residents, was a perfunctory affair, a performance of conformity and consent.

At the Estación Central meeting, attendees not only voiced their objections to vacuous participation policies and forced evictions. They also called attention to the less apparent, enduring forms of insecurity and deterioration that had driven the destruction of their neighborhoods long before expropriation notices and bulldozers arrived. Many of them centered their comments on the idea of "urban decay [*deterioro urbano*]." They questioned official definitions of decline, as well as the notion that planning interventions were aimed at stopping deterioration in downtown neighborhoods. One local shop owner exclaimed, "Decay in the city center is not accidental, it's intentional!" Another resident talked about how insecurity and abandonment had "devalued the zone" to the advantage of real estate speculators. But it was Efraín, a veteran community organizer, who most directly challenged planners' "simple answers to complex problems," as he put it. Drawing on his experience as a longtime resident of the west side of downtown, which he called a "rotting heap of humanity [*pudridero humano*]," he contested the widespread assumption that urban renewal was aimed at countering urban decay. Hinting at the irony of plans that aimed to recuperate a zone by displacing its residents, he admonished the administration: "Do not construct a single housing unit; instead please stop the decay, because that is what is weighing us down [*nos está agobiando*]!"

For Efraín and many others at the Jorge Eliécer Gaitán Theater that day, officials had deployed discourses of decline and insecurity to usher in real estate agendas while contributing to the deterioration of central areas through years of regulation and zoning. This is what Efraín, concluding his statement as attendees applauded, called "misdevelopment [*maldesarrollo*]." Urban decay, for him, was not the result of the abandonment of the state or the lack of intervention, but rather of long-established, destructive planning regimes.

The Archaeology of Decay

Not long after the Estación Central meeting, I met with Efraín at a small café in front of the Jorge Eliécer Gaitán Theater. Originally trained as a sociologist, he had become a hardened activist involved in neighborhood politics, NGO work on waste management, and, more recently, antieviction campaigns in downtown Bogotá. He had lived for decades in one of the city center's most "deteriorated" neighborhoods, San Bernardo, near El Cartucho (see chapter 2). Over the previous decade, Efraín had witnessed the destruction of El Cartucho, the construction of the monumental Tercer Milenio Park, and the shock waves of crime, poverty, and abandonment that had followed the urban project.

As we spoke about long-running government plans for downtown renewal, Efraín said that officials had for years "hidden information" about the fate of his neighborhood so that it would "continue to rot away" and people would sell their properties at lower prices. The imagery of "putrefaction [*pudrimiento*]," which he had also used at the Jorge Eliécer Gaitán Theater, was closely linked to his work as a grassroots organizer and environmentalist. Since the 1990s, Efraín had been dedicated to local participation movements around neighborhood waste recycling in central districts. This was a main economic activity in his own neighborhood as well as in other downtown districts, including the now defunct El Cartucho. Such waste work had been typically associated with urban decline and marginality, primarily through the figure of the *desechable* (disposable), as waste pickers are often degradingly called in Bogotá. Efraín, however, called attention to the critical knowledges that emerged from inhabiting amid *deterioro* in a degraded, decomposing environment.

For him, it was necessary to understand "urban rot" as a process and make visible "how the material conditions of decay expand."[1] This was not unlike the process of sorting waste, he noted, because "garbage forms only when debris [*residuos*] is mixed; without mixing there is no garbage."[2] According to Efraín, something like an "archaeology of decay" was critical to sort things and people and unearth the "nucleus of decomposition" that was at the heart of deteriorating neighborhoods such as his own. It would make apparent the human and material layers of rotting terrains, from illicit activities and street commerce to the circulation of weapons and the exacerbation of urban poverty. Further excavation, he noted, would also show how "decay . . . also starts to diminish" along certain routes and at different times of the day, as types of people and activities gradually shift: "Streets for the commerce of trinkets [*baratijas*] emerge, zones of poverty, but not of indigence, where people arrive to sell all kinds of things."

The archaeology of decay, Efraín said, was ultimately about examining "different degrees of decay [*grados de deterioro*]." Efraín's attention to gradations was a way not only of producing more nuanced descriptions of processes of deterioration but also of grounding the technical concept of decay in inhabitants' intimate knowledge and sensorial experience of their changing environs. Implicit in Efraín's talk of degrees was the unsettling of the norms, or what Paul Kockelman calls "comparative grounds," in relation to which urban places appeared to be declining.[3] Grading, gradations, and gradients, Kockelman argues, are central to how people inhabit, make sense of, and act in the world.[4] They are semiotic, phenomenological, and material processes that do not simply reflect shared experiential and epistemic backgrounds but rather "performatively constitute" them, "changing [people's] assumptions about the world."[5] Such systems of valuation and their underlying grounds are inscribed in things, embodied by actors, and encoded in laws and regulations.[6] Furthermore, built environments are pervaded by signs that index practical understandings of gradations and values.[7] At stake here are the affordances of urban worlds, the relational and emergent properties that both open and close possible uses and modes of dwelling.[8]

When Efraín pointed to the graduated intensities of urban decay, to shifting grounds of practice and perception, he was making apparent the power-laden, transformative effects of official norms. He had been suspicious, for instance, of a raucous business that had recently appeared on his block. Like other illicit activities in the area, it had been ignored by the nearby police station while residents' trivial misdemeanors and code violations were swiftly sanctioned. Efraín hinted at how governmental technologies to interpret and regulate urban decay—what planners also offhandedly called an entire neighborhood's "level of decay"—were themselves driving deterioration and pushing people to abandon the area. Such epistemologies impinged on people's understanding of the city, their modes of dwelling, and the very materiality of urban space. Efraín had been vocal about such dynamics in his activist and political networks. On one occasion, he had brought up the issue with a city councilor. The politician had tried to dissuade him from conspiratorial thinking. "He told me that there wasn't really a perverse plan of rotting," Efraín recalled. He responded with a more subtle critique: "So I told the politician, 'Well, that's even worse, because it still occurs, so what we have here is a structural logic that creates decay. And people who want to leave, sell for any price to get out, and that only benefits the real estate business, people who don't mind that the place is rotting beyond measure.'"

Efraín's call for an archaeology of decay was representative of local critical knowledges of renewal and deterioration and their inextricable connections to the violence of legal and property regimes. In one sense, and as the city councilor suggested, Efraín's mention of hidden agendas and wide-ranging collusions—common tropes among downtown residents facing eviction—resonated with conspiratorial understandings of urban development. In this regard, anthropological literature shows how conspiracy theorizing has become a central mode of knowledge and critique through which people make sense of the opaque and mediated workings of global power.[9] But while many downtown residents conjured shadowy agents and wondered about how they pulled the strings of urban development, theirs was not primarily an attempt to "assert epistemic certainty" over an unknown and estranged reality, to borrow from Dominic Boyer.[10] Downtown dwellers' theories of urban power were instead anchored to their intimate experience and even excessive knowledge of urban ruination. When they veered into conspiratorial thinking, it was more "to disrupt knowledge": to unsettle planners' certainties about urban decay and assumptions about order, security, and value.[11]

In this chapter, I explore Efraín's archaeological sensibilities as a phenomenological regrounding of urban knowledge in the material and temporal experience of decay. At stake here is what I call a *ruinous knowledge*: an experiential epistemology borne out by the textures and rhythms of crumbling cityscapes and rotting neighborhoods. Anthropologists have increasingly turned their attention to ruins as critical sites for the study of the enduring violence and material traces of regimes of power, from the debris of colonialism and the rubble of capitalism to degraded landscapes and the wreckage of war.[12] This scholarship has illuminated the destructive undersides of notions of progress and their latent, layered, and differential material effects. Far from static remnants, such residues constitute what Ann Stoler calls "ruination": "an ongoing corrosive process that weighs on the future."[13] Building on this work, and on studies that probe into the possibilities and limits of life amid urban ruins, I examine the composition of knowledge amid decay.[14]

There are few concepts so integral to contemporary urbanism, yet so taken for granted, as decay, disrepair, and decline. Obsolescence and deterioration appear to be the very stuff of capitalist urbanization and its endless cycles of destructive accumulation.[15] In this regard, *deterioro* seems indistinguishable from similar notions such as "blight" in the United States. Yet critiques of blight in North American cities, as Andrew Herscher argues, have focused primarily on spatial and economic restructuring, failing to account for blight's central "relation to racial capitalism."[16] Similarly, the archaeology of decay and the ruinous knowledges on which it is grounded call for more capacious critiques of the sociocultural and political conjunctures that mediate deterioration. In Bogotá, this means situating decay not only in the city's trajectories of capitalist development but also, crucially, within violent regimes of law and citizenship and the social differences they engender.

In what follows I focus on ongoing plans to transform the neighborhoods of La Alameda and Santa Fe in the northwest edge of the city center. I show how urban dwellers' ruinous knowledges made visible the slow and sustained decomposition of the social and material infrastructures of everyday urban life. By attending to the protracted temporalities and banal materialities of urban renewal, residents illuminated the gradual, gradated, and inconspicuous enactment of unjust and violent legal orders. The ruinous qualities of this epistemic ground lent critical force to local understandings of planning strategies and denunciations of the city's politics of urban value. Much like the "displaced of Manzana Cinco" (see chapter 3), residents in these west-side neighborhoods called attention to the insecurities of city planning and the continuities between urban renewal and warfare. In one sense, the ruinous knowledges I follow below remained entwined with the normative orders of propertied citizenship as residents turned their attention to decay itself as the problem to be remedied. In their calls for "recovery," they thus reproduced the inequalities driving the slow violence of state-induced decay. At the same time, steeped as they were in the ruination of their immediate worlds, urban dwellers articulated incisive critiques in which the state and the law appeared inextricably linked to what Keisha-Khan Perry, in her work on Salvador da Bahia, calls the "violence of unequal urban development."[17] When they invoked the country's long-running armed conflict as a reference point for their dispossession, they did not employ the language of victimhood, of absent or illegitimate state actors, or of the violation of rights. Instead they articulated a more incisive critique in which state, law, and property appeared themselves as the origins of, not the solutions to, entrenched histories of violence and insecurity. Ruinous knowledges did not draw their force from liberal, middle-class regimes of citizenship but rather from the exact opposite: from rotting urban worlds and the ruination that lies at the core of planning and property regimes.

And this is the promise of such ambiguous subaltern epistemologies. By following the material traces of decay, residents called attention to how governmental logics are erected on and bring about destruction. Mediated by the imaginaries of Colombia's war, ruinous knowledges were keyed to the continuities between the devastation wrought by city planning and the country's long history of state violence and forced displacement in the countryside. They ultimately laid bare the "ruination [that] lies at the heart of modern regimes of knowledge," in the words of Yael Navaro-Yashin.[18] It is to these official epistemologies and their tacit systems of destructive interpretation and valuation that I turn next.

Chains of Decay

As in much of Latin America, the "discourse of downtown decay" attributed the decline of Bogotá's historic center to the overcrowding of impoverished rural migrants, the expansion of popular economies, and the departure of the middle and upper classes to new residential districts.[19] Urban renewal emerged as the main path for "recovery," further reproducing exclusionary ideals of governance, citizenship, and public space.[20] Similar to what Alejandra Leal Martínez shows in her work on Mexico City, downtown renewal became integrally connected to the "criminalization of the urban poor."[21]

In Bogotá, downtown deterioration became ensnared in the country's history of violence. Expert talk about "urban disorder" and "urban decay" can be traced back to the early twentieth century, when Bogotá became the main destination for rural migrants fleeing violence in the countryside. In the 1940s, modernist architects decried the "abandonment" and "filth" that these new inhabitants—Indigenous peasants, impoverished tenement dwellers, and informal market vendors—had brought to the city center.[22] Tellingly, they also noted how these "sordid" neighborhoods, located primarily on the west side of the city center, offered unparalleled opportunities for development and accumulation: "Their existence is a great fortune, a stupendous mine that the collective can and must take advantage of: it is called VALORIZATION."[23]

The relationship between social hierarchies, violent conflict, and urban (de) valuation was further cemented following El Bogotazo, the historic uprising of 1948 that partially destroyed the city center after the assassination of leftist presidential candidate Jorge Eliécer Gaitán (see chapter 1). In the aftermath, planners and architects celebrated the destructive power of the insurrection, arguing that it had finally opened the path to reverse the "horrendous disorder" of downtown and materialize existing plans for "expansion and beautification."[24] Urban disintegration appeared here again as a critical condition for progress and valorization. Proponents of a post-Bogotazo reconstruction plan wrote about valorizing the "unhygienic plots occupied by fruit trees" of the older blocks of downtown, many of them now burnt to rubble.[25] While the most ambitious reconstruction plans never materialized, ruination continued apace in the city center, constituting the urban equivalent of a scorched-earth tactic to prevent future urban revolts and make downtown less of a subaltern space.

The class and racial underpinnings of decay and its ties to security agendas became less overt in the following decades as planners and real estate developers rendered the concept into a technical artifact. Urban decay would be normalized as an objective condition amenable to expert diagnoses and intervention. A policy document from 1964, for instance, portrayed decay as a natural, self-driven process inherent to the city's rapid growth: "In cities of accelerated development, and such is the case of Bogotá, the transformation of its constructions is continuous, leaving some in disuse and others exposed to the action of decay [la acción del deterioro]."[26] In a late 1980s plan, officials wrote about "the systematic deterioration of [downtown's] environment" and identified three "main problems": the "expulsion of residents," the "excessive concentration of the tertiary sector," and the "generation of large urban voids."[27] Significantly, "residents" here referred to middle-class inhabitants, "tertiary activities" signaled the rise of informal and popular commerce, and "urban voids" appeared as natural occurrences and not as the outcome of previous rounds of demolition and displacement. Following Tania Li's work on development expertise, decay was "rendered nonpolitical," occluding relations of force, the role of specific agents, and political-economic structures.[28] As an official epistemology, according to Li, it had "far-reaching effects" not only in terms of expert conceptualizations and public discourse but also in the shaping of material environments and residents' everyday experience.[29] At the same time, the depoliticized materialization of decay was never complete, with both experts and residents recognizing and critically examining its contradictions and political openings.

The neighborhoods of La Alameda and Santa Fe epitomized the effects of such expert knowledges and their normalization of decay. Like most of downtown's west side, development in the area had been closely linked to wide-ranging processes of destruction. Most recently, the ambitious Estación Central plan, launched in 2007 and still underway in 2020, had led to the demolition of three city blocks for the construction of an underground bus station and future node of the city's rapid-transit bus system, Transmilenio. Planners envisioned a public-private partnership for the construction of a mixed-use, high-density complex above the station. After more than a decade, however, the city administration had built only bus roads and an underground walkway, leaving behind fields of rubble and abandoned buildings in expectation of the highly profitable real estate operation.

While infrastructural development proved effective in leveraging the first round of evictions and demolitions, as the plan became more real estate oriented and speculative, urban decay emerged as the main rationale. The scope and alleged urgency of the plan became directly tied to the expert diagnosis of decay as a naturalized, self-propelling phenomenon. One of the main findings of a 2012 technical supporting document (*documento técnico de soporte*, or DTS) was that the zone was undergoing a marked "process of deterioration."[30] The progressive nature of decay and its distinctive momentum required technical interventions that would both allow the area's supposedly natural obsolescence to run its course and remove the debris of the past through destruction and reconstruction. Planners described how land uses had shifted from residential to commercial, including repair shops and prostitution, and houses had been modified, stripped down, subdivided, and repurposed with "elements that are aggressive to architectural conventions and the environs."[31] The DTS also stated that the population had changed, "families had moved to modern or safer neighborhoods," and the "aesthetic features" and "identity" of a bygone era had been modified. "The development and better use [*aprovechamiento*] of this area," the document concluded, "requires allowing urban evolution to follow its course and eliminating obsolete systems to bring about new urban configurations."[32]

Cristina, one of the senior planners who coauthored the Estación Central DTS, described these processes as a "chain of decay [*cadena de deterioro*]." Some months after talking with her about her earlier experience as a planner on the Parque Tercer Milenio project (see chapter 2), I met her once again in her home office in north Bogotá to discuss her more recent work on Estación Central. As she sketched on a pad in her sparsely decorated studio—wooden shelves and dim lights, jazz playing in the background—she explained, "I have a diagram I put together [about urban decay]." She drew a standard x-y axis. "In a built-up urban sector that has existed for many years there are three moments, so to speak, three attributes: sense of belonging, investment, and economic activity." Cristina then traced a descending curve with the now nonexistent neighborhood of El Cartucho at the end. Drawing on her experience as one of the lead planners in the large-scale demolition of the central neighborhood in the 1990s and the subsequent construction of the monumental Parque Tercer Milenio, she continued: "[At the bottom is] El Cartucho; there was no sense of belonging, or if there was a sense of belonging it was of illegal people [*gente ilegal*], there was no licit economic activity, and public space was beyond repair." The result, Cristina explained, was that the stakes of intervention were much higher, and the state had to invest too many resources to "reverse" these processes and "detain the decay [*frenar el deterioro*]." Gesturing to a common narrative about governmental voids as a main cause of Colombia's history of armed conflict, she added, "The chain of decay in all these processes is a function of the absence of the state."[33] It was not surprising, then, that she and other functionaries described the demolition of El Cartucho as a "military operation" essentially aimed at regaining "territorial control."

At least three core assumptions were implicit in the notion of "chains of decay." First was the idea that decay was the result of a form of temporal causality: a

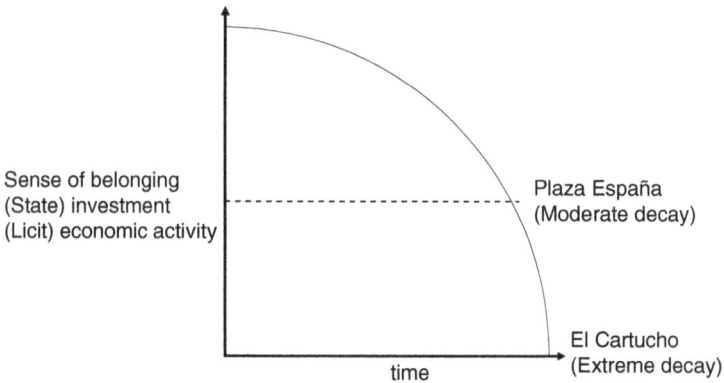

FIGURE 4.1. Diagram of "cycles of decay" based on Cristina's sketch. At the bottom on the far right is El Cartucho as an exemplar of irreversible decay. In the middle of the curve is the nearby area of Plaza España, which Cristina described as lacking state investment and a legitimate sense of belonging, but which still exhibited considerable economic activity. Created by the author.

linear chain of causes modulated by varying degrees of state presence, licit economic activities, and a legitimate sense of belonging. Second was the presupposition of an inherent contiguity—or "contagion effect," as some experts described it—so that chains of deterioration appeared not as discrete phenomena but as processes spread out in space and time. And third was the implication of a homology between the material and social attributes of urban space, such that deteriorating built forms necessarily entailed decaying human worlds (see chapter 2). Such assumptions proved to be widely shared among planners across the political spectrum. Cristina, for instance, had worked with Mayor Enrique Peñalosa (1998–2000), who became widely known for his aggressive security and public-space policies, epitomized in the erasure of El Cartucho. She had taken up the Estación Central plan during the administration of Samuel Moreno (2008–11), nominally a leftist mayor, whose term was mired in corruption scandals and largely aligned with the interests of the construction sector. She continued to work on the plan under the administration of Gustavo Petro (2012–15) and within its new policy frameworks against inner-city displacement and speculation. But even here, while progressive officials set out to create affordable, subsidized housing in the city center—ultimately with little success—they also vigorously pushed for what they called "urban revitalization," reproducing assumptions about the need to reconstruct and repopulate a deteriorated city center.[34] In describing to me their reinterpretation of the Estación Central plan, one of Petro's lead planners dismissed the existing houses and buildings as "not worth saving" and, with visible distaste, noted that these were mostly "cheap residences and tenements [*inquilinatos*]." While the future of downtown renewal may have been disputed, the past and present of decay were left intact.

These modes of expertise actively shaped sociomaterial worlds through what Michael Herzfeld calls the "management of time."[35] They enacted an urban temporality in which devaluation emerged as a natural historical process and state action and private investment as imperative solutions. Official epistemologies of decay can thus be viewed, following Laura Bear, as "forms of skillful making enacted within timescapes, which bring social worlds into being and link them to nonhuman processes."[36] Such institutional and expert mediation of downtown's rhythms of decay was further displayed in a PowerPoint slide created by the city government in 2010. Under the title "Curve of Decay," the diagram made apparent the sociopolitical and material implications of expert timescapes of decay. Depicting a curvilinear process similar to the one sketched by Cristina, the plotted trajectory showed once again El Cartucho at the bottom, while placing the renewed Eje Ambiental promenade at the top. The chart's directional arrows and overall organization presented a cyclical movement along axes of "deterioration" and "investment." The implication was clear: Decay inevitably transpires when the city is left to its own devices, and when that occurs, state action becomes increasingly costly and urgent. At work here was a praxis of intervention that was linked to the undoing of chains of decay and that legitimated widespread destruction, as in El Cartucho and Estación Central. As Cristina put it, commenting on the degree of deterioration in the area and the difficulty of containing or reversing it: "If you carry out an operation in a deteriorated zone and that operation is not large enough, then the surroundings will eat it up [*se la come el entorno*]."

Despite official portrayals of decay as a natural process devoid of politics, in moments of "professional intimacy" planners reluctantly recognized the entanglements between their work and urban deterioration.[37] At some point during her much-rehearsed and polished exposition of chains of decay, Cristina admitted, somewhat mortified, that older regulations had "unintentionally [*sin querer*] led to the deterioration of the city center" by promoting large-scale renovation and making it impossible for owners to develop their properties individually. Other planners often told me with frustration that they had made the same mistake again in the city's 2000 Plan de Ordenamiento Territorial, with zoning schemes that "froze up land." The fault, according to Cristina, lay in planners relying too much on norms and simply "waiting for things to happen"—namely, for investors and developers to arrive. Beyond a source of disappointment, however, such failures became a justification for planning expertise itself and for new rounds of state intervention aimed at fixing these allegedly technical errors. And

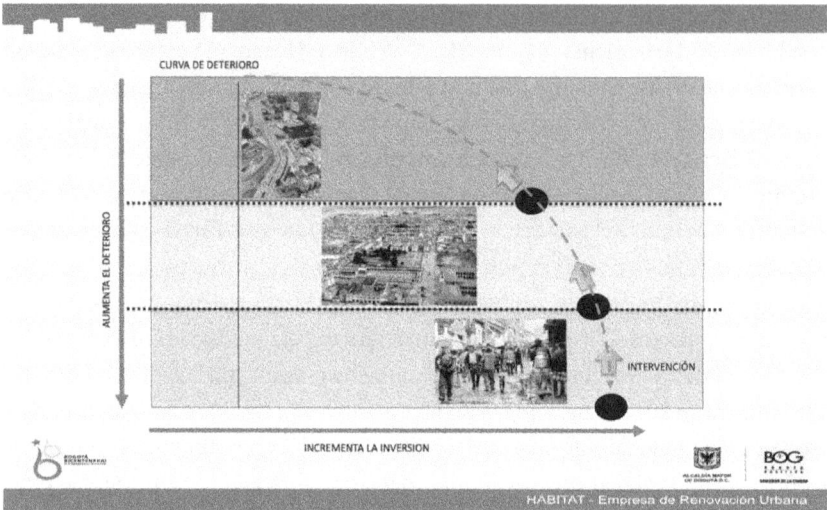

FIGURE 4.2. PowerPoint slide on the "curve of decay" from a presentation created by the city's Empresa de Renovación Urbana (Company of Urban Renewal). On the vertical axis, deterioration increases, and on the horizontal axis, investment increases. The curve is labeled "Intervention," and its trajectory starts from a picture of El Cartucho and ends in one of the city's emblematic downtown interventions, Eje Ambiental.

while most plans never came to fruition, things certainly did happen, as actors mobilized around the effects of urban zoning and regulations, compounding the destructive force of official epistemologies of urban decay.

Functionaries working on the ground became painfully aware of these contradictions and of how the Estación Central plan had mediated and catalyzed the dissolution of the neighborhood and the expulsion of its inhabitants. Marcela, a young social worker at the ERU who had been assigned to the Estación Central project, elaborated on the ways in which planning and bureaucratic action had created the conditions for social and material practices that intensified the area's decay. Marcela was openly critical of the ERU's work, and when we met at the company's offices, she avoided talking in her cubicle in front of her coworkers. She asked me to step into an empty office so we could talk "more calmly." With the office chatter still audible behind the room's panels, she explained how "the zone had started to deteriorate" after the city launched the plan: "We started to acquire properties and they start to empty out and get walled in, and then a process of decay begins in that area. And people's complaints are now [about] the zone's deterioration, the insecurity, and the absence of the state regarding social and security issues." According to Marcela, the intervention had exacerbated the area's existing conflicts around the drug trade, sex work, crime, and property to the point that she now feared for her life when she visited. The plan, she continued, had accelerated the "deterioration [of La Alameda] at a social level." It had caused property values to depreciate, worsened the prospects of fair compensation, and deepened the disputes between owners and tenants. Although Marcela blamed bureaucratic divisions, rigid regulations, and lack of political will for the rapid degradation of the neighborhood, she also recognized her unwitting complicity. Recalling her previous experience as a functionary at the national child protection and adoption agency, the Instituto Colombiano de Bienestar Familiar (Colombian Institute of Family Welfare), or ICBF, she offered a damning self-critique of how her bureaucratic work had contributed to ruining homes and lives: "[When I worked at the ICBF] they used to accuse me of stealing children to sell them. . . . Before I stole children and now I steal homes; what's the difference?"[38]

The extent to which planning routines had mediated urban decay was further illustrated by Rosa, a social worker specialized in planning, who had worked as an ERU contractor in the early stages of the land acquisition process. We met in the mezzanine of an office tower, just a few blocks from La Alameda and Santa Fe, where she was now a consultant on resettlement schemes for the national oil company Ecopetrol. Along with engineers, appraisers, and topographers, Rosa had carried out a local census and a land market study and had mapped the Estación Central zone. These knowledge-making practices, she explained, had prompted a host of strategies that had further eroded local socialities. Soon after her team started surveying properties, rumors of the intervention spread rapidly in the area, "generating expectations" about resettlement compensations and property sales.

One house, she recalled, had been owned by an elderly woman who passed away when expropriations started. Apparently she had been "made to sign [over the property]" before dying, and when Rosa's team arrived, more than ten people were living in the house: "No electricity, a broken entrance, full of excrement, full of trash." Eventually a person with a property deed surfaced, and city officials mediated between the owner and possessors (*poseedores*) and "facilitated the vacating of the house."[39] At another point in the process, Rosa and her team visited a cheap motel (*residencia* or *paga diario*) used frequently by sex workers. Initially they found sixteen residents, but the next time they came by, there were more than fifty people living in the crowded rooms and seeking resettlement assistance. The manager of the residencia, it turned out, had not paid rent in months to the landlord, Doña Eugenia, one of the oldest and most powerful landowners in the area—a *terrateniente*, as Marcela put it, who ran several bars and brothels. Ultimately, Rosa and her coworkers negotiated with the manager and helped Doña Eugenia regain control of the property. "The social work of resettlement," she noted, had in practice become a form of real estate brokerage.

Rosa left her job at the ERU "overwhelmed" and conflicted about the extent to which she had become embroiled in the "tangles [*enredos*]" and "mysteries" that shrouded land use and ownership in the area. In contrast to official normalizations of deterioration and the alleged imperative of intervention, she saw planning itself as an unmistakable link in local chains of decay. "What kind of planning are we generating?" she asked. The renewal plan, Rosa concluded, proved to be nothing more than property acquisition and negotiation mechanisms that had pushed deterioration to its culmination, "rashly expulsing people, for no reason."

Stratifying and Devaluing

Expert epistemologies of decay did not go unchallenged in La Alameda and Santa Fe. Drawing on their intimate knowledge and experiences of urban degradation, residents questioned official standards of value, theories of temporal causality, and ideologies of order and security. In doing so they revealed the workings of a different set of forces, causes, and rhythms. They did not simply critique the rationales for destructive urban intervention or the ways in which planning had accelerated the final stages of decay and destruction, as Marcela and Rosa suggested. Instead they went further and showed how deterioration itself had been associated with planning and legal regimes years before expropriations and demolitions were launched in the area. Urban dwellers illuminated the opaque and long-standing state practices that had slowly decomposed urban worlds.

The destructive effects of official valuations and regulations became most apparent from the vantage point of the people and places that had been most palpably at odds with expert characterizations. This was the case with Plaza 25, a six-story apartment building that planners described as "exceptional," an anomaly within the neighborhood's alleged cycle of decay. According to a functionary in charge of property acquisitions, Plaza 25 "was the only nice, well-maintained, and organized" building in the three blocks that the city had slated for demolition. Its 1980s smooth gray facade, red garage doors, and angular windows stood out among aging brick low-rises and the peeling stucco walls and broken roof tiles of older houses. While two government buildings and a taller residential tower on the same block were spared demolition, the city administration moved swiftly with the expropriation of Plaza 25, making low offers to owners for the obligatory sale of their apartments starting in 2009. It was as if the city had suppressed a categorical anomaly to further consolidate what Vyjayanthi Rao describes as "the

FIGURE 4.3.   Plaza 25 in 2013, empty and waiting to be demolished. Photo by the author.

murky, intermediate terrain of potential" of speculative urbanism.[40] Degrading the building was integral to leveling the terrain—symbolically and literally—and a condition of possibility for renewal: for "that which upgrades itself by downgrading others," to use Paul Kockelman's phrasing.[41]

For residents, their expulsion had been the culmination of a drawn-out process in which the state had devalued their properties through selective abandonment and oblique action, effectively "damaging the neighborhood [*dañando el barrio*]," as Cecilia, a former apartment owner, put it. Evoking imaginaries of war, she explained how authorities had previously "displaced" unsavory businesses to the "red zone" to the west, leaving streets "empty and ruined [*en la ruina*]." She mused, "It looks like, when the state is going to carry out urban renewal, they make sure it gets more and more ruined and decayed [*dañe y deteriore*] so they can kick people out." Eventually city officials in charge of the plan's so-called *gestión social* (social management) started visiting residents to inform them they would be expropriated, Cecilia continued, "despite not having the slightest idea of what the area was going to be used for." Remembering how, one by one, her mostly elderly neighbors came to terms with the "immense psychological and economic damage" of their expulsion, she noted that they had had no recourse: "People had simply been pushed out by the state, as if they had invaded [their own homes]."

Liliana, another former resident of Plaza 25, also elaborated on the destructive nature of official epistemologies by drawing on the ruinous knowledge gained from living in the decaying neighborhood. With the meager funds from her expropriation, she and her elderly father had moved into a low-income residential complex in Mosquera, a growing industrial and working-class suburb of Bogotá. In a few years she had gone from property owner in the city center to renter in an impoverished urban fringe. The spatial and phenomenological distance between her previous residence and her new environs reminded her every day of how much her "life of quality [*vida de calidad*]," as she put it, had been upended. In her old studio apartment in La Alameda, "everything was within reach": a density of amenities and opportunities, including her short walk to work as a secretary at a downtown bank. After her eviction, she had found work as a property manager at a subsidized housing project at the very edge of Mosquera. That is where we first met, at the end of an unpaved road that stopped at a barbwire fence, beyond which there were only empty pastures and downtown Bogotá's miniature skyline in the horizon. "I used to live there," she said, pointing to the distant mountains and tiny buildings.

Liliana shared an agonizing narrative about how the administration had devalued her property over the years, ending with her eviction and the demolition of her home. At the center of her account was a bureaucratic classification system known as *estratificación socioeconómica* (socioeconomic stratification) and its creation of differential geographies of urban value. The national government established the estratificación system in 1994 as a cross-subsidy mechanism (*subsidio cruzado*) for public utility charges. The aim was that affluent residents would offset the utility costs of lower-income populations. The classification, however, was not based on income level but on the "physical characteristics of housing and its surroundings."[42] For almost three decades, local estratificación committees have classified urban and rural areas across Colombia by *estratos* (the process is called *estratificar*) on a scale from 1 to 6, where estrato 1 is the poorest (or "low-low," according to the typology) and estrato 6 is the wealthiest ("high").[43]

As established by national law, field teams of *reconocedores* (surveyors) follow a standard methodology designed to grade the four main factors that determine the physical state of housing: structure, finishes, bathroom, and kitchen. This involves identifying and scoring multiple variables listed on a form, from the size of the construction and the quality of materials to the type of facade, furniture, and overall condition. Implicit in such valuations of material forms and their affordances are local and contextual knowledges about socioeconomic standing, class, neighborhood reputation, illicit activities, and insecurity.[44] Such assumptions are most apparent in evaluation categories such as "poor," "simple," "regular," "luxurious," "bad," "good," and "excellent," which the estratificación manual argues "may seem subjective" but are "precise descriptions, clearly distinguishable, that should not create any kind of confusion."[45]

Despite its technical aura and layering with statistics, the estratificación system is far from a neutral descriptor of given realities. Instead, and as anthropological work on the politics of measurement and commensuration has shown, estratos are generative of social worlds and relations of power.[46] They not only presuppose tacit norms and knowledges—what Kockelman calls "comparative grounds"—but are constitutive of semiotic, material, and experiential realities.[47] This has been evident in the social life of estratos beyond their original, allegedly progressive design. In addition to their adoption by a range of institutions for taxation, university tuition scales, and real estate transactions, estratos have been extensively appropriated and redeployed as markers of status and belonging— people talk of imagined estratos 0 and 10 to index sociospatial identities— ultimately reinforcing the inequalities and exclusions of Colombia's stratified society.[48]

Not surprisingly, Liliana had been very troubled when she discovered that the government had lowered the estrato of the Plaza 25 building from 4 (medium) to 3 (medium-low): "When I arrived in 1998, we were estrato four. And then one day the utility bill said, 'Restructured from four to three.'" Through a routine update, the city had reclassified the building and effectively declassed its residents. Although the recategorization lowered utility costs and property taxes, it also negatively affected property values, as estratos typically influence experts' property appraisals. "In 2004," Liliana recalled, "they decreased [my apartment's] cadastral appraisal [avalúo catastral] down to a third of the previous amount. My apartment was valued at eighteen million pesos [US$10,016] and they lowered it to six million [US$3,338]." According to her own calculations, her investment over the years had been close to US$47,000, and she had hoped to receive at least US$33,000 from the government. In the end, the city had only paid her US$18,000, an amount that made it impossible for her to relocate anywhere near downtown.[49]

For Liliana, the restratification of her building had been a clear indication that authorities "had already been paving the way" for expropriation, demolition, and reconstruction. She and her neighbors took issue not only with how the government had classified their properties but also with how official grading practices had themselves driven deterioration: "abandon to decay," in Liliana's words. In sharp contrast to narrow notions of economic value, residents centered a nuanced and expansive conceptualization of urban value. Following a rich body of anthropological scholarship, value here would be best viewed as emerging (and dissolving) through social, material, and semiotic action.[50] Elaborating on the creative and transformative potentials of value, residents described how they had cultivated, maintained, and projected their homes' worth over the years. This led them to denounce state modalities of commensuration as tools to undo processes of value creation and enable forced and unequal exchanges. Authorities had converted them into "trash," Liliana noted indignantly. They had treated them worse than "criminals," she said, evincing once again how entrenched repertoires of insecurity mediated the composition of ruinous knowledges. For her, the piecemeal violence of estratificación had fully surfaced when city officials finally carried out the eviction—what she described as a land grab, or *despojo*—"under threat and pressure" and with the police.

The dissolution of the meanings, socialities, and practices attached to the residents' homes was further brought into focus by Gerardo, another former resident of Plaza 25. Previously a taxi driver, he now helped his daughter run a small pizza shop in a garage in the middle-class Normandía neighborhood, in west Bogotá. Due to an outstanding mortgage loan at the time of his eviction, he had been left in an exceptionally precarious position and had to relocate to a room in a shared house. In addition to living in Plaza 25, Gerardo had acted as its longtime manager, making sure it complied with condominium regulations (*propiedad horizontal*) and was well maintained. Along with other neighbors, he had also collaborated with local authorities to improve policing and close two neighboring "drug houses [*casas de vicio*]." Preserving the property and building community, he explained, were critical to reaping the value of his apartment. This is what he described as the "future of the family patrimony [*patrimonio familiar*]," a term he and others used frequently and pointedly when describing their expropriation. The term *patrimonio* is used in Colombia and Latin America to refer to individual and collective property, typically generational and inherited. To call something *patrimonio*, as Elizabeth Ferry argues, "places limits on its exchange by classifying it as ideally *inalienable*."[51] In talking about the loss of his "essential, primary patrimony," Gerardo gestured in this direction. For him, dispossession had signified the destruction of an ensemble of things and experiences, the disintegration of social relations and a sense of self:

> [In that apartment] I projected my life. . . . I had to remove my paintings and put them in this business. [I had to throw away] my living room, dispose of my trinkets [*chucherías*] of many years, my memories. . . . Now I'm reduced to a room of four by three [meters] with a closet and bathroom, where I can barely fit a TV. I had a washing machine, I had a kitchen, I had my pots and pans, I had my living room, I had my paintings, I had my rugs, I had my memories, I had everything that is part of the life of a fifty-nine-year-old man, because I'm fifty-nine, I'm not a child. And these people come in and they destroy the life of a person.

This was not simply a romantic rendering of noneconomic value. On the contrary, Gerardo and his neighbors were acutely aware of the market implications of their valuation and critiqued the state's unjust offer accordingly. "We are not asking for millions of pesos, but only to be relocated in the area and in a home with similar characteristics," Gerardo explained. More than exchange, they sought a "replacement," or *vivienda de reemplazo* (replacement housing), an objective that would become fairly standard, yet rarely implemented, in later renewal plans.[52] The fact that this had not been possible confirmed for residents the politics of destruction and appropriation at the core of planning practices and their assessment techniques and reifications. As Liliana recalled, when functionaries told her she would not be able to stay in the neighborhood because it would become estrato 6, she replied, "Who told you that I am not able to live in estrato five or six? How is it that you define me in that way?" Besides perniciously undermining their sense of personhood, Gerardo noted, the gradual degradation of the building had ultimately "dismembered the community"—an expression redolent of Colombia's history of violence.

By drawing on their intimate knowledge of the slow decomposition of their homes, of the lived traces of decline, evictees had made apparent the material politics of expert systems of (de)valuation. Through an archaeology of the corrosive epistemologies of urban value, they had elucidated how planning knowledges and regulations had progressively ruined their building: how it had been devalued, emptied out, made to fall into disrepair, and dissolved into the landscape of rubble around it. In articulating their grievances, however, Plaza 25 residents also lamented the loss of propertied citizenship and its middle-class prerogatives. When Gerardo described the upkeep of the building and residents' earlier collaborations with authorities to confront the "insecure and depressed" surroundings, he reproduced the same ideals of security and order later called on by planners to evict them. Liliana, in turn, was especially indignant at the state's treatment of Plaza 25 owners because of their status as "upstanding citizens." Cecilia drove home these contradictions when she looked out the window of the downtown office where she worked as a secretary. Turning to the glitzy high-rises—the kind of building that would supposedly replace Plaza 25—she mourned, "For me this is the real city," not the decayed neighborhood she had last called her home.[53]

Forced Decline

In charting the rubble left by the neighborhood's alleged cycles of decay, the residents of Plaza 25 had nonetheless enacted an alternative timescape. For them, deterioration had been the result not of natural urban evolution, but rather of the work of specific actors, institutions, and regulations over an extended period. The archaeology of decay did not unearth an underlying logic, but rather brought to light a sociomaterial world grounded in forms of causality and accountability, knowledge and power, intimately tied to the destructive violence of city planning.[54]

Drawing on such archaeological sensibilities, Paulina, the social organizer who had warned residents about signing meeting attendance sheets at the Jorge Eliécer Gaitán Theater, offered one of the most compelling critiques of the politics of decay and the destructive violence of planning. As longtime property owners in the city center, she and her family had attained some semblance of middle-class security in previous decades. In recent years, however, the city had expropriated a commercial space owned by Paulina's mother near the San Victorino district for the construction of transit infrastructure. This loss, along with land use restrictions imposed on their other property and their main business, had translated into a drawn-out process of forced decline. She and her extended family now lived on the upper floor of what was once their successful billiard hall as they struggled to make ends meet on a dwindling income. The property was in La Alameda, only a few blocks from the Estación Central demolition site and just outside the boundary of the zone of intervention. In the early 2000s, however, planners had zoned the entire neighborhood for urban renewal due to its "deterioration" and "strategic potential."

The looming threat of eviction and the family's earlier expropriation, which Paulina was still contesting in court, had made her a self-taught expert in planning law. Originally trained as a veterinarian, she was now devoted to community organizing against urban renewal and downtown evictions. Every time I visited Paulina in the increasingly decrepit and lonely billiard hall, she was studying a new decree concerning property law, eminent domain, and the rights of dwellers in zones of urban renewal. She gathered all the official materials related to redevelopment plans for the area: pamphlets, leaflets, invitations to town hall meetings, official letters. She pored over these documents, bringing the papers close up to her eyes and looking through an exceptionally thick pair of glasses, her advanced myopia seemingly making her an incomparably sharp observer of the quotidian effects of legal minutiae. Her cultivation of legal and planning counterexpertise was firmly rooted in her inhabitation of and habituation to the decaying environment of her home, business, and neighborhood.

With salsa music in the background and a faint smell of cat urine in the room, Paulina talked passionately to me one day about the city's interventions in the neighborhood. "The problem of urban renewal for me is that urban renewal is a Machiavellian concept." She explained in detail how zoning regulations and urban laws had for years hampered property owners' use of their properties and their plans to renovate and transform them. At one point, she pulled out one of the many letters she had sent to the city government and read it out loud: "We are not against development, but in our areas we have had to suffer a great deal of deterioration caused by city administrations, with the implementation of limitations and restrictions on land uses, making us go from legality into illegality, [and all this] has only generated the closing of commercial establishments, the rise of empty properties, an increase of informality, and decay and more decay." Paulina talked about restrictions on alcohol sales, limitations on land use, and regulations on construction and remodeling. A late 1970s law, for instance, had established that only lots with an area of five thousand square meters or more could be subject to construction or expansion. "So what happened?" Paulina asked. "Who had five thousand square meters [of land]?" Only the several universities located in the area and large commercial owners, she explained. "And what did this generate?" she asked again. "Decay. And what did it force people to do? To sell." Small- and medium-size owners who did not sell sometimes allowed their properties to crumble so they could use them as parking lots. Since the 2000s, urban renewal zoning had further frozen development to create incentives for large-scale and comprehensive redevelopment—or, as Paulina put it, "so they could depreciate my property and give it to a constructor for greater profit."

Enrique, a good friend of Paulina's, lived closer to the zone's core of decay, as he himself put it, in the adjacent Santa Fe neighborhood. He had owned one of the many small printing and publishing shops that had lined a central street for decades but that had gradually disappeared as the area became a so-called red zone (*zona roja*). He had managed to keep his small press afloat by publishing miniature Bibles that sold well on the streets. Since the 1980s, the Victorian-style houses—originally built by European Jewish immigrants in the 1930s—had given way to a number of booming prostitution businesses and strip clubs. In 2001, a city decree officialized a so-called tolerance zone (*zona de tolerancia*) that allowed these businesses to expand and operate legally.[55] While the new zoning was intended to increase regulation and security, it hardened the area's "imaginary boundaries" as a place of marginality, paradoxically making it a "violent 'safe zone,'" to use Amy Ritterbusch's term, and rendering sex workers immobile and more vulnerable to violence.[56] According to Enrique, that was when the "kings of the business" arrived: former police and military, and people with links to drug cartels and paramilitary groups. This put into motion violent disputes over property and several modalities of land theft.

Early one morning, I joined Paulina and Enrique as they took photos of historic houses around the neighborhood, many of them recently back on the market. Paulina was going to attach the photos to a letter she had written, questioning officials' decision to remove the properties from the city's historic preservation list. She wanted to contest the portrayal of the area as irrevocably deteriorated, and to argue that it was technical actions such as the selective removal of historical preservation protections that had entrenched decay and enabled misappropriation and displacement.

Although Paulina picked up her son from school every day in the Santa Fe neighborhood, just a few blocks to the west from her billiard hall, she still seemed wary as we crossed the Avenida Caracas and things started to get "heavy [*pesadas*]." Enrique was more at ease navigating the rougher sides of La Alameda and Santa Fe. Not only did he live closer to the area, but with his blue-and-white Dallas Cowboys jersey and oversized baseball cap, the corpulent middle-aged man had an undeniable street presence.[57] Nonetheless he, too, was cautious not to cross Twenty-Fourth Street, another invisible border beyond which the *zona roja* or *zona de tolerancia* was in full ebullience: sex workers leaning next to motel doors, men walking hurriedly on the sidewalk, street vendors sailing through unconcerned, a scraggly street dweller crouching on an empty strip of pavement, and sharp-eyed squeegee kids waiting for cars at the intersection.

Pointing to a large house on a corner with reflective windows and a curved brick facade reminiscent of the neighborhood's older architecture, Enrique shouted over the street noise, "That one was just remodeled, more than forty rooms!" A brothel owner turned local politician, whose mother now owned several properties, had purchased this and other buildings a few years back, before he was shot down by his enemies. Property acquisitions, Enrique explained, followed a typical "paramilitary strategy": There would be an initial negotiation on the price, no documents or signatures, and often the use of intimidation; then a partial payment and transfer of the property; and, finally, a refusal to pay the rest of the sum.

At every corner we turned, Paulina and Enrique had a new story about property theft. A drug dealer and a group of bazuco addicts had forced an aging widow out of her house. A swindler had cheated a landlady into a series of loans that would eventually make her lose her low-rise apartment building. A well-known street criminal had taken over a crumbling residencia by killing its owner. These were some openly violent, scandalous cases of what Paulina attributed to an established "cartel or mafia of appropriations," which included lawyers, city functionaries, and armed enforcers. "People have formed cartels and they have friends in the office of the registry of properties, they have an entire team," she explained. "They know the floor area of this or that property, if it has any [legal] issues, and with all this information they start making their way in [*se van metiendo*]." Her billiard hall had also been in the sights of one such cartel. A local lawyer ran the scheme and had been harassing her through both legal and informal conduits for years. Long-running disinvestment and crippling regulations had made her property a "savory dish," one that land swindlers were "really hungry for [*le tienen un hambre*]."

Liquidating Space

The creation of the tolerance zone and the enactment of land use regulations had resulted in deterioration and displacement for some and in new opportunities for accumulation and appropriation for others—land cartels, prostitution business owners, and, ultimately, the city administration and developers. Critically reworking the expert notion of the cycle of decay, Enrique elucidated a politics of destruction and misappropriation: "It seems that everything is cyclical. [The place] starts all right, it has its highest point of beauty, and then they abandon it so they can liquidate the space. [This happens] so it can be appropriated either by the state [or by others] by simply leaving it there, totally abandoned." Abandonment here did not mean state absence but selective depreciation and revalorization enabled by planning institutions and instruments.

Enrique and Paulina's phenomenological elaboration of the materiality and temporality of urban deterioration was thus closely attuned not only to economic agendas but also to the continuities with broader patterns of violence and insecurity. In one sense, "liquidating space [*liquidar el espacio*]," as Enrique put it, pointed to the multiple techniques and drawn-out procedures through which properties had been both previously made illiquid and then liquidated and forced into exchange value under the predatory terms of land mafias and urban renewal. In a broader sense, it called attention to the destructive violence of planning and real estate regulations. Given the country's long history of land grabbing and armed territorial control, "liquidation" had unmistakable connotations linked to forceful eradication—a bureaucratic and financial attack on the neighborhood, a form of "urbicide."[58]

Back at Paulina's billiard hall, Enrique elaborated on the connection between armed violence and urban development. As we sipped reheated coffee from tiny plastic cups, Paulina's sister casually commented on the latest news about the government's peace negotiations with the FARC. Enrique interjected, "That has a lot to do with what we're talking about. I haven't found anyone who can tell me the difference [between what has happened here] and peasant displacement by paramilitaries." As I showed in the previous chapter, downtown residents often conceptualized urban eviction and renewal as forms of violence comparable to the actions of nonstate armed groups and guerrilla forces—such was the case with Margarita and her neighbors in Manzana Cinco who called the ERU "worse than the guerrillas." By focusing on paramilitarism, however, Enrique had located violence directly within the state—not as a result of state failures but rather as its continuation.

To illustrate his point, Enrique recounted a story that involved a *narcotraficante* (drug trafficker) who had been extradited to the United States and was serving a thirty-year prison sentence in New York. The tale ran as follows. A few years back, Enrique had worked as a contractor at a shopping mall construction project on the south side of downtown Bogotá, not far from the San Victorino and old El Cartucho neighborhoods. He became intrigued by the constant circulation of recycling pushcarts with oversized bundles and large plastic bags. The loads were unlike the junk and materials that waste pickers typically hauled around downtown. Although the construction foreman had warned him about speaking with the men moving the carts, one day Enrique recognized a young man from his neighborhood pulling one of the carts and asked him about the circulation of the furtive cargo. This is how he discovered that the drug boss was behind the development of the mall and had brought "three gangs from [the city of] Cali to depress the area [*deprimir el sector*] and buy on the cheap." The pushcarts were allegedly part of a scheme to dump the bodies of the people killed by the hired gunmen every week: owners, tenants, and anyone else who refused to vacate or sell or who tried to resist the takeover of the area.

Although the account was most likely embellished—Enrique was loquacious and had a story for every occasion—-the narrative alone was revealing. This particular drug boss had become widely known in Colombia for his close relations with the political establishment and Bogotá's elite. He was a gentleman criminal, both ruthless in wielding violence and well connected and savvy in his business enterprises. His real estate investments included a luxury resort near Bogotá that was visited by the city's aristocracy and was a frequent venue for political events. The story thus dramatized and amplified residents' critiques of decay as not natural or accidental but rather a political project in which urban plans blurred into forced displacement and violent destruction. "Like all that terrorism that [the drug dealer–developer] brought to that area," Enrique concluded, "people have been misappropriating places here, although in a subtler manner."

Residents often veered into conspiratorial thinking along these lines. "You would have to be a fool not to recognize that [the neighborhood's deterioration] was planned," Enrique told me. And yet he and others had done more than denounce a seemingly long-running, covert, and coherent strategy of urban displacement. Their ruinous knowledges centered on the convergence of sociomaterial effects and on strategizing actors that mobilized and exploited such effects. Far from opaque and distant powers, they tracked the proximate and tangible practices and techniques that had mediated and materialized decay—that "had rotted" the neighborhood, as Efraín once put it.[59]

Such attunement to the neighborhood's sociomaterial atmosphere—to the politics inherent to official valuations and incremental interventions—was further evinced in a brief exchange during one of our meetings at the billiard hall. "In order to buy our properties, they generate decay with regulations, they restrict building heights, they restrict land uses, they tie us down, so we can't grow vertically, so we can't develop our land, so we can't work in our properties," Paulina started indignantly. Enrique rejoined with a sarcastic grin, "But supposedly that isn't planned, no, those things are just random, it's just life, right?" It was "government, power, whatever you want to call it," he continued, "those with sufficient power," who used laws "as instruments of pressure" to simultaneously deteriorate and misappropriate. This was not the hand of a conspiratorial mastermind or a tentacular apparatus of governance, but rather the piecemeal work of multiple agents over prolonged periods of time and through the very materiality of the neighborhood and its temporal rhythms—chipping away at previous modes of sociality and livelihoods.

Ruinous Politics

I met Paulina again in 2016 to talk about neighborhood news over our usual cup of lukewarm coffee. This time the billiard hall seemed much darker and more cluttered. The tables were gone, as was a small commercial space for extra rental income that Paulina had built overnight and without a permit. The ceiling was falling apart, beams of light filtering through missing panels and illuminating piled-up furniture, tools, and materials. In a constant struggle to respond to zoning regulations and their constraining effects on the uses of her property, Paulina and her husband had set up an informal workshop in the back. Their shrinking income now came from the fabrication of billiard tables in what had been a de facto change of land use from commerce to manufacturing.

With her usual stoicism, Paulina picked up the conversation where we had left off a couple of years earlier. She told me about the most recent property swindles as well as the uncertainties that continued to surround the city's official renewal plan: the decay, depreciation, and insecurity—and not least the enduring threat of eviction—that emanated from the nearby demolition rubble. Toward the end of our conversation, she pulled out a marketing leaflet from two decades earlier, advertising the billiard hall in its glory days. It showed a polished facade, brand-new signage, two small storefronts in addition to the main entrance of the "billiard club, grill-bar," and pictures of several billiard tables in a well-maintained interior. The juxtaposition of the idealized portrayal on the brochure and Paulina's now-crumbling space, of "wish image and ruin," to use Susan Buck-Morss's

FIGURE 4.4. Marketing leaflet for Palatino billiard hall and bar and grill. Left: "Focus your sight on the perfect place for your company's social gatherings." Right: "Thirteen heated billiard tables and five pool tables at the service of ladies and gentlemen. A welcoming and safe place at your service."

FIGURE 4.5. Paulina's billiard hall in 2017. Photo by the author.

phrase, condensed the piecemeal, almost imperceptible processes of decline and decomposition that Paulina and other residents had been unraveling for years.[60]

The trajectories of urban destruction I have followed in this book are emblematic of rubble-strewn landscapes across the globe. These are the ruins of modernist planning, capitalism, environmental degradation, and violence—ruins whose material and affective afterlives and lingering sociopolitical effects scholars have increasingly shed light on.[61] As the contemporary global condition becomes defined in part by what Danny Hoffman describes as the ability to "learn to inhabit ruins," Paulina and her neighbors call attention to the forms of knowledge that are composed by dwelling *on* and *in* deteriorating urban worlds.[62] They help us understand the kinds of epistemic spaces and political critiques that emerge from the wreckage of urban transformations.

Through their ruinous knowledge, the inhabitants of La Alameda and Santa Fe revealed the everyday "rhythms, temporalities, and intensities" of urban destruction, to use Gastón Gordillo's terms.[63] They made apparent the ways in which planning epistemologies and their normalized techniques had driven the ruination of downtown homes and neighborhoods. Urban dwellers thus elucidated official assumptions about time, materiality, and value and how the "timescapes" of city planning had created the conditions for the gradual coalescing of strategies of dispossession, accumulation, and speculation.[64]

Like other downtown residents, those who lived in La Alameda and Santa Fe found traces of Colombia's long history of warfare in the decline of their neighborhood. As I showed in previous chapters, the materiality of downtown transformations has been closely bound to the shifting registers and experiences of violent conflict, from experts recrafting urban space into a terrain of military eradication (chapter 2) to property owners confronting bureaucratized eviction and demolition as forced displacement (chapter 3). In these instances, violence emerged as an external and exceptional force that had finally reached the city and unsettled its social, political, and legal order. The ruinous knowledge of the residents of La Alameda and Santa Fe, in contrast, located the logics of warfare in the very fabric of urban governance and development—a constitutive attribute of urban life, value, and forms. For them, the material remains of downtown planning and renewal indexed the interconnected spatiality and temporality of violence. Like postwar ruins, the decaying city was a product of what Hiba Bou Akar calls the "overlapping geography of past and present conflict."[65]

To further clarify the political significance of such ruinous knowledges, it is useful to return to Efraín's notions of urban rot and the archaeology of decay. The critical excavations that Efraín called for and that the residents of La Alameda and Santa Fe put into practice were aimed at uncovering the city's rotten undersides. At stake here was the foundational destructiveness of legal and political orders—that underlying violence that Walter Benjamin famously identified as "something rotten in the law."[66] Yet far from a metaphysical principle, this rotting force was instantiated in the "shards, debris, or rubble," as Yael Navaro-Yashin puts it, that was left behind by planning regulations and interventions.[67] This is what made Efraín's archaeological analytic particularly appropriate. It evoked what Shannon Dawdy calls "social stratigraphy"—that is, the layered palimpsest of "past events and structures that produced the shared conditions under which residents live."[68] Drawing on their sustained and intimate awareness of urban decay, the residents of La Alameda and Santa Fe charted the material accretion and corrosive effects of a set of practices, structures, and experiences over time. Their talk of planned annihilation and hidden agendas was thus not primarily about making visible distant and opaque networks of power. Rather, it was about illuminating a proximate yet muted constellation of epistemic practices and material processes that had enabled the gradual enclosure, devaluation, and ruination of the neighborhood.[69]

The archaeology of decay resonates with modes of opposition employed by urban dwellers caught amid global displacements, from the "politics of staying put" (to use Liza Weinstein's phrase) and everyday tactics of negotiation to practices of accommodation and legal maneuvering.[70] Yet as urban scholars have noted, such contestations have often paradoxically reinscribed exclusionary discourses of progress and civility. The practices of dissent I explored in the previous chapter are a case in point. Like the residents of La Alameda and Santa Fe, the "displaced of Manzana Cinco" gestured to the destructive violence of urban bureaucracy. In their legal battle and appeals for redress and reparation, they upheld idealized versions of state legitimacy and individual property rights. For them, the violence they had suffered was the result of a misuse and deformation of the law and a failure to protect their entitlements.

The grounded knowledges I have tracked in this chapter also partially reproduced the oppressive orders they had opposed. Residents often reified their experiential knowledge of ruination and portrayed decay as the cause of urban ills, assimilating it to criminal disorder and reinforcing existing social hierarchies. At the same time, for these residents on the west side of downtown Bogotá, navigating decay and assigning accountability entailed what Michael Herzfeld calls a "ceaseless reckoning with materiality."[71] This is a reckoning I have disentangled here, following locals' archaeological attunements and their sorting through "differential modes of decay," as Ghassan Hage puts it in a call for ethnographies of the "tempo" and "spatiality" of decay.[72] Such sifting through the epistemic and material contours of decay brought to light the politics of violent destruction written into city plans and laws and into ideals of property and citizenship.

But what urban imaginaries do such ruinous politics afford? Can other futures besides the desolate spaces and exclusionary dreamscapes of urban renewal emerge from the debris of dispossession and demolition?[73] These issues became central to planners, developers, and downtown residents in the aftermath of the Manzana Cinco and Estación Central projects and as the national government and the FARC embarked on a peace process in 2012. In what seemed like the beginning of an elusive transition to a postwar era in Colombia, the question of how and what to rebuild out of the residues of violent destruction permeated the country's public consciousness and shaped urban sensibilities.

Tellingly, in his inauguration address at the Plaza de Bolívar in January 2012, Mayor Gustavo Petro talked of a new paradigm of territorial planning (*ordenamiento territorial*) as the pillar of a more humane and progressive city. "We do not want to see more processes of urban renewal like the one that exists two blocks from here or the one that took place one block down the street," Petro told the crowd, pointing to surrounding neighborhoods.[74] "[These were plans] where the poor were expelled from the city center by the state with fraudulent prices [*precios de estafa*] to carry out large real estate projects, excluding traditional inhabitants [*población tradicional*]," the newly elected mayor continued as the crowd cheered. "Jairo Aníbal Niño [a local writer and former resident of Manzana Cinco] died as a result of one of those processes," Petro concluded in a more somber tone. "That is not the urban renewal we want."

A few months later, back at the Estación Central meeting at the Jorge Eliécer Gaitán Theater where I started this chapter, María Mercedes Maldonado Copello, Petro's secretary of planning (*secretaria de planeación*), elaborated on the administration's new vision for "urban revitalization [*revitalización urbana*]." Maldonado Copello cited Manzana Cinco as an example of how the administration had expropriated land and "projected more profitable land uses and higher building allowances [*edificabilidades*]," essentially acting as an intermediary for real estate developers. "In the administration," she asserted, "we now question today that the role of the public sector is to simply valorize land in this way."[75] The city government would now move "toward projects that are truly associational [*asociativos*], initiated by property owners themselves, and committed to overcoming the distrust and forms of resistance that the previous model created."

But as much as rubble and ruins can become the grounds for the composition of critical knowledges and insurgent practices, they also "form boundaries and limits to what can be imagined and what can be done," as Danny Hoffman argues.[76] In the following chapters I examine such contradictions and their materialization in new modes of expertise and urban transformation, and I track the ways in which the residues of violent regimes of governance, citizenship, and property live on in progressive epistemologies and plans to remake downtown Bogotá.

Part III

THE LIMITS OF URBAN EXPERTISE

TERRITORY BY DESIGN

Just when the team of city planners was leaving the office for the day, a phone call came in from the Alcaldía. The mayor's press office had requested an interview with the experts working on the revision of the city's Plan de Ordenamiento Territorial (Territorial Ordering Plan), or POT. It was October 2011, and I had spent almost three months at the Secretaría Distrital de Planeación (City Planning Department) following the Grupo POT, as the group of planners was informally known. After some friendly wrangling about who would do the interview, three group members left for the appointment. On his way out, Ernesto, a senior architect and urban designer, asked if I wanted to tag along. Although the secretary of planning had supported my role as visiting anthropologist—with desk and office chair included—both the planners and I were still trying to make sense of our relationship. "Are we supposed to be your tribe?" one of them had recently joked. Ernesto's invitation was encouraging.

We squeezed into a taxi and made our way through rush-hour traffic from the Secretaría, a concrete modernist structure just outside the city center, to the Palacio Liévano, a French Renaissance-style building flanking the historic Plaza de Bolívar to the west and housing the Alcaldía's main offices. Once inside the office—an elegant room with high ceilings that had been subdivided into cubicles—two press officials explained they were writing a piece on the "topic of territory" for the administration's institutional newspaper. This would not be an article for "técnicos [experts]," one of the journalists stressed, but rather for anyone interested in understanding the "vision" of the Territorial Ordering Plan. "'What is the POT? What is its purpose? How does it affect me as a citizen? Why are you revising it?'" he continued. "We want to tell a story about the history of territorial ordering [*ordenamiento territorial*]."

This was a question that Diego from the Grupo POT was more than happy to answer. An architect in his thirties, he had specialized in urbanism and written his master's thesis on the history of modernist planning in the city of Cali. Diego traced Bogotá's "tradition of territorial planning" back to the Plan Piloto (1950) designed by modernist architect and planner Le Corbusier in the late 1940s and its convergence with agendas to radically reconstruct and modernize the city after the 1948 Bogotazo uprising. But as migrants streamed into the city in the "post–Le Corbusier" decades, Ernesto chimed in, "the city lacked instruments to organize its population." What this meant, he explained, was that the state lost ground and "private actors led [processes of urban development], obtaining the greatest profits."

As the journalists' attention drifted, Diego and Ernesto brought the conversation back to the POT and to legislation from the 1980s and 1990s, and to Colombia's 1991 constitutional reform, which recentered territory as a key governmental category. The POT emerged as a crucial "instrument to regulate and manage territories," Diego said.

"And so, what is your vision?" one of the journalists interjected, pushing them to get to the point.

"The wager is to redensify the city; [in other words,] we're betting on a dense and compact model," Ernesto replied. While the first version of the POT in 2000 had already established this "vision," mirroring global planning trends, the instruments employed to materialize this "city project [*proyecto de ciudad*]" had failed. Most urban renewal plans, the Grupo POT experts explained, had remained on paper, and the ones that had been carried out, such as Parque Tercer Milenio, had *de*-densified the city center rather than attracting new populations and private investments, as officials had originally envisioned. Planners had "marked [*manchado*] deteriorated areas [for renewal on their maps]," Diego noted, but instead of putting into motion redevelopment processes, they "froze building permits, they froze up the zones, and everything went downhill" (see chapter 4).

With the current revision of the POT, Diego continued—now more animated, seeing he had piqued the journalists' interest—planning would be firmly anchored in "the reality of the city, because you can't change the world with the stroke of a pen [*de un plumazo*]." And the reality, Ernesto added, was that densification was already occurring, albeit through "lot-by-lot [*predio a predio*]" development. Old houses and low-rises were being demolished at an increasingly rapid rate, and buildings were going up as high as construction codes allowed. For the Grupo POT planners, this process was haphazard and extractive: It did not follow broader planning guidelines, it ignored existing infrastructural conditions, and it generated value primarily for developers and landowners, not for the

city or the neighborhoods where it occurred. Taking issue both with decontextu-
alized visions of urban renewal and with fragmentary processes of lot-by-lot densification, the Grupo POT called for a mode of planning attuned to the realities
of the "city's range of distinct behaviors." They proposed "differential treatments
and interventions" across urban zones and less focus on regulations and codes,
"because the city isn't made simply by the force of norms [*la ciudad no se hace a
punta de normas*]."

The city needed flexible and effective planning and management instruments
(*instrumentos de gestión y planeación*), the Grupo POT experts insisted. Ernesto
explained that the group was redesigning something called *edificabilidad* (build-
ability, or "floor area ratio" in anglophone planning terminology) as the POT's
main instrument. They were retooling edificabilidad—the ratio of a building's
floor area to the area of the parcel of land on which it is built—into a capacious technique to regulate variable development intensities across urban space,
intervene in the volume and shape of construction, and capture value for public
infrastructure. The modified POT would thus ultimately seek to modulate and
distribute urban densities. This was critical to moving away from planning for an
elusive "ideal city" to planning for the "possible city."

After the meeting ended and as we trailed behind the last downtown commuters in the chilly Bogotá night, the enthusiasm of the presentation waned as
the Grupo POT experts talked about the uncertain fate of the POT modification project. The end of the mayoral term was months away, and approval of the
revised plan by the city council was unlikely. As we crossed the Plaza de Bolívar,
Andrés, the group's data-savvy geographer, tried to lighten the mood and asked
us, "Have you ever wondered why the plaza is inclined?" Previously, the historic
square had had four water fountains in a sunken center surrounded by steps
marking the uneven topography. A 1960s renovation had unified the surface
and made the east-west slope almost imperceptible through the construction of
an expansive, warped plane. As we continued walking to the legendary downtown Pastelería Florida for a debriefing over hot chocolate, Diego and Ernesto
entertained Andrés's provocation—they were used to his humorous penchant
for obscure facts—and speculated about how the plaza's smoothed inclination
lent force to the surrounding state architecture. Looking back at the exchange, it
revealed what I would come to understand as a mode of planning aimed at knowing and remaking territory as a pliable sociomaterial volume.

Managing Volumetric Densities

The Grupo POT was critical of an epistemology of surfaces in which mapping and
zoning took precedence. This is what Doreen Massey calls "space-as-surface": a

cartographic imagination in which space is "continuous and given" and overtly tied up with projects for spatial colonization and mastery.[1] In downtown Bogotá, the demolition of El Cartucho and the construction of Parque Tercer Milenio had embodied these modes of knowledge (see chapter 2). Planners had marked what they called a "polygon of intervention [*polígono de intervención*]" and set out to domesticate the area's allegedly unruly topography. It was a territorial technology imbued with military-strategic logics and centered on the flattening of a rugged and disorderly space. In the case of Tercer Milenio, the unwieldy terrain had ultimately escaped planners' control and continued to live on in the park's empty expanses, deserted underground levels, and fearful landscape.[2]

The revision of the POT was an attempt at retooling technologies for more effective sociomaterial interventions. Critical to such redesigns was the reconceptualization of territory in the language of urban density.[3] While planning in Bogotá had been long concerned with density—what I described earlier as policies for the rarefaction of disorderly crowds and the creation of modern densities (see chapter 1)—with the modification of the POT, the concept took on unprecedented centrality in both expert circles and public opinion. Partly a reflection of global "smart growth" policies, the ideal of a "dense and compact city" emerged as a recipe to spur economic development and alleviate housing and environmental crises.[4] Surfaces here were "filled with spatiality," to borrow Clancy Wilmott's term, and "solidified" into a three-dimensional and dynamic sociomaterial arrangement.[5] Planners in Bogotá took up density as a more sophisticated and effective technology to track the ways in which people and things "occupied territory." Yet as a supposedly neutral metric of urban form, its political effects and limitations remained occluded.

In this chapter, I argue that far from a stable, descriptive category, density is a profoundly generative practice. Contrary to its usual treatment as a "self-evident" concept, I follow Vyjayanthi Rao and adopt "a socially and culturally inflected understanding of density."[6] I also build on Colin McFarlane's call to study the "multiple spatialities of density" and its ideological and political substrates.[7] McFarlane develops the notion of "topological density" as a fundamental counterpart to "topographical, linear, or numerical" views.[8] In this manner, he points to the "malleable, plastic nature of density both as a political tool and as a geographic imaginary and form."[9] From this perspective, planners' calculative (or topographical) orientations toward density in Bogotá were ultimately linked to the making and ordering of urban territory.[10] "In a topological frame," John Allen argues, "power relationships are not so much positioned in space or extended across it, as compose the spaces of which they are a part."[11] With urban densities as their central objects of knowledge and intervention, planners recomposed the materialities and geometries of urban territory. Instead of a bounded and fixed backdrop to be conquered, experts became engaged with the "instabilities and fluctuations of state territory," its "ambiguity and uncertainty," in the words of Penelope Harvey.[12]

Planners reconceptualized the city as a shifting assemblage of densities and redefined the parameters of urban territory and how it would be governed. Earlier downtown plans had aimed to secure urban perimeters, delineating "decayed" areas for state intervention and real estate development. With the revision of the POT, experts now sought to manage urban volumes.[13] In contrast to the two-dimensional renderings of zoning maps, the city emerged here as a volumetric process—the constant coming together and spreading out of people and material structures.[14] Density thus became a powerful device to simultaneously conjure, harness, and regulate space in multiple dimensions.[15] It represented a more complex engagement with the "materiality of territory," or what Stuart Elden calls "volumetric territory."[16]

What this meant ranged considerably throughout the POT's long-running revision across different city administrations. The Grupo POT's revision project was launched during the administration of Samuel Moreno (2008–11) and largely sought the technocratic harnessing of densities for "efficient" and "sustainable" growth. Like his predecessor Luis Eduardo Garzón (2004–7), Moreno was only nominally a leftist mayor. During his time in office, he did not introduce substantive reforms and remained close to the city's real estate and infrastructure development sectors.[17] By the end of his term, he was found responsible for one of the largest corruption scandals in Bogotá's recent history, ultimately landing in jail along with a network of local politicians and contractors. Within this context and partly to separate themselves from the mayor, planners presented the revision of the POT as a highly technical, nonpartisan, and untainted project. Following the suspension of this modification project, the administration of Gustavo Petro (2012–15) launched a new revision project that more directly confronted real estate interests. The POT revision now promoted participatory and inclusionary densification in the inner city and wide-ranging visions centered on housing and environmental justice. This modification project was ultimately blocked, and a new group of planners returned to the drawing board after the reelection of Enrique Peñalosa (2016–19). For Peñalosa, who had decreed the original POT during his first term in 2000, this was the opportunity to deepen reactionary public-space policies and expand the reach of real estate interests, sidelining planning laws' more progressive applications.

Despite these contrasting visions, however, territory-as-density reappeared in every case as a taken-for-granted epistemology: a naturalized sociomaterial dynamic subject to expert assessments and experimentation. As an unquestioned urban grammar, it both limited and obscured political agendas.[18] Compared to the overt bids for spatial control and the forceful displacements of earlier renewal plans, redensification seemed an innocuous technical instrument. As a city official once explained during a public presentation of the POT modification project, the main challenge was to undo "imaginaries" of renewal as a "process that razes entire areas of the city" and leads to "evictions and social conflicts." Instead, he suggested, the city had to "reposition [renewal] as a logical urban process [*un proceso lógico de la ciudad*]." As seemingly neutral descriptors of urban realities, "density" and "territory" would thus serve to render urban renewal an unquestioned phenomenon. But as performative categories with material effects, such technical concepts inevitably enacted specific political projects. Contrary to what the expert suggested, "social conflicts" were not defused but rather relocated and submerged in the management of dense volumetric territories. In this sense, the focus on "complex volumetric geographies," as scholarship on volumetric politics has shown, did not lead to the "weakening or dilution of the logics of territorial control," but rather to their reconfiguration.[19]

Planning and managing densities resemble what architectural theorist Keller Easterling describes as the "operating system for shaping the city."[20] Drawing on informatics, Easterling calls attention to the kinds of power that reside not in the "content" but rather in the "medium" of spatial production. From special economic zones to telecommunications networks, these "infrastructure spaces" operate as a "content manager dictating the rules of the game in the urban milieu."[21] In Bogotá, planners themselves often employed cybernetic language, describing new planning instruments as a "self-regulating system." In the following sections, I track how densification became an unobtrusive yet consequential "spatial software."[22] The epistemics of density not only actively shaped sociomaterial forms and relations but also tacitly imposed limits on urban imaginaries and politics. Even progressive planners who attempted to "hack" such technical platforms and make them more inclusionary and redistributive, continued to operate under the rules and protocols of urban densification as a naturalized process.[23] Finally, by reconceptualizing planning as the management of fluid volumetric densities, experts remained beholden to the securitized logics of territory and property. Territory-as-density ultimately reproduced Colombia's longer history of governmental technologies aimed at expanding territorial control and entrenched regimes of ownership and development.

Planning the "Real City"

Writing about the so-called "independent republics" of the 1960s—the rural enclaves of peasants fleeing partisan violence that led to the creation of the

FARC—sociologist José Jairo González Arias argues that "Colombia is a country whose territory surpasses the nation, and its society is more solid than the state."[24] He evokes a textured and expansive sociomaterial topography that exceeds the workings of an idealized technocratic apparatus and of the body politic itself. Variations on this theme, as I mentioned earlier in this book, have been common in academia, among bureaucrats, and in public opinion, including in the board-rooms where Bogotá planners discussed the revision of the POT.[25]

By the end of 2011, the Grupo POT held meetings almost every afternoon until late at night as they rushed to submit the revised plan for approval at the city council before the end of the mayoral term. Planners were "in the barracks [*en acuartelamiento*]," as they called this period of intense work. During the day, the group worked in a temporary, windowless office that had been set up in a semi-deserted mezzanine of the concrete, boxlike structure that housed the offices of the Unidad Administrativa Especial de Catastro Distrital (public land registry) and a citizen services center where throngs of people paid bills and carried out official procedures, or *trámites*. The building was connected through a glass-and-concrete tunnel to the Secretaría Distrital de Planeación, a taller gridded tower where offices were also flooded with people submitting requests and checking on their trámites. The two structures formed the Centro Administrativo Distrital (City Administrative Center), a modernist monument to bureaucratic manage-ment built in the early 1970s.

The Grupo POT planners—most of them consultants hired exclusively for the revision project—had found themselves in a paradoxical position: They were at once thrust into the core of the city's overwhelmed bureaucracy and cut off from it in their lonely office, where internet and phone connections broke down fre-quently and rolls of maps were strewn across desks and cabinets. But not having a direct phone line had advantages, Andrés once noted, "because we can avoid meetings." Diego agreed: "One of the good things that came with this workspace is that we were removed from the day-to-day [trámites] that take place upstairs [in the main office tower]." Looking at the cubicle divisions and overhead fluo-rescent lights, he said, "We didn't have a window, but we had time. We had time to discuss, to debate. The layout of our workstations [open cubicles with an open space in the middle] allowed us to unroll plans on the floor, sketch, all that." More than anything else, this "relative distance" offered experts a vantage point from which to understand the contradictions of daily planning procedures and policy implementation.

The more time I spent with the Grupo POT planners, the more I found that their work was shaped by something like an ethnographic sensibility. Being "neither totally inside the institution nor really outside of it," as Diego put it, they aimed to track the uses and conflicts associated with everyday planning

FIGURE 5.1A. The Secretaría Distrital de Planeación and the citizen service center building where the Grupo POT's office was located. Photo by the author.

FIGURE 5.1B. Planner at work in the mezzanine cubicles. Photo by the author.

practice. This is what they called "planning from reality." Significantly, they recruited collaborators from within the Secretaría—seasoned functionaries and bureaucrats—who offered critical insights based on their grounded experiences. The Grupo POT's intervention was thus informed by what Douglas Holmes and George Marcus call "para-ethnography": "the *de facto* and self-conscious critical faculty that operates in any expert domain as a way of dealing with contradiction, exception, facts that are fugitive."[26] For Diego, functionaries' critiques and interpretations, their "marginal ways of knowing,"[27] as Holmes and Marcus put it, were "especially useful because when you have that kind of help [from insiders], you learn about what's really going on inside the institution." So even while Grupo POT experts carved out time for reflection, theirs was not the "mental space . . . inhabited by technocrats in their silent offices," in Henri Lefebvre's words.[28] Instead, their "phenomenology of expertise," to use Dominic Boyer's term, was defined by sustained collaborations around the messy realities of planning-in-action.[29]

Like other office workers, the Grupo POT planners spent considerable time in front of their computers processing data, creating maps, and editing the text of the revised plan. Yet their screen work was constantly punctuated by meetings, presentations, and discussions as well as ongoing conversations among each other and with friendly bureaucrats during breaks and lunches. Following these routines revealed not only the socially mediated and materially situated nature of their work but also the extent to which Grupo POT planners aimed to unravel the specific circumstances in which planning unfolded. They took on the role of experts of urban expertise, as they became immersed in and critically analyzed the ways in which planning knowledge was composed, negotiated, and materialized. At stake here, beyond the institutional and technical contexts that animated planning, were experts' "habituated patterns of interaction," as Keith Murphy puts it in his study of Swedish designers.[30] Murphy offers a close-up portrayal of how everyday "patterns of talking" and "habits of thought" mediate designers' creative, "form-giving" practices and instantiate broader cultural and political imaginaries—what he calls a "cultural geometry."[31] Although planners in Bogotá did not craft things as tangible as design objects, they did approach their work as if they were giving form to the city as a scaled-up, dynamic object.[32] Like the creative practices of designers and architects—and many of the planners at the Secretaría had actually been trained in these disciplines—theirs were mediated by specific ways of talking and thinking with other planners, designers, policymakers, real estate developers, and the larger public. These sustained interactions became integral to planners' rendering of the city as a volume to be modeled and, ultimately, to the reproduction of long-standing "power-geometries" of territorial control and security.[33]

During the Grupo POT's meetings with senior planning officials "upstairs [*arriba*]," usually in a boardroom that overlooked the city's rolling landscape of brick and cement, one recurring interaction revolved around the administration's "lack of teeth" in the face of the city's "lot-by-lot" development. Many evenings, after rushing from their mezzanine office through the glass-and-concrete tunnel and up to the eighth floor via the unfailingly congested elevator, the Grupo POT experts discussed new instruments to finally "get ahold of the city's dynamic [*agarrar la dinámica de la ciudad*]." Central to these conversations was what policymakers and scholars often described as Bogotá's profound "fragmentation."[34] This referred both to the piecemeal character of construction and to the fractured nature of underlying social, legal, and political structures. As Andrés often remarked, lamenting the recalcitrance of Bogotá's urban development trends, "The main problem is that Colombians have a very low capacity to associate with one another." He gestured in this way to broader representations of Colombia's history of sociopolitical conflict and its deep-seated divisions. What emerged from these exchanges, in one sense, was the idea of a broken sociomaterial terrain shaped by the whims of the real estate market and its operators—from entrenched landowning elites and developers, to the politically connected urbanizers of informal settlements (also known as *urbanizadores piratas*), to small-scale builders and autoconstructors. In another sense, planners recognized that plans and regulations themselves had critically contributed to urban fragmentation and disorder.

Not only did urban regulations vary significantly across the city's geography due to local-level zoning and planning mechanisms, but they had also accumulated over time, creating inscrutable amalgams of building codes and rules. Crucial in this regard was a zoning figure called urbanistic consolidation (*consolidación urbanística*). Real estate development within a zone under consolidación was supposed to follow the area's "original regulation." This meant that construction might be regulated by a forty- or fifty-year-old decree, including all the modifications the decree had undergone—many of them contradictory and incomplete—over the span of several decades. Deciphering these complex legal landscapes required what planners, lawyers, and developers called a form of "juridical archaeology [*arqueología jurídica*]."[35] The sedimentation of legal frameworks became not only a significant space for contestations over development but also one of the main obstacles to the implementation of more recent planning instruments such as the POT. In one memorable meeting, the Grupo POT experts projected an up-to-date map of the areas that were covered by the treatment of consolidación (*tratamiento de consolidación*). One of the Secretaría's senior officials, a young Ivy League–trained economist named Catalina, could not hide her astonishment as she looked at the almost completely yellow map on the PowerPoint slide. "So what you're telling me," she said, "is that the POT basically doesn't apply to anything that's in yellow?" Satisfied with the persuasiveness of their presentation, Grupo POT experts confirmed that nearly 70 percent of the city's building permits were issued under the figure of consolidación. As things stood, they concluded, most of the "built city [*ciudad construida*]" was beyond the purview of the POT's instruments and regulations.

To make matters worse, one of the main planning tools designed to counter the unruly and patchwork densification of consolidación—the *plan parcial* (partial plan)—had proved to be a failure. Planes parciales aimed to bring together property owners, developers, and the state for the comprehensive development and redevelopment of urban land. In contrast to lot-by-lot development, planes parciales were meant to promote "the urbanistic development of a specific area with the corresponding road infrastructure, green areas, amenities, and public services," as urban legal scholar and practitioner Juan Felipe Pinilla Pineda explains.[36] Additionally, planes parciales assigned a series of charges to developers—for example, the financing of public infrastructure—seeking to distribute the rents generated by urban development in a more equitable manner. Yet very few planes parciales had been implemented since the figure was established in the late 1990s. Significantly, the instrument had been used only on the city's outskirts (*planes parciales de desarrollo*), on vacant land with few to no inhabitants and where ownership was concentrated in a few hands. As Catalina, the senior planner, once quipped about planning on empty land, "Well, it's pretty easy to get cows out of the way, isn't it?" Within the built city, no plans (*planes parciales de renovación*) had yet been implemented, and many of the projects under consideration were being strategically deployed by developers to change land uses, obtain permission for more intensive development, and compel property sales by locals through state-backed expropriations.

With planes parciales stalled, a vacant land shortage within city limits, and shrinking expansion areas in the periphery, the demands for real estate translated into increased lot-by-lot development. The fact that construction was taking place in areas of consolidación meant that it was regulated by older decrees, which typically allowed greater building heights and did not impose development exactions or strict guidelines regarding public space and infrastructure. Developers had thus been rapidly acquiring and demolishing old houses and small apartment buildings for the construction of high-rises. "The city is building itself up [*la ciudad se construyendo sobre sí misma*], constructing its second story," planners often noted with a sense of urgency, evoking a densifying terrain beyond the control of authorities.

For the Grupo POT, urban territory thus emerged as an unwieldy assemblage of people and things mediated by an equally unruly palimpsest of urban laws and regulations. Planning became a matter of tracking, managing, and reshaping this sociomaterial formation and its shifting dynamics. The older versions of the POT, Diego once argued, contained a "vision" of the "desired city" that "simply crashed against reality." In their efforts to return to the "real city," he explained, the Grupo POT had considered two alternatives. First was "modeling the city based solely on urban dynamics, on the recognition of reality." But this approach, taken to its full expression, Diego admitted, "[means that] you're not really planning, you're only following existing urban trends." What the Group POT aimed for instead was a "middle ground." In the face of the city's haphazard and fragmented densification (*densificación desordenada*), they were trying "to go down the middle, tying [*amarrando*] things together."

At stake here was a critique of long-standing engagements with the city as a static, two-dimensional territory ready to be controlled and transformed: planning as a blueprint to be materialized in space. The Grupo POT experts sought instead to work with and harness existing urban processes in their active, volumetric manifestations. Not only did their approach infuse planning with pragmatic sensibilities, but it also marked a shift away from the overtly securitized modes of territorial control that had permeated planning in Bogotá. Rather than the conquest of an unruly terrain, for them it was about "tying" back together a broken sociomaterial topography. In doing this, however, territory-as-density emerged as a naturalized sociomaterial dynamic. It became an unquestioned urban grammar through which planners reinscribed a particular epistemology of the city as the ongoing agglomeration of people and things.[37] In their efforts to manage and adjust densification patterns, as I show below, planners ultimately evacuated the political complexities and modes of agency that mediated sociomaterial processes. Territorial control reemerged here as a more insidious technical exercise around the very conditions of urban transformation: It sought primarily to steer urban development, leaving intact and further occluding the conflicts surrounding governance, property, and development.

Cybernetic Densities

As the drawn-out revision of the POT gained visibility, notions of density and densification began to circulate far beyond planning circles. During these years it was not uncommon to see posters on home windows with the phrases "No to densification!" and "Yes to densification!" Densification, understood as the spontaneous filling in and building up of space, had captured the imagination of developers, property owners, and residents. Urban growth and agglomeration appeared as natural, almost inevitable tendencies that could be either fostered or impeded. Earlier frameworks had aimed to control density in space, whether through the destruction of unruly crowds and their physical environments or through the assembling of new, desirable populations and structures. In these more recent approaches, urban territory itself appeared as an expression of the ebbs and flows of densities.

The shift from density *in* territory to density *as* territory was spectacularly embodied in the construction of Colombia's tallest skyscraper, the BD Bacatá. The sixty-seven-story building began construction in 2011 and was marketed as the world's largest crowdfunded building. Over the course of several years, close to four thousand small to midrange investors purchased fiduciary shares in the project. With BD Bacatá, urban crowds reemerged not as a threat to be suppressed or replaced, as in earlier decades, but rather as a "tellurian force" that could be channeled through financial tools.[38] Far from requiring the expulsion of unruly multitudes for its creation, the BD Bacatá project sought to manage and capitalize on existing flows and concentrations of people.

One of the developers behind the project, a middle-aged Spanish expat from Barcelona called Daniel, made this point when I interviewed him in his downtown office in 2012. He had left Spain during the 2008 real estate crisis, looking unsuccessfully for new markets in Portugal and Poland. A chance encounter with another European developer at an airport, however, led him to Colombia. Upon arriving in the capital in 2010, Daniel was struck by the "dynamism" but also the relatively "neglected state" of many areas in the city. He was drawn to the city center, which he said reminded him of the downtown districts of Madrid and Barcelona during Spain's boom of the late 1990s. "For us," he told me, "[Bogotá's] Calle 19 [the future site of BD Bacatá] is the Calle de Pelayo of Barcelona in the 1990s." Both avenues "have masses and masses of people walking up and down the street." With a streetscape packed with "low-profile" storefronts and restaurants but relatively "higher-profile" pedestrians, he was certain the avenue would change rapidly in the next few years.

In this view of densification, BD Bacatá would unlock and materialize the power of the existing "masses" of passersby and anonymous "crowds" of investors. It would transubstantiate low- and mid-profile urban dwellers into global citizens and tourists. One of the promises of the project was to make real estate investors out of regular and working-class citizens: the gentrification of the urban mass, so to speak. This spectacular rendering of densification, furthermore, would be inscribed in the building's architecture. In contrast to the city's widespread use of brick, the project had a decidedly "international vocation," Daniel noted. This was reflected in the use of concrete, steel, and glass, and in the project's unique division of labor: Spanish design, Colombian construction, and North American marketing. The global icon would be inserted into downtown's urban fabric to allegedly have a rippling effect on its surroundings. It would be a "drop of oil, with a contagious effect," Daniel mused. Tellingly, in visualizing this path to a new urban age, he evoked the immiscibility of oil—a qualitatively different and incommensurable form of urban density compared to the city center's existing densities.[39]

Small developers and property owners also came to view the city as a densifying terrain ready to be reaped. Nelson, a young architect turned developer, had been successful in the reconstruction of several properties within a city block in central Chapinero, a bustling commercial and aging residential neighborhood a few miles north of downtown. He had graduated from the prestigious architecture school of the Universidad de los Andes in 2002, right in the middle of a "construction crisis." After a few years of dim professional prospects, by 2005, when the real estate industry started to recover, he decided to use family capital to go into lot-by-lot development on his own. "I started looking [for potential sites]," Nelson explained in his office in one of the four buildings he had recently built and where he also lived. He became interested in an area near the recently reconstructed Fifty-Third Avenue. The expansion of the avenue had "reactivated" the once "depressed sector," he said, and young professionals, couples, and "higher-profile" businesses had been increasingly trickling into the neighborhood.

Over six years, he had acquired several properties—from low-income retirement homes and cheap student residences to semiabandoned houses—and assembled enough land for the construction of six- and seven-story buildings. For Nelson, everything in the process had been "hard work [*un camello*]": negotiating with multiple owners, creating designs for highly irregular lots (*lotes irregulares con muchas muelas*), and navigating changing building codes to build as much as possible. Despite recognizing the work that went into reassembling the block and creating a demand for small, stylish apartments through his brand— what he described as "nice" and "flexible spaces"—Nelson portrayed densification as an inevitable and irreversible process. "These are not family sectors," he explained causally, but rather areas for single people and investors looking for new central spaces. As we toured the buildings and visited his newest construction site—the largest lot he had so far managed to put together—he pointed to a mid-century, four-story apartment building and said, "This one is in danger [of disappearing] in the next five years; it's a shame because it's a very good building." He then turned to an aging low-rise: "This one is also in danger of extinction [*en vía de extinción*]." Significantly, the phrase evoked a naturalized ecology of densification in which buildings died out and inexorably gave way to new, denser, and "higher-profile" sociomaterial assemblages.

Projects like Daniel's and Nelson's largely eluded a key value-capture mechanism, known as *plusvalía*, or state participation in land value increments, by following older regulations under the consolidación treatment.[40] They were also not subject to other urbanistic contributions, such as the improvement of public infrastructure or the creation of urban amenities. This was critical in the case of BD Bacatá and its impacts on its surroundings—from the increase of traffic in an already gridlocked corner of downtown to the rising flow of wastewater into decrepit sewage systems. As one city official warned during a long session in the planning boardroom, "We can't have Bacatás going up all over the city!"

For Grupo POT experts, however, densification was a reality that could not be ignored, much less prevented. Once again planners evoked a form of pragmatic planning that acknowledged and intervened in the "city's actual dynamics," rather than aspiring to create urban realities *ex nihilo*. In this sense, they would seek to shape—temper, stimulate, order—densification through planning logics based on incentives, self-adjustment mechanisms, and a minimal set of rules. Ultimately, planners aimed to generate public goods and some measure of redistribution through the expert management of densification. Central to city officials' revision of the POT, therefore, was the creation of mechanisms to do away with legal loopholes, recognize densification trends, and, most importantly, obtain part of the value created through densification for public investments. The key vehicle to this end was edificabilidad, a figure that Grupo POT experts centered in almost all their presentations.

In its most basic expression, edificabilidad was the technical designation for the relationship between the permitted area of construction in a plot and its original area. The Grupo POT had expanded the concept, making it a key planning and financial mechanism. They had reconceptualized it as an algorithm that would require developers to contribute the equivalent in cash of 1 square meter for every 5.6 square meters of construction when the built area surpassed an established threshold.[41] Beyond its technical dimensions, edificabilidad constituted a mode of thinking about and giving form to urban territory. In their elaboration of the notion, experts evoked a landscape of volumetric densities whose modulations could be planned and redirected toward the construction of a more "orderly" and "balanced" city.

Andrés enacted these forms of knowledge during one early Saturday meeting with representatives of the Consejo Territorial de Planeación Distrital (Territorial Council of City Planning), or CTPD, a citizen organization for planning participation established by law in the 1990s. For planners, the stakes of talking in front of the small audience of community leaders, local politicians, and urban professionals were not very high. As we stood outside the nondescript government building, waiting for the meeting to start, Andrés causally mentioned that the CTPD "had a voice but not really a vote."[42] As a mostly non-expert yet politically active group, however, the CTPD tested planners' capacity to communicate their vision of an allegedly more realistic and less legally and technically convoluted POT.[43]

One of the CTPD members, a middle-aged man dressed in his weekend sweatshirt who took short sips of coffee from a small plastic cup, introduced the "compañeros técnicos [expert comrades]" who had come to share their progress on the revision project. Andrés took the microphone and walked toward the front of the small meeting room, which looked more like a classroom. "This is a moment in which the city has a lot of data available, a battery of data it didn't previously have," he said. He explained that the data were instrumental in reaching a "balance between the public and the private," between public infrastructure and real estate development and land uses. The concept of edificabilidad would play a crucial role because it provided "the leverage for [public] projects across urban zones." He continued: "Explained simply, it means that if I have a plot, edificabilidad is the number of times I can build the area of that lot." Andrés stepped back and pointed to the table in front of him. "If this table is my lot, it's like taking this table and putting another one there. Edicabilidad one. Edificabilidad two, well, it's building two tables. But if the norms say I have to leave fifty percent of the lot empty or have some setbacks, I could build the two tables but it's going to be higher; it would maybe be four stories." He then reiterated the fact that most of the city was built without making contributions. Higher edificabilidad meant more people, and this created an "unbalance," a "deficit" in terms of parks, roads, and other amenities. "One of the main bets [of the POT] is to have a share in the city's edificabilidades," Andrés noted as he leaned on the table. "Whoever wants to pass the [established edificabilidad] limit will have to pay, because we don't have the money to provide roads, public space, and amenities that those new edificabilidades require."

Turning to a slide with a graphic of a city block—a series of heterogenous volumes with intersecting planes—Andrés elaborated on the methodology that Grupo POT planners had used to establish edificabilidad thresholds. Drawing on the city's cadastral database, they had calculated the geometric medians for each block's construction areas and set them as edificabilidad targets. "You reach this point without paying," Andrés said. "Beyond that point," he explained, more animatedly, "is where the real planning exercise [ejercicio de planeación] says, 'We would like this sector to have edificabilidad five, which is very high edificabilidad, in some cases reaching fifteen stories.'" Pointing to the upper bound on the graphic, he continued: "When you go beyond that point and want to reach higher, well, you're going to have to contribute to the rest of the city." In addition to the cash payment (the equivalent of 1 square meter per every 5.6 square meters), greater building rights would require the construction of public spaces and amenities. Ultimately, Andrés explained, the edificabilidad instrument

FIGURE 5.2A. BD Bacatá under construction in 2017. Photo by the author.

would accomplish what plusvalía, with its heavily legalistic approach, had not. It was a critical "adjustment to the method [through which the city] captures increasing urban values."

During a meeting at the Secretaría boardroom a few days earlier, Susana, a senior planner overseeing the POT revision, had described edificabilidad as an instrument that would make planning more "operational" and "grounded." She stressed that "this is a POT of opportunities, not of restrictions" and called attention to a planning logic aimed at mobilizing existing densification potentialities

Edificabilidad - Aportes

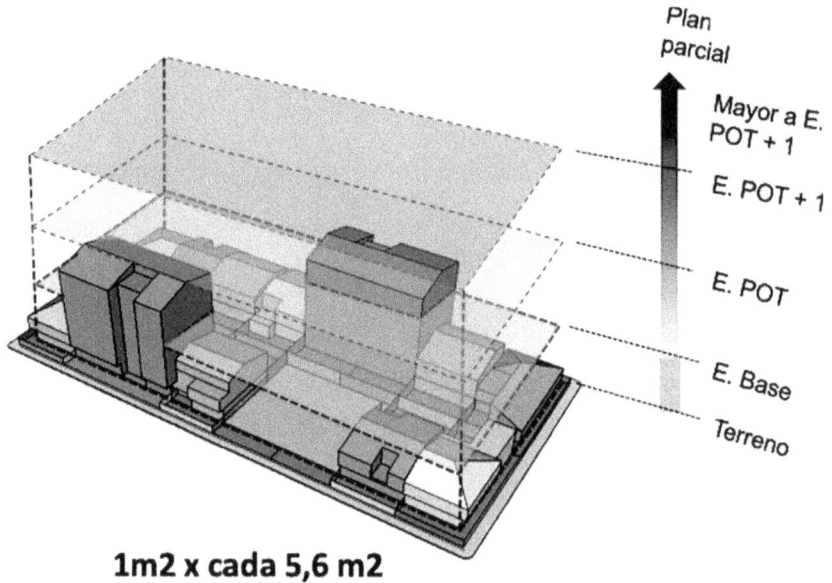

Plan parcial

Mayor a E. POT + 1

E. POT + 1

E. POT

E. Base

Terreno

1m2 x cada 5,6 m2

FIGURE 5.2B.   Edificabilidad diagram. Created by the Grupo POT in 2011.

to create more "equitable" and "orderly" urban spaces. The Grupo POT experts had thus created a "sociospatial strategy [*estrategia socioespacial*]" that established edificabilidad limits across city districts based on existing public infrastructure and amenities. Within this scheme, planners had identified two key "zones of opportunity," or "pockets [*bolsas*]," for intensive densification. "These pockets will be the palace of the market!" Andrés exclaimed during the same meeting, noting the potential for significant densities given local conditions and the funds obtained through edificabilidad. As Javier, a Grupo POT legal expert, put it, edificabilidad would ideally become a "self-regulating instrument" that fully acknowledged the "dynamic" and "unplannable" nature of urban realities. Experts thus reenvisioned the POT as a data-driven platform that both tracked and intervened in the city's volumetric shifts. The envisioned outcome would be the almost automatic production of the necessary material conditions for densification or its efficient regulation, depending on the realities of different urban zones.

Despite their pragmatic sensibilities, Grupo POT planners had ultimately subscribed to an overtly technical approach that naturalized densification and left unquestioned its politics and forms. Although they had opposed developers' speculative mining of density, experts had still approached densification as a taken-for-granted phenomenon waiting to be harnessed. In this context, the edificabilidad proposal embodied a mode of cybernetic planning "centered on a model of feedback-driven adaptive systematicity" and aimed at "manag[ing] dynamic, real-time environmental inputs," to borrow Dominic Boyer's definition of the "cybernetic imagination."[44]

Planners, however, were not unaware of the problems created by this approach. Would these instruments not simply "trail behind the city's trends," one city planner asked, instead of more substantively "transforming it"? At one official meeting, Catalina, the senior planner, was even more vocal about her misgivings. She worried that by focusing on the provision of the local infrastructures—the creation of "self-sustaining zones"—they would ultimately reproduce the city's "logic of perpetual inequity." In what sounded like an admonition, she exclaimed, "What we need is to transfer [resources] to the zones that are in real need!" The proposal's lack of direct engagement with deeper political questions was something that several other Grupo POT experts acknowledged, although less openly. Fernando, a public official who had worked alongside the team, once told me, off the record, that he felt "they were letting the private sector act and not demanding enough as [the] public sector." During one of our final conversations, Diego reluctantly admitted that the revision project had failed to articulate a policy for affordable housing and thereby address one of the city's most critical problems. Andrés, who was usually enthusiastic about the edificabilidad mechanism, also became concerned about how it "tied [contributions and investments] to real estate dynamics" and how this would limit redistribution to zones with less intense densification patterns.

During the revision of the POT, technical considerations had ultimately overshadowed the sociopolitical contexts of planning. Cybernetic planning had privileged the idea of the efficient management and taxation of densities. In doing so, the revision project had continued to treat densification as a natural urban trend, accepting its forms and relations as paradigmatic. As a result, planners had addressed substantive political questions—for example, about access to housing and redistribution—only timidly and as ex post facto issues. Density emerged as a technical platform that further obfuscated the city's contentious conflicts over property and belonging. Despite commitments to greater state intervention in land markets and public funding of collective goods, state-backed real estate development had continued to be at the core of planning visions. Far from a transformative project, the POT revision implied the expansion and refinement of territorial techniques and their more subtle and encompassing reinscription into the language of densification.

The Contradictions of Progressive Planning

By the end of 2011, the Grupo POT planners were coming to terms with the looming failure of the revision project. After several months of busy routines and long work sessions, the team's mezzanine cubicles were now eerily still. With their contracts expiring in a few months, experts were looking ahead to new jobs and consultancies, while career bureaucrats were preparing for the change of administration. During this period, Grupo POT members came to accept the political limitations of their technocratic approach and the extent to which it had contributed to the revision's demise. On our way back to the office from the group's usual lunch spot one day, Diego lamented how "mere politics" had blocked the plan, while he described himself and his colleagues as "técnicos" who had nothing to do with the world of "personal interests and ambitions." After a few steps he added, "Although as técnicos we are also political in the sense that we have a particular vision of the city." It was the tenuousness of this vision that Diego and others had come to reluctantly blame, at least in part, for the collapse of the revision. Looking back on their work, Andrés was openly critical about the gap between the group's technical work and its political resonance: "Nobody wants to be planned, and least of all politicians." For him, the modification project had failed to "allow [social and political actors] to play their part [in the planning process]" and "grab them [agarrarlos] through technical knowledge."

If the Grupo POT planners had embraced the ideals of liberal technocracy and sought to stay above ideological frays through their pragmatic commitments, the new group of experts under the incoming Petro administration were intent on repoliticizing the POT. In contrast to the previous team's focus on the micropolitics of implementation and technical adjustments, these experts set out to directly confront entrenched development patterns and economic interests. These two opposing planning factions were no strangers to each other. For years, the soon-to-take-office cadre of planning academics had been critical of practitioners' moderate and market-friendly interpretation of Colombia's progressive planning frameworks. Técnicos, in turn, portrayed these critical planners as "too radical," as a veteran and well-respected planner once told me, and overzealous about financial redistribution mechanisms, or what he called the "urbanism of additions and subtractions."[45] Many of these practitioners, who had been for years ensconced in governmental institutions and private-sector consultancies, dismissed activist planners for being "destructive," "rhetorical," and "preachy."

The new administration was thus viewed by many as a seismic shift in planning logics. It represented the waning dominance of *doers*, to borrow again the language of former mayor and champion of técnicos Enrique Peñalosa (see chapter 2), who legitimized their expert interventions by appealing to pragmatic imperatives. In question here was planning's long-standing reliance on what Ananya Roy aptly calls the "tyranny of practicality" and its silent complicity with the violent workings of property and development regimes.[46] The election of the Petro administration, in turn, would test the promise of a form of activist planning aimed at transforming territorial ordering through vigorous political commitments to social justice.

The stakes of this transition, as well as its less visible continuities, were dramatically exposed during the final months of the Grupo POT's now-struggling revision project. One afternoon in October 2011, soon after the mayoral elections, the team was informed about a long-awaited meeting with the new administration's top planning adviser. Rosario was a well-known academic who specialized in urban law and had gained prominence among environmental and housing activists. She was both well respected and disdained in urban planning circles. Many técnicos and developers, especially those with ties to the construction sector, considered Rosario to be polarizing in her positions. "She loves anything that means developers have to pay [the state]," one functionary once quipped. Other officials with a more activist bent silently admired her unwavering critiques of "neoliberal development," as one seasoned bureaucrat put it, commenting on her antagonistic relationship with the Cámara Colombiana de la Construcción (Colombian Chamber of Construction), or CAMACOL. She had also been a vocal adversary of the POT revision, voicing her critiques both from her academic platforms and in her consultancies with environmental agencies. Not surprisingly, Grupo POT experts waited for her in the boardroom with apprehension. "So now we have to pay our respects to her?" one of them asked.

Rosario walked briskly into the room, accompanied by another well-known urban scholar. The cold and curt greetings made it impossible for anyone to ignore the tense atmosphere. After two Grupo POT experts clicked through their PowerPoint presentation, Rosario launched into what seemed more like a cross-examination than a government transition meeting. "Will Planning Zonal Units disappear?" "How do you define the central district?" "What about maintenance of the sewage system?" Planners responded, defensively and unsure about where she was going with her line of questioning. Rosario finally revealed her main point of contention when the discussion arrived at the instrument of edificabilidad and its proposed "contributions [*aportes*]," in space or cash, of 1 square meter for every 5.6 square meters of construction. "Where does that charge [*carga*] come from?" she asked, testing the group. Experts scrambled to justify the number, implying it was what developers had considered a reasonable percentage of their sales. Rosario countered: "We have to stop playing the political game of asking developers if they're willing to pay." She then stressed developers' meager contributions in terms of public space and the staggering differences between requirements for development in vacant land and those for construction within the built city. While Grupo POT experts would have in principle agreed with these points, Rosario pushed further and insisted on the need to increase the scope and scale of exactions on development. For her, current attempts were "too modest" and there was still a lot of room to produce the public space and housing that the city needed through more aggressive financial and densification policies. "We need to stop giving away regulations [*regalar la norma*]," she reprimanded the meeting's assistants, "and [recognize] there is a significant margin for more verticalization."

At this point her companion, who had thus far remained silent, interjected with some realpolitik: "Are you still really presenting this revision project to the city council? Because [this term] is over . . ."

"Of course we are; we still have three months left," Catalina, the most senior official at the meeting, replied bluntly.

Rosario turned to her friend and echoed his deflating comment: "Yes, you're right, this is not going to pass." A politically savvy lawyer who advised the secretary of planning tried to dissipate the tension: "Look, we'll submit the project to the council and it's the best of both worlds [if it's approved]: You can blame us for the revision and you'll have new regulatory instruments for your administration." Although the discussion did not go further, the exchange was revealing of the distance between both groups. The Grupo POT had dealt with the political ramifications of their proposal too late and too little. For Rosario and her new cohort of critical planners, political questions about redistribution and equity were at the core of technical interventions. Significantly, however, the meeting had also made apparent the extent to which this more ambitious and progressive agenda would reproduce the grammar of territory-as-density. By relying on existing conceptions of densification and its expert management, planning for sociospatial justice once again risked naturalizing development and property as unquestioned categories. Such assumptions, as progressive planners would themselves later admit, ultimately limited their political agendas and even resulted, in some cases, in the paradoxical favoring of real estate interests.

I met Rosario again several months later, in August 2012; she was now a senior official in the Petro administration working to shift the city's planning apparatus. For most of this first year of the term, Rosario and a new team of urban experts had been creating an agenda for what they now called urban revitalization (*revitalización urbana*). Planners aimed to reduce the influence of large-scale developers and focus instead on small construction firms and redevelopment partnerships with residents. The administration also set ambitious goals for the construction of thousands of units of subsidized housing, a significant proportion of which it

would seek to assign to victims of the armed conflict—an important postconflict reconciliation gesture—and locate within central districts.⁴⁷ Planners thus
imagined a densified inner city, which they called the expanded center (*centro
ampliado*), with mixed-uses, affordable housing, and robust public infrastructure. It was a potentially radical vision that promised to unsettle the dominance
of the real estate sector, reverse deep-seated patterns of urban segregation, and
prevent further ecological destruction stemming from sprawling urbanization
in the city's peripheries. By the end of the term, however, the city had made only
a few symbolic conquests, such as the construction of two subsidized housing
complexes on public land in the city center, while its more wide-ranging goals
had proven largely elusive.

"The worst mistake . . . [was] to move from academia to the public sector,"
Rosario sighed as she sat at the far end of the meeting room table. She was hinting at the mounting obstacles the administration was facing with its planning
agenda, from the stark opposition of the private sector and the national government to managerial weaknesses within the city government and the mayor's own
combative style of governing.⁴⁸ Beyond such barriers, however, her account of
the city's planning disputes revealed the extent to which radical urban visions
had been themselves entwined with and limited by the grammar of territory-as-
density. According to Rosario, the real estate sector, the national Ministerio de
Vivienda, Ciudad y Territorio (Ministry of Housing, City, and Territory), and
their supporting "epistemological communities"—allied academics and professionals working within the public sector—had for years "eroded" the country's
so-called urban reform laws of the late twentieth century (Law 9 of 1989 and
Law 388 of 1997). These legal frameworks had introduced a range of planning
instruments with the promise of promoting the "social function of property," an
ideal cemented in Colombia's 1991 constitution that aimed to subordinate individual property rights to collective interests. They expanded planning authority to undercut real estate speculation through eminent domain (*extinción del
derecho de dominio*), the mandatory development of vacant land (*desarrollo prioritario*), and the capture of added value (*participación en plusvalías*). Ultimately,
such measures were meant to unsettle what María Mercedes Maldonado Copello
describes as Colombia's "myth of absolute property" and its long-standing tradi-
tions of civil law and individual rights.⁴⁹

For Rosario and her colleagues, the previous POT revision had been yet
another weak interpretation of the urban reform laws: Based primarily on the
physical or "urbanistic [*urbanístico*]" understanding of territory, the plan had
been mostly aligned with real estate interests. "I always tell my students that
planning per se [doesn't have an objective] because plans can be either mainly

regulatory or more interventionist: Either the plan simply accompanies the private sector's contested interests and follows the market, or the plan intervenes," she explained. The administration's new proposal would aim to do the latter and recover the POT's central mandate. "[The POT] is really about land uses and you shouldn't be afraid of that. It's about how activities are distributed in the territory and how land rents are redistributed," Rosario asserted as she paused for a moment to look at her buzzing mobile phone. And yet, while critical planners decidedly embraced the POT as an "institutional space for the struggle of political forces and very concrete urban interests," as Rosario put it, their political agendas ultimately unfolded within the entrenched grammar of density. Plans for affordable housing, public space, and environmental sustainability would once again rely on harnessing what Rosario described as the city's "strong dynamic of densification and growth."

At their most radical, new plans for inclusionary densities challenged the prerogatives of property development as well as long-held assumptions about planning and the creation of economic value. "The POT," Rosario explained, "will require [land] transferences [*cesiones*] for public space [within the built city], and if we manage to include the [significant] percentages for required subsidized housing [we are currently considering], we will really be intervening in the use of land." Recentering the access to housing and equity inevitably went against what she called the "popular imaginary according to which the state [is meant to] valorize land." The new POT would open a space for the "arrival of the other [*el otro*], of the unknown urban poor who had been confined to the periphery, into the [densifying] inner city," Rosario argued, even if this entailed "devaluing land." At the same time, and as would become increasingly apparent, such progressive plans continued to adopt density and its assumptions about urban sociomateriality as their points of departure. "I don't know if we are going to reorganize densification, but at the very least, we are going to bring more social inclusion to the process. We are going to stick the poor [*meter pobres*] into an area [the inner city] which I am sure is going to transform radically," Rosario said, concluding our conversation as she prepared for another meeting. More than transforming territorial imaginaries, the implication here was that planning would stretch the logics of property and development to make them more inclusionary. Experts would continue to manage volumetric assemblages, but now with the aim of "stick[ing] the poor" inside, as Rosario tellingly put it, evoking the normalized and depoliticized physics of density. The enduring influence of territory-as-density as a mode of knowledge and intervention would not only limit urban imaginaries but, as experts would later admit, lead to intractable contradictions in the use of progressive planning instruments.

Cake Buildings and Volumetric Designs

In August 2013, Mayor Petro decreed the administration's new version of the POT, known as the Modificación Excepcional del Plan de Ordenamiento Territorial (Exceptional Modification of the Territorial Ordering Plan—Decree 364), or MEPOT, after much debate and despite the active opposition of the construction sector and its allies in the national government. Lucía, another scholar turned functionary who had overseen the formulation of the revision, described the MEPOT as moving closer to an actual "turn in the politics of territorial ordering." If previous modification projects had continued to follow the "[real estate] market's signals," Lucía told me a few years later, looking back on her time in the Secretaría, the MEPOT had aimed to "generate a better city," one with less sociospatial segregation and urban sprawl. Densification, however, would still appear as the main path toward such urban ideals. The MEPOT's promotion of an inclusionary city hinged on the intensive densification of a large central area, the so-called extended center: more than eleven thousand hectares, or approximately 25 percent of Bogotá's total area. Although the plan conceptualized density as a sociospatial process to be actively intervened in and more decisively molded, densification still emerged as a naturalized dynamic whose benefits were waiting to be reaped.

The conflicts surrounding inclusionary densification surfaced early in the revision process when the national housing ministry issued a decree (Decree 075 of 2013) restricting municipal regulations for the production of affordable housing on urbanized land. "So, we came up with something else," Lucía explained. In a similar vein to the previous revision's edificabilidad proposal, the MEPOT would create incentives linked to greater floor-area-ratio allowances. But in addition to introducing general urban contributions (*cargas urbanísticas*) linked to public space and infrastructure, the plan established guidelines so that a percentage of construction areas could be devoted to affordable housing (*vivienda de interés prioritario*) or translated into an equivalent payment to a municipal urban housing fund. Additionally, the percentages of required affordable housing would be lower if developers constructed the housing on-site or within the limits of the extended center. As Lucía explained, "It was a mechanism to gradually generate small affordable housing projects mixed in with other uses, with housing of other socioeconomic strata, [to] transform the stigma of segregation this city has so deeply interiorized."

The MEPOT's promises were short-lived. In March 2014, less than seven months after the MEPOT was decreed, an administrative tribunal suspended the plan indefinitely on procedural issues: It had been a *leguleyada*, or legal sleight of hand, as one city official put it. Lucía told me that the city administration followed the legal defeat with a "shock strategy" of its own, seeking to recover the "territorial vision" inscribed in the MEPOT. A key component within this new regulatory tactic was Decree 562, issued by the city government in December 2014. Although the areas it covered were less expansive compared to the MEPOT, the decree made similar commitments to promoting "densification with urbanistic contributions" in central districts that were either "frozen in time" or developing lot by lot without making contributions to the city—such as the infamous BD Bacatá skyscraper. The decree represented an evolution of financial instruments, Lucía noted, and of "volumetric regulations." Its generous building allowances would be tempered not only by infrastructural and housing contributions but also through elaborate codes on building setbacks and "terraced volumes [*volumetría escalonada*]." Decree 562 and its contestations would be materialized in what several planners called "[wedding] cake buildings [*ponqués*]": the ziggurat-like tiered towers that started dotting the Bogotá skyline in 2015.

Opposition to the Skyscraper Decree, as it became known, was fierce and quickly jumped from the legal battlefield to the public sphere. News media published reports, and opinion columns warned that the regulation would unleash chaos and destroy the city's "social fabric."[50] The country's leading newspaper,

FIGURE 5.3. A "cake" building rising behind older structures in a central neighborhood northwest of the city center, 2018. Photo by the author.

El Tiempo, featured a video news story on its YouTube channel in which an eminent architect toured buildings erected under Decree 562. He described the "aggressiveness" and the "threatening" nature of their designs and decried the "deep wounds" they had left behind.[51] CAMACOL commissioned a short film titled *The Dark Side of Skyscrapers in Bogotá*, which circulated widely on You-Tube and among planning and development circles under the hashtag #ojoal562 (#keepaneyeon562).[52] Using colorful stop-motion animation, the developer-backed video argued that the regulation would benefit property owners, con-structors, and the administration at the expense of "the city and its citizens, who will lose, who will have to live in the insufferable chaos of Bogotá, which will be worse when it feeds off this decree." In denouncing the decree's deleterious effects, it called for planned densification of the kind that had failed throughout Bogotá's modern history, and it willfully ignored the fact that the city had already been densifying in these areas with no obligations or contributions. Elite owner-ship and long-running development interests informed these critiques, as did ideologies of segregated, expansionary, and low-density residential urbanism.

In the end, large-scale developers had sought to preserve their high-profit and fairly unregulated construction activities in the built city. The city admin-istration, in turn, had sought to destabilize the entrenched political economy of the construction sector. As Sonia, another former high-ranking official and university professor, explained to me, "While CAMACOL and the national gov-ernment trained their sights on us, we educated small and midsized developers

FIGURE 5.4. Still from *The Dark Side of Skyscrapers in Bogotá* (Magic Markers Producciones SAS 2015).

about the decree. [Our aim was] to diversify the kind of constructor that took on these projects." The decree was less beneficial, Sonia continued, for large-scale developers that already owned extensive areas of land, had very high financial expectations, and operated with complex administrative structures. But many developers, both small and large, rushed to request building permits under the decree: In fifteen months, around nine hundred had been approved, and many others were still under consideration.[53] According to Sonia, the administration collected around US$63 million in these months, while the total funds obtained through other value-capture mechanisms over the course of the previous twelve years had been US$46 million. Contrary to the fear of excessively tall, predatory skyscrapers, she added, most buildings had been around twenty stories high.

A few years later, however, after returning to her university position and with the benefit of hindsight, Sonia had come to terms with the contradictions of her work in the administration. We talked at length about the limitations of progressive planning one afternoon in 2018 in her duplex apartment. She lived in an affordable enclave, or *conjunto residencial*, of narrow, brick townhouses, much like the ones the administration had envisioned for the extended center and had been unable to materialize. As a young planner who had entered the city government right after finishing her doctorate in urban studies, she had been invested in the administration's ambitious housing and inclusionary redevelopment plans—her main fields of expertise. After seeing the gradual collapse of the administration's policies, she had been left wondering how the politics of implementation had undermined radical planning agendas. "I have a self-critique," she confessed pensively, "and it's that we focused on the large objectives and forgot the procedures [*trámites*], everything that passed underneath. [It's critical to understand] how the bureaucratic machine moves, because the devil is in the details, in the technical details of the chain of urbanistic procedures and land development." Operational flaws, Sonia and many of her colleagues argued, had critically undermined Decree 562, in particular the delayed creation of a related regulatory decree that finally came out in April 2015 (Decree 138) and established the guidelines for the production of affordable housing. For more than four months, Decree 562 had thus created considerable financial incentives without the complementary affordable housing requirements. "So it was a mistake," Sonia admitted, "because it unleashed a building permit boom partly because developers wanted to get permits before the Priority Interest Housing [subsidized affordable housing] decree came out."

As Petro's term concluded in December 2015, the most visible outcome of the government's contested plans had been the sprouting of "cake buildings" across a handful of central neighborhoods. Very little subsidized housing had been produced within the extended center, and the considerable funds that the administration had collected remained in the city's treasury without a clear destination. Yet the technical shortcomings of Decree 562 pointed to a deeper problem. Despite their critical reenvisioning of planning logics, experts had continued to conceive of and intervene in the territory in reductive and depoliticized terms—as a volumetric assemblage of densities. While plans for redistribution and desegregation pushed the boundaries of traditional planning and development, they still operated within the confines of its entrenched imaginaries. The MEPOT's and Decree 562's political impetus had been constrained by something similar to the previous proposal's cybernetic approach: Planners had aimed above all to anticipate and modulate densification as a self-generating and recursive sociomaterial dynamic. Instead of seeking to transform the territory of planning—its underlying logics of control and ownership—they had continued to plan the territory, redesigning its forms and relations within the established coordinates of state and development logics.

Beyond the Horizon of Territory?

The reelection of former Mayor Enrique Peñalosa for a second term starting in 2016 marked a regressive reinstantiation of territory-as-density. Only a month after taking office and signaling his allegiance to the construction sector and landowning elites, Peñalosa repealed Decree 562. By 2018 the city was back to business as usual: Unfettered lot-by-lot rebuilding in the inner city had gathered momentum, and the administration had started calling for the intensive urbanization of vacant land on the city's outskirts. Lucas, a planner who until recently had worked in an architecture firm, talked to me in his office at the Secretaría about the inevitability of densification and the need to both stimulate and regulate its patterns outside central districts. "Bogotá is already a very dense city," he said, "and it is one of the few cities in the world that is still densifying. Not even Dhaka is densifying like us."

In its own project to revamp the POT, the new administration did not entertain questions about different types of densities and lopsided distributions, let alone about housing segregation. Peñalosa's planners returned instead to the drawing board to "review each zone, block by block of the city," Lucas explained, "using parametric design." In what planners presented as an unreservedly technical approach, they would now seek to create a template for the efficient modeling of urban densities across the city's varying conditions of public infrastructure. Sitting at his desk, Lucas turned to his computer to show me a video that the Secretaría had made to illustrate the city's approach to densification. Opening with a black screen, the video's computer-generated animation depicted the settlement

FIGURE 5.5. Lucas running the Planning Department's visualization of urban growth. Photo by the author.

of the entire region of the Sabana de Bogotá from an imagined year 0 to 2050. Set to a mellifluous nocturne by Chopin, the video juxtaposed two scenarios. First it showed the accelerated and chaotic urbanization of the Sabana under the title "If the City Grows Without a Project"; then it displayed a slower and more orderly expansion, "If It Grows with a Project." The video, Lucas explained, was made by "taking the city's growth algorithm for the past fifty years and reproducing it, making it run along wherever the topography allowed."

The animation enacted a distinctly reified understanding of densification as a forceful and naturalized sociomaterial dynamic. It also offered a compelling alibi for a planning rationale aimed at creating new land markets for the real estate sector. In Lucas's phrasing, "Sooner or later this will end up happening, for good or for bad, but the proposal is that it be planned correctly." Unbridled urban growth across a variable topography emerged here as an inevitable outcome, so that all that planners and citizens could hope for was to anticipate and organize this urban sprawl—what planners now called "dense expansion." In marked contrast to the MEPOT and Decree 562, and "the monsters it generated in the middle of neighborhoods," as another planner in the Peñalosa administration put it, this outlook not only justified but urgently called for the urbanization of exceptionally valuable expansion land (*suelo de expansión*) in north Bogotá. Opening such land for urban development would constitute nothing short of the most profitable opportunity for the real estate sector in the city's contemporary history. Additionally, this "dense expansion" would encroach on and threaten the connectivity of an important and contested area that regional environmental authorities had declared a natural reserve in 2011.[54]

Despite its contrasting agenda, this most recent iteration of the POT made apparent the shared centrality of density to Bogotá's shifting planning models. As an urban epistemology and sociomaterial ideology, it proved a common thread in divergent expert frameworks, both obscuring and limiting the politics of urban intervention. In this sense, Lucas's parametric and algorithmic urbanism gave full expression to the idea of density as a detached, agentive reality that planners had to bring under the reins of calculative and managerial techniques.[55] And it was precisely by conjuring density as an unwieldy yet generative sociomaterial process that experts, across the political spectrum, enacted specific urban realities and normalized particular political agendas.

What is most significant about the epistemics of density is that it replicated the long-standing relationship between urban planning and territorial control. Planning knowledges centered on densification moved beyond earlier approaches that conceptualized urban space as a static surface to be bounded, smoothed, and tamed. These latter interventions, which defined planning in Bogotá during much of the twentieth century, brought together the logics of militarism and developmentalism with projects to discipline the city's unruly crowds and terrains. As I showed in previous chapters, this resulted in the contested materialization of urban frontiers and voids, a history that paralleled the conflict-ridden production of a national territory and its unreachable corners.[56] With the rise of density as a central planning logic, experts now conceptualized urban territory not as a tabula rasa ready to be filled with the wide-ranging visions of urban modernity, but rather as a dynamic sociomaterial formation to be administered and gradually modulated. Experts all but abandoned the language of security so integral to planning practices in previous decades, turning instead to the imagery of distending volumes and solidifying assemblies of things and people. Instead of creating blueprints for new realities, planners would now seek to give form to the city's unfolding materialities and try to steer them, at their most progressive, toward redistributive and inclusionary outcomes.

Yet far from leaving behind the logic of territory, such approaches recast it in the language of density. As the taken-for-granted medium of urbanism, territory-as-density naturalized specific sociomaterial relations and political-economic assumptions. Cyphered in the epistemology of density were once again the entrenched territories of the state, property, and development.[57] For all their pragmatic commitments, the city's new plans were "still modernist urbanism," as Javier, the Grupo POT's legal expert, once told me. Planners bounded densities in space and translated them into quantifiable magnitudes, ultimately seeking to render them into "controllable futures," he further noted. Their attempts to reshape the city's volumetric densities—from the narrowly technical to the more progressive and political—had thus tacitly reinscribed the univocal vision of territory as the product of modern sovereignty and as a space to be parceled out according to the logics of individual ownership and market dynamics. Even apparently radical agendas aimed at reversing deep-seated patterns of urban segregation and exclusion—most notably the Petro administration's plans for subsidized housing in the inner city—became subordinated to the assumptions of territory-as-density. They emerged as collateral effects of the densifying landscape of real estate development, rather than the transformative political projects planners had intended: a reordering of sociomaterial elements—for instance, Rosario's quip about "stick[ing] the poor" inside central districts—within a fundamentally unchanged structure.

At stake here, ultimately, was planning's enduring entanglements with colonial and modernist projects aimed at redressing what Vincent Gouëset calls Colombia's "deficit of territoriality."[58] This was reflected in the notion of ordenamiento territorial, which was institutionalized in the 1991 constitutional reform as a means to attain "national integration."[59] Ordenamiento territorial took on particular significance as the alleged solution to the country's deep-rooted and violent conflicts over land and governance. Sociologist and historian Orlando Fals Borda, who famously stated that Colombia was not a nation but a "country of regions," echoed such promises after having served as a member of the commission for territorial ordering at the 1991 constitutional assembly. He saw ordenamiento territorial as a potential platform for a grassroots reconstruction of administrative institutions from the ground up—what he called "reordered zones" or "peace zones"—and as a critical step in the "search for peace and good governance" and a resolution to the country's so-called "voids of power."[60]

Such visions not only resonated with progressive urban plans such as those of the Petro administration; they were also taken up in the landmark negotiations that led to the peace agreement with the FARC in 2016. "Territorial peace," peace commissioner Sergio Jaramillo argued in a public talk in 2013, would follow a "logic of integration and inclusion, based on a new alliance between the state and communities to construct together institutional infrastructure [institucionalidad] in the territory."[61] But despite acknowledging a "plurality of uses and appropriations of territory," geographer Alice Beuf notes, ordenamiento territorial continued to reproduce, in practice, a "reductive conceptualization [of territory] . . . as an instrument of domination in the service of development."[62] Progressive and emergent postconflict rearticulations of territorial ordering were thus still very much *territory by design*. Experts imagined a unitary territory to be known, managed, and reshaped: the territory of the state, property, and development.

A central question in this regard is whether and how city planning can move beyond what Arturo Escobar, in a critique of urban design and habitability, calls "heteropatriarchal capitalist colonial modernity."[63] Following his earlier and influential work on the "colonizing politics of development knowledge," Escobar turns to design, broadly construed, as a crucial site for decolonial struggles and the remaking of lifeworlds.[64] Drawing on his long-running scholarly and activist work with Afro-Colombian communities in the country's Southwest around processes of regional ordenamiento territorial and local ecological, cultural, and socioeconomic struggles, Escobar asks, "Can design be reoriented from its dependence on the marketplace toward creative experimentation with forms, concepts, and materials?"[65] Extending this question in the terms of this book, one could ask whether urban planning and design can be untethered from deep-seated epistemologies of security, order, and development. What would planning look like if its horizon were not territory—in the singular—and territorial control? For Escobar, the answer lies unequivocally outside the realm of liberal modern epistemologies and their inherently destructive and "defuturing" effects. Expanding world-making imaginaries to render them truly transformative— what Escobar calls "autonomous" and "transitional" design—thus necessitates a radically different grounding. This is what he describes as non-Western, place-based, "relational ontologies" emerging from the experiences and knowledges of Indigenous, peasant, and Afro-descendant groups. Of central importance for Escobar is subalterns' own making of alternate territories, those "other territorialities" that starkly oppose the expanding territory of capital and the state and embody "strategies for the persistence of the place-based and communal weave of life."[66]

In the context of contemporary sociopolitical and ecological crises, the attention to "new territorialities" and their liberatory potential is undoubtedly urgent and far exceeds academic debates—something that is clearly attested to by Latin American social movements and their sustained engagement with territorial politics in the past decades.[67] At the same time, however, burgeoning calls for the decolonization of planning and territory risk replicating the persistent "dualisms of modernity," as Kiran Asher argues, as well as "reify[ing] . . . the 'non-Western' and other 'Others'" on which many of these critiques rest, not to mention modernity and the state itself.[68] Such slippages may lead to what Silvia Rivera Cusicanqui describes as the "cooptation and neutralization" of counterhegemonic agendas, something that in Colombia and elsewhere in Latin America has been most visible in the codification of multiculturalism and territorial autonomy in the law.[69] In this regard, Rivera Cusicanqui reminds us that "there can be no discourse of decolonization, no theory of decolonization, without a decolonizing practice."[70] In Bogotá, as I have shown in this chapter, progressive planning did not sufficiently reckon with the materiality of territory, its underlying violence and security-laden contours, and the political-economic conditions that historically shaped ordenamiento territorial in Colombia. New urban rhetoric about social justice and inclusion thus came dangerously close to enacting "the policy of changing everything so that everything remains the same," as Rivera Cusicanqui puts it.[71]

These contradictions call for analyses of urban planning and development not only as discursive or epistemological constructs but as conflict-ridden and sociospatially mediated processes that are materialized in wide-ranging ways. As much as planning is born out of this "political wrangling," as Ajantha Subramanian argues about development policy, so, too, are local communities shaped by their struggles against and alliances with state officials, experts, and economic actors.[72] Far from representing unitary worldviews and experiences, let alone overarching political and economic interests, subaltern groups are shot through with divisions and hierarchies. Reimagining urbanism as an anticolonial and desecuritized project must therefore begin with the study of the conjunctures—historical, political-economic, epistemic, and material—within which specific forms of colonial capitalist modernity are enacted and contested in the making of urban worlds.[73] In Bogotá, this entails tracing the specific circumstances through which planning is shaped by state officials, developers, experts, and city dwellers. Of critical importance here is what Subramanian calls the "sedimented forms of power and protest" through which people signify and materialize strategies of rule, rights claims, and modes of belonging.[74] It is these obdurate sediments and their materialization through territory, security, and dispossession that I have been probing in this book to better understand the emergent potentials and entrenched limits of urban imaginaries. Urbanism as warfare, from this vantage point, is far from finished and all-encompassing. Rather, it is a paradoxical and irregular epistemic and sociomaterial space that is continually redefined.

I turn next to another, more localized and allegedly progressive plan in Bogotá to look at how the making of urban knowledge presses against the limits of security and violence while reinscribing their "stubborn materiality," to use Donald Moore's phrasing.[75] At stake here is the very possibility of a "dissenting design imagination," to borrow from Escobar again, in which experts and non-experts "think communally and relationally."[76] Such planning and design spaces, and their potential for epistemic multiplicity, transformative imaginaries, and the co-construction of new urban worlds do not unfold in a vacuum. They are mediated by the layered repertoires and materialities of territorial control and propertied citizenship so central to Colombia's enduring political violence and elusive post-conflict era. Contemporary plans in Bogotá and their alternative visions, I argue in the following chapter, reveal the entrenched workings of what Rivera Cusicanqui calls a "political economy of knowledge," in which hierarchies, modes of domination, and everyday violences are woven into collaborative and inclusionary schemes and their everyday materialities.[77]

6

PROGRESSIVE FICTIONS

"Let him work! You should be out catching thieves!" It was an April morning in 2012, and university students were shouting at a group of police officers who had surrounded a street vendor. The young man was sitting on top of his cart, undaunted by the commotion. As the crowd grew, the officials' expressions went from authoritative to concerned. Residents joined the chorus demanding that the police "suspend the procedure." It soon became apparent that more was at stake in the otherwise routine affair. The so-called "restitution of public space [*restitución de espacio público*]" had stirred latent fears of displacement in a neighborhood besieged by urban renewal.

Alex, the vendor, had been rolling his makeshift cart, or *chaza*, along the Eje Ambiental walkway and the stagnant waters of its stepped canal: on one side, the Universidad de los Andes, the country's most elite private university, and on the other, the neighborhood of Las Aguas, also known as Germania, nine blocks of old tenements and aging houses, self-built shacks, small stores, cheap cafeterias, and modest low-rise apartment buildings. The confrontation with the police had occurred in front of the demolition site of the Manzana Cinco renewal plan, on the southern edge of the neighborhood, where piles of rubble were a daily reminder of the recent wave of dispossession and destruction (see chapter 3). It was not surprising, then, that when a police officer justified the procedure by saying that the university president himself had filed a petition (*derecho de petición*)—an improbable yet savvy rhetorical move to defuse students' complaints—some of the locals present immediately turned to an "urban revitalization plan" known as Progresa Fenicia (Fenicia Progresses), which the university had been recently promoting in the neighborhood.

"I've been here for sixty years and now the university also wants to kick us out!" Manuel, the owner of a small restaurant in Las Aguas, shouted from the back of the crowd. For him, the removal of the vendor from the walkway was indistinguishable from what many residents saw as a new threat of eviction under Progresa Fenicia. Manuel, like many others in the area, was a "possessor" (*poseedor* in Colombian legal terms): He had inherited his house, but he did not hold a legal title to it. The street vendor himself lived with his family in one of the neighborhood's residences, a precarious living arrangement that offered little assurances to tenants. Others in the neighborhood had been longtime renters who had never seen their landlords again, while some had been squatting in abandoned properties for decades, and others had arrived, violently displaced from the countryside, and built shacks on city grounds on the hillside. These residents, along with more affluent apartment owners, shared similar concerns about their uncertain fate, especially after witnessing the swift round of expulsions in the nearby Manzana Cinco project, where the dust of demolition had not yet settled. The fight to keep the vendor on the street pointed to the mounting conflict around livelihoods and property rights between the university and residents.

As the circle of people grew, it became clear that the vendor would not be removed, at least not on this occasion. Several law students engaged police with incisive questions and long-winded arguments to the point that the officers, possibly now concerned about upsetting the powers-that-be on campus, decided to withdraw. The fact that it had been university students who had derailed the police procedure—something that the street vendor later acknowledged with gratitude—was significant. It encapsulated the ambivalences that had characterized university-neighborhood relations for years. While residents often resented the university's elitism and the rising costs associated with its encroachment on the largely working-class neighborhood, many in the area had also benefited from its money-spending crowds, employment opportunities, and outreach programs. And although gates and guards separated the university campus from its surroundings, students and staff found varied services and spaces for socialization in Las Aguas. Such intimate proximities and stark social distances would be reproduced and magnified with the university's Progresa Fenicia revitalization plan and its alleged goal of bringing "progress" to the residents of Las Aguas. More broadly, they pointed to the shifting yet enduring workings of security as the medium for struggles over urban space and belonging.

An Orangutan in a Frock Coat

Los Andes launched the Progresa Fenicia plan in 2010 as a radical shift from previous downtown renewal projects, including Manzana Cinco, whose razing unfolded just steps from campus and became a poignant reminder of the threat of eviction among neighboring residents. "The university wanted to do things differently," Carolina, a senior university administrator explained to me in her airy office, "starting not with a spatial plan but rather with people." An architecture professor and longtime campus planner, Carolina was also candid about the university's own missteps in its earlier expansion plans in Las Aguas. "We had an absolutely physical vision," she told me, "and that was a mistake."

Property acquisitions over the years had culminated in an earlier project known as the Triángulo de Fenicia (Fenicia Triangle), launched in 2008 by Los Andes and Ospinas & Co.—one of Colombia's largest construction firms and an organization with deep ties to the university, its president at the time, and the board of trustees. Soft-spoken and diplomatic, Carolina lamented that she and her colleagues had approached this previous plan simply as "real estate development" mainly for the university's benefit and not as a "comprehensive program with the community." Such limitations, she suggested, had ultimately led the university to withdraw the Triángulo de Fenicia plan in 2009 and return to the drawing board to create the community-based Progresa Fenicia.

But Carolina also hinted at how the initial plan was more than mere oversight, and the subsequent decision to cancel arose from more than just a change of heart: Appreciating land values and rising discontent in the area had led to a "deadlock" that spurred the university administration to change gears. As Miguel, an architect and campus planner, put it, university leadership realized that "the way things were unfolding, the [Triángulo de Fenicia] plan was not going to work out." Participatory development and inclusionary planning became a practical necessity, something that many residents would come to suspect was a ploy to take over the neighborhood by other means: a "Trojan horse of development," to use Faranak Miraftab's words.[1] The tensions between ideals of inclusion and collaboration and strategies for land control and accumulation would thus become a central feature of Progresa Fenicia and demarcate lines of contention both within the university and in Las Aguas in the years to come.

Progresa Fenicia became well known within Bogotá's planning circles as a blueprint for inner-city renewal without displacement. Much like progressive planners who attempted to retool the city's POT and its modes of territorial governance (see chapter 5), university planners set out to test the possibilities of a new model of inclusionary densification. While the POT had been concerned mainly with top-down technologies to reassemble territories, populations, and land uses, Progresa Fenicia engaged residents directly and sought to transform social and property relations from the ground up. Far from a campus expansion plan based on buying out residents or the state-driven reconstruction projects of previous decades, Progresa Fenicia envisioned the creation of a new dense and mixed neighborhood through "partnerships" and "joint construction" with locals. The languages of territorial insecurity and control, decay and recovery, receded into the background, and urban renewal, now more frequently called "revitalization," was recast as a means toward social integration and community development. Las Aguas became a laboratory in which campus planners, university professors, urban consultants, and students contributed to the production of new forms of knowledge alongside, but also often at a distance from, residents and property owners. Such progressive epistemologies aimed to turn the page on the city center's history of destruction and displacement and—in line with nascent postconflict discourses in Colombia—rectify long-standing injustices through the remaking of urban spaces and socialities.

Yet the Progresa Fenicia team's visions about the university's role within the city and in relation to Colombia's tentative postconflict futures were plagued with contradictions. In one sense, Los Andes's plan resonated with what has become the increasingly central yet often unacknowledged role of higher education institutions within circuits of speculative development linked to the so-called creative and knowledge economies. This is what urban scholar Davarian Baldwin, writing about universities in the United States, describes as the "rise of Univer-Cities" and their exploitative relationship with the racialized urban poor that often surround urban campuses.[2] In another sense, Los Andes's new planning team—which now included legal scholars, social workers, management faculty, anthropologists, development studies professors, financial experts, and planners and designers—reframed the university's intervention in Las Aguas as a collaborative community-investment program that would secure the permanence of residents and improve their lives and livelihoods.

Despite the radical turn this suggested within Bogotá's trajectories of downtown renewal and displacement, university experts' reliance on liberal ideals of progress and technical knowledge reinscribed entrenched modes of territorial control, inequality, and difference. As I elaborate in this chapter, expert epistemologies for the participatory and inclusionary reconfiguration of physical spaces, land values, and social relations inevitably clashed with the materiality and lived experience of deep-seated insecurities and conflicts. Planners failed to engage directly with the social and political-economic fault lines that had shaped the working-class neighborhood. The disavowal of these broader conjunctures—from the entanglements between technocratic knowledge and state violence to the layered histories of forced migration and urban dispossession—undermined collaborative endeavors and risked making them complicit in the long-running banishment of downtown's urban poor. As one resident aptly put it during a community meeting organized by Los Andes, "This is the same thing as Manzana Cinco; they want to kick us out. The only difference is that they want to do it *more elegantly.*"

Progresa Fenicia's social promise was predicated on the alleged benefits of real estate development and individual property, categories charged with class and racial overtones and suffused with the legacies of Colombia's violent struggles over land. Much like national postconflict reconstruction discourses based on ideals of economic development and entrepreneurialism, this was not a plan to undo structural inequalities and promote forms of collective solidarity, but rather a promise of inclusion into existing arrangements of power.[3] As Tania Li notes, liberal reformism too often "counts on growth" to solve historical injustices, when what progressive mobilization requires is "a commitment to distribution fought for on political terrain."[4] A similar sentiment had permeated university planners' own moments of skepticism and disillusionment after working for years on Progresia Fenicia—it was "coming up against the limits of the paradigm of development and profitability," one expert confided, having questioned at times why he and his colleagues had even embarked on the plan. One professor who had grudgingly agreed to contribute the plan's qualitative analysis had more serious misgivings. "Participatory frameworks," he complained to me during a quiet conversation in one of the campus's courtyards, "are ideological placeholders [*comodines*]." Increasingly frustrated with the potential implications of the plan, he described the university's recent expansion into the neighborhood as "imperialism and colonialism" and suggested an outcome resembling "eugenicist terraforming"—a race- and class-inflected reshaping of human and material topographies.

In this chapter, I follow the discussions and encounters brought about by the Progresa Fenicia plan among faculty, administrators, consultants, and residents, as well as the social and material frictions and realignments that accompanied the plan. I explore the commitment to ideals of "progress," "participation," and "inclusion" as expressions both of a particular history and politics of knowledge production and of university planners' situated experiences as middle- and upper-class professionals largely insulated from the violences of property and development. I avoid reducing university planners' attempts at collaborative planning to hidden agendas or "false consciousness"—that is, to mere conduits for class domination, as the disgruntled professor suggested above. Instead I illuminate the conjunctures that shaped experts' approaches to knowledge production and that prevented them from recognizing the plan's larger sociopolitical context and its reverberations across a terrain of violence and insecurity.[5]

I also avoid portraying the inhabitants of Las Aguas as a homogenous mass or as passive victims. As Catalina Muñoz and Friederike Fleischer argue, residents actively gave meaning to the Progresa Fenicia plan and recontextualized it within the neighborhood's sociopolitical history through their embodied experiences and everyday narratives.[6] Whether it was middle-class owners protecting their privileges and gaining leverage in future negotiations or impoverished dwellers opposing what they saw as their eventual expulsion, for them much more was at stake than the technical reshuffling of square meters and land uses to benefit a generic individual property owner. In repoliticizing the intervention, residents called attention to how the neighborhood had been intimately tied to the specters of land violence and misappropriation, from the threats of gangs and the uncertainties of illegal tenure to the struggles over local governance and the anxieties of widening inequality. Residents thus produced critical knowledges about local citizen struggles, state authority, and the political significance of the material transformations of their homes and neighborhood.[7] The idea of Las Aguas as a real estate partnership and vertical condominium thus inevitably seemed out of touch. Progresa Fenicia emerged as a sanitized vision that clashed with the lived reality of downtown as a landscape of legal, property, and bodily violence.

Bringing together the main threads of this book, I examine in this chapter how Progresa Fenicia reenacted urbanism as warfare in the language of equitable progress and inclusionary development. In the context of downtown's trajectories of renewal and displacement, the university plan shifted away from militaristic spatial control while echoing human security discourses prominent in Colombia's convulsed postconflict era.[8] Yet as scholars have pointed out, interventions aimed at protecting and aiding communities have in practice often merged militarization and development, expanding modalities of governance to manage "disorderly" populations.[9] So although Progresa Fenicia was far from enacting overt modes of militarization and policing, it brought to light the subtle and intractable connections between progress and insecurity, development and violence—something reflected in Los Andes's own place within Colombia's history of technocratic governance and warfare.

These contradictions foreground another central theme of this book: the politics of (in)security as a mediating force in the production and materialization of urban knowledge. In previous chapters, I detailed how social actors mobilized epistemologies linked to Colombia's long-running armed conflict both to legitimate plans of reconstruction and dispossession and to resist such projects as incarnations of state violence and forced displacement. Progresa Fenicia brought into focus the dynamic, dialectical quality of such topographies of urban knowledge. As university planners moved away from visions of renewal centered on security and order, residents responded by calling forth the everyday violences of urbanization. This process exposed the trenchant hierarchies and power differentials that shaped the plan's allegedly collaborative and inclusionary modes of knowledge production. It revealed the ideals of property and progress that underpinned the vision of a mixed-use, high-rise development and their intimate connection with the sociopolitical and institutional structures behind Colombia's conflicts over governance, land, and citizenship.

Progresa Fenicia highlights the complex ties between elite liberal knowledge and the country's foundational violences and colonial legacies. Both an embodiment of enlightenment and propriety and a key node of power within class, racial, and political-economic hierarchies, Los Andes recalls Liberal politician Darío Echandía's famous description of Colombian democracy as "an orangutan in a frock coat."[10] From this point of view, I examine how scholars, administrators, and consultants both disavowed and reckoned with the university's role as a vehicle for projects of nation making, modernization, and capital accumulation. Anxieties about epistemic violence under the veneer of cosmopolitan politesse and detached narratives of neutrality and progress are central to my analysis and not least to my own positionality as an Universidad de los Andes alumnus and US-based scholar.[11] They call attention to the ways in which forms of expertise, from progressive planning to anthropological research, reproduce assumptions about racialized and impoverished communities as subjects waiting to be incorporated "into the comforts and privileges of property and citizenship," as Ryan Cecil Jobson puts it.[12] Looking at the sociomaterial conditions that shaped the composition of progressive urban knowledge in Progresa Fenicia ultimately points to the limits of planning expertise as an epistemology tied with violent histories of state making, development, and citizenship. It also raises crucial questions about the possibility of a mode of planning beyond the security-laden roots of colonial and modernist governance, one that centers the transformation of the epistemic and material structures of urban governance and belonging.

A University with Its Back to the City

The creation of Los Andes brings us back, full circle, to the emblematic event of the destruction of El Bogotazo (see chapter 1). Its foundation can be traced to November 1948, when more than fifty aristocratic men signed the university's "declaration of principles." This was only months after the El Bogotazo uprising had left downtown Bogotá in ruins and as political violence swept across the country. The momentous juncture was no coincidence. As Mario Laserna Pinzón, the university's main founder, explained, "The 9th of April [of 1948] was the best argument for the foundation of the Universidad de los Andes."[13]

The son of a wealthy Conservative family, Laserna Pinzón had studied in North American and European elite universities such as Columbia, Princeton, and Heidelberg. After graduating in mathematics from Columbia University, Laserna Pinzón returned to Colombia to create a nonpartisan, nonreligious private university modeled after US liberal arts colleges. The idea was to promote a form of "technological humanism," as one of the university's founding members put it, to overcome the country's profound social and political divisions.[14] It was as if the explosive violence of El Bogotazo had finally made the devastation of rural warfare visible to urbane *letrados*—those nation-building, lettered elites Ángel Rama wrote about[15]—who were now, according to one history of the university, "compelled to descend to the harsh terrain of the reality that surrounded them."[16]

But as Los Andes settled at the base of the city's iconic Cerros Orientales (Eastern Hills), overlooking the expanding historic center from the old working-class industrial periphery of Las Aguas, the "descent to reality" looked far more like an ascent out of the quagmire of Colombia's history of sociopolitical violence. The university rose as a center of technocratic expertise—the future training ground of policymakers, state planners, and business leaders—with administrators declaring the institution "apolitical" and "neutral."[17] It aspired to embody a technical ethos through which its *técnicos* would be able to stay above the fray of political violence and offer an alternative to vitriolic partisanship and social conflict. As cofounder Francisco Pizano de Brigard recalled, "In a certain way, we did not want to build a new university but rather a new nation."[18]

In practice, this vision for a new Colombia was anything but neutral. While Los Andes's appeal to academic independence seemed like a legitimate response to bipartisan interference in public universities, the discourse of technical transparency enabled specific political orientations and disavowals. The university remained close to the country's social, political, and religious establishments. It followed elites' regressive rejection of student organizing—a pillar of university life at Latin American public universities—and it channeled Cold War anti-Communism and fears of leftist activism on campus. More broadly, Los Andes's technocratic ethos was heavily indebted to the United States, not only in its emulation of the lofty ivory tower but also with its strong ties to US funders and their geopolitical agendas. With the support of the Rockefeller Foundation, as historian Amy Offner shows, Los Andes became the country's top center for economic planning and policy starting in the late 1950s.[19] University economists, in the spirit of Lauchlin Currie's work and the Alliance for Progress, focused on questions of economic growth and rural-to-urban migration, contributing to the era's paradigmatic merging of urban development and counterinsurgency (see chapter 1). Behind Los Andes's status as an independent and depoliticized institution ultimately lay concrete political commitments to the "superiority of the private sector" and the technocratic management of reality, all within an elite refusal of meaningful sociopolitical transformation.[20]

Los Andes's contradictory politics, as a supposedly progressive and independent force of change bounded by liberal technocracy and class and racial hierarchies, were nowhere more apparent than in the material configuration of the campus over time. The location of the university—perched at the base of the landmark hills of Monserrate and Guadalupe, two of Bogotá's main tourist and pilgrimage sites, and beside independence leader Simón Bolívar's country house, the historic Quinta de Bolívar—was charged with unique political and cultural significance. The vertical topography of the forested urban edge became an ideal medium to carve out a space of cultivated knowledge making that was separate from the unruly city below.[21]

The character of the buildings where classes were first held in 1949 was revealing. The university administration initially rented and later purchased several structures that had been property of the Hermanas del Buen Pastor (Sisters of the Good Shepherd), a Catholic religious order founded in France that had expanded across Latin American cities in the nineteenth century with the mission of rehabilitating "delinquent" women. The nuns' colonial-style convent, asylum, and penitentiary would house some of the university's early offices and classrooms. Los Andes continued climbing up the hill and stretching sideways through the acquisition of several other properties that had been vital to this working-class, industrial periphery: the Germania Brewery and its warehouses; the Richard hat factory and Richard textile manufacturing plant, later turned into a religious hospital and asylum with an attached chapel; and the Fenicia glass and bottle factory, which would give the renewal plan its name decades later. The conservative and elitist roots of Los Andes's modernizing agendas were congealed in the campus's traditional religious and industrial architecture: technocratic enlightenment inhabiting the material shells of institutions of social discipline and reform. The cloister of *técnicos letrados* would thus sit above a reality it either disavowed or would manage at a distance and on its own terms.[22] A piece of graffiti in the 1980s, which became a well-known expression in local circles, put it best: "[The University of los Andes] facing Monserrate and with its back to the country."

This did not mean that the university envisioned a campus severed from its surroundings. On the contrary, Los Andes would become a critical force in the reshaping of the east side of downtown Bogotá and of planning expertise more broadly. Early on, the university rendered Las Aguas and other surrounding historic and working-class neighborhoods into objects of technical knowledge and intervention. Crucial in this regard was the creation in 1964 of the Centro de Planificación y Urbanismo (Center for Planning and Urbanism), or CPU, within

FIGURE 6.1. Germania Brewery, 1951. Photo by Saúl Orduz. Fondo Saúl Orduz/ Collección Museo de Bogotá.

the Faculty of Architecture and Design. The mission of the CPU, according to its first director, was to "promote and carry out studies related to the problems of territorial ordering, and urban and metropolitan development."[23] Among its many research projects on zoning, housing, and development, the CPU led key urban renewal studies in downtown Bogotá in the 1960s in coordination with the city administration of Virgilio Barco.

One of these studies, a precursor to the Fenicia plan, was completed in 1967. In line with the densification discourse of Lauchlin Currie and Mayor Barco (see chapter 1), CPU researchers presented Las Aguas as "an ideal sector for urban concentration, capable of containing a significant number of inhabitants." They recommended "its urban remodeling [*remodelación urbana*] with the aim of improving current land uses." For university researchers, this meant primarily "land uses for middle-income housing and adequate facilities for cultural and educational institutions."[24] The class and racial overtones of such a proposal were apparent in the photographs appended to the study. A panoramic view of old rooftops and smokestacks included the caption "Confusion of housing and industry." Close-up views of peasant markets—*campesinas* with children in arms and foodstuffs arranged on the sidewalk—were described as "improvised" and stood alongside other photos of hillside erosion and improper waste disposal. Overall, CPU architects overlooked the realities of urban labor, housing, and popular economies and portrayed them instead as "problems" that required a technical solution through the consolidation of a middle-class university and residential district. If the university had been born from the ashes of El Bogotazo to "rebuild the nation," its first steps beyond its walls suggested a rebuilding in its own image and far from the grounded realities of urban life. At stake here were the same politics of detached, gentlemanly civility and institutional entrench-ment through which urban elites had long ignored the complexities of Colombia's sweeping violence and its integral connections to modern citizenship, property, and governance. University planners' proposals to "improve current land uses" disregarded downtown's history of working-class struggle over space and belong-ing. This was a striking disavowal for a university founded in the aftermath of the widespread destruction of El Bogotazo and amid unprecedented rural displace-ment to the city as war raged in the countryside.

Although the 1967 renewal plan was never implemented, fragments of its vision for a densified, middle-class neighborhood materialized in the following decades. The old Fenicia glass factory was demolished in the late 1960s, and pri-vate developers erected two thirty-one-story residential towers, the Torres Feni-cia, in its place. Owners increasingly let aging houses collapse, repurposing plots as parking garages to serve the university's growing population. Flanking modest cafeterias and corner shops, a large car-armoring plant became a blunt reminder of the area's industrial past and of its variegated land uses and piecemeal transfor-mations. By the 1980s, a few middle-class apartment buildings had been erected on the western edge of the neighborhood, and residents continued to add floors to their self-built homes for additional rental income, while others assembled precarious shacks on the vacant public land on the eastern slope. During this period, Los Andes crept out of its hillside enclave more decidedly. Together with the neighboring Universidad Jorge Tadeo Lozano and Universidad de América, by the 1980s and 1990s the university had become a central actor in the city's plans to reverse "urban deterioration," "recover public space," and attract new middle-class residents to the city center.[25] Los Andes gradually turned toward Las Aguas and into the several blocks known as Germania, which the university eventually renamed Fenicia. These decades were marked by significant construc-tion both within and outside the university campus, the almost doubling in size of its student body, and transformative public works such as the construction of the nearby Eje Ambiental (1996–2001)—the walkway that had partially uncov-ered and canalized the Río San Francisco—and the renovation of the Parque Espinosa (2005), a small park on the north side of campus.[26]

Most notably, in 2007 the university inaugurated a main university building on the other side of the Eje Ambiental, moving directly into Las Aguas. Developed in a vacant lot that had long operated as a parking garage next to the 1970s Torres Fenicia, the ten-story glass and metal structure would now house the Facultad de Administración (School of Management) in the very core of the neighborhood. For many, the building epitomized the university's increasing encroachment in the area. Residents often remarked on its "ugly architecture," particularly the building's north and south windowless black facades, evidence of Los Andes's indifference to the people living under its shadow. Further compounding the sense of elite intrusion, the building was named after one of Colombia's richest men and the university's most important benefactor, Julio Mario Santo Domingo. The name was resonant. Starting in the mid-twentieth century, the Santo Domingo family had consolidated its control over the Bavaria brewing company, originally founded by German Jewish immigrant Leo Kopp, and subsidiaries such as the Fenicia bottling factory in Las Aguas. With its armed security guards and watchdogs, the glittering Santo Domingo building, or Bloque SD (SD Block), seemed to point to the return of the capitalist landowner. It was the replay of the history of industrial patronage and authority that had loomed over the working-class area for decades: The ivory tower rose as a "new smokestack" in the changing neighborhood.[27]

FIGURE 6.2.   SD building on the far right, and the main campus on the left. Photo by the author.

The Bloque SD would operate as the main outpost from which administrators and faculty devised and launched the Progresa Fenicia plan. "The university has always been facing Monserrate with its back turned toward the city," Carolina, the senior university administrator, said, invoking the well-worn adage, "and we need to reverse that!" Inevitably, however, this alleged reversal under Progresa Fenicia, and its promises of inclusion and collaboration, would be set against the backdrop of decades of technocratic indifference, material encroachments and inequalities, and tacit university control over the fate of the downtown neighborhood and its residents.

"You're Not Neighbors!"

In late November 2011, a group of residents walked up to the Bloque SD to attend a public meeting organized by the Progresa Fenicia team. For most of them, this was their first time walking past campus guards and watchdogs and into a university building. As one elderly woman entered the tall atrium through the electronic turnstiles, she looked up in awe and whispered, "*Qué bonito* [how beautiful]," while others behind her noted with contempt how they had never been invited into the massive structure despite living under its towering presence.

The roughly sixty neighbors assembled in a lecture hall on the eighth floor, where a handful of professors and university administrators presented the Progresa Fenicia plan and answered questions. Alejandro, a middle-aged professor of public management and policy, addressed the audience with the calm of an approachable professor and the blasé tone of a seasoned bureaucrat: "Last year we told the city government, 'We want to change the focus of the Fenicia plan and have a new focus in which we take people into account [*que tenga en cuenta a la gente*].'" He clicked to the next PowerPoint slide: "What we did was rethink the scheme and create an entire program called Progresa Fenicia that tries to work with residents to improve their economic, social, and urbanistic conditions."

A mother calmed a crying baby in the back as residents followed the presentation with a mix of concern, confusion, and lack of interest. Collecting "information" about the neighborhood, Alejandro explained, had been vital to confirm the viability of the project. "We need to know who *they* are," he said, inadvertently making apparent the distance between university planners and residents. "[We need to know] who *we* are!" he added, quickly switching to the first person, stepping back into a conversational, more intimate tone. Preliminary "diagnostics" and a "census" had showed that the project was possible, Alejandro continued, and it was now necessary to refine and deepen that information to ensure that "we don't have to leave [the area], that those of us who want to stay can stay."

Over the course of the meeting, the rhetoric of collaborative knowledge and associative planning unraveled. The setting itself, with residents sitting behind the classroom's long white tables and professors and planners lecturing in front, was revealing of the hierarchies that underpinned the exchange. The meeting restaged bureaucratic *socialización* (socialization), as procedural participation is known in policy circles in Bogotá, through a form of educational authority: the imparting of knowledge on the unlearned. As Progresa Fenicia team members took to the stage to describe the "components" of the plan and the "diagnostic work" they had thus far carried out, the tensions between the coproduction and extraction of knowledge became more apparent.

Miguel, a lead architect from the campus management office, began by recognizing that urban renewal in Bogotá had largely "gotten off on the wrong foot [*entradas con el pie izquierdo*]": "[This is when promoters] launch a project with a *render* [architectural rendering], that's spectacular and shines—"

"Pardon me, what's a *render*?" Alejandro interjected, nudging Miguel to use less technical jargon, as residents snickered in the back.

"Excuse me, good question, it's an image of a project, a drawing that gives an idea of the future [in a particular place], and it's typically large towers with a lot of glass that don't include what used to be there and those who used to be there." He assured the audience that Progresa Fenicia would reverse this tendency through a form of "collective construction" that recognized "diversity" in the neighborhood: "This place we call the *barrio*, the community, is not a single thing; diverse communities are located here, and they are not easily aggregated, but they all share the same space." University experts, Miguel continued, had a "great responsibility" to learn from residents' "knowledges, experiences, stories" and to use that "great mass of knowledge" in the creation of a vision for a future with a place for everyone.

Two unspoken assumptions were embedded in the presentation. The first was that it would be professors and planners who would assemble this body of knowledge and establish the corresponding epistemic categories. And the second was the idea of urban reconstruction as an a priori, inescapable process. "Transformations will keep on happening [whether we like it or not]," as Miguel put it, compelling residents to participate in downtown renewal rather than question its foundations. University planners' interactions with residents tacitly centered a particular worldview. With their talk of inclusionary redevelopment, they projected middle-class ideals of citizenship and progress as universal, unquestioned aspirations. At stake here, following feminist theory, was a distinctive "standpoint," a privileged position that permeated knowledge production, defined the questions that mattered, and simultaneously obscured the situatedness of planning expertise.[28] Despite its progressive intentions, Progresa Fenicia enacted a form of knowledge from the *center*, which ultimately revealed more about university planners' presuppositions about liberal values of property and governance than about residents' urban experiences and understandings. This mode of seeing failed to recognize that residents themselves had for decades elaborated forms of knowledge from the *margins* about state displacement and oppression closely linked to Los Andes as its powerful landowning neighbor and occasional employer.[29]

It was thus unsurprising that residents had been wary of a "census of living conditions" that the university had piloted months earlier. At some point Silvia, an administration professor specializing in community development, took the microphone and reviewed the several activities—community meetings, workshops, focus groups, and the census—that Progresa Fenicia had organized to understand the "conditions" and "needs" of the population. Significantly, such exercises had portrayed residents' lived realities as "problems" requiring the "design of adequate proposals" to find "solutions."[30] Silvia pulled up a slide that gave a bird's-eye view of the neighborhood and its estimated 1,628 residents. She noted, for instance, that 55 percent of workers in the area were independent: "If we are thinking about a model of economic development that allows people who want to stay to actually be able to stay in the zone, we have to understand who those independent workers are." While Silvia was acutely aware of the difficulties of the redevelopment partnership and was committed to illuminating the many obstacles residents would face, she did not question the assumptions behind the plan or the imperative to participate. Silvia concluded her intervention by admitting that "the census had had significant coverage in some blocks, but very little in others." She called on the silent crowd to help improve and supplement the information available to the Progresa Fenicia plan. For her and her colleagues, the key was to gather more knowledge about the neighborhood and create mechanisms to include as many people as possible in the project. Obscured were questions about the necessity itself of renewal and the very terms in which residents and their homes would be conceived and incorporated into the plan.

These tensions became apparent with the intervention of Camilo, the team's legal expert. A savvy and knowledgeable consultant, lecturer, and lawyer, Camilo was one of Progresa Fenicia's main architects and a passionate critic of the city's recent history of exclusionary renewal. In our many conversations about the plan over lunch, he would describe himself as the "man *without* a suitcase." Far from negotiating sale prices with property owners—a common role for real estate lawyers, not to mention legal swindlers and scammers—Camilo had been developing a methodology to determine the "juridical situation [*situación jurídica*]" of properties so that residents could become partners in the project. Attempting to be as didactic as possible, Camilo explained to the audience the color-coding system, or "traffic light," that the team had devised, as he showed a map of the neighborhood's more than five hundred land parcels: green meant no restrictions to become a partner in the plan; yellow represented a legal condition easy to solve, such as shared tenure; gray was lack of information; and red pointed to a complex situation such as ongoing lawsuits, foreclosures, or possession. Sensing some unrest among attendees, Camilo stressed that it was critical to establish "properties' legal *aptitude* to be part of the project."

An elderly man stood up and waved his arms with exasperation, interrupting the presentation. "This is a violation of confidential information and of our freedom. You never consulted with us."

Camilo tried to be conciliatory. "Your opinion is very valid. We understand the perception of a transgression of privacy, but to be totally clear, this information is public, and anyone can access it." In any case, he added, it was still crucial for residents to cooperate and "validate" the information. Alejandro stepped in to appease the audience, explaining that the planning team had gathered data with the sole purpose of "designing a proposal that would allow us to redevelop the area, to secure local residents' permanence, and to make sure that people would stay and develop [*permanecieran desarrollándose*]." Shifting the responsibility back to residents, he argued that the success of the plan and its promises of permanence and inclusion depended on them: "If we all contribute, we all win [*todos ponemos, todos ganamos*]." He called on residents to refrain from selling their properties and consider instead their future gains as owners within a dense, redeveloped neighborhood. "But the project is not viable," he warned, "if we open spaces for intermediaries who want to speculate."

More was at stake in these exchanges than a disagreement over the mechanics of the redevelopment partnership. It was the underlying power differentials— the structuring conditions of the meeting and of any potential partnership—that were at the center of residents' increasing discontent. A visibly upset homeowner, for instance, raised concerns about residents' "economic capacity" to become partners in the project. He slowly but insistently asked about the steps the university would take to examine the issue. Every time Alejandro attempted to respond, the man interrupted with a reformulation of the question. "You're not the only ones who can speak here!" the man finally protested. He was voicing a sense of inequality between the university and local dwellers over the control of the terms of the discussion.

In contrast to university planners' newfound desire to know their neighbors, residents had for years tracked Los Andes's moves within the area, in particular its property purchases, making it difficult to reconcile everyday material realities with the idea of a redevelopment partnership. The university's proposal appeared as elite indifference or, at its worst, cynicism—a form of epistemic violence.[31]

One man articulated this fundamental lopsidedness later in the meeting.[32] Using paused and formal speech—seemingly gesturing to the genre of the professorial lecture and its politics of decorum and knowledgeability—the man pointed out the contradiction between the "principles" that planners talked about and the "university's behavior": "If you walk around the area, you'll find that the university has acquired several large properties. The university has expanded rapidly: Take this building where we are right now, or the new library, or the communal park, which is practically the university's property. All of this shows no reciprocity. What trust or assurance can we have?"

An elderly woman, one of the many retirees who lived in the neighborhood, stood up next, visibly agitated. "What does the Universidad de los Andes want?" she asked. "What does it want? You tell me! What does it want? [Does it want] to rebuild all of this? [Does it want] to take our homes away from us?" Alejandro spoke into the microphone again, in his most conciliatory voice, assuring the attendees that the university only wanted people to remain in the neighborhood and become partners in the project. He then added, invoking a sense of commonality, "We [professors and administrators] also want to stay here, as neighbors [*como vecinos*]," to which a man in the back immediately retorted, "You're not neighbors; you live in the north!"

Alejandro, with Miguel now backing him, tried to appease the crowd by going over the mechanics of the redevelopment partnership once again. They started by reminding the audience that Los Andes was a "university, not a real estate company" and that Progresa Fenicia was not a "rent-seeking scheme." Instead, to "escape the commercial logic," the plan included multiple modes of association so that property owners could obtain new apartments at no additional cost. By tripling the neighborhood's density, Miguel stressed, "[the real estate profits brought in by] new residents would pay for urban improvements and for local dwellers' new apartments." For residents, however, such technical assurances were moot, as their concerns lay with the broader and long-standing power differentials that had structured the relations between the university and the neighborhood.

Pointing to this underlying history of material conflicts, a middle-aged apartment owner commented on what he saw as the contradictions inherent to the promise of inclusionary revitalization, and he invoked the specter of land grabbing and dispossession. "I work in the Indigenous sector," the man declared, "and this is how Indigenous communities have lost their territory." He drew out the connection by calling attention to the epistemic and political-economic struggles at the core of the plan: "You talk a lot about how the university has scientists and we're all aware that this is one of the highest-ranked universities in Latin America. But the community also has its *saberes*, its knowledges. So, I respectfully would like us to open a space, not for information, but for us to work together." At stake for him were the material conditions of knowledge production. Not only had the university established the epistemological parameters of urban revitalization, the man concluded, but professors and administrators inevitably remained beholden to the larger economic forces shaping the project. "You are professors, but you are not the owners of the university," the man concluded, "and when large investors enter the scheme, how can we be sure the terms of the partnership will not change?"

Epistemic Dissonance

The friction between the material politics of expert knowledge production and the neighborhood's everyday realities and *saberes* intensified in the following months. As rumors about the plan continued to circulate among residents, university planners held weekly "executive meetings" on a top floor of the Bloque SD and expanded their presence in the neighborhood through surveys, town halls, and social outreach. By this point the Progresa Fenicia team had accepted my presence as a regular "observer" and, eventually, as a collaborator in the organization of academic events related to the plan. This had happened not without ambivalence on their part. Some university experts seemed uncomfortable with the idea of having a tagalong anthropologist with undeclared allegiances, while others, for whom Progresa Fenicia was primarily a research endeavor and a form of epistemic experimentation, were more than welcoming. As Camilo, the team's legal expert and my closest friend in the group, once told me half-jokingly, "I will always be happy to be your object of anthropological research."

If my relationship with the planning team was permeated by the tensions between knowledge production and its unspoken politics, so was the preparation and implementation of the plan itself. In experts' everyday routines, the plan's broader political contexts and ramifications lurked uncomfortably—repressed and submerged—in the background. They inevitably resurfaced time and again only to be reluctantly acknowledged or willfully ignored. This was apparent, for instance, in the everyday spatiality of the planning process. While experts talked every week about collaborative knowledge and associative development, they did so from the heights of the Bloque SD meeting room. The impulse to plan *alongside* residents stood at odds with experts' continued gaze from above. As Miguel, the lead architect, once told me, looking out into the neighborhood from an SD balcony, "Down there it's very similar to the country's situation with all its conflicts but at a micro scale; that's the challenge we're taking up with the intervention."

Such dissonances were further materialized with the university's acquisition of two houses in the area to set up Progresa Fenicia social outreach programs and meeting spaces. The paradox of serving the community while further expanding property control was not lost on all the experts. As the planning process advanced and conflicts deepened, planners occasionally sought to mitigate such jarring contrasts. In one meeting, for example, team members cautioned that university architects affiliated with the project had been taking photographs of the neighborhood as they worked on their initial designs. "This is just going to make people more nervous," one expert noted, calling for all contact with residents and documentation of the area to be closely monitored. Tracking such contradictory orientations toward the project and following planners' reckoning with the contentious undersides of the progressive plan became central to my ethnographic work. This reckoning, I should clarify, was theirs as much as it was mine. Being similarly positioned to them in terms of class, race, and sociocultural background, I was equally confronted with the complicities and disavowals of my own epistemic praxis. In this sense, my analysis here emerges as much from following university experts' practices as from my own process of learning about the plan and recognizing its unsettling implications and underlying paradoxes.

Tensions within the planning team came to a head when Progresa Fenicia recruited a group of university ethnographers to assist in deepening the information previously gathered through a preliminary census. Ideals associated with the "collective construction of space [*construcción colectiva espacial*]" came up against what experts called a "viable financial model." For Tomás, a professor in

FIGURE 6.3. Architects at work in Las Aguas. Photo by the author.

the social sciences, and José, a doctoral student, the plan presented a problematic contradiction between the ethics of collaborative knowledge and the plan's real estate imperatives. As coordinators of the new qualitative study—which included home visits and interviews—they viewed their role within the plan with discomfort and wariness. During an initial meeting between them and the Progresa Fenicia team, Alejandro suggested that the group imagine the ethnographers as "vendors of options [to enter the project]" and residents as "clients." Embracing an extractive approach to knowledge production, the team's financial expert added that the social researchers should not "miss any opportunity to get [*sacar*] more information out of residents." I glanced over to Tomás and José and saw them wince, as another professor quipped, "That sounds like an insurance broker." From Alejandro's managerial perspective, the study was a key instrument of negotiation. Tomás and José, for their part, were reluctant to frame their participation in such terms. As Tomás later warned in the meeting, "Our role will not be to try to get people to sign on to the project." After a moment of silence, Alejandro restated his point, seeking to placate the social scientists: The objective of the survey, he said, "is getting information that will assist us in making decisions, period."

The tensions between extracting information, negotiating development partnerships, and collaboratively composing urban knowledges continued to reappear in the day-to-day ethnographic work. In an early meeting with the four recent anthropology graduates hired to carry out the fieldwork, Tomás urged the young women to remember that they were not "real estate brokers." The aims of their ethnographic study, however, had already been the result of a compromise. While Tomás and José had originally envisioned open-ended, semistructured interviews as their main methodology, others on the planning team insisted on gathering specific data about ownership, income, and land use. In one sense, the study had thus ended up looking more like a standard socioeconomic census (*censo socioeconómico*) with actionable questions about property and tenure. At the same time, the new ethnographic survey opened spaces to make visible other social realities within the neighborhood.

Tomás and José advised the fieldworkers to "avoid unitary stories" and "reject the assumption that everyone who lives in the same conditions has the same narrative." They insisted on the need to reconstruct people's "temporal orientations" and "senses of place" by attending to their "life plans [*planes de vida*]." In his work on community- and place-based design, Arturo Escobar follows the idea of planes de vida conceptualized by Colombian Indigenous and Afro-descendant peoples as a promising path to envision alternative futures outside the parameters of capitalist modernity.[33] For Tomás and José, something similar was at stake in Las Aguas. "The biggest challenge," Tomás told the four young researchers, "is to understand how two different life logics [*lógicas de vida*]"—those of the university and the neighborhood—"coexist in the area." Ethnographers thus deployed the notion of planes de vida to repoliticize knowledge production within Progresa Fenicia. In doing so, they strategically reified the neighborhood as the embodiment of urban precariousness and informality.[34] Contrary to their initial call to attend to the multiple narratives within the neighborhood, Tomás and José demarcated, as sharply as possible, the lines of difference between the plan's assumptions and the everyday realities of insecure labor, tenuous ownership, and lived uncertainty in Las Aguas. For them, this "quotidian economy [*economía de la cotidianidad*]" was at odds with the long-term temporal horizon and stability necessitated by the redevelopment partnership.

This epistemic disjuncture became apparent in discussions about tenements (*inquilinatos*). A common living arrangement in downtown Bogotá for decades, inquilinatos had been traditionally defined as "shared housing," where, according to a 1970s university study, several households rented and "shared communal spaces such as patios, hallways, yards . . . kitchen, bathrooms, and laundry."[35] As elites moved out of the city center during the twentieth century, dilapidated estates were subdivided and repurposed as precarious rentals by absentee owners.[36] Inquilinos and the increasingly deteriorated structures they inhabited would become integral to class-inflected and racialized representations of downtown decay. Although shared housing continued to be a key modality of residence in central areas in later decades, it was increasingly working-class property owners or poseedores themselves who would rent out rooms within their homes. Shared housing unsettled dominant assumptions about ownership and residence, posing a direct challenge to Progresa Fenicia. Not only did such arrangements house the neighborhood's most impoverished residents and represent a main source of income for homeowners, but they did not fit neatly with the ideology of individual property so central to the plan.[37]

During a meeting in early March 2012, Tomás and José gestured to such deep-seated tensions between local forms of housing and the plan's property partnership scheme. They referred to the case of a two-story house from the early twentieth century in which several families had lived for years without a property title. Each family had its separate living space and shared common areas, and although they were all relatives, they paid rent to the older couple that lived on the upper floor. The social scientists argued that the house was an "inquilinato" and that it exemplified the "subsistence economy" of many neighborhood residents who lived on precarious incomes and lacked basic utilities. To further illustrate such deprivation, José recalled how, during their first visit to the house, the young fieldworkers had been shocked to discover that it was flooded with sewage from a burst pipe.

Miguel, the campus architect, objected to their description. "I'm not sure that we should call this an inquilinato. It isn't really on the market so it would require a different treatment within the plan."

"In terms of its internal organization," Tomás insisted, somewhat irritated, "it does operate as an inquilinato."

"Sometimes they call this *allegamiento*," Miguel noted, referring to a situation where *allegados* (relatives) share housing.

"But they pay rent and share services and space," José interjected. The fact that the families shared the house as kin but also paid rent emerged as an anomaly within the plan's categories. It was neither individual property nor rental space.

The "legal solution," Camilo suggested, "would be to consider all the tenants as poseedores, but that would make the whole thing a mess." It would entail a legal procedure through which the residents could obtain shared ownership over the house given the prolonged absence of a property owner. At stake here was not only change in tenure but also the transformation of social relations and kinship dynamics. This ultimately raised questions about what the plan could offer in the renovated neighborhood to extended working-class families such as this one. It was apparent to the experts that new units in an apartment building would not work. As planners considered the problem for a few minutes, José broke the silence by sarcastically pointing to the limits of the plan's allegedly progressive property scheme: "[Can the plan offer] progressive inquilinatos?"

Tomás and José's deployment of the notion of *inquilinato* was deliberately political. It drew attention to those who were "most vulnerable" and who lived in the most precarious conditions. But other Progresa Fenicia team members seemed wary of the category's implications. If they "discovered" too many inquilinatos, Miguel intimated, they would have to devise impossibly robust policies to relocate all impoverished tenants or create alternatives for them to become homeowners. For many university experts, the focus was therefore on individual property owners and their various forms of tenure and livelihoods. For them it was imperative to recognize the neighborhood's heterogeneity and the multiplicity of actors that were well positioned to become part of the plan. This afforded a space of negotiation and compromise. More than inquilinatos, they talked, for example, about productive households (*viviendas productivas*), where tenants were recast as sources of income and owners or possessors came to the fore. Such perspectives ultimately privileged ideals of capitalist productivity and individual ownership in line with the plan.

Throughout the planning process, the construction of epistemic categories produced certain kinds of inhabitants while making others less visible, and it rendered certain forms of ownership and belonging legible while obscuring others. Despite their skepticism of Progresa Fenicia, even the social scientists had reproduced the power dynamics of the university-led plan by imposing the reified category of inquilinatos. As one of the young ethnographers commented after a morning interview with a tenant, "[Our supervisors, Tomás and José,] seem to already know what they're going to find"—namely, "informality" and "marginality." Despite political differences within the planning team, the production of knowledge was thus largely a unidirectional process led by experts, one that left little space for local actors' self-representations. Residents' grounded knowledges of urban land and ownership, of long-standing histories of conflict and violence, not only remained out of sight but were subsumed under categories mapped onto them from above.

Progressive Fictions

With planning events and social outreach in full swing by late 2012, the Progresa Fenicia team set up a voicemail box to get feedback from residents. Soon afterward, Camilo listened to a disturbing recording. The voice at the other end did not comment on increased costs of living, replacement housing, or the risks of partnering with the university. Instead the anonymous caller made a short and blunt threat: "If you keep on messing with the neighborhood you're going to get bombed." More than he was concerned about the threat, Camilo was unsettled by the irruption of the talk of violence.

Over the previous two years, university planners had crafted a narrative about progress, participation, and collective improvement. Far from the destructiveness of previous downtown plans and their security-centric rhetoric, they had recast renewal—what they now called revitalization—as a platform for inclusionary community building and development. Yet such reframings had immediately struck many residents as *puro cuento* (stories or cheap talk). While Progresa Fenicia team members typically interpreted such reactions as lack of trust or as misrepresentations of the university's intentions, for locals something more significant was at stake. For them these were not simply lies but rather, following urban geographers D. Asher Ghertner and Robert Lake, dangerous "land fictions": "social stories" that not only reinvented "land qua commodity but land as a particularly socially indexed commodity, one that promises to transform its uses and hence its users in ways that align with desirable social imaginaries of value."[38] In this regard, a homeowner and longtime street vendor who worked in the neighborhood told me candidly, "This isn't going to be for the poor. . . . We have been taught to live differently. [If the project becomes a reality] I will probably say, 'How nice,' but I won't be able to stay."

FIGURE 6.4. Progresa Fenicia participatory design workshop. Photo by the author.

Residents interpreted the university's progressive land fictions through the experience of pervasive and long-standing conflicts over urban property and space. For most people, ownership had been gained through sustained struggles, which often turned violent, with rival land claimants as well as local authorities. From this vantage point, the bombing threat that had shocked Camilo was not so surprising. It was a manifestation of the violent undersides of property regimes and a reminder that the university's incursion did not happen in a vacuum. Its role as the promoter of the plan—however well-intentioned and conciliatory— emerged as a bid to consolidate authority within the neighborhood's patchwork trajectories of territorial control. Moreover, the speculative uncertainties created by Progresa Fenicia catalyzed local divisions and hardened power differentials. Behind the veneer of participatory negotiation, and beyond expert representations of a space of properties and land uses, lay a fractious terrain of disputes, misappropriation, destruction, and displacement.

Unbeknownst to most students, faculty, and staff who walked through Las Aguas daily, visited its cafeterias, and used the area's makeshift parking lots, the neighborhood had long been a destination for people fleeing violence in rural areas. A family of seven, for example, had been displaced from their land in Marinilla in the department of Antioquia in the early 2000s under the pressure of both guerrilla and paramilitary forces. I met the father—his campesino past still visible in his worn work clothes and rugged hands—while following the Progresa

Fenicia ethnographers during one of their field visits. The family rented a dilapidated colonial-style house across the street from the Bloque SD. Part of its orange tile roof was collapsing, its courtyard was cluttered, and two of its four rooms had been repurposed as sewing shops where the family worked. The interview proceeded as usual with questions about occupation, tenure status, income, and cost of living. But when one of the anthropologists asked about his arrival to Las Aguas, the man stopped, and his voice quivered. He talked about how "*paracos* [paramilitaries] were sanguinary to the core" and described the violence he had seen before fleeing: children with signs of torture, a cracked head, a campesino dragged by an SUV. "Every day these images come back," he told us. After one of the young ethnographers uncomfortably turned back to her script and asked about his family's opinion about the plan, the man simply stated, "We want [the university] to let us live here, to live in peace."

The university's focus on property development and its lack of attention to these grounded histories made it unwittingly complicit in local land conflicts and displacements. Such entanglements never reached the planning table, with experts either treating them as mere anecdotes or remaining oblivious to their occurrence. One revealing story involved a family of six who had been recently displaced from Huila, a department in southwestern Colombia. With the help of Eduardo, a longtime possessor of a small parking lot, the family had settled into a vacant house owned by the city in the main entrance to the neighborhood. Family members could be seen every afternoon selling arepas and chorizos to passersby from a small grill on the sidewalk. Eventually authorities evicted them, and the university acquired the house, demolished it, equipped it with a shipping container turned planning office, and created an urban vegetable garden in the back. Gesturing to the imagery of sustainable urbanism, the cutting-edge Progresa Fenicia office had ironically contributed to the family's renewed displacement. While I was chatting one afternoon with Eduardo about his own struggle to remain in place, the newly evicted mother and grandmother walked by and asked if we knew of any other vacant houses in the neighborhood. "So many abandoned houses in downtown," the elderly woman complained. "How about that big gray house on Twenty-First Street; isn't that one empty?" her daughter asked. Eduardo recalled how a young man who had been a tenant there had taken over the house a few years earlier. He was not sure if the man was still there, but he could assure the women of one thing: "If you are going to take over a house like that, you have to be ready to stand your ground with your life."

Residents who arrived in the neighborhood escaping rural violence—from the older generations who fled La Violencia in the mid-twentieth century to recent arrivals caught in the crossfire of paramilitary, guerrilla, and state violence— had not merely "resettled" in the city. More than "adaptation, integration, and

FIGURE 6.5. The university's planning office/container on the site of the previously squatted-in house. Photo by the author.

assimilation," as Andrés Salcedo Fidalgo importantly argues, at stake here were processes of "reconstruction" linked to the recomposition of social relations and the "production of spaces."[39] At the same time, agonistic practices associated with rural property conflicts were translated and rematerialized in the construction of urban housing—what residents often called their ranchos, a throwback to the rural smallholding. In Las Aguas, the possession of land through gradual improvements (*mejoras*) and its constant defense from legal and extralegal threats of expulsion echoed through urban dwellers' everyday experience. But such practices and conflicts did not simply migrate from the countryside into the city with the displaced families who squatted in abandoned houses or built shacks on the hillside. Rather, as I have been arguing in this book, they were integral to the city's modern regimes of property and development. The logics of land and state violence were at the very core of urban knowledges and their sedimentation in downtown spaces. For residents of Las Aguas, such material histories unsettled the university's progressive fictions, bringing to light the underlying and contradictory politics of appropriation.

Sara, an elderly single mother of a disabled adult son, elaborated on the intimate connection between the logics of violent (dis)possession and her path toward home ownership.[40] She had bought her small rancho in the 1980s at a very low price from a taxi driver who had received threats and decided to leave. "But I had it very hard too," Sara recalled pensively, sitting in the sparsely stocked cafeteria she ran out of her small living room. Since her arrival, her clean and well-organized home and cafeteria had collided with the street's aesthetics: its "dingy bars, brothels, and clouds of smoke." Almost immediately after moving into her house and reconditioning it for her modest business, she was pressured by local drug dealers and brothel owners to aid in their illicit operations. Her refusal increased animosity from neighbors, leading up to a critical event in the 1990s: "They put a revolver to my chest. It was a woman who ran a repair shop across the street, one of the toughest families in the area." This was part of an attempt to get her to leave the neighborhood and give up her house. "But I went back up to them," she continued, "and I told them they would have to buy my house or kill me." Tensions had resurfaced more recently when the house next to hers was abandoned by its owners and "people tried to invade it." Sara decided to "take charge of the property," carrying out repairs and making sure no one got in. Other residents looking to appropriate the house "declared a war" against her and accused her of "hiding thieves and drugs" behind the restored facade. In the end, the house remained vacant, its entrances sealed, with Sara claiming she had only been trying "to benefit the community."

Other residents similarly pointed to the dangers associated with home building and ownership. A street vendor explained how the remodeling of the first

FIGURE 6.6. Las Aguas homeowner and her stalled remodeling project. Photo by the author.

two floors of her auto-constructed home had antagonized some neighbors, "people who think they own the barrio." When they saw construction materials and the changing appearance of her home, they sent city officials to inspect the construction—an oblique threat to her tenure. Another property owner had endured more overt attacks from a family who had been after her house: They threw bricks on her roof every week, both to scare her and to deteriorate the well-kept structure. Conversely, a local store owner with no legal title took great pains to build up and improve his house in order to have more legal security and avoid expropriation. And yet another homeowner with a unique penchant for vernacular design had incorporated security features into his house—such as concealed lookout openings—to "keep an eye on the street" and prevent squatting in neighboring structures and the theft of electrical wiring and exposed metal pipes. In all these cases, urban property was imbued with the conflicts and insecurities associated with the threat of dispossession. Sara concluded her story about the trials of home ownership by commenting on the university's plan and gesturing to the country's broader currents of land violence: "You know, I really pity those poor peasants who get thrown off their lands."

For Ramiro, an attorney and newspaper editor who owned a small two-story house, it was difficult to disentangle Progresa Fenicia from the lasting threats of downtown displacement. "I just hope the same thing doesn't happen [to us] with the university plan," he told me as he recounted his beleaguered path toward property ownership in the city center. His early life had been marked by state dispossession. He was born to a family of watchmakers, and his parents had bought a small colonial-style house in the historic Santa Bárbara neighborhood near the Plaza de Bolívar after years of living in inquilinatos and rentals. Ramiro and his family lived there "until the Banco Central Hipotecario [state mortgage lender] started to dismember the neighborhood [in the early 1980s]" for a state-led renewal plan (see chapter 1). "[Authorities] started buying houses . . . just like [the Universidad de] Los Andes is doing now!" Ramiro noted. The family opposed the plan fiercely and was "the last in the block" to accept the forced purchase.

Displaced by renewal, in the late 1980s Ramiro and his family arrived in Las Aguas, where they clung to their precarious middle-class status amid poverty and criminal bands vying for control. "It was a very tough area when we arrived," he recalled. Given this history, Ramiro found university experts' detachment from downtown territorial struggles and property violence troubling: "Do they really want us as neighbors [in the future development]? I don't think so." For him, the fact that power differentials had been left intact—with the university dictating the terms of the participatory planning process and establishing the parameters of land values—preserved the violence of exclusionary property regimes and tacitly devalued his sense of ownership and belonging. This was the continuation of the "expulsion of *raizales* [original populations]" he had experienced earlier in his life, what he remembered as a violent urban dismemberment but now under the promise of progressive revitalization and its fictions of inclusionary development.

Between Equals?

Eventually local dissent became impossible to ignore. Apartment owners in Multifamiliares Calle 20 (Multifamily Twentieth Street), a building complex constructed in the 1980s, emerged as the most visible force opposing Progresa Fenicia. In one sense, their mobilization was an expression of middle-class anxieties exacerbated by the plan. The uncertain future of renewal and its lingering threat of displacement deepened existing sociospatial divisions. Apartment buildings such as Multifamiliares had already been visibly separated from Las Aguas's older houses, tenements, and hillside shacks. They stood at the edges of the neighborhood, near main avenues and close to the campuses of Los Andes and the Universidad Jorge Tadeo Lozano. Surrounded by fencing and facing the renovated promenade of the Eje Ambiental, Multifamiliares had been an island in the working-class neighborhood. Residents of the modest apartment complex had also been deeply unsettled by the razing of Manzana Cinco that had unfolded directly across from the complex's main gate (see chapter 3). The plan and its calls for progress had thus unsettled what residents viewed as their hard-gained yet fragile social status and security. To reassert such distinctions, some apartment residents occasionally expressed disdain toward the people living past Twenty-Second Street and up the hill. During planning meetings, they often rejected the idea of relocating to shared buildings "with those people from up there." Some went as far as sending letters to officials at the Secretaría de Planeación, one functionary recalled, complaining about Progresa Fenicia and arguing that "the project should get rid of those people who live in shacks and tenements and leave us alone."

At the same time, apartment residents and nearby property and business owners created alliances with the broader community—including poorer homeowners, poseedores, and inquilinos. Not only was this a strategic move to catalyze opposition to the plan, but it also reflected a shared history and political consciousness around property struggles and belonging. Aligning with downtown-wide calls against "urban displacement" and "the defense of territory," the rising movement against Progresa Fenicia deployed repertoires of land violence that rematerialized Las Aguas as a battlefield closely linked to urban and national territorial conflicts. The name adopted by the opposition group, Comité No Se

Tomen Las Aguas, was revealing in this regard: Translating both to "Do not drink the waters" and "Do not take over the waters," it conjured the physical takeover of the neighborhood—an image resonant with the country's history of armed invasions of towns and villages. It represented Las Aguas as a kind of commons—the Waters—and the university as a sophisticated urban land grabber.

Under the banner of No Se Tomen Las Aguas, property owners and residents organized panels, film screenings, and town halls about the dangers of urban renewal. At the height of its activities in 2013, the group called for a march against the university's intervention. Residents carried torches and lit a small fire in the open space in front of one of Los Andes's main entrances. This protest would later be known by participants and Progresa Fenicia staff as the Marcha de las Antorchas (March of the Torches). Redolent of Bogotá's history of political violence, this had been the name of a massive manifestation against bipartisan violence led by leftist Liberal politician Jorge Eliécer Gaitán in 1947, one year before his assassination. The emblematic procession is said to have drawn around one hundred thousand people to the city center through highly coordinated grassroots organizing across working-class neighborhoods. This "river of fire," as Gaitán described the procession at the time, would become a symbol of the contained power of the urban masses as well as a foreshadowing of the undercurrents of urban violence that would surface during the Bogotazo uprising.[41] By deploying these repertoires of contention, No Se Tomen Las Aguas members sought to repoliticize the university plan and draw attention to the material histories of urban power and inequality that had shaped Las Aguas. Yet the mobilization of these histories, particularly in the hands of middle-class property owners, was replete with contradictions. The idea of a commons overrun by the university not only occluded frictions and struggles *within* the neighborhood but also tacitly reproduced normative ideals of ownership and citizenship. This was brought home to me by Nancy, one of the leaders of No Se Tomen Las Aguas.

Nancy and her partner, a downtown alderman (*edil*), were property owners in Multifamiliares, and although they no longer lived in the neighborhood, their ties to Las Aguas and the city center ran deep. The couple had built their legal clientele and political base, which were closely entwined, in the neighborhood and surrounding areas. Nancy was the embodiment of a downtown lawyer—for many university experts she represented the proverbial *tinterilla* (ink spiller). She litigated modest lawsuits, mostly for impoverished residents, and became closely involved with land disputes in the city center. Nancy had also become a regular dissenting voice at university town halls. She was always present in these gatherings and often made her way into smaller tenant and property-owner meetings carrying a folder of *poderes*—powers of attorney given to her by residents.

As a main organizer of No Se Tomen Las Aguas, Nancy had drawn on her long-running experience as a legal and political broker to widen local participation beyond the parameters established by Progresa Fenicia. For her, one of the group's main "social conquests" had come after the Marcha de las Antorchas when the city administration agreed to host a series of roundtables with community organizations and university planners. With the mediation of the city's Veeduría Distrital (Oversight Office), participants discussed guarantees for resettlement on the blocks on which they resided, an allocation of funds to mitigate the economic impacts of renewal, and the temporary suspension of rising utility costs in the renewed neighborhood.[42] These negotiation points would ultimately make it into the decree that sanctioned the Progresa Fenicia plan in 2014, as well as into subsequent regulations for the "protection of original property owners and dwellers."[43] Nancy was proud not only of the outcome but of the fact that No Se Tomen Las Aguas had been mentioned by name in one of the decrees. For her, this was a form of recognition and respect that had been all but absent in the university's participatory planning. Apartment residents and homeowners gradually accepted Progresa Fenicia—as the neighborhood's propertied middle class, Nancy herself admitted, they were well positioned to benefit from redevelopment. At the same time, Nancy continued to represent Las Aguas's most impoverished neighbors in their negotiations with the university, often acting as a vocal opposer in public settings.

After years of seeing only her public persona as a defender of the poor and witnessing planners' discomfort with her "double agenda," I was finally able to meet with Nancy in her downtown office in 2018. Located in a modernist mid-rise on the edges of the historic La Candelaria, her tiny law firm consisted of two cubicles brimming with legal volumes and court cases in leather binders. Nancy started by pointing out the enduring power differentials that surrounded the Progresa Fenicia plan as well as the university's initial disregard for local organizations. "I'm still very upset with the university," she told me, "because this is like a mosquito dealing with an elephant." Yet in describing the redevelopment conflict, Nancy traced her activism and professional beginnings not to property disputes but rather to *cocinol*: white gasoline used for cooking by the urban poor from the 1960s to the early 1990s. As a young law student, she had lived with her parents and sister in a house in Las Aguas not far from her apartment at Multifamiliares. In her daily walk to the Universidad Libre—a decidedly middle-class and secular university founded by Liberals in the late nineteenth century, where Jorge Eliécer Gaitán would serve as president in the 1930s—Nancy was always shocked by the long lines of women and children waiting to fill large plastic jugs (*bidones*) with cocinol. "It was almost like a punishment for the community, it seemed terrible to me," she recalled. Nancy probed further and realized that cocinol was at the center of neighborhood politics. The national Ministerio de Minas y Energía (Ministry of Mines and Energy) distributed the fuel to working-class homes that lacked propane gas or electric stoves. "So people got a *carné* [official card], and if they didn't have it," Nancy said, "well, they couldn't get the cocinol." As in other neighborhoods, the Junta de Acción Comunal (Community Action Council), or JAC, of Las Aguas became the key mediator in the distribution of the cards and the fuel. The access to cocinol, Nancy explained, "was part of the political, partisan pressure at the time in Bogotá, through the JACs."

Cocinol opened a contentious space of political engagement, government corruption, and illegal trade. Dubbed the "blue coca" by the newspaper *El Tiempo* in 1993 in reference to Colombia's explosive drug trade, the volatile gasoline not only was a leading cause of burns in the city but also became a sought-after commodity for clandestine networks that siphoned cocinol from delivery trucks and diluted the remaining load with petrodiesel or water.[44] In their role as local managers of beneficiary lists, members of JACs also allegedly manipulated cocinol distribution for individual gain and, most importantly, as a source of political capital. Cocinol was at the center of emblematic protests during those decades, such as a 1983 "pro-cocinol march" in the city center in which thousands of working-class residents protested cocinol scarcity.[45] In later years, calls for the transition from cocinol to natural gas in *barrios populares* also led to social mobilizations, such as the 1993 Paro Cívico de Ciudad Bolívar, a civic strike in Bogotá's largest working-class district.[46]

According to Nancy, cocinol became "a way to group people in relation to a necessity or, better, to instrumentalize them." She said these last words with a critical tone. Nonetheless, Nancy's career had been built precisely by harnessing cocinol mobilizations in Las Aguas. Amid government discussions in the early 1990s to eliminate the distribution of the cooking gasoline and promote the use of propane gas cylinders, she helped organize residents to oppose the initiative and its increased costs for families. "I started to fight and so I organized the community," Nancy recounted with excitement, "and we would go to the Ministerio de Minas . . . it was a lot of people, we would go in buses." This first experience in community activism, however, had ultimately frustrated her. "After all those meetings and so much time dedicated to the community," she continued, "in the end gas companies started to give away propane stoves and people started to change their stance and stop fighting for cocinol." While she admitted that it was important to "not fear change"—the shift to propane would eventually pave the way for the provision of affordable natural gas in many low-income neighborhoods—Nancy continued to see the process as an example of strategies to "debilitate social mobilizations." Most importantly, the episode foreshadowed the contradictions that would define her personal and professional paths as a savvy neighborhood broker in the years to come.

By the end of the 1980s, Nancy became a member of the neighborhood JAC as two local actors vied for its control: on one side, one of the largest landowners in the area, an emerald trader and "far right Conversative," and, on the other side, a Multifamiliares resident and member of the leftist Union Patriótica party. While she avoided siding with either one of the political groups, she realized "that the local fights around cocinol were [really] about powers, the micropowers [in the neighborhood]." Seeking to stay outside the "struggle of partisan powers" and following the generic goal of "defending my barrio," she became a visible political actor on the east side of the city center, serving as edil three times. She worked actively for years to legalize informal settlements, prevent state displacements of people occupying public lands, and assist poseedores in titling their homes. Pointing to a shelf behind her that was packed with files, she told me she had helped "legalize at least eleven downtown barrios." One of her sharpest memories of these struggles was when she helped 153 families resist eviction in the Vereda Monserrate, up the hill from Las Aguas, and negotiate resettlement agreements with state officials. "With other JAC leaders, children and women, we didn't let them evict them by making a very long cordon," Nancy said, stressing her activist resolve. "When the bulldozer arrived, I saw a woman with her child in her arms get on and I made her get off so I could get on, as a police officer hit me in the back with his baton." Here, too, however, she was ultimately disillusioned with the movement when "some social leaders went to the Alcaldía thinking they would get a better settlement and they started to divide the community."

Nancy brought her narrative back full circle to Progresa Fenicia and suggested that the university had also co-opted and divided the community, just as local political leaders had done in the cocinol years. Instead of cheap fuel, now it was with the promise of property and propriety. Becoming increasingly aware of local political dynamics, she explained, university planners had "joined forces with the president of the JAC . . . generating discord." They had co-organized social events and outreach for the poorest inhabitants, tenement dwellers, and squatters on public land. "[This is the] population that is going to end up busted [*reventados*] and that will end up being displaced," Nancy told me. For her, the plan's social programs "did not have much value or impact," but rather "attracted people by giving them 'candy,' just like every private and public agency does to obtain benefits." The imperative, she insisted, was to negotiate "between equals [entre iguales]," a phrase that would become a new slogan for the latest wave of opposition to the plan. "Sometimes they use people's vulnerabilities," Nancy argued, "because people see them [university staff] as gods. They're unemployed, they haven't even finished elementary school, they're not professionals, so they see a god and a savior."

In 2018, Nancy and her allies held several Entre Iguales meetings so "the most vulnerable" could learn to deal with university functionaries "without fear" and "with knowledge [of the value of their] patrimony and land." In an important strategic move, No Se Tomen Las Aguas countered the university's influence on the JAC and got one of their own elected as president. For Nancy, this led to a crucial reorganization of the board following "criteria of defense, not of subjection to the university, so that they don't see the Junta [the JAC] as henchmen or foot soldiers, but rather with the dignity each one of us deserves." Her talk of dignity illuminated the deeper politics that underlay her opposition to the university. For Nancy, even with the broadening of participation and inclusion, and despite her own adherence to the plan—"Because to tell you the truth, [Progresa Fenicia] benefits me, as well as people in the building," she admitted—the university had continued to reproduce insidious forms of social difference and epistemic hierarchies, part of the class warfare so integral to the history of downtown. Beyond the veneer of progressive appropriateness, Nancy suggested, university experts, "who are all very intelligent and educated, sometimes consider that because one is from the barrio one doesn't have the same preparation, and they're wrong!" Entre Iguales was thus partly aimed at defying what she saw as everyday forms of condescension and authority. For her, the personal and the political were inseparable, such as when planners did not acknowledge her experience as an attorney and litigant and treated her as a manipulative tinterilla. "If Sánchez [the surname of a university expert] calls me Nancy, well, I call him Sánchez," she said, indicating her refusal to call him "Doctor"—the form of address typically used for attorneys and professionals in Colombia—as he had not given her the same deference. "Because you see, it's the struggle between equals." Such struggles thus descended into everyday practice, into the ordinary "treatment [*tratamiento*]" of people and its classist undertones.

For Nancy, her activism was thus about cultivating a particular kind of knowledge in opposition to the university's dominant epistemic assumptions. This is what she called a "clandestine knowledge." Yet her critiques of Progresa Fenicia and her long-running activities as a neighborhood lawyer and politician implicitly reproduced the hierarchies and normative values integral to the university's liberal progressivism. In describing her work, she reinscribed ideals of pedagogical authority and social progress not unlike those enacted by the university. "People's lack of education is so serious," she asserted, "that they become aggressive, unreceptive, mistrustful—it's a very complicated conflict of knowledge." No Se Tomen Las Aguas and Entre Iguales had thus aimed to "educate people, form them politically." In the face of accusations about her own political and economic interests as a neighborhood broker, Nancy again invoked ideals of educational betterment as her main alibi. Far from chasing after court cases and extracting funds from impoverished families, she argued, she had "educated people about having savings, doing [fundraising] bazaars and parties, so they could start saving and creating funds." With these funds, families would gradually pay their legal fees in installments, "even with coins!"

Much as experts rationalized financial planning and pathways to ownership, Nancy justified the brokering practices at the heart of her neighborhood activism as a way of helping people "to learn to value their patrimony, have juridical security with their title, and negotiate fairly." Her critique of Progresa Fenicia ultimately foregrounded ideals of educational integrity and social improvement rather than the political-economic structures she had initially found so perilous for her "vulnerable" clients.[47] "The university is not playing a leading role in formation and education. What is the education they are leaving behind for such a violent and aggressive society?" she said as she described the planning team's alleged manipulation of poor residents and influence over the JAC. Mirroring her aspirations to be on the same footing—in terms of status and influence— as elite experts, she also elevated middle-class visions of educational progress as the response to violent conflict. And like the university, Nancy, too, had to deal with the conflict-ridden undersides and repercussions of her incursion into local ecologies of power and poverty. Noting the conflicts that emerged from the recent takeover of the JAC as well as the circulation of rumors about her exploitation of residents' vulnerability for political and economic gain, she talked about her "deteriorated image" and gestured to the latent dangers she was now facing: "This has been very risky for our security; we still have threats [hanging over us]."

The Paradoxes of Progressive Displacement

"For me only what is real is possible," Camilo told me, reflecting on his work in Progresa Fenicia and on the plan's limitations—especially the uncertainties surrounding the fate of inquilinos and squatters. It was 2019, a year after the city administration had approved the plan's first Unidad de Actuación Urbanística (Unit of Urbanistic Action), a zone of two blocks where the reconstruction process would begin. With negotiations underway, resettlement and expropriation had become more tangible possibilities. Camilo, however, was reassured by the fact that most property owners in this area had agreed to the plan, and when he had any qualms about the process, he reaffirmed his commitment to "incrementalism" and "pragmatism."

In one sense, notions of the real, and therefore of the possible, had indeed expanded after years of planning and negotiation. Progresa Fenicia had not only incorporated measures aimed at securing the permanence of residents but had also become the blueprint for citywide regulations for the "protection of dwellers [*protección de moradores*]." Yet university planners' conceptualizations of the reality of urban transformation and its possible futures had been refracted through their situated experiences and material conditions. Looking through such ideological lenses had largely occluded the neighborhood's fractious social terrain and its deep running entanglements with histories of violence and displacement. From experts' vantage point, Las Aguas appeared as a sociomaterial ensemble of agents and spaces that could be reordered into a densified and valorized real estate development.

When university planners did recognize the centrality of conflict within the plan, they couched it in managerial terms and as a matter of coordinating individual "interests and stakeholders." One of the main architects of Progresa Fenicia, Juan Felipe Pinilla Pineda, argued in a scholarly article that the plan was best viewed as a "consensus-building process."[48] For him, the university emerged as a neutral mediator ideally positioned for "conflict management."[49] Although self-critically recognizing the limits of Progresa Fenicia's "land pooling" efforts and its almost exclusive focus on landowners, the university's managerial vision inscribed a sanitized understanding of conflict that glossed over the existing power differentials integral to Las Aguas and Los Andes's shared history.[50] At work in the university's "consensus building" was what Laura Nader calls "controlling processes": "the mechanisms by which ideas take hold and become institutional in relation to power."[51] While Progresa Fenicia stood in stark opposition to downtown's trajectories of securitized renewal, it nevertheless entrenched established ideological and material arrangements of governance, property, and development—arrangements closely linked to the country's history of land violence and displacement.

For many residents, such disavowal of conflict, as well as its sanitized rendering as something to be "overcome," appeared to be a bid for control over knowledge production and the very terms of urban transformation. As I have shown in this chapter, residents had experienced urban reality differently, something that made them wary of the university's progressive promises. For them, the material and sociopolitical contours of urban life were inseparable from property violence and local contestations over authority. This of course included the university, which, despite claims of neutrality as a nonprofit institution of higher education, was a key node in local and national circuits of governmental power and capital accumulation. In a letter to the Secretaría Distrital de Planeación, Astrid, a resident of Multifamiliares, described the university as an "oligarchic mafia." She read the letter out loud to me, her elderly mother, and two neighbors as we sat in her narrow living room one afternoon. When Astrid uttered the words "oligarchic mafia," she snickered, as if she had transgressed an unspoken boundary of decorum. But one of the neighbors, a retiree and apartment owner, went further and compared the plan to "paramilitary displacement" and agroindustrial land grabs in the countryside. He recounted how, in his many trips to the northern regions of Cesar and Magdalena, he had seen African palm oil plantations push out populations and crops. "Land dispossession," he noted, had resulted from "projects" presented by investors and approved by the Ministry of Agriculture. He emphasized the word "project"—the term used by university planners to refer to Progresa Fenicia—and drew a parallel between the real estate partnership and the use of "investors" and "frontmen [*testaferros*]" in rural land grabs. "They also offer them [opportunities to participate], but in the end they make them leave," he continued. "In Cesar, they kill them."

By pointing to the neighborhood's deeper undercurrents of sociopolitical conflict, residents contested the university's dominant epistemic frames and its technocratic brand of progressive urbanism. Such counterhegemonic knowledge, however, was not an alternative, subaltern epistemology—a separate "logic of life," as Tomás and José, the team's social scientists, conjectured in their critical contributions to the plan. It did not represent a reality beyond modernity and capitalism that would radically open new urban possibilities.[52] Nancy's activism and brokering shows instead how local opposition unfolded within the parameters of capitalist development and through normative views of progress and citizenship. Neighborhood mobilization was contradictory, with activists such as Nancy simultaneously leveraging their own interests and middle-class aspirations while struggling to shift the plan's lopsided power structures. Other homeowners skillfully assessed their opportunities within the plan, pressing for better conditions to either remain as resettled apartment owners or exit while capturing the highest value for their land. Local opposition and negotiation, in this sense, were irrevocably connected to ideals of propertied citizenship and to the alleged inevitability of urban development. This again resonates with Nader's calls to examine "how central dogmas are made and how they work in multiple sites" and to follow the "microprocesses" through which "individuals and groups are influenced and persuaded to participate in their own domination or, alternatively, to resist it."[53]

The contradictory nature of these epistemic struggles was brought home to me during a conversation with Alex, the street vendor harassed by the police, with whom I opened this chapter. Alex had long lived in a tenement in the neighborhood, and I asked him what chances he saw in avoiding displacement and staying in the area as a tenant. "Tenant?" he immediately fired back, standing in front of his chaza full of candy and snacks. "No, I see myself as a homeowner; if that doesn't happen then we're really not accomplishing anything, are we?" At work here was the expert reinvention of Las Aguas as commodified land to be pooled in a fiduciary trust and reassembled as a denser and more valuable urban space. This was a "value project" that would supposedly enable the transition from impoverished tenement dweller to socially ascendant property owner.[54] For Alex, ideologies of individual ownership and commodification had catalyzed both his opposition to and, eventually, his support for the plan.[55]

Such contradictions were not lost on planners—more so as negotiations dragged on and new oppositions and frictions surfaced. Visibly frustrated, Camilo gave me a pessimistic update on Progresa Fenicia over the phone in 2021. After years of working out agreements and conditions for cooperation, he explained, "a demolishing dose of Colombia reality had arrived." The plan's approved Unidades de Actuación Urbanística remained in a stalemate, while the "theory of a university conspiracy" had gained force among a new group of vocal property owners and allied political actors. Some of these were shadowy figures, Camilo suggested, questionable brokers with their own speculative interests and clientelistic strategies in play. For his part, he had become the target of accusations of corruption—a "white-collar thief," the rumor went—as well as the recipient of numerous requests for official information. This new "merciless legal strategy" had bogged down the plan in red tape.

It was clear that the plan was not going to happen "Los Andes–style [*al estilito de los Andes*]," Camilo said in a self-deprecating tone, referring to the university's technocratic politesse. Neighborhood tensions and inequalities had surfaced more visibly with the COVID-19 pandemic and amid the massive social protests that swept through Colombia's major cities between 2019 and 2021 (see the epilogue). Not only did many small businesses suffer and some disappear with the temporary closure of the university, but also, Camilo noted, "other strange things started to happen." A resident who had become a vocal ally of the plan and undeclared enemy of No Se Tomen Las Aguas had been murdered in his home in Las Aguas. The suspicion was that family disputes over land were behind the crime. That same year, a well-known business owner who had actively participated in the planning process was detained by the police during a large drug raid in his neighborhood store. For Camilo, this strained atmosphere, along with the renewed attacks on the plan, had made the latest round of negotiations a "small hell [*un pequeño infierno*]." But his misgivings did not stop there. Sensing a deeper disenchantment, I asked him whether he had doubts about the plan itself.

"Of course I have doubts," Camilo replied. "Developers are only in this for the financial deal; they don't care if people are going to live or not [in the new development] or if they used to inhabit [the area]. The [real estate] paradigm is concerned only with itself."

The conflicts over urban knowledge traced in this chapter ultimately point to the limits and contradictions of planners' progressive fictions. Not only did narratives of inclusionary property and progress clash with the political-economic realities of Las Aguas, but they also made apparent the trajectories of state and land violence that had been woven into sociomaterial relations. What experts envisioned as an "example of peaceful coexistence and development for the entire country"—an aspiration that mirrored Colombia's emergent postconflict sensibilities—risked compounding the social and political violences integral to the creation of land markets and its implied transformation of property relations. The plan's promise of social justice was ultimately dependent on the expansion of real estate dynamics and regimes of individual ownership and entrepreneurial citizenship embodied in the figure of the partner and proprietor. So while Progresa Fenicia undoubtedly represented a move away from the securitized expulsion of previous renewal plans, it nevertheless preserved the conditions of Bogotá's urbanistic warfare, constituting a form of progressive displacement. The imperatives of development, property, and urban intervention were left intact— their deep-seated violences and conflicts disavowed—such that progressive agendas of urban inclusion emerged as new routes toward dispossession, ones in which urban dwellers themselves actively took part.[56]

Considering these paradoxes, one of the most radical statements I heard during my time with the Progresa Fenicia team did not question the plan's consensus-making procedures or participatory techniques but rather challenged the assumption that renewal was inevitable or even desirable. During a walk around the neighborhood with the design team, led by a well-known professor and famously grandiloquent creator of several downtown buildings, an architecture student voiced her concerns about the plan. As if knowing she was crossing an unspoken line, she wondered quietly, audible only to me and a couple of students, whether the university should consider simply not intervening in Las Aguas at all.

EPILOGUE

In late August 2018 I witnessed an unlikely scene just steps away from Parque Tercer Milenio in the formerly infamous El Bronx, or La L, the roughly two blocks that had become a bustling drug market since the disappearance of El Cartucho in the late 1990s. The city administration had organized a cultural event dubbed Graffitón: Arte y Transformación (Art and Transformation), part of an ongoing effort to rebrand the area after its almost complete demolition in 2016. That year, more than two thousand law enforcement agents had stormed into the area by order of Mayor Enrique Peñalosa. The operation aimed to dismantle three microtrafficking organizations, or hooks (*ganchos*), and "rescue" hundreds of children and homeless drug addicts who had been allegedly caught in their grips. It was also the completion of what Peñalosa had begun years earlier with the demolition of El Cartucho in his first mayoral term.

The officer in charge of the takeover was a veteran counterinsurgency police colonel who had participated in emblematic military raids of guerrilla camps and cocaine laboratories in the countryside. Intelligence reports warned of the presence of the ganchos' heavily armed foot soldiers (*saiyayines*), as well as an elaborate network of counterintelligence and underground escape routes. Authorities employed surveillance and drones for terrain reconnaissance, and special forces swooped into the area, hidden in unmarked commercial trucks. News coverage described a form of military swarming: "The official troops overwhelmed the zone in minutes and units Alfa, Charly, Bravo, and Delta concentrated on each one of the 'ganchos' and 'Sayayines,' while snipers and a team of special forces secured the area."[1] Weeks later, a senior official explained to me that police had deployed "security rings" and the government had scheduled helicopter flyovers to "demonstrate overwhelming force." But the police squads did not encounter gunfire, only unarmed crowds of destitute residents. Accounts of the confrontation were nonetheless thoroughly militarized. In a news interview, the city's secretary of security (*secretario de seguridad, convivencia y justicia*) had remarked on the tactical use of debris: "Filling up the place with garbage was a strategy, using it as a barricade to isolate people, [especially] law enforcement."[2] Protesters were portrayed as an army of addicts, social debris that had been weaponized by drug leaders. And the built environment became a target of military intervention: "criminal architecture," as another newspaper put it.[3] The consensus among city officials was that every building had to be demolished, that "a total physical transformation" was required to overcome the area's history of violence and illegality.

By 2018, officials had designated two remaining historic buildings—La Facultad and La Flauta—and the street between them, La Milla, as the starting point for the rebirth of El Bronx. A temporary archway built with scaffolding announced this much at the entrance of the Graffitón event: "El Bronx is reborn and alive again [El Bronx renace, revive]." A group of city architects from the Empresa de Renovación Urbana (Company of Urban Renewal) had recently described the renovated area to me as an emergent node for a creative economy through which "vulnerable populations, the unemployed, people with a history of addiction, could be reintegrated into social life." El Bronx: Distrito Creativo (El Bronx: Creative District), as it had been renamed, would be a hub for the creative and artistic industries allegedly merging social welfare and city branding agendas. Yet the paradoxes of this approach became uncomfortably visible during the evening of El Graffitón.

Officials carefully managed the entrance to the supposedly public event, which was cordoned off with a gate, as they distributed a flyer with punched-out holes that could be used as a spray-paint stencil. Inside La Milla, organizers had set up a tent with instructional material about street art, a stage with music equipment, and a large vehicle in the middle of the road wrapped in black fabric. El Graffitón was meant to be a celebration of street art, a practice that not only brought up conflicts associated with urban renewal but also pointed to the city's entrenched police violence. In the previous years, Diego Becerra, a sixteen-year-old graffiti artist who had been shot by the police in 2011, had become one of the symbols of police abuse in Bogotá, his face now memorialized in murals on overpasses and walls. In what aspired to be a decisive shift, the city administration had now organized a public competition to select four graffiti artists for an art residence and a public installation during El Graffitón.

In the culminating act, organizers unveiled the shrouded vehicle: "a cool surprise," a city functionary had told me earlier with a grin. Beneath the cover was

FIGURE E.1.   Shrouded antiriot vehicle at El Graffitón. Photo by the author.

a black armored vehicle, the kind used by the feared riot police Escuadrón Móvil Antidisturbios (Mobile Antidisturbance Squad), or ESMAD, and the same type that had been deployed to capture El Bronx and displace its inhabitants two years earlier.[4] Graffiti artists and event goers—including children—spray-painted the antiriot vehicle as concert lights strobed and Los Angeles rock band Rage Against the Machine's antipolice anthem "Killing in the Name" blasted through the street. Yet the irony of the scene was not lost on all the attendees. As a video of the event later showed, at some point one man stepped in front of the vehicle and scrawled a message on the pavement: "Everything wrong / I don't give a shit about the graffitón / circus for rich people."[5] It was a blunt dismissal of the administration's empty gesture: mostly middle-class people defacing the instrument of violence that had been integral to the destruction of El Bronx, in the name of a rebranded, palatable expression of urban marginality.

But as with the plans I have analyzed in the preceding pages, the remaking of El Bronx into a "creative district" was not seamless. The violent expulsion of its inhabitants and the destruction of its built forms did not eradicate the urban knowledges and politics that had animated what Amy Ritterbusch and El Cilencio call its "street-connected community."[6] And even events like El Graffitón did not fully co-opt local oppositional practices, nor did such practices become disentangled from the forms of governance they opposed. As programs to rebrand El Bronx continued in the following years, one initiative illustrated the contradictory relationship between planning initiatives and local critical knowledges and practices. A hip-hop collective, Free Soul, which had emerged from the streets of El Bronx, became a central activist movement after the neighborhood was captured and destroyed by the state. After being displaced, the group of young rappers received support from the city administration to embark on "memory work" around their life on the street.[7] With the collaboration of more than 120 former inhabitants, they built a scale model of the area. A form of "social cartography," the model salvaged the everyday experiences of violence and solidarity that had been erased through demolition and dispossession.[8] In 2017, the miniature neighborhood was exhibited in the Museo Nacional de Colombia (National Museum of Colombia), where Free Soul also shared their stories with visitors, and it is now part of the museum's permanent collection. As Andrés Góngora, a curator and anthropologist involved in the process, explains, the model was a "potent testimonial object" that contested "institutionalized memory."[9]

But Free Collective's interventions did not stop there. In 2019, the Foundation Gilberto Alazate Avendaño, the city agency in charge of cultural programming for El Bronx: Distrito Creativo, invited the collective to co-design a museum in the neighborhood's last ruin.[10] The building, known as the Esquina Redonda (Round Corner), became the Co-Laboratorio de Creación y Memoria (Co-Laboratory of Creation and Memory). It would be a space to counter dominant narratives about urban decay and marginality through "different memory and artistic practices" such as "guided visits through the ruins of El Bronx," concerts that recalled the "street art festivals" that used to take place in the area, "local history workshops," and "talks about drug prohibition, harm reduction, and the present circumstances of street inhabitants [habitantes de calle]."[11] Echoing the country's post-peace-agreement projects of truth, memory and reparation, urban renewal in El Bronx had become a site of reckoning, opening "spaces for resistance and memory," as Francisca Márquez and Andrés Góngora put it.[12] At the same time, these oppositional knowledges had been supported by the same state institutions that had destroyed the neighborhood. Subaltern critiques thus became entangled with the violence of urban planning.

While these destabilizing remnants and "provoking spaces" questioned official urban trajectories and brought to light silenced histories, they also took the form of a fetishized ruin-turned-museum within the elite makeover of the area.[13] Yet in contrast to other contestations of urban renewal, it was precisely such materializations in the ruined landscape that gave force to former inhabitants' epistemic engagements. Such ruinous knowledges had been integral to local imaginaries of El Bronx. Urban dwellers had not only traditionally referred to the area as "La L," a reference to its physical layout, but had also called it simply "the piece" or "part [*pedazo*]."[14] And it was precisely the attention to leftover fragments—both in material and epistemic terms—that brought to light submerged currents of urbanistic violence, made apparent the ingrained contradictions of city making, and ultimately opened a site for other ways of knowing and learning about the city.[15]

The kinds of critical knowledges embodied in Free Soul's scale model and its ruinous museum surfaced forcefully during a series of historic protests that engulfed Bogotá and other cities across Colombia between 2019 and 2020 and again in 2021. The protests, known as the Paro Nacional 21N, started on November 21, 2019. Not since El Bogotazo and the civic strikes of 1977 and 1993 (see chapter 1) had the city seen such massive mobilizations. Unlike previous protests, the Paro Nacional 21N lasted for weeks at a time and brought together a diverse set of populations, and it rippled through urban spaces as never before. The protests began as broad opposition against right-wing President Iván Duque's social and economic reforms and their deepening of stark inequalities, as well as the government's sabotaging of the 2016 peace agreement with the FARC and the growing violence against community leaders and activists. Such structural undercurrents of state violence became even more central to the Paro after a critical event on November 23, 2019, which involved once again one of the country's key vehicles of urban militarization: the ESMAD and its antiriot tanks. As downtown protests continued unabated, the ESMAD was deployed in full force to disperse the crowds. With the street now turned into a battleground, eighteen-year-old high school student Dilan Cruz was shot by an ESMAD agent as he ran away from the squad.[16] Cruz's death in the hospital two days later sent shock waves through the city. Thousands took to the streets to participate in *cacerolazos*, hitting pots and pans (*cacerolas*) as they marched.[17]

Mobilizations went on for weeks not only in the city center but also in working-class and middle-class neighborhoods across Bogotá. The crowds paid homage to Cruz as they centered their struggle against state violence and injustice. The ESMAD escalated its attacks on protesters in scenes that resembled urban warfare: youths running through streets and seeking refuge as police motorcycles and ESMAD tanks and agents corralled them in their own neighborhoods. Mobilizations continued in 2020 and surged again in 2021, with previous grievances now exacerbated by the economic crisis of the COVID-19 pandemic and the state's militarized response to both the protests and the public health crisis.[18]

The activist networks forged during months of protest continued to expand across geographies of class and race, within and beyond Bogotá. Afro-Colombian and Indigenous groups energized the uprisings and evinced the connections between the urban *estallido social* (social explosion), as the Paro became known in 2021, and the longer history of injustice and violence in Colombia. The Misak, an Indigenous community of the Cauca region in the Southwest of the country, emerged as a key force in this regard. Marching for days to the capital, the Minga Indígena—as Indigenous community action spaces are traditionally called— arrived for the closing of the 2020 Paro in October. The following day, the Misak descended on the city's airport to denounce rising violence and displacement in their territories. The protest, they stated in a communication, was aimed at "calling for the unity of social, popular, ethnic, student, labor union, urban, and rural sectors against policies of war [*políticas de guerra*]."[19]

The social and political effects of the 2019–21 mass protests are still unfolding, as shown by the historic election in 2022 of former Mayor Petro as Colombia's first leftist president after decades of bipartisan and right-leaning rule. While the significance of the country's renewed forms of organizing and activism is the subject of ongoing debate and analysis, the mobilizations revealed something central to the arguments of this book: Urban materiality and infrastructure emerged as the medium for forms of knowledge and action inextricably tied to the country's enduring history and politics of insecurity. The renewal plans described in the previous chapters showed how warfare shaped both expert intervention and critical opposition to speculation and displacement. This was a war waged in epistemic and physical terrains, and one that became easily occluded in the sedimentation and reassembling of urban space. With the protests, it was as if the undertow of urbanistic violence had risen and left tangible marks on the material contours of the city.[20]

As in other historic urban protests going back to El Bogotazo, the destruction of certain infrastructures became central to the struggle against everyday inequities and violence. Besides financial institutions and government buildings, Transmilenio bus stations also emerged as key targets, with dozens dismantled and damaged during the protests. While the rapid-transit system had been celebrated as one of the city's successes of the past decades, it had also become emblematic of the privatization of public services and its resulting sociospatial injustices. Like urban renewal, Transmilenio was predicated on a public-private alliance. The state built the infrastructure, and companies operated the buses, reaping the benefits of an essential public service. According to one report, the Paro came after years of "overcrowding, high fares," and "large areas of the city underserved by public transit."[21]

Also notable was the burning of one-third of the city's small neighborhood police stations, known as Comandos de Atención Inmediata (Immediate Attention Commands), or CAIs, in 2020. Amid rising police repression, state forces had killed dozens of protesters and injured hundreds, while many remained disappeared or illegally detained. The destruction of the CAIs, a quotidian infrastructure of urban policing, became a tangible condemnation of police vio-lence.[22] But activists went further and reinscribed the material remains of the stations with memorials to those who were killed and with emergent visions of police abolition (one of the Paro's main demands was the elimination of the ESMAD). In the hours after burning the stations, residents and protesters came together to transform several CAIs into people's libraries (*bibliotecas populares*). One of these was in the working-class neighborhood of La Gaitana in the north-west district of Suba. Renamed by locals as the Cultural Center Julieth Ramírez—after an eighteen-year-old student who had been shot the night before, during the protests—the small command was covered with murals and signs, some of which read, "peace and education," "life first," and "a center for reclusion and torture turned into a center for creation and culture." The boxy concrete structure, now without tinted windows and with its walls charred, became an open space where volunteers distributed donated books.

As scholars have noted, urban space and infrastructure took a new and central place during the Paro.[23] Mobilizations involved new modes of appropriating pub-lic space as well as the expansion of the city's traditional "circuits and points of gathering and confrontation," as Sergio Montero and Isabel Peñaranda describe them.[24] This included musical and artistic performances, street teach-ins, and neighborhood assemblies (*asambleas barriales*). As the remaking of the CAIs suggests, the urban character of the protests had a distinctive material dimen-sion. This became apparent with the central role that street art, graffiti, and post-ers played during the Paro. Over months of protest, certain places in the city became critical nodes for organizing. In the sprawling working-class district of Kennedy, for example, protesters established a key point of gathering around a large Transmilenio bus hub, the Portal de las Americas, in 2021. During several weeks, people organized street assemblies, collective food preparation in "com-munity pots" (*ollas comunitarias*), cultural events, and medical attention points. This is also where the ESMAD carried out some of its most violent attacks against activists and the so-called Primera Línea, a front line of protesters who protected others in the crowd with makeshift shields, helmets, and masks. Activists eventu-ally covered the sign at the station's main entrance with posters, renaming it the Portal de la Resistencia (Portal of Resistance).

Over the course of the Paro, as journalist Ana Puentes reports, "dozens of street artists backed by hundreds of youths launched into the streets to fill the ground and walls with urban art."[25] Such "imprinting" on public space, and its transgressive qualities, was on full display at another main point of protest, the Monumento a los Héroes (Monument to the Heroes), in northeast Bogotá.[26] The rectangular stone monolith had been built during the dictatorship of General Gustavo Rojas Pinilla in the mid-twentieth century as a memorial to Colombia's independence fighters and its armed forces. A large statue of the Liberator, Simón Bolívar, stood on the north side of the monument, its walls emblazoned with the names of independence battalions and battles. The tower was emblematic of a national, militaristic historical narrative, to the point that it had been originally designed to house a military museum—a project that never materialized.

So when thousands of protesters took over Héroes and covered it with murals, posters, and graffiti, they were collectively building an "antimonument," as one of the activists put it.[27] Below the monument's main metal sign, "Bolivar Libertador," large red block letters of the same size now read "Oppressor." Protesters set Bolívar's statue on fire and partially toppled it until the city administration eventually removed it. Behind where the statue used to stand, street artists created a large mural that showed an Afro-Colombian woman, her hand stretched out and palm open, with a bloody inscription: "no más sangre [no more blood]." On the opposite end of the tower, another mural depicted a woman looking intently, a weapon visible over her left shoulder, and a black-and-red cloth covering the lower part of her face. Underneath the image was a large painted sign that read, "guerreras ancestrales [ancestral fighters]."

The murals were an inversion of the patriarchal history of independence struggles embodied in the monument. They unsettled the conservative and militaristic foundations of national projects and linked them to the present of state violence. On another side of the Héroes tower, activists painted a cadaveric portrait of former right-wing President Álvaro Uribe Vélez, framed by a large sign reading, "enemigo público [public enemy]." On the opposite side, below the names of historic battles, a version of one of the signature murals of the Paro stretched across the wall: "6.402 héroes." This was a reference to the number of so-called false positives (falsos positivos): impoverished men executed by the military and presented as guerrilla fighters killed in combat. This practice was widespread during the Uribe Vélez administrations and had recently been investigated by Colombia's Jurisdicción Especial para la Paz (Special Jurisdiction for Peace).

For months, as activists overlayed posters, scrawled slogans, and painted murals, the monument became a canvas for both the grievances and the visions of the future that animated the Paro. One of the street artists involved in the making of the antimonument explained its political significance: "The Héroes Monument will remain in people's collective memory, and it will make collective denunciations transcend: the understanding that people are tired of the war and that art has been a form of healing and a form of constructing truth and avoiding repetition."[28] Yet the final fate of the monument was revealing of the limits of such modes of intervention in urban space. The political meanings that had been attached to Héroes—activists' denunciations of violence and injustice through the very materiality of the city—would be undone through the banal workings of bureaucratic action and infrastructure development.

In late September 2021, a demolition crew started to take apart the tower, working from top to bottom, chipping away at the limestone with its decades-old engravings and months-old murals. The removal of Héroes had been planned since 2010 as part of the long-awaited construction of the metro system's first line. In 2019 the city had launched a public competition for the design of a new monument connected to the metro station. The winning project envisioned a series of panels with an open space in the middle: It proposed the "void as monument."[29] That same year, the city requested that only Bolívar's statue be considered patrimony worthy of preservation and that the rest be demolished.[30] Earlier proposals within the administration to preserve some of the mural and graffiti-covered slabs of stone had been dismissed. Conservative sectors decried the idea of enshrining vandalism, while the pressures of the metro project and its promises of progress and valorization took precedence.

The final scene of destruction captured the essence of urbanism as warfare, of administrative violence and its perfunctory operations. If the figure of front-line protesters with construction helmets had been demonized during the Paro, as Manuel Salge Ferro and Luis Gonzalo Jaramillo E. point out, those same helmets, now on demolition workers, became potent signifiers of the "imperative of the administrative apparatus of the state."[31] The controversies over toppled and defaced spaces during the protests gave way to the seemingly uncontroversial attack on the antimonument and its critical knowledges of urbanistic violence. It was the creation of a void that, like the other voids of urban renewal, erased the footprints of the city's sociomaterial battles.

Yet as I have shown throughout this book, Bogotá's urban struggles—along with their echoes of the country's larger violent conflicts and tentative moves toward reconciliation—continually rematerialize in subaltern epistemologies and progressive planning. And while these modes of knowledge and political engagement seek to move beyond security paradigms, they also remain uneasily linked to normative orders of governance, citizenship, and development, and their violent undersides. Such contradictions were again illuminated by the city's new Territorial Ordering Plan (POT), finally approved at the end of 2021 after more than a decade of debate and failed proposals. Responding to the city's history of displacement, segregation, and inequality, the new POT established concrete measures for the "protection of urban dwellers [protección a moradores]" amid Bogotá's ongoing urban transformations. More broadly, it introduced the notion of care (cuidado) as one of the main through lines for the city's policies, programs, and projects. Whether it was to address gender inequalities, health crises, or environmental degradation, the vision for a citywide system of care (*sistema distrital de cuidado*) emerged as a central planning epistemology that placed renewed emphasis on the production and location of vital infrastructures as well as the distribution of socioeconomic resources.[32]

But here again, as in the progressive fictions I have analyzed in this book, it is yet to be seen how a Bogotá Cuidadora (Caring Bogotá), as planners have now called the city, can move beyond frameworks centered on territorial control, market-led development, and violent property regimes. Such contradiction was perhaps most clearly embodied in the figure of Claudia López, the city's first woman and lesbian mayor (2020–23) and a well-known critic of paramilitarism in her career as an academic and congresswoman. Yet during the Paro, as Alejandra Azuero Quijano notes, it was as if the city had "two mayors."[33] At times López's incendiary tweets criminalized the protests and encouraged the ESMAD's heavy-handed tactics. At other moments, she condemned the police's use of excessive force and called for accountability. Most ironically, as the administration delegitimized the Paro's vibrant forms of community organizing and mutual care, it also sought to institutionalize notions of care through the POT.

If anything, then, Bogotá's planning epistemologies call attention to the intractable entanglements between progressive planning and the city's sedimented histories of urban insecurity and its exclusionary regimes of governance, property, and citizenship. They take us back to the crucial question of how urban knowledges are grounded and take form: how the retrofitting of urban worlds and its political promises are both made possible and limited by the histories, materials, and experiential horizons within which they unfold. They compel us to reimagine planning beyond itself, certainly not as a practice of reordering and disciplining space, but also not as a reformist strategy to simply make the city more inhabitable and inclusionary. At stake here, in short, is the possibility of envisioning radical urban knowledges aimed at the dismantling of the colonial and securitized roots of planning—that is, at the very abolition of urbanism as warfare.[34]

Acknowledgments

If writing is shaped by experiences that reach far back before typing is even on the horizon, it is hard to say when this book began. One beginning is when I started visiting downtown Bogotá regularly while in high school and later as a college student at the Universidad de los Andes in the late 1990s. As it was for many residents of north Bogotá, El Centro was both a fabled and a feared space. It crystallized Colombia's histories of violence and oppression but also epitomized urban inventiveness and endurance. Far from Bogotá's privileged spaces and their long-standing aspirations of order and distinction, the city center embodied a motley juxtaposition of people, stories, and things. From revered colonial and republican buildings, busy elite officials, and wandering tourists to the improvised spaces of precarious workers and street dwellers, hustlers and dealers, bohemians and artists, this was a place of overlapping difference and friction. I would like to think there are traces of these years of (self-)discovery in the preceding pages. At the very least, my ethnographic sensibility in this book is indebted to my formative downtown itineraries and to the time spent with fellow travelers at the now-closed cafeteria La Puerta de La Calendaria, a literal and metaphorical doorway into the historic center.

Another origin story, closer to when this project began: Between 2001 and 2004 I worked as an assistant to the mayor's office and was charged with recording, transcribing, and editing mayoral interventions to create short booklets, *Apuntes de la alcaldía* (Notes from the administration), for the general public. Taking the role of an uninitiated ethnographer of urban policy, I navigated the city through the eyes of experts and administrators—a prefiguring of my research for this book. I remain grateful to Alicia Eugenia Silva Nigrinis, then chief of staff, and urbanist Rafael Obregón Herrera, for their always reliable and savvy guidance. Thanks also to Francisco Ruiz Peronard and Tomás Martín Jiménez, with whom I shared many good times in government offices and as we zipped across the city in Francisco's purple Renault Twingo. This period sparked my interest in the critical study of governmental knowledge and introduced me to the planning and policy networks that are at the core of this ethnography.

At Harvard University, I benefited from the invaluable support of several mentors in social anthropology. Kimberly Theidon gave me the necessary *ánimos* and academic grounding to undertake my research project. She helped me understand the stakes of my questions in relation to Colombia's history of armed conflict and humanitarian intervention. I was fortunate to learn about the anthropology of development, citizenship, and the state with Ajantha Subramanian. Her always critical and sharp analyses were indispensable to my thinking around expertise, space, and power. Ever since welcoming me to Harvard, Michael Herzfeld became an essential guide to anthropological thought and ethnographic writing. Our conversations about the anthropology of knowledge and urbanism have been critical to my arguments in these pages. Finally, as someone who is interested in urban planning as a site of critique and praxis, I am very grateful to have been a student of Susan Fainstein. She reminded me to always keep in focus the material outcomes of urban interventions and their implications in the making of a just city.

At Harvard, I learned from and enjoyed the company of many people: Muhammad Arafat, Alejandra Azuero Quijano, Sai Balakrishnan, Naor Ben-Yehoyada, Kerry Chance, Aryo Danusiri, Juana Dávila Sáenz, Namita Vijay Dharia, Alex Fattal, Nancy Khalil, Julie Kleinman, Ekin Kurtiç, Jennifer Mack, Andy McDowell, Jared McCormick, Lisanne Norman, Sanjay Pinto, Vipas Prachyaporn, Esra-Gökçe Şahin, Benjamin Siegel, J. P. Sniadecki, Claudio Sopranzetti, Stephanie Spray, Nicolás Sternsdorff-Cisterna, Julia Yezbick, Dilan Yildirim, and Emrah Yildiz, among others. Marianne Fritz, Susan Farley, and Cristina Paul provided continuous logistical assistance and morale during my doctoral studies. I've been lucky to share a friendship with Jyothi Natarajan and Anand Vaidya over our journey from the East Coast to the West Coast. Anand was always willing to comment on long chapter drafts and help me find the thread, and my first attempt at putting some of my research into writing was under Jyothi's exceptional editorial guidance. Thanks also to María Ospina Pizano, Simón Parra, Seth Pipkin, Chikako Francis, Andy Francis, and other friends around Boston.

Many people in Bogotá, many more than I can name here, made this book possible. María Camila Uribe Sánchez and Alejandro Rodríguez Caicedo kindly plugged me into the city's planning networks at the start of my study. Cristina Arango Olaya welcomed me unconditionally to the city's Secretaría Distrital de Planeación, where I carried out months of ethnographic research. City planners, policymakers, and officials not only tolerated the ethnographer among them but became close collaborators and friends who taught me enthusiastically about planning and design practice. Thank you especially to Hernando Arenas Castro, León Espinosa Restrepo, Armando Lozano Reyes, Carmenza Orjuela, Geovanni Patiño Torres, Alfy Tovar Sepúlveda, Eduardo Restrepo González, Rafael Sáenz Pérez, Sandra Samaca Rojas, Julio César Vega Angarita, and Antonio Velandia Clavijo. Outside the planning department, I was lucky to learn from seasoned urbanists who shared their time and helped me navigate the past and present of planning in Bogotá. Thanks to Patricia Acosta Restrepo, Mario Avellaneda

González, Claudia Carrizosa, Yency Contreras Ortiz, Clemencia Ibañez, María Mercedes Maldonado Copello, Leonel Miranda Ruiz, Mario Noriega, Dorys Patricia Noy Palacios, Liliana Ospina Arias, María Cristina Rojas Eberhard, Carmenza Saldías Barreneche, José Salazar Ferro, Claudia Silva Yepes, Otto Quintero Arias, Diana Wiesner, and many others who shared their knowledge and insights.

I carried out a significant part of my research at the Universidad de los Andes, where I had been an undergraduate more than a decade earlier. This was a peculiar homecoming: Here I was at a radically expanded campus doing ethnography both within and about an institution that was increasingly embracing its role as a downtown redeveloper. Many thanks to the faculty, staff, consultants, and students who supported my work and accepted my shifting positionality as an alumnus, outside critic, and invited researcher. Julieta Lemaitre Ripoll and Isabel Cristina Jaramillo Sierra kindly endorsed a key institutional affiliation through the Centro de Investigaciones Sociojurídicas (CIJUS). Claudia Velandia Gómez and Oscar Pardo Aragón opened the doors for my participation in the urban and campus revitalization project Progresa Fenicia. I am very grateful to university experts and staff for their continued support throughout my research: Victoria Caicedo Medina, Franklin Combariza Luna, Luis Díaz Matajira, David Díaz Rivera, Clemencia Escallón Gartner, Natalia Franco Borrero, Tatiana García, María Angélica López Torrado, Manuela Mattos, Giovanni Perdomo Sanabria, Yezid Rodríguez Martínez, Maurix Suárez Rodríguez, Roberto Suárez Montañez, Astrid Reyes, Silvia Tibaduiza Sierra, and others in the university community. I am especially grateful to Juan Felipe Pinilla Pineda for his always critical insights about urban law and his keenness to become an autoethnographer of planning.

My deepest gratitude to all the people from Las Aguas, Santa Inés, La Alameda, and Santa Fe who shared with me their experiences and included me in their projects of knowledge making and dissent. It was in conversations with them that I articulated some of the central analyses of this book. Thank you to Camilo Arango Trujillo, Ricardo Ávila, José Vicente Cantor, Germán Madrid, Edgar Montenegro, Julián Neira, Doris Patricia Niño Pérez, Gloria Pinzón, Adriana Rodríguez Restrepo, Amelia Sanabria de Suárez, Saúl Suárez Niño, José Torres Torres, and many others. I am indebted to Helena Gallo Bernal, who taught me like no one else about counterexpertise and local politics in downtown Bogotá.

I also want to thank the many supportive scholars and researchers I met along the way: César Abadía-Barrero, Rolf Abderhalden Cortés, María José Álvarez-Rivadulla, Emma Shaw Crane, Mark Healey, Cymene Howe, Clara Irazábal-Zurita, Sergio Montero, Ingrid Morris Rincón, Diana Ojeda, José Antonio Ramírez Orozco, Andrés Romero, Andrés Salcedo Fidalgo, Luisa Sotomayor, and Erik Vergel Tovar, among others. Alejandra Leal Martínez, Nitzan Shoshan, and Antonio Azuela de la Cueva invited me to Mexico City for an extremely helpful discussion about early chapter drafts with a remarkable group of scholars at the Universidad Nacional Autónoma de México and El Colegio de México. I thank them for the generosity and insights. My colleagues, friends, and students in Portland have made these years both academically engaging and sufficiently detached from writing and teaching. Thank you to the Honors College community at Portland State University for a welcoming, engaging, and supportive academic home. Many thanks to Mrinalini Tankha and Alpen Sheth for all the good times in the Pacific Northwest.

My sincere thanks to Dominic Boyer, editor of the Cornell University Press Series on Expertise: Cultures and Technologies of Knowledge, for his interest in this project and his encouragement throughout. Many thanks to Jim Lance, Karen Laun, and Bethany Wasik for their expert guidance during the editorial process, and to Eric Levy for his meticulous copyediting. I also thank Lilia Noger-Onstott for proofreading an early version of the manuscript and Varsha Venkata-subramanian for creating the index.

This book, which is in many ways about home, would not exist without the support of my family. All my gratitude to my parents, Clemencia and Alberto, and my siblings, Natalia and Juan Camilo, whose love and companionship has kept me going. Thank you to Ana María and Juan Felipe and to my wonderful nieces and nephews, María, Isaac, Raquel, Juan José, and Valentina. And many thanks to Clara, Gabriel, and Andrée, for their optimism and warmth.

I dedicate this work to Ivette, Guillermo, and Aurora: makers of worlds of hope. Thank you for all the love, wisdom, and imagination you bring to our life together.

Research and writing were carried out with the generous funding and intellectual support of the Wenner-Gren Foundation, the Social Science Research Council and Open Societies Foundation (Drugs, Security and Democracy Fellowship), the Inter-American Foundation, the American Council of Learned Societies, Harvard University, and Portland State University. An earlier version of chapter 4 appeared as "The Archaeology of Decay: Ruinous Knowledge and the Violence of Urban Planning," *American Anthropologist* 125, no. 3 (2023): 505–18. Previous material and arguments included in chapters 1, 2, 3, and 6 appeared in "Material (In)securities: Urban Terrain, Paperwork, and Housing in Downtown Bogotá," *Anthropological Quarterly* 93, no. 1 (2020): 1491–522. Earlier versions of sections of chapter 5 appeared in " 'The Miracle of Density': The Socio-Material Epistemics of Urban Densification," *International Journal of Urban and Regional Research* 44, no. 4 (2020): 617–35, and "An Anatomy of Failure: Planning After the Fact in Contemporary Bogotá, Colombia," in *Life Among Planners: Practice, Professionalism, and Expertise in the Making of the City*, ed. Jennifer Mack and Michael Herzfeld (University of Pennsylvania Press, 2020).

Notes

INTRODUCTION

1. I am following John Austin's (1975) conceptualization of speech acts as "performatives" that have concrete social effects. I am also drawing inspiration from Ludwig Wittgenstein's reflections on grammar as linguistic patterns and uses that are radically grounded in experience and inextricably connected to "life-form[s]" (1953, 7). In a passage that is particularly relevant to my thinking about urban grammars and spaces, Wittgenstein conceptualizes language as a city: "a maze of little streets and squares, of old and new houses, and of houses with additions from various periods; and this surrounded by a multitude of new boroughs with straight regular streets and uniform houses" (7).

2. This is Foucault's (2003, 16) inversion of Clausewitz's famous dictum, "War is the continuation of politics by other means." My analysis is closely related to scholarship on the everyday entanglements between planning practices and militarism, particularly in the context of colonial violence and sectarian and ethnonationalist conflict (Çelik 1997; Yiftachel 2006; Weizman 2007; Crane 2017; Bou Akar 2018).

3. Virilio 1994, 18.

4. The most common terms for "renewal" within planning circles are *renovación* and the more technical *redesarrollo* (redevelopment). I use "renewal," "renovation," and "redevelopment" interchangeably and reserve "revitalization" (*revitalización*) for the self-described progressive renewal plans launched since the early 2010s (see chapters 5 and 6).

5. See Andrés Salcedo Fidalgo's (2015) illuminating analysis of internal displacement in Colombia and the production of urban space.

6. Goldstein 2010, 488.

7. Graham 2010.

8. It is important to note here that after 9/11, the United States' war on drugs under Plan Colombia (1999) was reframed as part of the broader war on terror. Drug eradication and counterinsurgency were recast as counterterrorist efforts: As María Clemencia Ramírez (2019, S138) observes, "Guerrillas came to be known as 'narco-terrorists,' peasant coca growers were criminalized, and the US view of Colombia exclusively through a national security lens was reinforced."

9. Coaffee 2016.

10. In his ethnography of environmental risk in Bogotá, Austin Zeiderman usefully identifies the convergence of multiple and overlapping dangers, or what he aptly terms "hybrid threats" (2016, 82–88). Similarly, Javier Auyero develops the notion of "concatenated violence(s)" to conceptualize the interconnections between wide-ranging modalities of violence and harm (2015, 89). More broadly, Nancy Scheper-Hughes and Philippe Bourgois write about a "violence continuum" and what they call the "little violences" of everyday life (2004, 19).

11. For scholarly discussions of this notion in Colombia, see, e.g., Uribe Tobón 1990; Ramírez 1997; Blair Trujillo 2009.

12. The literature in this field is extensive, but for a milestone of what came to be known as "violentology," see Comisión de Estudios Sobre la Violencia 1987. For an illuminating analysis of the emergence of violentology as a field of expertise and institutional practice, see Villaveces-Izquierdo 1998.

13. For an account centered on the ordinary and experiential dimensions of violence, see Jimeno and Roldán 1998.

14. Boyer and Lomnitz 2005.

15. Jimeno 2001, 239.

16. See Serje 2005; Uribe 2017.

17. Goldstein 2010.

18. For an anthropological study of "vernacular security," see Bubandt 2005.

19. On the concept of "vernacularization" in the context of human rights discourses, see Goodale and Merry 2007; Merry 2009.

20. Martin Heidegger's article "Building Dwelling Thinking" (1971), which I am paraphrasing, has been widely influential in architecture circles. While the relationship between Heidegger's thought and his involvement in the German Nazi Party are beyond the scope of this book, it is crucial to recognize what architectural theorist Neil Leach (1998, 35) describes as the "violence repressed" within his phenomenological elaboration of dwelling in connection to ideas of national identity and homeland.

21. Mumford 1961, 44.

22. Mumford 1961, 388–89.

23. See, e.g., Rama (1984) 1996; Kagan 2000.

24. For a detailed political-economic history that also acknowledges the militaristic overtones of Haussmann's renovation plans, see D. Harvey 2003.

25. Wright 1991; Rabinow (1989) 1995; Çelik 1997.

26. M. Davis 2006, 205, 109.

27. Rabinow (1989) 1995, 9. See also Holston 1989.

28. Rabinow (1989) 1995, 9.

29. Rabinow (1989) 1995, 149, 12. According to Rabinow, his analysis is a continuation of Michel Foucault's work on the emergence of modern welfare (8). In this sense, it is intimately connected to Foucauldian conceptualizations of governmentality, biopower, and security as distinctive forms of governing populations and structuring spaces. In his lectures in the Collège de France, Foucault was particularly interested in the relationship between security apparatuses and town planning: "Sovereignty capitalizes a territory, raising the major problem of the seat of government, whereas discipline structures a space and addresses the essential problem of a hierarchical and functional distribution of elements, and security will try to plan a milieu in terms of events or series of events or possible elements, of series that will have to be regulated within a multivalent and transformable framework" (2007, 20).

30. As Rabinow ([1989] 1995, 11) explains, "The problem that social thinkers, reformers, architects, engineers, and emperors posed for themselves was one of bringing both norms and forms into a common frame that would produce a healthy, efficient, and productive social order."

31. See, e.g., Foucault (1966) 1973; Said 1979; de Certeau 1984; Mitchell 1988. For a dialectical critique of modern sight based on Walter Benjamin's work, see Buck-Morss 1991. On the role of "visualism" in anthropological knowledge, see Fabian 1983.

32. J. Scott 1998. For a critique that shows how planning instruments create opacity rather than transparency and legibility, see Hull 2012b.

33. Haraway 1988, 581.

34. See Herzfeld 2005; T. Li 2005.

35. See Mitchell 2002. For an alternative representation of planners, see Peattie 1987. For literature on the reflexive and situated character of planning expertise, see, e.g., Schön 1983; Suchman 1987.

36. Drawing inspiration from actor-network theory and new materialist theories, social scientists have countered human-centered accounts of social life that do not sufficiently

recognize the agency and qualities of things and material networks. While I build on this work, I do not emphasize nonhuman agency but rather highlight the relational dynamic between social actors' discursive performances and the constitution of urban materialities (Navaro-Yashin 2012). More than materiality, then, the main concern here is the *materialization* of urban security (Barad 2003, 810; Aradau 2010; Appadurai 2015). This is what Arjun Appadurai has described as a "mode of materialization": the mediations—ideational and practical—through which "matter comes to matter" (233–34). Adopting this perspective usefully refocuses attention on the status of human action and political accountability within complex techno-material assemblages.

37. See, e.g., Smith 1996; Samara 2010; Perry 2013; D. Davis 2013; Gledhill 2015; Larkins 2015.

38. Smith 1996.

39. Gledhill 2015, 49.

40. Gledhill 2015, 19.

41. Gledhill 2015, 107.

42. Perry 2013, 157.

43. Caldeira 2000, 19. See also Low 2003.

44. Caldeira 2000, 38.

45. In a major contribution to this discussion, Brazilian urban scholar and activist Raquel Rolnik (2019) offers a sweeping critique of global housing policy and finance as forms of "urban warfare" and "colonization." Although this book adopts a related perspective, instead of taking up warfare as an analytical category or metaphor, I attend to its grounded uses, deployments, and materializations by a range of urban actors. Here the emphasis is on how urbanism is rendered into a mode of warfare.

46. See, for example, Lakoff and Collier 2008; Gusterson and Besteman 2010; Goldstein 2010; Masco 2014; Jusionyte 2015; Ghertner et al. 2020; Al-Bulushi et al. 2023. Scholarship on Colombia has importantly added to these discussions by examining articulations of security in diverse fields such as ecotourism (Ojeda 2012), environmental risk (Zeiderman 2016), business politics (Moncada 2016), and marketing (Fattal 2018).

47. This ethnographic scholarship includes works on urban fortification and segregation (Caldeira 2000; Low 2003), rights and citizenship (Goldstein 2012), neoliberal development (O'Neill and Thomas 2011), mobility (Monroe 2016), and environmental risk (Zeiderman 2016). In close relationship to this literature, Zoltán Glück and Setha Low (2017, 289) have noted the centrality of "the scale of the city" for "the anthropology of security" and the need to further theorize and develop an "urban-focused analysis of 'security.'"

48. On the politics of "vertical urbanism," see, e.g., O'Neill and Fogarty-Valenzuela 2013; Harris 2015; Graham 2016. For an analysis of highway, bridge, and tunnel networks as security infrastructure, see Weizman 2007. On urban surveillance and technology-infused spaces, see Graham 2011.

49. Suchman et al. 2017, 984.

50. Murphy 2016, 443.

51. My formulation here builds on Henri Lefebvre's influential work on the "social production of space" and his "conceptual triad" of "spatial practices," "representations of space," and "representational spaces" (1991, 33). I am particularly interested in a phenomenological exploration of the closely entangled composition of urban knowledges and materialities.

52. Murphy 2016, 443.

53. Nader 1969, 292. See also Hannerz 1998.

54. Nader 1969, 292.

55. See Bourdieu 1977.

56. Boyer 2008. See also Holmes and Marcus 2005.

57. Boyer 2015b, 99.

58. Boyer 2015b, 99.

59. Boyer and Howe 2015.

60. Taussig 2003, 152.

61. Pérez Fernández 2010.

62. Berney 2017.

63. Alcaldía Mayor de Bogotá 1998, 466.

64. Elden 2017, 219. For a materialist and affective theorization of terrain, see Gordillo 2018.

65. Elden 2010.

66. Jaramillo 2006.

67. On insurgency in urban citizenship and planning, see Holston 2008; Miraftab 2009.

68. For a discussion of the city as palimpsest, see Huyssen 2003.

69. Aihwa Ong (2005, 339) defines "ecologies of expertise" as "novel combinations of mobile knowledge and actors connected to diverse sites and labors."

70. I met most residents thanks to a combination of referrals and introductions from officials and experts, contacts made during public events and planning outreach activities, and serendipitous encounters in downtown neighborhoods targeted by renewal. Although some of the residents were established community leaders long involved in struggles against displacement, many others had only just become engaged in antirenewal activism as a result of more recent waves of expropriation and eviction.

71. Amar 2013, 15. For analyses of the notion of "human security," see also Duffield 2001; Gledhill 2015.

72. Amar 2013, 27. It is worth noting that Michel Foucault's (2003) discussion of the shifts from sovereignty and discipline to biopower have inspired somewhat linear narratives based on the evolution of governmental technologies in the West. Despite often suggesting such a sense of progression, however, Foucault also writes, "So, there is not a series of successive elements, the appearance of the new causing the earlier ones to disappear. . . . In reality you have a series of complex edifices in which, of course, the techniques themselves change and are perfected, or anyway become more complicated, but in which what above all changes is the dominant characteristic, or more exactly, the system of correlation between juridico-legal mechanisms, disciplinary mechanisms, and mechanisms of security" (2007, 8).

73. Bogotá's rigid class stratification is organized around a geographical imaginary in which the South is poor and the North is affluent (cf. Uribe Mallarino 2008).

74. See Fortun and Cherkasky 1998.

75. For an anthropological discussion of "recursivity," see Kelty 2005.

76. Corsín Jiménez 2017, 455.

77. Rao 2006. See also Holston 1991, 2008; Simone 2010; Roy 2011; Caldeira 2017.

78. Rao 2009, 371, 377.

79. Herzfeld 2006.

80. Suchman 2011, 3.

81. Billé 2017. See also Elden 2013; Harris 2015; Graham 2016. In relationship to the notion of "density," see Rao 2007, 2015a; McFarlane 2016.

82. Stoler 2016, 27.

83. On the political possibilities of fragmentary, makeshift urbanism, see Simone and Pieterse 2017; McFarlane 2021.

84. This is what Gordillo (2014, 26), in his historical ethnography of rubble and destruction in the Argentinian Chaco, evocatively calls the "debris of violence."

85. On the notion of "reverberation" in the study of violence, see Navaro et al. 2021.

86. I draw inspiration from scholarship on ruins and its call to explore the "social after-life of structures, sensibilities, and things" (Stoler 2013a, 9).

1. DOWNTOWN GROUND ZERO

1. Vignolo 2013.

2. Castro Roldán and García 2015.

3. Agreement 174 of 2005 (City Council Agreement).

4. Vignolo 2013.

5. This was a program led by the city administration's Office for Peace, Victims, and Reconciliation (Alta Consejería de Paz, Víctimas y Reconciliación) and incorporated into Petro's government plan, *Plan de Desarrollo Bogotá Humana, 2012–2016.*

6. Quoted in *Revista Arcadia* 2019.

7. *El Tiempo* 2019a.

8. *El Tiempo* 2019a.

9. Quoted in *Revista Arcadia* 2019.

10. Rama (1984) 1996, 10.

11. Rama (1984) 1996, 12.

12. Rojas 2002, 29.

13. Trouillot 1995.

14. Huyssen 2003.

15. Dawdy 2016.

16. For a conceptualization of "residues of violence" in Colombia, see Fanta Castro 2015; Acosta López 2016.

17. Navaro et al. 2021, 8.

18. Navaro et al. 2021, 8.

19. Navaro et al. 2021, 10.

20. See, e.g., Weizman 2007; Aradau 2010; Rodgers and O'Neill 2012; Bou Akar 2018.

21. Delgado 2007, 156.

22. Aprile-Gniset 1983, 93.

23. Aprile-Gniset 1983, 91.

24. *El Espectador* 2021.

25. Medina 1984, 69.

26. See Alape (1983) 2016 for a monumental oral history of El Bogotazo.

27. Quoted in Braun 1985, 160.

28. Braun 1985, 158.

29. Alape (1983) 2016, 291–96.

30. Alape (1983) 2016, 643.

31. Alape (1983) 2016, 650.

32. Aprile-Gniset 1983, 19.

33. Colón 2005.

34. Tarchópolus 2022.

35. Oelze 2016, 102.

36. Alape (1983) 2016, 109–13.

37. Alape (1983) 2016, 110.

38. Alape (1983) 2016, 305.

39. Aprile-Gniset 1983, 34–36.

40. Arango et al. 1948, 11.

41. Quoted in Aprile-Gniset 1983, 49.

42. Sáenz Rovner 1992.

43. Niño Murcia and Reina Mendoza 2010.

44. Palacios 2006, xiii. See also Uribe 2017.

45. Decree 1370 of 1948.

46. Decree 1286 of 1948.

47. Aprile-Gniset 1983, 211–12.

48. Gusterson 2004. See also Low and Maguire 2019.

49. Sánchez-Beltrán 2022.

50. Aprile-Gniset 1983, 206.

51. DAPD 1964, 31.

52. Quoted in J. Dávila 2000, 172.

53. Quoted in J. Dávila 2000, 172.

54. Sandilands 1990.

55. Brittain 2005.

56. In her study of development policy in Colombia and the United States, Amy Off-ner (2019, 102) explains how Currie "set himself against the signal projects of the early National Front [governments]" with an "economic plan that proposed to accelerate urban migration and liquidate small farmers." In addition to his conviction about the futility of making campesinos "compete with large-scale, capitalist-intensive agriculture," Currie also critiqued dominant frameworks focused on "aided self-help housing" (promoted by agencies such as the Instituto de Crédito Territorial and El Centro Interamericano de Vivienda y Planeamiento Urbano) (102–3). For him, not only were these wasteful programs, but they also tended to concentrate public resources and rising land values in the hands of middle-class beneficiaries. Such was the case of Ciudad Kennedy in Bogotá, a housing development on the city's western edge that was constructed with the support of the Alliance for Progress and that Offner brilliantly dissects in her book (2019, chap. 3). On housing development and its centrality to ideologies of middle-class democracy, see also López-Pedreros 2019.

57. CID 1969, 19.

58. López-Pedreros 2019, 14.

59. For my account of this history, I rely primarily on Torres Carrillo (1993) 2013; and Pinilla 2014.

60. Torres Carrillo (1993) 2013, chap. 3.

61. Offner 2019, 99.

62. Offner 2019, 99.

63. Torres Carrillo (1993) 2013, 132.

64. Torres Carrillo (1993) 2013, 132.

65. Pinilla 2014, 26.

66. Valencia Tovar 1969, 121.

67. Valencia Tovar 1969, 121.

68. Valencia Tovar 1969, 121.

69. Saldarriaga Roa 2000, 131.

70. Currie 1975, 41. In later years, and after the implementation of projects such as the emblematic Ciudad Salitre in west Bogotá, Currie (1989) himself commented on the failure to include low-income residents, materialize ideas of public ownership, and capture value for social purposes. He considered these projects missed opportunities.

71. Everett 1998.

72. This was despite his initial appeal to leftist movements and working-class voters and his historic legalization of the Confederación Sindical de Trabajadores Colombianos (Union Confederation of Colombian Workers), an organization aligned with the Colombian Communist Party. See Restrepo Jaramillo 2016.

73. See Gill 2016 for an anthropological study of antiunion violence, counterinsurgency, and working-class activism in Colombia.

74. Gallón Galindo 1979, 129.

75. Gallón Galindo 1979, 150.

76. Jaramillo 2006.

77. See, e.g., Rodríguez Silva et al. 2004; Jaramillo 2006; de Urbina González 2012.

78. León Palacios 2008.

79. León Palacios 2008, 195.

80. *Alternativa* 1974, 24.

81. *Alternativa* 1975, 7.

82. *Alternativa* 1975, 7.

83. *Alternativa* 1975, 7.

84. *Alternativa* 1975, 7.

85. *Alternativa* 1975, 7.

86. *Alternativa* 1975, 7.

87. See Sarmiento Rojas 2017 for a detailed analysis of the struggles around heritage and memory in the renewal of Santa Bárbara.

88. Botero Montoya 2006, 28.

89. Botero Montoya 2006, 27–28.

90. Quoted in Hurtado Muñoz 2011, 30.

91. *El Tiempo* 1992.

92. Agreement 9 of 1977 (City Council Agreement).

93. Molano Camargo 2010, 134. See also Alape 1980; Torres Carrillo (1993) 2013.

94. Molano Camargo 2010, 122.

95. Molano Camargo 2010, 136.

96. Molano Camargo 2010, 137.

97. Molano Camargo 2010, 120.

98. Molano Camargo 2010, 133. See Ranajit Guha's (1983) 1988 classic essay on the "prose of counterinsurgency."

99. Molano Camargo 2010, 133. See also Alape 1980.

100. See Fattal 2018 for a revealing anthropological study of media and guerrilla warfare in Colombia.

101. Juzgado Tercero Penal del Circuito Especializado de Bogotá 2010, 59.

102. See, e.g., Vega Cantor 2016.

103. For a detailed account, see M. Maya Sierra 2005.

104. Bou Akar 2018, 37.

105. Bou Akar 2018, 37.

106. On urban residues and the Palace of Justice, see also Fanta Castro 2015, 91; Acosta López 2016.

107. T. Maya Sierra 2007, 14.

108. T. Maya Sierra 2007, 42.

109. T. Maya Sierra 2007, 14.

110. Alape 1997, 41.

111. Caicedo 1990, 14, quoted in T. Maya Sierra 2007, 14.

112. Caicedo 1990, 14, quoted in T. Maya Sierra 2007, 14.

113. Two artistic interventions in the palace in the following years pointed to the history that the building still occluded—first in ruins and then reconstructed. In March 1988, a group known as Movimiento Obrero Estudiantil Nacional Socialista (MOENS) bombed a theater performance during Bogotá's emblematic theater festival, the Festival Iberoamericano de Teatro. MOENS was the first incarnation of one of Colombia's largest paramilitary organizations, Autodefensas Campesinas de Córdoba y Urabá. By the

time of the bombing, the group had already massacred dozens of workers and union members in the Antioquia region (Rutas del Conflicto 2019). A few days after MOENS's attack against the Bogotá theater festival, the Catalonian theater troupe Els Comediants took over the ruins of the palace for a street performance titled *Dimonis*. A carnival of performers dressed as demons descended on the burned building and the Plaza de Bolívar and danced in the middle of an audience of one hundred thousand people with music and fireworks. *Dimonis* not only represented the reclaiming of urban space but also, in keeping with the group's own post-Franco roots, constituted "a response . . . to the murderous terror of fascist fire," as a local news report described the performance (Orozco 1988, 6). More than a decade later, another artistic performance, now in the recently inaugurated palace, called for a reckoning with Colombia's history of state violence. In 2002, hundreds of empty wooden chairs slowly crawled down a corner of the building, commemorating the victims of the attack and the recapture of the palace. The intervention by Colombian artist Doris Salcedo evoked the silence and forgetfulness that had characterized the aftermath of the episode and its materialization in urban space. The chairs, as María del Rosario Acosta López (2016, 35) aptly puts it, were "witnesses to an absence" (see also Zeiderman 2016, 58–59).

114. T. Maya Sierra 2007, 22.
115. T. Maya Sierra 2007, 42.
116. Trouillot 1995, 30.
117. Trouillot 1995, 30.
118. *El Espectador* 2016.
119. Centro de Memoria, Paz y Reconciliación 2012, 4.
120. Roca 2012, 9.
121. Roca 2012, 10.
122. Centro de Memoria, Paz y Reconciliación 2012, 13.

2. THE CITY AS TERRAIN

1. See Zeiderman 2016, 150–56, for an account of the encampment.
2. Bazuco is similar to crack cocaine. It is made from coca paste and other chemical byproducts of cocaine production.
3. References to martial arts and Japanese manga are common descriptors of the code of violence in downtown ollas. Besides the allusion to the Chinese martial arts tradition of the Shaolin Temple, street enforcers and hitmen are known as Sayayines or Saiyayines, the extraterrestrial warriors in the manga comic *Dragon Ball*.
4. Gordillo 2014, 25.
5. Gordillo 2014, 10.
6. Stoler 2016, 347–48.
7. The notion of "warscape," discussed by Nordstrom (1997, 37–39) (see also Hoffman and Lubkemann 2005), calls attention to how violence shapes places and ordinary lives beyond the war zone.
8. Virilio 1994, 45.
9. Virilio 1994, 46.
10. See, e.g., Berney 2017; Franco Calderón 2010; Robledo Gómez and Rodríguez Santana 2008; Zeiderman 2016.
11. Donovan 2008, 43.
12. D. Harvey 2006.
13. Here again I am building on Gordillo's work and his move away from conceptualizations of "creative destruction" that "subsume [destruction's] negativity to a creative affirmation" (2014, 81). In conversation with the work of Henri Lefebvre and David Harvey, he

writes instead about the "destruction of space" and "destructive production" as processes that need to be explored in their own terms and in all their complexity and variation (81).

14. Clausewitz (1832) 1989, 109.

15. See Gordillo 2023 for a theorization of "hostile terrain" as the material and affective grounding for revolutionary politics.

16. Weizman 2007, 186.

17. Weizman 2007, 5.

18. Weizman 2007, 262. For critical analyses of the geographies of occupation in Palestine that move beyond the narrow scope of security and that consider a broader range of actors and quotidian practices see, e.g., Harker 2020 and Rabie 2021. For a textured ethnography of urban planning and development in Beirut and their complex roles in propagating the logics of warfare, see Bou Akar 2018.

19. Graham 2011. For a discussion of the political challenges of an anthropology of the "forever war" and its "security encounters," see Glück 2024. See Al-Bulushi, Ghosh, and Grewal 2023 for an important call to decenter Euro-American geographies of militarism and state security in the anthropology of security.

20. The Israel Defense Forces' near obliteration of Gaza between 2023 and 2024 has taken the urbanization of warfare to new urbicidal extremes. In addition to what international law and human rights organizations have denounced as the genocidal killing of tens of thousands of civilians since 2023 (see, e.g., Human Rights Watch 2024), approximately 66 percent of Gaza's structures had been damaged or destroyed by September 2024, according to a United Nations assessment (UNOSAT 2024). For a longer history of urbicide in Palestine, see Abujidi 2014.

21. Graham 2011, 138.

22. Elden 2017, 223. See also Gordillo 2018.

23. See Hoffman 2019 for an illuminating analysis of security interventions and urban terrain, and for his emphasis on security operations' dependency "on the blunt instruments of instituting lines and violently carving shapes in urban space" (S105).

24. Navaro-Yashin 2012, 5. In a similar vein, Gordillo (2018, 54) coins the notion of "affective geometry" to analyze "how bodies are affected by and affect terrain." His "materialist phenomenology" is thus also committed to bringing together human experience and the physical dimensions of terrain.

25. Despite his penetrating critique of the militarized effects of planning, Weizman (2007) tends to portray the relationship between planning knowledge and warfare primarily as one of ideological mystification, a form of political "camouflage" (91).

26. See, e.g., Mejía Pavony 1999; Carbonell Higuera 2010.

27. Carbonell Higuera 2010, 227.

28. Carbonell Higuera 2010, 236.

29. Quoted in Carbonell Higuera 2010, 236.

30. Carbonell Higuera 2010, 236.

31. Carbonell Higuera 2010, 238.

32. Carbonell Higuera 2010, 237. See also Jaramillo 2006.

33. Carbonell Higuera 2010, 238.

34. Morris Rincón 2011, 26.

35. *Cartucho* is also the name of the lily flower, which evokes both the gardens of the neighborhood's bourgeois past and spaces of death, given the flower's symbolic association with funerals.

36. I am expanding on Navaro-Yashin's (2012, 27) conceptualization of "affective geography" as "the merging of the forces, energies, and affective potentialities of human beings, with their natural, built, and material environment" (see also Gordillo 2018). Affective geographies, I argue, are inextricable from individuals' epistemological orientations.

37. Quoted in Morris Rincón 2011, 37.

38. According to Morris Rincón (2011, 54), the term *gancho* originates from the colored clips or hooks used to pack bazuco doses. Different *jíbaros* (drug dealers), their foot soldiers, and their products were identified by specific colors—for example, *gancho azul* (blue hook) or *gancho amarillo* (yellow hook).

39. Bedoya Lima 2002.

40. Official representations of El Cartucho did not distinguish among the inhabitants of these buildings—impoverished renters, bazuco smokers, and dealers—and criminalized them all as members of the ganchos. Moreover, such accounts disregarded the complex political and social roles that ganchos performed within the neighborhood.

41. *El Tiempo* 1999.

42. Caldeira 2000.

43. Salcedo Fidalgo 2015.

44. For an intimate account of the relationship between urban life and violence in the Colombia of the late 1980s, see Braun 1994.

45. See, e.g., Safford and Palacios 2002; Serje 2005; Palacios 2006; Uribe 2017. For a broader theorization of how the "margins" are constitutive of state practices, see Das and Poole 2004.

46. Serje 2005. See also Ramírez 2011; Uribe 2017.

47. Serje 2005.

48. Gordillo 2018, 55.

49. Roitman 2014, 13.

50. Cepeda Ulloa 2000.

51. In his work as an international consultant, Peñalosa speaks regularly at academic, policy, and expert venues. He gave a TED Talk about one of his most widely known projects, the Transmilenio Bus Rapid Transit system, in 2013 ("Why Buses Represent Democracy in Action," September 2013, TEDCity2.0).

52. J. Dávila 2000.

53. *Proa* 1947, 7.

54. McCann 2011, 119.

55. United Nations Conference on Human Settlements 1976b, 2–3.

56. F. Scott 2016, 228.

57. F. Scott 2016, 233.

58. United Nations Conference on Human Settlements 1976a, 16.

59. See, e.g., Ferguson 1990; Mitchell 2002; Li 2007.

60. Clausewitz (1832) 1989; Foucault 1980c; Virilio and Lotringer 1983. On the military origins of logistics, see Cowen 2014.

61. This is what Foucault (1980b, 196) defined as "strategies of relations of forces supporting, and supported by, types of knowledge."

62. Clausewitz (1832) 1989, 71.

63. Kornberger 2012, 93.

64. Kornberger 2012, 98.

65. This is the Foucauldian idea of power as a relational field that has strategic effects and operates beyond individual agency and intentionality (Foucault 1980a, 203–24). I am interested here, in contrast, in the contingent and performative character of strategizing.

66. As Masco (2014, 35) argues, "theatricality" is central to the creation of military theaters of operation and the enactment of their boundaries.

67. On the politics of aesthetics, see the influential work of Jacques Rancière (2006). For a scholarly analysis of the role of aesthetics in urban governance, see Ghertner 2015.

68. On the links between Colombian regions and racial and cultural hierarchies, see Wade 1993.

69. Williams 1975, 46.

70. Williams 1977, 132.

71. Weizman 2007, 12.

72. Experts' adherence to this environmental determinism was itself revealing of the politics of material affordances (Gibson 1979; Dokumaci 2020): a fixing of the emergent and variable relationalities between people and their environments.

73. Elyachar 2010. See also Simone 2004.

74. But as Erika Robb Larkins (2015, 149) points out in her ethnography of favela pacification in Rio de Janeiro, such militarized policing strategies also deployed tactics to garner community support. Building public amenities, she notes, has been central to Rio's recent policing interventions, which resonate closely with the global counterinsurgency strategy of "clear, hold, build."

75. On the World Bank's "involuntary resettlement" policies, see Cernea 1988.

76. I am in conversation here with Zeiderman's work on the politics of security in Bogotá and his insights about the connections between disparate security logics, from risk management to crime control, and what he calls an "entanglement of diverse dangers" (2016, 82). His account, however, positions environmental risk as an encompassing technology of urban governance, and not enough is said about how logics of warfare and policing continue to shape urban models of intervention. In writing about El Cartucho, he argues that a "shift from center to periphery was encouraged by the progress of the Urban Renewal Program" (15). What I found, instead, was that many of the tactics employed in the Tercer Milenio had in fact originated in experiments to govern urban and rural peripheries. Additionally, even as autoconstructed peripheries became primary targets of state intervention, downtown continued to be a key focus of urban anxieties and policies. What this suggests, then, is a dialectical relationship between center and periphery in which urban security logics are continually reassembled and hybridized across time and space.

77. Fassin and Pandolfi 2010, 9.

78. On the emergence of "human terrain" in the US military and its relationship to anthropology, see R. González 2010.

79. Fassin and Pandolfi 2010, 10.

80. R. González 2010, 116.

81. Taussig 1999.

82. See Bornstein 2012 for an analysis of humanitarian and development aid through a critical engagement with Marcel Mauss's theorization of the gift.

83. See Mawdsley 2012.

84. *El Tiempo* 2000.

85. *El Tiempo* 2005b.

86. It is important to note here that a common pejorative term for unhoused people in Colombia is "disposable" (*desechable*).

87. *El Tiempo* 2005a.

88. Stoetzer 2018, 308.

89. See Abderhalden Cortés 2007. The performance was called *Prometeo*, and it was based on Heiner Müller's version of the myth of Prometheus. The project was part of a larger initiative called C'undúa, which was funded by the administration of Antanas Mockus from 2001 to 2003. *Prometeo* was carried out as a symbolic reckoning with the displacements caused by Tercer Milenio, reflecting in part the new administration's more ambivalent positions with regard to the plan. From 2003, Mapa Teatro's work on El Cartucho–Tercer Milenio was no longer funded by the city government. On Mapa Teatro's artistic experimentations and their sociopolitical significance during this time, see Taylor 2009; Till 2012.

90. Abderhalden Cortés 2007.

91. Corsín Jiménez 2014, 343.
92. Pérez 2020.

3. THE VIOLENCE OF BUREAUCRACY

1. Benjamin 1969, 12.
2. Gutierrez Sanín 2001, 69.
3. Gupta 2012, 33. See also Herzfeld 2009; Graeber 2015.
4. Urbina Vanegas 2015, 237.
5. Gledhill 2015, 3.
6. With their focus on bureaucratic artifacts, residents pierced through representation of "the state" as a coherent and unitary entity, tracking instead "the techniques that enable mundane material practices to take on the appearance of an abstract, nonmaterial form" (Mitchell 1999, 77).
7. Chu 2014, 360.
8. I am in conversation with the growing anthropological literature on bureaucratic and legal materiality (Riles 2006; Navaro-Yashin 2007; Hetherington 2011; Hull 2012b; Mathur 2016; Pérez 2016) as well as with scholarship in legal geography (Braverman et al. 2014).
9. Nakassis 2013, 403.
10. See McFarlane 2011 for an illuminating analysis of geographies of urban knowledge, learning, and dwelling. See Ingold 2000 for an anthropological elaboration of the Heideggerian perspective on dwelling.
11. Ahmed 2006, 3.
12. I am drawing here on critiques of the phenomenological anthropology of space and place (such as Ingold's [2000]) and the lack of sufficient attention to the critical role of sociopolitical relations and mediations (Myers 2000; Corsín Jiménez 2003). For a review of the rich and changing engagements between anthropology and phenomenology, see Dejarlais and Throop 2011. More broadly, I am inspired by critical reworkings of classical phenomenology and their exploration of the ways in which social processes and political practices inflect embodied perception and experience. This includes scholarship on critical race and postcolonial theory (going back to Frantz Fanon's influential work), critical theories of space inaugurated with the work of Henri Lefebvre, and queer and gender studies (e.g., Ahmed 2006).
13. Hoffman 2007.
14. I follow here Jonathan Shapiro Anjaria and Colin McFarlane (2011, 7), who conceptualize "urban navigations" as the ways in which "people actively move through, practice, cope with, seek to dominate, and learn how to live in the city."
15. See Pérez Fernández 2010; Berney 2017.
16. Braun 1985; Rojas 2002.
17. Quijano 2000.
18. Appelbaum 1999, 132; Farnsworth-Alvear 2000.
19. Roldán 2003, 136.
20. Roldán 2003, 135.
21. For a study of "fragmented sovereignty" in urban Colombia, see Gill 2016.
22. D. Harvey 1989, 8.
23. The ERU had its first incarnation in 1999 during the Peñalosa administration. At the time, it was a government program directly under the supervision of the mayor's office and devoted exclusively to the creation of Parque Tercer Milenio (see chapter 2). In 2004, it was reconstituted as a municipal company with its own budget, an independent organizational structure, and a wide-ranging mandate aimed at "channeling private-sector

initiatives" to increase both "urban competitiveness" and "citizens' quality of life" (Agreement 1 of 2004, Concejo Distrital de Bogotá).

24. In Spanish, *manzana* means both "apple" and "city block."

25. Pérez Ballén 2015, 71.

26. In other respects, the comedy was also arguably a middle-class idealization of working-class and peasant cultures.

27. Quoted in Peña Ardila 2012, 108.

28. Peña Ardila 2012, 109.

29. *Semana* 1983a, 1983b. See Peña Ardila 2012, 20.

30. The term "pariah capitalist" was coined by historian Marco Palacios (2006, 203) in his analysis of the "emergent bourgeoisie" of the drug trade of the 1980s.

31. See Duarte 2015.

32. Aya Uribe 2012. Conceptualizations of the urban sensorium can be traced back to Georg Simmel's ([1903] 1995) and Walter Benjamin's (2002; see also Buck-Morss 1991) works on the sensorial and aesthetic experience of urban modernity. I build here on this literature and on scholarship focused on the politics of urban sensory regimes (see, e.g., Goonewardena 2005; Rancière 2006; Ghertner 2015; Jaffe et al. 2020).

33. Similar to the Brazilian *jeitinho* (finding a way), understood as a form of bureaucratic manipulation (Holston 2008, 226), and the Indian *jugaad* (making do), viewed as a tactic of urban improvisation (Ranganathan et al. 2023, 33), *rebusque* points to "the hybridity, ingenuity, and opacity of political practices and gray ethical stances practiced by ordinary people in their everyday lives" (Ranganathan et al. 2023, 34).

34. In pointing to one of the block's most affluent residents and holding up a form of middle-class respectability, here, too, they paradoxically reinscribed the social hierarchies they were opposing.

35. Calvo Isaza and Saade Granados 2002.

36. For a history of coffee in Colombia, see Palacios 1979. On the relationship between political ideology and smallholding regimes, see Bergquist 2017. In addition to these works, I draw inspiration from Lowell Gudmundson's argument about how coffee smallholding constituted an "anti-left, petty-bourgeois reformism for the cold war era" (1989, 225).

37. Stewart 2011, 446.

38. Stewart 2007, 129.

39. I am in conversation with the growing scholarly literature in geography and anthropology on affective, urban atmospheres (see, e.g., Anderson 2009; Stewart 2011; Edensor 2012; Gandy 2017), and I draw inspiration from the way in which such works hold in productive tension materiality and meaning, things and subjects. I am interested in illuminating what Matthew Gandy (2017, 365) describes as the "politics of urban atmospheres" and their "historically constituted cultural and sociotechnical constellations."

40. On the contentious history of land boundaries and peasant mobilization, see LeGrand 1986.

41. The concept of "primitive accumulation" was famously coined by Karl Marx (1977) to describe the violent roots of capitalist development (e.g., land enclosures, slavery, conquest, and robbery). The notion has inspired extensive scholarship in agrarian and peasant studies, political economy, and critical urban studies, including David Harvey's (2006) influential theorization of processes of "accumulation by dispossession" under global neoliberalism. In the case of Colombia, authors have employed the lens of primitive accumulation to analyze the histories and geographies of violent dispossession and the contradictory processes of state formation in the context of the armed conflict (see, e.g., Ojeda 2012; Gómez et al. 2015; Vargas and Uribe 2017; Ballvé 2020). I build on this literature to explore the links between dispossession in the rural frontier and the urban core and,

more importantly, to illuminate the ways in which people encounter, render sensible, and critique these forces in everyday urban life.

42. See Salcedo Fidalgo 2015.

43. Hermer and Hunt 1996.

44. Hermer and Hunt 1996, 465.

45. Blomley 2002.

46. The misspelling of "private," whether intentional or not, was also illustrative of the opposition to the formalism of bureaucratic language.

47. See Ranganathan et al. 2023, 24, for a discussion of "middle-class respectability politics" in the context of global urban development conflicts and corruption narratives.

48. Navaro-Yashin 2012, 20.

49. Navaro-Yashin 2012, 20.

50. Legal anthropologists have long studied the various deployments of laws in social, political, and military disputes. As Sally Falk Moore explains, since at least the 1960s and 1970s the law "was understood [by anthropologists] to be usable in a great variety of ways by people acting in their own interest" (2001, 101). But with Margarita it was not only that she attended to legal process, politics, and agency; she also brought into focus the experience of legal practice as a form of violence.

51. Das 2007, 163.

52. See, e.g., Das 2007; Gupta 2012; Hull 2012b.

53. On the material mimicry of legal forms, see Ellison 2018.

54. Tate 2015.

55. Tate 2015, 236.

56. Stoler 2009, 52.

57. For theorizations of archives as instruments of power and control, see Foucault (1966) 1973; Derrida 1995; Trouillot 1995.

58. On archiving as an imperative in the context of democratic transitions, see Bickford 1999.

59. See Mbembe 2002 for a discussion of the "tactile" and "material" status of archives.

60. Law 975 of 2005.

61. Riaño Alcalá and Uribe 2016.

62. Riaño Alcalá and Uribe 2016, 9.

63. Law 975 of 2005.

64. Riaño Alcalá and Uribe 2016, 8.

65. Law 1448 of 2011.

66. Weizman 2017, 64. Alan Sekula (2014) originally used the term in his analysis of photographic counterarchives. Significantly, he drew inspiration from forensic anthropologist Clyde Snow and his work on victims of state violence across Latin America and beyond.

67. For an illuminating historical ethnography of archival activism in Latin America, see Kirsten Weld's (2014) study of postdictatorship Guatemala.

68. Weld 2014, 15.

69. As anthropological work has pointed out, beyond a narrow scope of the law, counterforensic practices are productive in a broad political and affective sense (Azuero Quijano 2023; Bozçali 2024).

70. Theidon 2012, 390.

71. Theidon 2015, 324. Since the early 2000s, the state has negotiated paramilitary demobilizations and struck the landmark peace accord with the FARC insurgency, bringing the country closer to a postconflict landscape. And yet violent conflict is far from over, with the operations of a new generation of paramilitary groups, FARC dissidents, and the ELN guerrillas. In this context, and as has been the case for decades of peace accords with

older armed groups, postagreement Colombia is exemplary of the contradictory temporality of an elusive peace yet to come.

72. Valverde 2014, 69.

73. Clarke 2019, 10.

74. Castillejo Cuéllar 2007.

75. See, e.g., Shaw and Waldorf 2010; Hinton 2011.

76. Jimeno 2007, 188.

77. Jimeno 2007, 180.

78. Theidon 2010, 100.

79. Theidon 2010, 100.

80. Hull 2012a, 255.

81. Herzfeld 1992, 20; see also Weber 1978.

82. Cody 2013, 205.

83. Cody 2013, 14.

84. Ricoeur 1984, 65. In their ethnography of urban corruption, Malini Ranganathan, David L. Pike, and Sapana Doshi (2023, 3) explore the urban "'plot' as land and as story" and conceptualize emplotting as "a semantic and sensory framework used by ordinary people to morally assess spatial change in late capitalism."

85. Tate 2007.

86. Gill 2016, 24, 25.

87. Antonio Gramsci ([1971] 1992, 235) likened hegemony, or "the superstructure of civil society," to "the trench-systems of modern warfare." He wrote about "war of maneuver" and "war of position" as two dialectically connected forms of struggle: the former more "tactical" and conjunctural, and the latter more "strategic" and comprehensive (234–35). In this context I understand Manzana Cinco's "epistemic maneuvers" as tactical forms of dissent that operate within a dominant paradigm of knowledge. Crucially, this hegemonic epistemology is warfare itself and its structuring of sociopolitical relations and material worlds.

88. I am in conversation with Gramscian critiques of ideology as "false consciousness," such as in the work of Raymond Williams (1977) and William Roseberry (1994). For an important contribution to this debate in anthropology, see Sopranzetti 2017.

89. Williams 1977.

90. Roseberry 1994, 361.

91. For a discussion of how evicted residents participate in hegemonic visions of urban beauty, see Harms 2012.

4. RUINOUS KNOWLEDGE

1. In her work with agricultural practitioners in Colombia, Kristina Lyons similarly illuminates "the potential for decay to reveal itself not only as erasure, but as a process that can be generative of different kinds of knowledge, different forms of organizing, and different practices" (2020, 39).

2. Writing about waste pickers in Rio de Janeiro, Kathleen Millar makes the important point that "garbage ceases to provoke abjection the moment perception shifts from the amorphous mass of detritus to its identifiable contents" (2018, 58).

3. Kockelman 2016b.

4. Kockelman 2016a, 2016b, 2016c.

5. Kockelman 2016b, 404–5.

6. Kockelman 2016c, 347.

7. See Murphy 2015 for a related discussion on the making of material forms as processes of "crafting and naturalizing *signs*" (217).

8. Kockelman 2016c, 350; see also Gibson 1979; Ingold 2000. I am most interested in Arseli Dokumaci's call to "politicize and historicize affordances" (2020, S100).

9. See, e.g., West and Sanders 2003.

10. Boyer 2009, 331.

11. Boyer 2009, 331.

12. See, e.g., Navaro-Yashin 2012; Stoler 2013a; Gordillo 2014; Tsing 2015.

13. Stoler 2013a, 9.

14. See, e.g., J. Collins 2015; Harms 2016; Hoffman 2017; Stoetzer 2018; Schwenkel 2020.

15. D. Harvey 2006.

16. Herscher 2020, 59.

17. Perry 2013, 91.

18. Navaro-Yashin 2009, 7.

19. Jaramillo 2006.

20. Cf. Carrión 2005.

21. Leal Martínez 2016, 556; see also Gandolfo 2009.

22. Amorocho et al. 1946.

23. Amorocho et al. 1946, 16.

24. Arango et al. 1948.

25. Arango et al. 1948, 19.

26. Alcaldía Mayor 1964, 1.

27. Bonilla et al. 1988, 31–32.

28. Li 2007, 7.

29. Li 2007, 7.

30. ERU 2012, 17.

31. ERU 2012, 35.

32. ERU 2012, 35.

33. Serje 2005; Tate 2015.

34. These contradictions were even more apparent in the left-leaning administration of Luis Eduardo Garzón (2004–7) and its reinvigoration of urban renewal with the Plan Zonal del Centro (2007). Paralleling what Austin Zeiderman (2016, 26) describes as the "overarching imperative [of security] across the political spectrum" in Colombia, progressive planners' attempts to redefine renewal remained conditioned by security and order-inflected views of decay.

35. Herzfeld 2009, 136. Herzfeld's (2009) study of urban management, historic preservation, and temporality in Rome is an interesting counterpoint to what I describe here.

36. Bear 2016, 490.

37. Herzfeld 2020, 19.

38. This was a reference to the alleged complicity of Colombian institutions such as the ICBF with exploitative international adoption schemes.

39. *Posesión* is the legal term for continuous use and occupation of a property without legal title.

40. Rao 2015b, 19.

41. Kockelman 2016b, 411.

42. DANE 2015, 19.

43. The other levels are estrato 2: low; estrato 3: medium-low; estrato 4: medium; and estrato 5: medium-high.

44. Tamayo Arboleda and Valverde 2021, 693.

45. DANE 2015, 33.

46. See, e.g., Hankins and Yeh 2016.

47. Kockelman 2016b, 398.

48. Uribe Mallarino 2008. See A. Dávila (2016, 123) for a subtle analysis of *estratos* in Bogotá and their complex relation to the "denial of racism" and "the continued valorization of whiteness" under an entrenched ideology of *mestizaje*.

49. Currency amounts are based on the average exchange rate for 2012.

50. Munn 1992; Graeber 2001; Elyachar 2005.

51. Ferry 2005, 13.

52. See Kockelman (2016a, chap. 3) for a discussion of use value through the analytic of "replacement."

53. Cf. Harms 2016, 15.

54. For a contrasting use of the notion of "archaeology" among bureaucrats and experts in urban law, see Pérez 2016.

55. Decree 400 of 2001. The decree was a response to a court order originated by an *acción de tutela* (a direct citizen claim to constitutional rights sanctioned by Colombia's 1991 constitution) presented by a resident in another Bogotá neighborhood. The administration was compelled to "establish tolerance zones in the capital city to avoid the illegal practice of prostitution and related economic activities beyond their limits." Tolerance zones were thus initially a response to local moral discourses and deep-seated conflicts between longtime residents, sex workers, and brothel owners (Salcedo Fidalgo et al. 2010). Eventually they would acquire a more legalistic character and, in a later iteration in Santa Fe in 2006, a fairly progressive tone aimed at creating a "pact" for mutual respect and for the defense of sex workers' rights. In practice, however, the talk of rights and equality did not map onto the reality of the area, with its deepening conflicts over territorial and economic control and violence against sex workers and street dwellers (129–30).

56. Ritterbusch 2016, 429–30.

57. While gender also played a role in how Paulina and Enrique related to urban space and danger, violence in the area was mostly directed at women and transgender sex workers (Ritterbusch 2016). "Los muchachos," as Enrique miscalled transgender sex workers, were being killed every week in the midst of violent territorial disputes—this is something a brothel doorman confirmed on our first stop walking down to Santa Fe. Further complicating the role of gender dynamics was the fact that the two main property and prostitution-business owners in the area were middle-aged women.

58. While most scholarly uses of "urbicide" refer to violence against cities in war and postwar contexts and implicitly draw a contrast with peacetime urbanity, I follow Herscher (2007) in understanding the violence of urban destruction as integral to projects of urban modernity (see also Benjamin 2002). For a comprehensive volume in this vein, see Carrión Mena and Cepeda Pico 2023.

59. I follow here Tania Li's important point about how, beyond assuming notions of conspiracy or overly "consistent, strategic effects," it is crucial to recognize that actors "take note of these effects and build them into their plans" (2007, 287n22). In this book I have pushed this line of inquiry to explore the performative dimensions of urban strategy (see chapter 2) as well as the complex ways in which strategic effects are mediated by people's interpretations, experiences, and practices (cf. Bou Akar 2018).

60. Buck-Morss 1991, 211.

61. See, e.g., Navaro-Yashin 2012; Gordillo 2014; Tsing 2015; Hoffman 2017; Bou Akar 2018.

62. Hoffman 2017, 4.

63. Gordillo 2014, 82.

64. Bear 2016.

65. Bou Akar 2018, 37.

66. Benjamin 1978, 286.

67. Navaro-Yashin 2009, 7. I am inspired here also by Nancy Fraser's (1991) call to attend to the political and institutional dimension of legal violence, as well as by Nicholas Blomley's (2003, 133) insight that "the violences of law are socially selective."

68. Dawdy 2016, 140.

69. In his discussion of "enclosure of value," Kockelman (2016a, 7) argues that "processes that create, interpret, and reveal value are concomitant with processes that capture, carry, and reify value."

70. Weinstein 2017. See also Roy 2009; Zhang 2010; Harms 2016.

71. Herzfeld 2009, 64.

72. Hage 2021, 8.

73. These questions, as well as most of the literature on ruins I draw on here, are inspired by Benjamin's (1978, 2002) insights on the critical and revolutionary potential of destruction.

74. Petro was referring to the Tercer Milenio and San Victorino interventions.

75. For a brief account of some of Maldonado Copello's ideas on planning and land policy, see Fernandes and Maldonado Copello 2009. More on this in chapter 5.

76. Hoffman 2017, 6. See also Stoler 2009; Gordillo 2014.

5. TERRITORY BY DESIGN

1. Massey 2005, 4. De Certeau (1984, 121) writes about how the "map" is an objectifying figure that "colonizes space" and stands in contrast to the "tour," which is a grounded and practice-based approach to space.

2. On the liveliness and dynamism of "terrain," see Elden 2017; Gordillo 2018.

3. A key question I take on in this chapter is how territory, as a political and sociospatial category, "become[s] articulated as design" (Suchman 2021, 18)—that is, as a matter of giving form to sociomaterial densities (cf. Murphy 2016). I heed in particular Lucy Suchman's call to "question design's modern/colonial genealogies, and design's capture within dominant modes of neoliberal capitalism" (2021, 31; see also Escobar 2018). This requires attending to the particular conjunction between urban planning, design, and territory in the context of Colombia's history of struggles over modern sovereignty.

4. Economist Edward Glaeser has articulated influential prodensity discourses in academia and beyond. For a critical review, see Peck 2016.

5. Wilmott 2020, 157.

6. Rao 2007, 229.

7. McFarlane 2016, 632.

8. McFarlane 2016, 631.

9. McFarlane 2016, 644.

10. In addition to drawing on Elden's (2010, 812) conceptualization of territory as a "political technology" that is "produced, malleable, and fluid," I follow here a rich body of scholarship that explores Colombia's nation-building process as the fragmentary, contradictory, and incomplete materialization of modern ideals of territory. This includes studies on the tensions between state-driven processes of territory making and the local geographies and histories of countervailing territorialities (see, e.g., Serje 2005; Escobar 2008; Ng'weno 2007; Ballvé 2020), as well as critical analyses of the politics of ordenamiento territorial (see, e.g., Fals Borda 1996; Asher and Ojeda 2009; Beuf and Rincón Avellaneda 2017). More broadly, my ethnographic approach to territory, territorial ordering, and the afterlives of security is informed by Donald Moore's illuminating work on territory in Zimbabwe as the product of "historical sedimentations, at once discursive and material" of geographies of violence and dispossession (2005, 12).

11. Allen 2011, 284.

12. P. Harvey 2012, 77, 78.

13. This formulation is inspired by Stuart Elden's article "Secure the Volume," where he reconceptualizes security in terms of "circulation and power" in volumetric geographies (2013, 49). I use the term "managing" to draw attention to "calculative techniques" (49) and their centrality to such less overt modes of securitization. This resonates with Foucault's (2007, 21) thoughts on security and town planning as mainly concerned with the organization and regulation of a "milieu" or "a set of natural givens—rivers, marshes, hills—and a set of artificial givens—an agglomeration of individuals, of houses, etcetera." Particularly relevant to my discussion of density is his mention of "overcrowding" and "miasmas" as key objects of intervention for early town planners (21). I follow a related line of thinking to explore the links between security, in an expanded sense, and planning as the management of territory-as-density. Yet Foucault's use of "milieu," as Elden (2021, 4) points out, fails to "capture the specifically material aspects" of volumetric geographies.

14. For literature in anthropology and geography on volumetric spatialities and their politics, see, e.g., Weizman 2007; Elden 2013, 2017, 2021; Graham 2016; Billé 2017, 2020.

15. While building codes and urban norms have historically regulated volumetry (*volumetría*), heights, and edificabilidades of construction in Bogotá, the lens of density as proposed in the POT modification projects entailed a much more substantive citywide treatment of the physical dimensions of urban space and represented a broad planning and policy objective.

16. Elden 2017, 219.

17. For an analysis of the politics of leftist governments in Bogotá, see Eaton 2021.

18. Density, in this sense, is part of what Ananya Roy (2016, 205) calls the "universal grammar of urbanism": hegemonic urban concepts originated in the global North that obscure historical and geographical difference across urban worlds.

19. Billé 2020, 5.

20. Easterling 2014, 13.

21. Easterling 2014, 14.

22. Easterling 2014, 13.

23. Easterling (2014, 21) writes about spatial activism as follows: "Exposing evidence of the infrastructural operating system is as important as acquiring some special skills to hack into it." Hacking as a form of dissent, however, reproduces the computational paradigm and its assumptions. As Shannon Mattern (2013) argues in her critique of "smart urbanism," political mobilization around urban data production still entails "facing the city as a computational problem" and "uphold[ing] the algorithmic ethos." My analysis explores the similar problem of how planners seeking to rework density into more progressive arrangements ultimately reproduced epistemological assumptions about the city as a volumetric territory.

24. González Arias 1992. Karl (2017) offers a perceptive historical analysis of the notion of "independent republics" and their role in the trajectories of violent conflict in Colombia.

25. Extolling the virtues of political decentralization, for instance, former minister and Bogotá Mayor Jaime Castro stated in 1998, "Decentralization . . . will one day allow us to say that we have as much territory as we have a State, because until now the expanse of the first has been far superior to the authority of the latter" (quoted in Ballvé 2020, 51). In a similar vein, former Vice President Gustavo Bell responded to a 2002 massacre in the town of Bojayá, Chocó, with the declaration, "Colombia has more geography than state" (quoted in Serje 2005, 45).

26. Holmes and Marcus 2005, 237.

27. Holmes and Marcus 2005, 241.

28. Lefebvre 1991, 6.

29. Boyer 2005, 43–44. My use of "planning-in-action" echoes Donald Schön's (1983) discussions of planners and related practitioners as immersed in forms of "reflection-in-action."

30. Murphy 2015, 133.

31. Murphy 2015, 132, 171.

32. Despite the increasing influence of data and financial instruments within the profession, planners often brought designerly sensibilities into their work—what Diego described as the need to "sketch out ideas [echar lápiz]." The rise of techniques to reshape density arguably point to the enduring role of architecture and design within city planning even as computer-based, algorithmic approaches of parametric design have taken precedence.

33. Massey 2005, 100.

34. Pergolis 1998. For a theorization of the politics of urban fragmentation, see McFarlane 2021.

35. Pérez 2016.

36. Pinilla Pineda 2010, 353.

37. Roy 2016. Amin and Lancione (2022, 4) have discussed the tacit politics of dominant "urban lexicon[s]" and the importance of exploring "critical grammars for the city."

38. In her work on Lima, Daniella Gandolfo (2020, 157–58) offers a conceptualization of the "tellurian forces" associated with working-class masses and how they historically clashed with modernist architecture and planning. Building on her analysis, my research suggests a form of planning that seeks to domesticate and exploit the "tellurian power" of downtown's crowds and what elites and officials typically characterized as their unwieldy activities and forms of organization.

39. The speculative nature of BD Bacatá became apparent as its developer filed for liquidation in 2018 amid not only serious financial issues but also accusations of corruption tied back to investigations in Spain. The building itself, partially inhabited by 2021, has been the subject of ongoing scrutiny, with residents denouncing problems with utilities, flooding, and poorly built (and unfinished) areas. See Agencia de Periodismo Investigativo 2021.

40. In the tradition of nineteenth-century political economist Henry George, Martim Smolka of the Lincoln Institute of Land Policy—an influential organization among planners in Colombia and Latin America based in Cambridge, Massachusetts—defines plusvalía in the following terms: "Value capture refers to the recovery by the public of land value increments (unearned income or plusvalías) generated by actions other than the landowner's direct investments" (2013, 8). In Bogotá, this involved a complex calculus of the potential value added by new urban norms in terms of changes in land uses or building allowances. Overall, collections through plusvalías in Bogotá have been very low as a result of the technical difficulties in determining value increments within the city's convoluted and shifting legal terrain. In many cases, moreover, because older norms contain greater building allowances, planners often find a "minusvalía [loss of value]" under new regulations, as an expert once told me, making it impossible for the administration to share in the economic value produced by urban development.

41. The ratio (1 to 5.6 square meters) had been established through direct negotiations with the Cámara Colombiana de la Construcción (Colombian Chamber of Construction), or CAMACOL.

42. The CTPD is in charge of channeling wider inputs from communities and localities across the city, which it then uses as a basis to produce a nonbinding "concept [concepto]" about the POT. Although this concept can have an impact on the social and political reception of the plan, the POT's fate is ultimately decided in the Concejo de Bogotá (Bogotá City Council).

43. In another sense, the meeting exemplified the stark opposition between technocratic conceptions and alternative visions of territory circulating among citizens and activists—what the CTPD called the "social construction of territory." See Duque Franco 2010 for an analysis of these tensions.

44. Boyer 2015a, 163.

45. "Technical" planners saw themselves carrying forward the tradition of modernist planning and what they called "quality urbanism [*urbanismo de calidad*]" or "well-designed" urban spaces. Many of these professionals had studied in Spain and followed closely the civic ideals imprinted on urban revitalization projects made famous by the city of Barcelona, replicating what Manuel Delgado (2007, 38) calls the Catalonian capital's "myth of public space" and its instrumental role in the "capitalist reappropriation of the city." Generally speaking, these planners—many of them architects and urban designers—moved through institutional spaces such as the Escuela de Arquitectura y Urbanismo (School of Architecture and Urbanism) at the Universidad Nacional, the Departamento Nacional de Planeación (National Planning Department), and CAMACOL. Critical and activist planners, in turn, had less of a background in architecture and were more closely connected to interdisciplinary urban studies and policy research centers such as the Instituto de Estudios Urbanos (Institute of Urban Studies) at the Universidad Nacional, the Centro Interdisciplinario de Estudios sobre el Desarrollo at the Universidad de los Andes, and the Lincoln Institute of Land Policy. In contrast to técnicos' focus on physical forms and their tacit alignment with developmentalist ideologies, activist planners centered questions of land, redistribution, and property and value.

46. Porter et al. 2021, 117. With some exceptions, técnicos typically espoused center and center-right ideological positions and supported market-led reforms.

47. While the Petro administration had pledged to build 70,000 units of Vivienda de Interés Prioritario (Priority Interest Housing), or VIP, between 2012 and 2016, by the end of the term only 11,638 units had been constructed.

48. Eaton 2021, 15.

49. Maldonado Copello 2003, 215. Maldonado Copello herself was one of the most influential academics turned officials during the Petro administration, serving as director of planning and director of housing during the term. She has been a leading expert in urban law, planning, and land policy in Colombia since the 1990s. In addition to her affiliations with local universities, her work has been supported by the Lincoln Institute of Land Policy and is central to critical and activist planning networks in Colombia. For a contrasting vision focused on modern planning and development, see Salazar Ferro 2018.

50. *El Tiempo* 2018.

51. *El Tiempo* 2019b.

52. Magic Markers 2015.

53. *El Tiempo* 2016a. For a comprehensive analysis, see Contreras Ortiz 2019.

54. Reserva Forestal Regional Productora del Norte de Bogotá D.C., "Thomas Van der Hammen," Agreement 11 of 2011 (Corporation Autónoma Regional de Cundinamarca—CAR).

55. According to Simone and Pieterse (2017, 78) the rise of data-driven, parametric urbanism creates "interfaces between the 'data city' and 'real city' [that] are uncertain even as the pragmatics of these calculations emphasize the sense of stability and order brought to bear on the 'real city.'" In these terms, urban density is a key parametric function that aims to "stabilize" unwieldy and complex urban processes (84).

56. Serje 2005, 144.

57. I follow Blomley's conceptualization of territory not only as the material expression of state sovereignty but also as the taken-for-granted instantiation of property regimes, or what he calls "the territorialization of property" (2016, 605).

58. Gouëset 1999, 92.

59. Serje 2005, 139.

60. Fals Borda 1999, 86, 84.

61. Quoted in Beuf 2019, 2.

62. Beuf 2019, 2.

63. Escobar 2019, 134.

64. Escobar 2018, 61.

65. Escobar 2018, xvii.

66. Escobar 2018, 74.

67. Beuf 2019, 5.

68. Asher 2019, 214. For a discussion of decoloniality in the context of urban planning, see, e.g., Ugarte 2014.

69. Rivera Cusicanqui 2012, 99–100.

70. Rivera Cusicanqui 2012, 100.

71. Rivera Cusicanqui 2012, 101.

72. Subramanian 2009, 145.

73. This is what Kiran Asher (2020, 950), writing about territorial struggles in the Colombian Pacific and responding to Escobar, describes as the "key political economic and cultural political conjunctures" that illuminate "how Afro-Colombian struggles, state power, and neoliberal development *shape each other* in paradoxical and uneven ways."

74. Subramanian 2009, 250.

75. D. Moore 2005, 210.

76. Escobar 2018, 198, 196.

77. In her critique of decolonial studies and its reproductions of structural inequalities in academia and beyond, Rivera Cusicanqui (2012, 102) calls attention to the "economic strategies and material mechanisms that operate behind discourses," which she terms the "political economy of knowledge."

6. PROGRESSIVE FICTIONS

1. Miraftab 2004.

2. Baldwin 2021, 6.

3. For more on the continued forms of extractivism and dispossession under Colombia's "postconflict development" paradigms, see Ojeda and González 2018.

4. Li 2014, 184–85.

5. I follow here what Tania Li (2014, 18) calls a "conjunctural approach." Inspired by the thought of Antonio Gramsci, Henri Lefebvre, Raymond Williams, Doreen Massey, and Gillian Hart, among others, Li notes that attending to conjunctures "means rejecting the liberal concept of the self-sovereign, strategizing subject" to "foregroun[d] practices, taken-for-granted habits, and material configurations" (18).

6. Muñoz and Fleischer 2022.

7. At stake here was the recognition of what Nicholas Blomley (2003, 132) calls the "violences of property": the implied and overt, legal and corporeal violences through which property regimes are founded and reproduced. More broadly, residents' critical knowledges pointed to the materiality of housing as a key "site of struggle over the making and remaking of the political" (Elinoff 2016, 612; see also Holston 1991).

8. Dating back to a 1994 UN Development Program report, "human security," according to Chowra Makaremi (2010, 108), was aimed at "redefining security as 'humane' and

broadening the use of the concept from exclusive military threats to economic, social, and environmental threats." In practice, Makaremi argues, "the concept of human security has been remilitarized in humanitarian interventions, promoting notions of emergency and safety as moral grounds for political action" (108). See also Amar 2013.

9. Duffield 2001.

10. Quoted in Gutiérrez Sanín 2001.

11. Such forms of "epistemic violence," Santiago Castro-Gómez (2002) argues, are integral to the history of the social sciences in Latin America and their crucial role as vehicles for hegemonic projects of nationhood and citizenship.

12. Jobson 2020, 265. I echo here the renewed sense of urgency that abolitionist and decolonial reckonings have taken in anthropology and urban planning. For this discussion in anthropology, see, e.g., Harrison 1997; Shange 2019; Jobson 2020. For urban planning, see, e.g., Miraftab 2009; Bates et al. 2018; and Porter et al. 2021.

13. Quoted in Bell Lemus et al. 2008, 54.

14. Bell Lemus et al. 2008, 67.

15. Rama (1984) 1996.

16. Bell Lemus et al. 2008, 55.

17. Bell Lemus et al. 2008, 81.

18. Quoted in Bell Lemus et al. 2008, 73.

19. Offner 2019, 122–30.

20. Offner 2019, 131.

21. I follow Steven Gregory's (2020, 81) call to "attend to the symbolic meanings that verticality obtains through the spatial practices of religious, political, and cultural elites." Gregory writes about how Columbia University, along with other elite institutions, "harnessed geography" (94) as a strategy of control in the Morningside Heights neighborhood in New York City.

22. On the simplifying optics from above, common in modernist modes of governance and planning, see the well-known works of de Certeau (1984) and J. Scott (1998).

23. Universidad de los Andes 1972, 12.

24. Centro de Planificación y Urbanismo 1967.

25. Bonilla et al. 1988.

26. Muñoz and Fleischer (2022, 44–45) offer a useful analysis of campus maps during these years, showing the shift from an almost pastoral image of a self-contained hillside campus to renderings that increasingly integrated the surrounding urban fabric.

27. Writing about urban universities in the United States, Baldwin (2021, 36) argues that "with the decline in manufacturing, the 'bell towers' of higher education were targeted as the new 'smokestacks': the signals of a thriving urban economy after the fall of factories." While nothing comparable to the US back-to-the-city movement of the late 1990s and early 2000s happened in downtown Bogotá, university campuses undoubtedly served as anchors for middle- and upper-class land uses and socialities. More recently, with the expansion of the campuses of Los Andes, the Tadeo Lozano, Universidad Central, and the Universidad Externado de Colombia, and their more active participation in urban renewal plans, universities have emerged as key players in the city center's rising real estate markets (see de Urbina González 2012).

28. On feminist standpoint theory, see Harding 2004.

29. I follow here Black feminist scholars Patricia Hill Collins (1986) and bell hooks (1984) and their foundational theorizations of the production of knowledge from the perspective of the "outsider within" who is aware of both "margins and center."

30. According to Tania Li (2007, 7), "The practice of 'rendering technical' confirms expertise and constitutes the boundary between those who are positioned as trustees,

with the capacity to diagnose deficiencies in others, and those who are subject to expert direction. It is a boundary that has to be maintained and that can be challenged."

31. In addition to recognizing its integral role in colonial modernity's regimes of knowledge (Castro-Gómez 2002), my use of "epistemic violence" here follows standpoint theory once again and its attention to oppressors' "systemic ignorance" (Harding 2004, 5). This is what David Graeber (2015, 45), in a later variation of such critiques, describes as the "structural stupidity" of those in power. As Progresa Fenicia shows, such forms of ignorance do not indicate an absence of knowledge. On the contrary, it is precisely the technical production of knowledge that deepens the obliviousness to facets and experiences of social life. As one faculty member and collaborator in the plan put it, it was hard to imagine a place more studied and "overdiagnosed" than Las Aguas—from student theses to classroom fieldwork to robust research and social engagement programs. The more experts thought they knew about Las Aguas and its people, the more they obscured internal differences, underlying political-economic conditions, and locals' epistemic practices.

32. Graeber further discusses the violence of bureaucracy as an expression of "highly lopsided structures of imagination" (2015, 72).

33. Escobar 2018, 74.

34. This engagement with informality resembles what Ananya Roy (2005, 147–48) describes as its "[strategic use] by planners to mitigate some of the vulnerabilities of the urban poor."

35. Zorro and Reveiz 1974, 14.

36. Jaramillo 2006, 10.

37. In an important contribution to the anthropological literature on property, Katherine Verdery (2003, 13) calls attention to the fact that "property is a process (of making and unmaking certain kinds of relationships)." Writing about Romania's postsocialist transition, she reflects on changing property regimes and their effects on social and power relations. Verdery argues that "property specifies what things have what kind of value and who counts as a person" and that it "sets up inclusions and exclusions," ultimately becoming a "powerful idiom in processes of appropriation" (18). Progresa Fenicia struck many residents in Las Aguas as potentially leading to such forms of appropriation and dispossession. As a contentious transformation of property regimes, furthermore, it bore troubling resemblances to the violence of changing land rights so central to the country's armed conflict (Gutiérrez Sanín and García Reyes 2016), as well as to the ambiguous and uncertain promise of property in what Meghan Morris (2019) aptly terms the "shadow of the post-conflict."

38. Ghertner and Lake 2021, 17.

39. Salcedo Fidalgo 2015, 208.

40. In her work on land conflict in Colombia's Urabá region, Morris (2017, 49) importantly calls for more careful ethnographic theorization of the "intimate relation" between histories of dispossession (*despojo*) and the politics of possession (*posesión*).

41. Alape (1983) 2016, 69.

42. Pinilla and Arteaga 2021, 46.

43. Decrees 420 and 448 of 2014.

44. *El Tiempo* 1993.

45. *Voz* 1983.

46. Forero Hidalgo and Moreno Camargo 2015. See also Medellín Pérez 2024.

47. As Tania Li (2007, 282) argues, improvement, as a key governmental logic, "directs the conduct of 'small people' while leaving radical political economic inequalities unaddressed." Something similar was at work in both planners' and Nancy's interventions in Las Aguas.

48. Pinilla and Arteaga 2021, 51.

49. Pinilla and Arteaga 2021, 51.

50. Pinilla and Arteaga 2021, 50.

51. Nader 1997, 711.

52. For Escobar (2018, 226), radically new ways of being and envisioning the world are necessary to move beyond the "established politics of the possible and the real." In line with his theorizations of ontological difference, he suggests that new urban imaginaries would have to emerge from outside the city—namely, by "introduc[ing] a peasant view of the soil into the city, reconstituting the apartment building and the neighborhood as what could be called rurban territories" (Escobar 2019, 136). Instead of looking outside toward idealized urban peripheries or rural enclaves—with the usual pitfalls this entails in terms of reifying difference and reproducing dualisms (Asher 2019)—Progresa Fenicia turns our attention to the dialectical shaping of urban planning and politics within specific political-economic and sociomaterial contexts. From this vantage point, imagining new urban realities and possibilities requires above all an analysis of power structures, of how certain ideas and arrangements become hegemonic, and of their contradictory unraveling through the everyday practice and materiality of politics.

53. Nader 1997, 712.

54. Ghertner and Lake (2021, 17) have elaborated the notion of "value projects" as follows: "What holds together the multiple regulatory, legal, and narrative land fictions we explore, then, is their function as value projects that evoke and emphasize particular commodity registers of land and draw in willing subjects seeking to remake the world through the modified relationships and roles they promise to enact."

55. It is worth noting here the echoes of longer histories of land titling in Latin America's peripheral settlements and of their deeply contradictory absorption of urban dwellers into regimes of property and debt. See, e.g., Gilbert 2002 for a critique of urban titling policies made famous by Peruvian economist Hernando de Soto.

56. In her piercing critique of the paradoxes of progressivism in an antiracist school in San Francisco, Savannah Shange (2019, 15) writes, "Carceral progressivism functions as a pinnacle of efficiency for late liberal statecraft because the discursive narratives (e.g., liberation) and material gains (e.g., a justice-themed public high school) of redistributive social movements are cannibalized and repurposed as rationales for dispossession."

EPILOGUE

1. *El Tiempo* 2016b.

2. León and Arenas 2016.

3. Marín Correa and Flórez Suárez 2016.

4. The national government rebranded the ESMAD in 2022 as the Unidad de Diálogo y Mantenimiento del Orden (Unit of Dialogue and Order Maintenance), or UNDMO, part of President Petro's campaign promise to eliminate the ESMAD. The UNDMO is a striking example of the paradoxes of progressivism, in this case of "progressive policing." People still refer to riot police as the ESMAD, and violent repression of protests is still the usual governmental response.

5. Andres Felipe 2018.

6. Ritterbusch and El Cilencio 2020, 212.

7. Márquez and Góngora 2023, 14.

8. Márquez and Góngora 2023, 14.

9. Márquez and Góngora 2023, 16.

10. Other participating institutions included the Museo Nacional de Colombia (National Museum of Colombia) and the city's Instituto Distrital para la Protección de la Niñez y la Juventud (Institute for the Protection of Childhood and Youth), or IDIPRON.

11. Márquez and Góngora 2023, 16–17.

12. Márquez and Góngora 2023, 17.

13. Márquez and Góngora 2023, 20.

14. Márquez and Góngora 2023, 11.

15. On learning and the city, see McFarlane 2011 and Corsín Jiménez 2017. On the epistemic and political promises of "fragment urbanism," see McFarlane 2021.

16. For spatial and visual analyses that establish the intentional killing of Dilan Cruz with a "non-lethal bean bag" fired to the head by an ESMAD agent, see Fiorella 2019 and Forensic Architecture Team 2023.

17. Peñaranda and Gómez-Delgado 2019.

18. Ojeda and Pinto García 2020.

19. Alvarado 2020.

20. Alejandra Azuero Quijano (2023, 21) conceptualizes the Paro as an "epistemic explosion [*estallido epistémico*]" that reshaped "politics, conditions of the sensible, and modes of knowing." Her illuminating analysis of the phenomenological ramifications of the event resonates closely with my interest in how the Paro shattered the city's sedimented history of warfare and opened spaces to counter the "normalization of state violence" (44).

21. Waterhouse 2019.

22. The second wave of protests had been set off by the death of a man under police custody at a CAI.

23. See, e.g., Waterhouse 2019; Montero and Peñaranda 2020; Azuero Quijano 2023.

24. Montero and Peñaranda 2020.

25. Puentes 2021.

26. Caldeira 2012.

27. Quoted in Sanabria Ortiz 2021, 38.

28. Quoted in Sanabria Ortiz 2021, 40.

29. Salge Ferro and Jaramillo E. 2021.

30. Salge Ferro and Jaramillo E. 2021.

31. Salge Ferro and Jaramillo E. 2021.

32. The most concrete manifestation of this new paradigm took the form of a "feminist care policy" implemented through so-called Manzanas del Cuidado (Blocks of Care): public buildings constructed in poor neighborhoods to "address gender and class inequalities and alleviate care burdens on women" (Álvarez Rivadulla et al. 2024).

33. Azuero Quijano 2023, chap. 3.

34. On "abolitionist planning" understood as "abolishing planning," see Porter et al. 2021, and as a practice inherently at odds with professional planning, see Dozier 2018.

References

Abderhalden Cortés, Rolf. 2007. "The Artist as Witness: An Artist's Testimony." *E-misférica* 4 (2). http://hemisphericinstitute.org/journal/4.2/eng/artist_presentation/mapateatro/mapa_artist.html.

Abujidi, Nurhan. 2014. *Urbicide in Palestine: Spaces of Oppression and Resilience.* Routledge.

Acosta López, María del Rosario. 2016. "Las fragilidades de la memoria: Duelo y resistencia al olvido en el arte colombiano (Muñoz, Salcedo, Echavarría)." In *Resistencias al olvido: memoria y arte en Colombia*, edited by María del Rosario López Acosta. Universidad de los Andes.

Agencia de Periodismo Investigativo. 2021. "El desplome financiero de seis mil inversionistas por el edificio más alto de Colombia." March 13.

Ahmed, Sara. 2006. *Queer Phenomenology: Orientations, Objects, Others.* Duke University Press.

Alape, Arturo. 1980. *Un día de septiembre: Testimonios del Paro Cívico Nacional, 1977.* Ediciones Armadillo.

Alape, Arturo. (1983) 2016. *El Bogotazo: Memorias del olvido.* Ocean Sur.

Alape, Arturo. 1997. *Río de inmensas voces . . . y otras voces.* Planeta.

Al-Bulushi, Samar, Sahana Ghosh, and Inderpal Grewal. 2023. "Security Regimes: Transnational and Imperial Entanglements." *Annual Review of Anthropology* 52 (1): 205–21.

Alcaldía Mayor. 1964. *La renovación en Bogotá.* Alcaldía Mayor de Bogotá D.E.

Alcaldía Mayor de Bogotá. 1998. *Formar Ciudad: 1995–1998.* Alcaldía Mayor.

Allen, John. 2011. "Topological Twists: Power's Shifting Geographies." *Dialogues in Human Geography* 1 (3): 283–98.

Alternativa. 1974. "'Derrotamos la Avenida de los Serruchos." No. 16, September 16–29.

Alternativa. 1975. "Cómo encontrar cartas del ELN en un colchón." No. 31, April 28–May 5.

Alvarado, Abel. 2020. "Grupo de indígenas protesta en el aeropuerto El Dorado de Bogotá." *CNN*, October 23. https://cnnespanol.cnn.com/2020/10/23/grupo-de-indigenas-protesta-en-el-aeropuerto-el-dorado-de-bogota.

Álvarez Rivadulla, María José, Friederike Fleischer, and Adriana Hurtado Tarazona. 2024. "Making the State Care: The Role of Political Willingness and Brokerage in Bogota's New Feminist Care Policy." *City* 28 (5–6): 637–58.

Amar, Paul. 2013. *The Security Archipelago: Human-Security States, Sexuality Politics, and the End of Neoliberalism.* Duke University Press.

Amin, Ash, and Michele Lancione. 2022. "Introduction: Thinking Cities from the Ground." In *Grammars of the Urban Ground*, edited by Ash Amin and Michele Lancione. Duke University Press.

Amorocho, Luz, Enrique García, José J. Angulo, and Carlos Martínez. 1946. "Bogotá puede ser una ciudad moderna." *Proa* 3:15–26.

Anderson, Ben. 2009. "Affective Atmospheres." *Emotion, Space and Society* 2:77–81.

Andres Felipe. 2018. "Graffiti en El Bronx Distrito Creativo | Preview #Graffitón." YouTube video, 1:08, August 31. https://www.youtube.com/watch?v=e5XVeyuFPDc.

Anjaria, Jonathan Shapiro, and Colin McFarlane. 2011. *Urban Navigations: Politics, Space and the City in South Asia*. Routledge.

Appadurai, Arjun. 2015. "Mediants, Materiality, Normativity." *Public Culture* 27 (2): 221–37.

Appelbaum, Nancy. 1999. "Whitening the Region: Caucano Mediation and 'Antioqueño Colonization' in Nineteenth-Century Colombia." *Hispanic American Historical Review* 79 (4): 631–67.

Aprile-Gniset, Jacques. 1983. *El impacto del 9 de abril sobre el centro de Bogotá*. Centro Cultural Jorge Eliécer Gaitán.

Aradau, Claudia. 2010. "Security That Matters: Critical Infrastructure and Objects of Protection." *Security Dialogue* 41 (5): 491–514.

Arango, Jorge, Herbert Ritter, and Gabriel Serrano. 1948. "Reconstrucción de Bogotá." *Proa* 12:11–20.

Asher, Kiran. 2019. "The Risky Streets of Ontologically Redesigned Cities: Some Comments on Arturo Escobar's Rurbanization Research Program." *Geoforum* 101:212–14.

Asher, Kiran. 2020. "Fragmented Forests, Fractured Lives: Ethno-Territorial Struggles and Development in the Pacific Lowlands of Colombia." *Antipode* 52 (4): 949–70.

Asher, Kiran, and Diana Ojeda. 2009. "Producing Nature and Making the State: Ordenamiento Territorial in the Pacific Lowlands of Colombia." *Geoforum* 40:292–302.

Austin, John. 1975. *How to Do Things with Words*. Edited by J. O. Urmson and Marina Sbisà. Harvard University Press.

Auyero, Javier. 2015. *In Harm's Way: The Dynamics of Urban Violence*. Princeton University Press.

Aya Uribe, Edgar Ferney. 2012. *Don Chinche: Sensorium urbano y experiencias televisivas en la ciudad de Ibagué*. Sello Editorial Universidad del Tolima.

Azuero Quijano, Alejandra. 2023. *El paro como teoría: Historia del presente y estallido en Colombia*. Herder.

Baldwin, Davarian L. 2021. *In the Shadow of the Ivory Tower: How Universities Are Plundering Our Cities*. Bold Type Books.

Ballvé, Teo. 2020. *The Frontier Effect: State Formation and Violence in Colombia*. Cornell University Press.

Barad, Karen. 2003. "Posthumanist Performativity: Towards an Understanding of How Matter Comes to Matter." *Signs: Journal of Women in Culture and Society* 28 (3): 801–31.

Bates, Lisa, Sharita A. Towne, Christopher Paul Jordan, et al. 2018. "Race and Spatial Imaginary: Planning Otherwise." *Planning Theory & Practice* 19 (2): 254–88.

Bear, Laura. 2016. "Time as Technique." *Annual Review of Anthropology* 45:487–502.

Bedoya Lima, Jineth. 2002. "Rockets, al mejor postor." *El Tiempo*, July 7.

Bell Lemus, Gustavo, Patricia Pinzón de Lewin, Lorenzo Morales Regueros, and David Rojas Roa. 2008. *Historia de la Universidad de los Andes, Tomo 1: Inicios, 1948–1977*. Universidad de los Andes.

Benjamin, Walter. 1969. *Illuminations*. Translated by Harry Zohn. Schocken.

Benjamin, Walter. 1978. *Reflections: Essays, Aphorisms, Autobiographical Writings*. Schocken.

Benjamin, Walter. 2002. *The Arcades Project*. Harvard University Press.

Bergquist, Charles. 2017. "La izquierda colombiana: Un pasado paradójico; ¿un futuro promisorio?" *Anuario Colombiano de Historia Social y de la Cultura* 44 (2): 263–99.

Berney, Rachel. 2017. *Learning from Bogotá: Pedagogical Urbanism and the Reshaping of Public Space.* University of Texas.

Beuf, Alice. 2019. "Los significados del territorio: Ensayo interpretativo de los discursos sobre el territorio de movimientos sociales en Colombia." *Scripta Nova: Revista Electrónica de Geografía y Ciencias Sociales* 23. https://revistes.ub.edu/index.php/ScriptaNova/article/view/22452.

Beuf, Alice, and Patricia Rincón Avellaneda, eds. 2017. *Ordenar los territorios: Perspectivas críticas desde América Latina.* Universidad de los Andes, Universidad Nacional de Colombia, Instituto Francés de Estudios Andinos.

Bickford, Louis. 1999. "The Archival Imperative: Human Rights and Historical Memory in Latin America's Southern Cone." *Human Rights Quarterly* 21 (4): 1097–122.

Billé, Franck. 2017. "Introduction: Speaking Volumes." Theorizing the Contemporary, Society for Cultural Anthropology, October 24, 2017. https://culanth.org/fieldsights/1241-introduction-speaking-volumes.

Billé, Franck. 2020. "Voluminous: An Introduction." In *Voluminous States: Sovereignty, Materiality, and the Territorial Imagination*, edited by Franck Billé. Duke University Press.

Blair Trujillo, Elsa. 2009. "Aproximacíon teórica al concepto de violencia: Avatares de una definición." *Política y Cultura* 32:9–33.

Blomley, Nicholas. 2002. "Mud for the Land." *Public Culture* 14 (3): 557–82.

Blomley, Nicholas. 2003. "Law, Property, and the Geography of Violence: The Frontier, the Survey, and the Grid." *Annals of the Association of American Geographers* 93 (1): 121–41.

Blomley, Nicholas. 2016. "The Territory of Property." *Progress in Human Geography* 40 (5): 593–609.

Bonilla, Liliana, Carolina de Botero, Fernando Jiménez, Nicolás Rueda, and José Salazar. 1988. *Preinversión: Plan zonal del centro.* Fonade.

Bornstein, Erica. 2012. *Disquieting Gifts: Humanitarianism in New Delhi.* Stanford University Press.

Botero Montoya, Rodrigo. 2006. "Invocación a la modestia." *Conyuntura Económica* 36 (2): 25–29.

Bou Akar, Hiba. 2018. *For the War Yet to Come: Planning Beirut's Frontiers.* Stanford University Press.

Bourdieu, Pierre. 1977. *Outline of a Theory of Practice.* Translated by Richard Nice. Cambridge University Press.

Boyer, Dominic. 2005. *Spirit and System: Media, Intellectuals, and the Dialectic in Modern German Culture.* University of Chicago Press.

Boyer, Dominic. 2008. "Thinking Through the Anthropology of Experts." *Anthropology in Action* 15 (2): 38–46.

Boyer, Dominic. 2009. "Conspiracy, History, and Therapy at a Berlin Stammtisch." *American Ethnologist* 33 (3): 327–39.

Boyer, Dominic. 2015a. *Life Informatic: Newsmaking in the Digital Era.* Cornell University Press.

Boyer, Dominic. 2015b. "Reflexivity Reloaded: From Anthropology of Intellectuals to Critique of Method to Studying Sideways." In *Anthropology Now and Next: Essays in Honor of Ulf Hannerz*, edited by Thomas Hylland Eriksen, Christina Garsten, and Shalini Randeria. Berghahn.

Boyer, Dominic, and Cymene Howe. 2015. "Portable Analytics and Lateral Theory." In *Theory Can Be More Than It Used to Be: Learning Anthropology's Method in a Time of Transition,* edited by Dominic Boyer, James D. Faubion, and George E. Marcus. Cornell University Press.

Boyer, Dominic, and Claudio Lomnitz. 2005. "Intellectuals and Nationalism: Anthropological Engagements." *Annual Review of Anthropology* 34:105–20.

Bozçali, Firat. 2024. "Proving Injustice: Smuggler Killings, Impunity Work, and Vernacular Counterforensics in Turkey's Kurdish Borderlands." *American Anthropologist* 126 (4): 567–80.

Braun, Herbert. 1985. *The Assassination of Gaitán: Public Life and Urban Violence in Colombia*. University of Wisconsin Press.

Braun, Herbert. 1994. *Our Guerrillas, Our Sidewalks: A Journey into the Violence of Colombia*. University of Colorado Press.

Braverman, Irus, Nicholas Blomley, David Delaney, and Alexandre Kedar, eds. 2014. *The Expanding Spaces of Law: A Timely Legal Geography*. Stanford University Press.

Brittain, James. 2005. "A Theory of Accelerating Rural Violence: Lauchlin Currie's Role in Underdeveloping Colombia." *Journal of Peasant Studies* 32 (2): 335–60.

Bubandt, Nils. 2005. "Vernacular Security: The Politics of Feeling Safe in Global, National and Local Worlds." *Security Dialogue* 36 (3): 275–96.

Buck-Morss, Susan. 1991. *The Dialectics of Seeing: Walter Benjamin and the Arcades Project*. MIT Press.

Caicedo, Luis Javier. 1990. "¿Para qué Palacio sin Justicia?" *Magazín Dominical*, May 13.

Caldeira, Teresa. 2000. *City of Walls: Crime, Segregation, and Citizenship in São Paulo*. University of California Press.

Caldeira, Teresa. 2012. "Imprinting and Moving Around: New Visibilities and Configurations of Public Space in São Paulo." *Public Culture* 24 (2 [67]): 385–419.

Caldeira, Teresa. 2017. "Peripheral Urbanization: Autoconstruction, Transversal Logics, and Politics in Cities of the Global South." *Environment and Planning D: Society and Space* 35:3–20.

Calvo Isaza, Oscar Iván, and Marta Saade Granados. 2002. *La ciudad en cuarentena: Chicha, patología social y profilaxis*. Ministerio de Cultura.

Carbonell Higuera, Carlos M. 2010. "El Sector de San Victorino en los procesos de reconfiguración urbana de Bogotá (1598–1998)." *Cuadernos de Vivienda y Urbanismo* 3 (6): 220–45.

Carrión M., Fernando. 2005. "El centro histórico como objecto de deseo." In *Regeneración y revitalización urbana en las Américas: Hacia un Estado estable*, edited by Fernando Carrión M. and Lisa Hanley. FLACSO.

Carrión Mena, Fernando, and Paulina Cepeda Pico, eds. 2023. *Urbicide: The Death of the City*. Springer.

Castillejo Cuéllar, Alejandro. 2007. "La globalización del testimonio: Historia, silencio endémico y los usos de la palabra." *Antípoda* 4:76–99.

Castro Roldán, Andrés, and Daniel García. 2015. "La memoria colectiva y la muerte en el Cementerio de Bogotá." *Amerika: Mémoires, identités, territoires* 12. https://journals.openedition.org/amerika/6342.

Castro-Gómez, Santiago. 2002. "The Social Sciences, Epistemic Violence, and the Problem of the 'Invention of the Other.'" *Nepantla: Views from South* 3 (2): 269–85.

Çelik, Zeynep. 1997. *Urban Forms and Colonial Confrontations: Algiers Under French Rule*. University of California Press.

Centro de Memoria, Paz y Reconciliación. 2012. *Bogotá, ciudad memoria*. Alcaldía Mayor de Bogotá.

Centro de Planificación y Urbanismo. 1967. *Renovación urbana: Sector Las Aguas*. Universidad de los Andes.

Cepeda Ulloa, Fernando. 2000. "Espacios para la convivencia." *El Tiempo*, December 19.

Cernea, Michael M. 1988. *Involuntary Resettlement in Development Projects: Policy Guidelines in World Bank Financed Projects*. World Bank.

Chu, Julie. 2014. "When Infrastructures Attack: The Workings of Disrepair in China." *American Ethnologist* 41 (2): 351–67.

CID (Centro de Investigaciones para el Desarrollo). 1969. *Alternativas para el desarrollo urbano de Bogotá D.E.* Editorial Andes.

Clarke, Kamari Maxine. 2019. *Affective Justice: The International Criminal Court and the Pan-Africanist Pushback*. Duke University Press.

Clausewitz, Carl von. (1832) 1989. *On War*. Princeton University Press.

Coaffe, Jon. 2016. *Terrorism, Risk and the Global City: Towards Urban Resilience*. Routledge.

Cody, Francis. 2013. *The Light of Knowledge: Literary Activism and the Politics of Knowledge in South India*. Cornell University Press.

Collins, John F. 2015. *Revolt of the Saints: Memory and Redemption in the Twilight of Brazilian Racial Democracy*. Duke University Press.

Collins, Patricia Hill. 1986. "Learning from the Outsider Within: The Sociological Significance of Black Feminist Thought." *Social Problems* 33 (6): s14–32.

Colón, Luis Carlos. 2005. "El saneamiento del Paseo Bolívar y la vivienda obrera en Bogotá." *Revista Urbanismos* 2:104–15.

Comisión de Estudios Sobre la Violencia. 1987. *Colombia: Violencia y democracia*. Universidad Nacional de Colombia.

Contreras Ortiz, Yency. 2019. *Renovación urbana en Bogotá: Incentivos, reglas y expresión territorial*. Universidad Nacional de Colombia.

Corsín Jiménez, Alberto. 2003. "On Space as Capacity." *Journal of the Royal Anthropological Institute* 9 (1): 137–53.

Corsín Jiménez, Alberto. 2014. "The Right to Infrastructure: A Prototype for Open Source Urbanism." *Environment and Planning D: Society and Space* 32 (2): 342–62.

Corsín Jiménez, Alberto. 2017. "Auto-Construction Redux: The City as Method." *Cultural Anthropology* 32 (2): 450–78.

Cowen, Deborah. 2014. *The Deadly Life of Logistics: Mapping Violence in Global Trade*. University of Minnesota Press.

Crane, Sheila. 2017. "Housing as Battleground: Targeting the City in the Battles of Algiers." *City & Society* 29 (1): 187–212.

Currie, Lauchlin. 1975. "The Interrelations of Urban and National Economic Planning." *Urban Studies* 12 (1): 37–46.

Currie, Lauchlin. 1989. "Bogotá, el 'deterioro' del centro, causas y soluciones." *Economía Colombiana* 215/216:27–32.

DANE (Departamento Administrativo Nacional de Estadística). 2015. *Metodología de estratificación socioeconómica urbana: Manual de actualización*. DANE.

DAPD (Departamento Administrativo de Planificación Distrital). 1964. *La planificación en Bogotá*. Talleres Editoriales del Distrito.

Das, Veena. 2007. *Life and Words: Violence and the Descent into the Ordinary*. University of California Press.

Das, Veena, and Deborah Poole, eds. 2004. *Anthropology in the Margins of the State*. School of American Research Press.

Dávila, Arlene. 2016. *El Mall: The Spatial and Class Politics of Shopping Malls in Latin America*. University of California Press.

Dávila, Julio. 2000. *Planificación y política en Bogotá: La vida de Jorge Gaitán Cortés*. Alcaldía Mayor de Bogotá.

Davis, Diane. 2013. "Zero-Tolerance Policing, Stealth Real Estate Development, and the Transformation of Public Space: Evidence from Mexico City." *Latin American Perspectives* 40 (2): 53–76.

Davis, Mike. 2006. *Planet of Slums*. Verso.

Dawdy, Shannon Lee. 2016. *Patina: A Profane Archaeology*. University of Chicago Press.

de Certeau, Michel. 1984. *The Practice of Everyday Life*. University of California Press.

de Urbina González, Amparo. 2012. "El Centro Histórico de Bogotá 'de puertas para adentro': ¿El deterioro del patrimonio al servicio de la gentrificación?" *Cuadernos de Vivienda y Urbanismo* 5 (9): 46–69.

Dejarlais, Robert, and Jason Throop. 2011. "Phenomenological Approaches in Anthropology." *Annual Review of Anthropology* 40:87–102.

Delgado, Manuel. 2007. *La ciudad mentirosa: Fraude y miseria del "modelo Barcelona."* Catarata.

Derrida, Jacques. 1995. "Archive Fever: A Freudian Impression." Translated by Eric Prenowitz. *Diacritics* 25:9–63.

Dokumaci, Arseli. 2020. "People as Affordances: Building Disability Worlds Through Care Intimacy." *Current Anthropology* 61 (S21): S97–108.

Donovan, Michael. 2008. "Informal Cities and the Contestation of Public Space: The Case of Bogotá's Street Vendors, 1988–2003." *Urban Studies* 45 (1): 29–51.

Dozier, Deshonay. 2018. "A Response to Abolitionist Planning: There Is No Room for 'Planners' in the Movement for Abolition." Progessive City, August 9, 2018. https://www.progressivecity.net/single-post/2018/08/09/a-response-to-abolitionist-planning-there-is-no-room-for-planners-in-the-movement-for-a.

Duarte, Mauricio. 2015. "Migración, televisión e identidad: Modos de ver trasnacionales en/desde Colombia." *Nexus*: 6–33.

Duffield, Mark. 2001. *Global Governance and the New Wars: The Merging of Development and Security*. Zed Books.

Duque Franco, Isabel. 2010. "Técnicos, ciudadanos y agendas privadas en la revisión del plan de ordenamiento territorial (POT) de Bogotá." *Scripta Nova: Revista Electrónica de Geografía y Ciencias Sociales* 14. https://revistes.ub.edu/index.php/ScriptaNova/article/view/1693.

Easterling, Keller. 2014. *Extrastatecraft: The Power of Infrastructure Space*. Verso.

Eaton, Kent. 2021. "Bogotá's Left Turn: Counter-Neoliberalization in Colombia." *International Journal of Urban and Regional Research* 44 (1): 1–17.

Edensor, Tim. 2012. "Illuminated Atmospheres: Anticipating and Reproducing the Flow of Affective Experience in Blackpool." *Environment and Planning D: Society and Space* 30:1103–22.

El Espectador. 2016. "Retiran placa que responzabilizaba a Plazas Vega por hechos del Palacio de Justicia." April 21.

El Espectador. 2021. "Sobrecostos, demoras y menos verde en peatonalización de la Séptima." June 19.

El Tiempo. 1992. "Santa Bárbara: Qué barbaridad." October 7.

El Tiempo. 1993. "Cocinol: La coca azul." November 28.

El Tiempo. 1999. "Colombia, un país secuestrado." May 31.

El Tiempo. 2000. "Rebelión en el Cartucho." March 2.

El Tiempo. 2005a. "Indigentes al matadero." April 30.

El Tiempo. 2005b. "La encrucijada de los indigentes del Cartucho." April 26.

El Tiempo. 2016a. "Caída de decreto de alturas no tumba 2362 licencias en trámite." February 22.

El Tiempo. 2016b. "Toma del 'Bronx': Historia de un operativo de película." June 4.

El Tiempo. 2018. "Un debate de altura." April 6.

El Tiempo. 2019a. "Beatriz González habla de los columbarios y de la reacción de Peñalosa." October 11.

El Tiempo. 2019b. "Los edificios que dejó el Decreto 562 del 2014." YouTube video, 3:56, May 5. https://www.youtube.com/watch?v=5P2C7FqLnU8.

Elden, Stuart. 2010. "Land, Terrain, Territory." *Progress in Human Geography* 34 (6): 799–817.

Elden, Stuart. 2013. "Secure the Volume: Vertical Geopolitics and the Depth of Power." *Political Geography* 34:35–51.

Elden, Stuart. 2017. "Legal Terrain—the Political Materiality of Territory." *London Review of International Law* 5 (2): 199–224.

Elden, Stuart. 2021. "Terrain, Politics, History." *Dialogues in Human Geography* 11 (2): 170–89.

Elinoff, Eli. 2016. "A House Is More Than a House: Aesthetic Politics in a Northeastern Thai Railway Settlement." *Journal of the Royal Anthropological Institute* 22 (3): 610–32.

Ellison, Susan. 2018. *Domesticating Democracy: The Politics of Conflict Resolution in Bolivia*. Duke University Press.

Elyachar, Julia. 2005. *Markets of Dispossession: NGOs, Economic Development, and the State in Cairo*. Duke University Press.

Elyachar, Julia. 2010. "Phatic Labor, Infrastructure, and the Question of Empowerment in Cairo." *American Ethnologist* 37 (3): 452–64.

ERU (Empresa de Renovación Urbana). 2012. *Documento técnico de soporte, plan parcial de renovación urbana "Estación Central."* Alcaldía Mayor de Bogotá D.C.

Escobar, Arturo. 2008. *Territories of Difference: Place, Movements, Life, Redes*. Duke University Press.

Escobar, Arturo. 2018. *Designs for the Pluriverse: Radical Interdependence, Autonomy, and the Making of Worlds*. Duke University Press.

Escobar, Arturo. 2019. "Habitability and Design: Radical Interdependence and the Re-Earthing of Cities." *Geoforum* 101:132–40.

Everett, Margaret. 1998. "Development Visions and 'Integration' on the Urban Frontier." *Political and Legal Anthropology Review* 21 (2): 1–10.

Fabian, Johannes. 1983. *Time and the Other: How Anthropology Makes its Object*. Columbia University Press.

Fals Borda, Orlando. 1996. *Región e historia: Elementos sobre ordenamiento y equilibrio regional en Colombia*. IEPRI, Universidad Nacional de Colombia, Tercer Mundo Editores.

Fals Borda, Orlando. 1999. "Guía práctica del ordenamiento territorial en Colombia: Contribución para la solución de conflictos." *Análisis Político* 36:82–102.

Fanta Castro, Andrea. 2015. *Residuos de la violencia: Producción cultural colombiana, 1990-2010*. Editorial Universidad del Rosario.

Farnsworth-Alvear, Ann. 2000. *Dulcinea in the Factory: Myths, Morals, Men, and Women in Colombia's Industrial Experiment, 1905-1960*. Duke University Press.

Fassin, Didier, and Mariella Pandolfi, eds. 2010. *Contemporary States of Emergency: The Politics of Military and Humanitarian Interventions*. Zone Books.

Fattal, Alexander. 2018. *Guerrilla Marketing: Counterinsurgency and Capitalism in Colombia*. University of Chicago Press.

Ferguson, James. 1990. *The Anti-Politics Machine: "Development," Depoliticization, and Bureaucratic Power in Lesotho*. Cambridge University Press.

Fernandes, Edesio, and María Mercedes Maldonado Copello. 2009. "Law and Land Policy in Shifting Paradigms and Possibilities for Action." *Land Lines*, July.

Ferry, Elizabeth. 2005. *Not Ours Alone: Patrimony, Value, and Collectivity in Contemporary Mexico*. Columbia University Press.

Fiorella, Giancarlo. 2019. "El segundo a segundo del disparo que mató a Dilan Cruz." *Cerosetenta*, December 3. https://cerosetenta.uniandes.edu.co/dilan-muerte-video/.

Forensic Architecture Team. 2023. "The Killing of Dilan Cruz." Forensic Architecture, September 6. https://forensic-architecture.org/investigation/the-killing-of-dilan-cruz.

Forero Hidalgo, Jymy Alexander, and Frank Molano Camargo. 2015. "El paro cívico de octubre de 1993 en Ciudad Bolívar (Bogotá): La formación de un campo de protesta urbana." *Anuario Colombiano de Historia Social y de la Cultura* 42 (1): 115–43.

Fortun, Kim, and Todd Cherkasky. 1998. "Counter-Expertise and the Politics of Collaboration." *Science as Culture* 7 (2): 145–72.

Foucault, Michel. (1966) 1973. *The Order of Things: An Archaeology of the Human Sciences*. Vintage.

Foucault, Michel. 1980a. "Confessions of the Flesh." In *Power/Knowledge: Selected Interviews, 1972–1977*, edited by Colin Gordon. Pantheon Books.

Foucault, Michel. 1980b. "*Power/Knowledge.*" In *Power/Knowledge: Selected Interviews, 1972–1977*, edited by Colin Gordon. Pantheon Books.

Foucault, Michel. 1980c. "Questions on Geography." In *Power/Knowledge: Selected Interviews, 1972–1977*, edited by Colin Gordon. Pantheon Books.

Foucault, Michel. 2003. *"Society Must Be Defended": Lectures at the Collège de France, 1975–1976*. Picador.

Foucault, Michel. 2007. *Security, Territory, Population: Lectures at the Collège de France, 1977–1978*. Palgrave Macmillan.

Franco Calderón, Ángela. 2010. *Impactos socioespaciales de la renovación urbana: La operación "tercer milenio" en Bogotá*. Escala.

Fraser, Nancy. 1991. "Force of Law: Metaphysical or Political?" *Cardozo Law Review* 13:1325–31.

Gallón Galindo, Gustavo. 1979. *Quince años de estado de sitio en Colombia: 1958–1978*. Editorial América Latina.

Gandolfo, Daniella. 2009. *The City at Its Limits: Taboo, Transgression, and Urban Renewal in Lima*. University of Chicago Press.

Gandolfo, Daniella. 2020. "In 'The Pit': Architecture and the Power of the Tellurian in Lima." *Journal of Latin American and Caribbean Anthropology* 25 (1): 145–67.

Gandy, Matthew. 2017. "Urban Atmospheres." *Cultural Geographies* 24 (3): 353–74.

Ghertner, Asher. 2015. *Rule by Aesthetics: World-Class City Making in Delhi*. Oxford Univerity Press.

Ghertner, D. Asher, and Robert W. Lake. 2021. "Introduction: Land Fictions and the Politics of Commodification in City and Country." In *Land Fictions: The Commodification of Land in City and Country*, edited by D. Asher Ghertner and Robert W. Lake. Cornell University Press.

Ghertner, D. Asher, Hudson McFann, and Daniel M. Goldstein, eds. 2020. *Futureproof: Security Aesthetics and the Management of Life*. Duke University Press.

Gibson, James. 1979. *The Ecological Approach to Visual Perception*. Lawrence Erlbaum.

Gilbert, Alan. 2002. "On the Mystery of Capital and the Myths of Hernando de Soto: What Difference Does Legal Title Make?" *International Development Planning Review* 24 (1): 1–19.

Gill, Lesley. 2016. *A Century of Violence in a Red City: Popular Struggle, Counterinsurgency, and Human Rights in Colombia*. Duke University Press.

Gledhill, John. 2015. *The New War on the Poor: The Production of Insecurity in Latin America.* Zed Books.

Glück, Zoltán. 2024. "Introduction—Anthropology and the Security Encounter: Toward an Abolitionist Anthropology in the Age of Permanent War." *American Anthropologist* 126:470–78.

Glück, Zoltán, and Setha Low. 2017. "A Sociospatial Framework for the Anthropology of Security." *Anthropological Theory* 17 (3): 281–96.

Goldstein, Daniel. 2010. "Toward a Critical Anthropology of Security." *Current Anthropology* 51 (4): 487–517.

Goldstein, Daniel. 2012. *Outlawed: Between Security and Rights in a Bolivian City.* Duke University Press.

Gómez, Carlos J. L., Luis Sánchez-Ayala, and Gonzalo A. Vargas. 2015. "Armed Conflict, Land Grabs and Primitive Accumulation in Colombia: Micro Processes, Macro Trends and the Puzzles in Between." *Journal of Peasant Studies* 42 (2): 255–74.

González, Roberto J. 2010. *Militarizing Culture: Essays on the Warfare State.* Left Coast.

González Arias, José Jairo. 1992. *Espacios de exclusión: El estigma de las repúblicas independientes, 1955-1965.* CINEP.

Goodale, Mark, and Sally Engle Merry, eds. 2007. *The Practice of Human Rights: Tracking Law Between the Global and the Local.* Cambridge University Press.

Goonewardena, Kanishka. 2005. "The Urban Sensorium: Space, Ideology and the Aestheticization of Politics." *Antipode* 37 (1): 46–71.

Gordillo, Gastón. 2014. *Rubble: The Afterlife of Destruction.* Duke University Press.

Gordillo, Gastón. 2018. "Terrain as Insurgent Weapon: An Affective Geometry of Warfare in the Mountains of Afghanistan." *Political Geography* 64:53–62.

Gordillo, Gastón. 2023. "Hostile Terrain: On the Spatial and Affective Conditions for Revolution." *Territory, Politics, Governance*: 1–16.

Gouëset, Vincent. 1999. "El territorio colombiano y sus márgenes: La difícil tarea de la construcción territorial." *Territorios* 1:77–94.

Graeber, David. 2001. *Toward an Anthropological Theory of Value: The False Coin of Our Own Dreams.* Palgrave.

Graeber, David. 2015. *The Utopia of Rules: On Technology, Stupidity, and the Secret Joys of Bureaucracy.* Melville House.

Graham, Stephen. 2010. *Cities Under Siege: The New Military Urbanism.* Verso.

Graham, Stephen. 2011. "When Life Itself Is War: On the Urbanization of Military and Security Doctrine." *International Journal of Urban and Regional Research* 36 (1): 136–55.

Graham, Stephen. 2016. *Vertical: The City from Satellites to Bunkers.* Verso.

Gramsci, Antonio. (1971) 1992. *Selections from the Prison Notebooks.* Edited and translated by Quintin Hoare and Geoffrey Nowell Smith. International Publishers.

Gregory, Steven. 2020. "Making the 'American Acropolis': On Verticality, Social Hierarchy, and the Obduracy of Manhattan Schist." *Annals of the American Association of Geographers* 110 (1): 78–97.

Gudmundson, Lowell. 1989. "Peasant, Farmer, Proletarian: Class Formation in a Smallholder Coffee Economy, 1850-1950." *Hispanic American Historical Review* 69 (2): 221–57.

Guha, Ranajit. (1983) 1988. "The Prose of Counterinsurgency." In *Selected Subaltern Studies*, edited by Ranajit Guha and Gayatri Chakravorty Spivak. Oxford University Press.

Gupta, Akhil. 2012. *Red Tape: Bureaucracy, Structural Violence, and Poverty in India.* Duke University Press.

Gusterson, Hugh. 2004. *People of the Bomb: Portraits of America's Nuclear Complex.* University of Minnesota Press.

Gusterson, Hugh, and Catherine Besteman, eds. 2010. *The Insecure American: How We Got Here and What We Should Do About It.* University of California Press.

Gutiérrez Sanín, Francisco. 2001. "The Courtroom and the Bivuoac: Reflections on Law and Violence in Colombia." *Latin American Perspectives* 116 (28): 56–72.

Gutiérrez Sanín, Francisco, and Paola García Reyes. 2016. "Acceso a la tierra y derechos de propiedad campesinos: Recorriendo los laberintos." *Revista Colombiana de Antropología* 52 (1): 91–116.

Hage, Ghassan. 2021. "Introduction: States of Decay." In *Decay*, edited by Ghassan Hage. Duke University Press.

Hankins, Joseph, and Rihan Yeh. 2016. "To Bind and to Bound: Commensuration Across Boundaries." *Anthropological Quarterly* 89 (1): 5–30.

Hannerz, Ulf. 1998. "Other Transnationals: Perspectives Gained from Studying Sideways." *Paideuma* 44:109–23.

Haraway, Donna. 1988. "Situated Knowledges: The Science Question in Feminism and the Privelege of Partial Perspective." *Feminist Studies* 14 (3): 575–99.

Harding, Susan, ed. 2004. *The Feminist Standpoint Theory Reader: Intellectual and Political Controversies.* Routledge.

Harker, Christopher. 2020. *Spacing Debt: Obligations, Violence, and Endurance in Ramallah, Palestine.* Duke University Press.

Harms, Erik. 2012. "Beauty as Control in the New Saigon: Eviction, New Urban Zones, and Atomized Dissent in a Southeast Asian City." *American Ethnologist* 39 (4): 735–50.

Harms, Erik. 2016. *Luxury and Rubble: Civility and Dispossession in the New Saigon.* University of California Press.

Harris, Andrew. 2015. "Vertical Urbanisms: Opening Up Geographies of the Three-Dimensional City." *Progress in Human Geography* 39 (5): 601–20.

Harrison, Faye Venetia. 1997. *Decolonizing Anthropology: Moving Further Toward an Anthropology of Liberation.* Association of Black Anthropologists, American Anthropological Association.

Harvey, David. 1989. "From Managerialism to Entrepreneurialism: The Transformation in Urban Governance in Late Capitalism." *Geografiska Annaler: Series B, Human Geography* 71 (1): 3–17.

Harvey, David. 2003. *Paris, Capital of Modernity.* Routledge.

Harvey, David. 2006. "Neo-Liberalism as Creative Destruction." *Geografiska Annaler: Series B, Human Geography* 88 (2):145–58.

Harvey, Penelope. 2012. "The Topological Quality of Infrastructural Relation: An Ethnographic Approach." *Theory, Culture & Society* 29 (4/5): 79–92.

Heidegger, Martin. 1971. "Building Dwelling Thinking." In *Poetry, Language, Thought*, translated by Albert Hofstadter. Harper and Row.

Hermer, Joe, and Alan Hunt. 1996. "Official Graffiti of the Everyday." *Law and Society Review* 30 (3): 455–80.

Herscher, Andrew. 2007. "Urbicide, Urbanism and Urban Destruction in Kosovo." *Theory and Event* 10 (2). https://doi.org/10.1353/tae.2007.0062.

Herscher, Andrew. 2020. "The Urbanism of Racial Capitalism: Toward a History of 'Blight.'" *Comparative Studies of South Asia, Africa and the Middle East* 40 (1): 57–65.

Herzfeld, Michael. 1992. *The Social Production of Indifference: Exploring the Symbolic Roots of Western Bureaucracy*. University of Chicago Press.

Herzfeld, Michael. 2005. "Political Optics and the Occlusion of Intimate Knowledge." *American Anthropologist* 107 (3): 369–76.

Herzfeld, Michael. 2006. "Spatial Cleansing: Monumental Vacuity and the Idea of the West." *Journal of Material Culture* 11 (1–2): 127–49.

Herzfeld, Michael. 2009. *Evicted from Eternity: The Restructuring of Modern Rome*. University of Chicago Press.

Herzfeld, Michael. 2020. "Shaping Cultural Space: Reflections on the Politics and Cosmology of Urbanism." In *Life Among Urban Planners: Practice, Professionalism, and Expertise in the Making of the City*, edited by Jennifer Mack and Michael Herzfeld. University of Pennsylvania Press.

Hetherington, Kregg. 2011. *Guerrilla Auditors: The Politics of Transparency in Neoliberal Paraguay*. Duke University Press.

Hinton, Alexander Laban, ed. 2011. *Transitional Justice: Global Mechanism and Local Realities After Genocide and Mass Violence*. Rutgers University Press.

Hoffman, Danny. 2007. "The City as Barracks: Freetown, Monrovia, and the Organization of Violence in Postcolonial African Cities." *Cultural Anthropology* 22 (3): 400–428.

Hoffman, Danny. 2017. *Monrovia Modern: Urban Form and Political Imagination in Liberia*. Duke University Press.

Hoffman, Danny. 2019. "Geometry After the Circle Security Interventions in the Urban Gray Zone." *Current Anthropology* 60 (S19): S98–S107.

Hoffman, Danny, and Stephen Lubkemann. 2005. "Introduction: West-African Warscapes: Warscape Ethnography in West Africa and the Anthropology of 'Events.'" *Anthropological Quarterly* 78 (2): 315–27.

Holmes, Douglas R., and George E. Marcus. 2005. "Cultures of Expertise and the Management of Globalization: Toward a Refunctioning of Ethnography." In *Global Assemblages: Technology, Politics, and Ethics as Anthropological Problems*, edited by Aihwa Ong and Stephen J. Collier. Blackwell.

Holston, James. 1989. *The Modernist City: An Anthropological Critique of Brasilia*. University of Chicago Press.

Holston, James. 1991. "Autoconstruction in Working-Class Brazil." *Cultural Anthropology* 6 (4): 447–65.

Holston, James. 2008. *Insurgent Citizenship: Disjunctions of Democracy and Modernity in Brazil*. Princeton University Press.

hooks, bell. 1984. *Feminist Theory: From Margin to Center*. South End.

Hull, Matthew. 2012a. "Documents and Bureaucracy." *Annual Review of Anthropology* 41:251–67.

Hull, Matthew. 2012b. *Government of Paper: The Materiality of Bureaucracy in Urban Pakistan*. University of California Press.

Human Rights Watch. 2024. *Extermination and Acts of Genocide*. December 19. https://www.hrw.org/report/2024/12/19/extermination-and-acts-genocide/israel-deliberately-depriving-palestinians-gaza.

Hurtado Muñoz, Valeria. 2011. "Análisis de la renovación urbana como estrategia de recuperación del centro histórico de Bogotá: Estudio de caso barrio Santa Bárbara colonial (Nueva Santa Fe), en el período 1976–2000." Bachelor's thesis, Universidad del Rosario.

Huyssen, Andreas. 2003. *Present Pasts: Urban Palimpsests and the Politics of Memory*. Stanford University Press.

Ingold, Tim. 2000. *The Perception of the Environment: Essays in Livelihood, Dwelling, and Skill*. Routledge.

Jaffe, Rivke, Eveline Dürr, Gareth A. Jones, Alessandro Angelini, Alana Osbourne, and Barbara Vodopivec. 2020. "What Does Poverty Feel Like? Urban Inequality and the Politics of Sensation." *Urban Studies* 57 (5): 1015–31.

Jaramillo, Samuel. 2006. *Reflexiones sobre las políticas de recuperación del centro (y del centro histórico) de Bogotá*. Documento CEDE 2006-40. Universidad de los Andes.

Jimeno, Myriam. 2001. "Violence and Social Life in Colombia." *Critique of Anthropology* 21 (3): 221–46.

Jimeno, Myriam. 2007. "Lenguaje, subjetividad y experiencias de violence." *Antípoda* 5:169–90.

Jimeno, Myriam, and Ismael Roldán. 1998. *Violencia cotidiana en la sociedad rural: En una mano el pan y en la otra el rejo*. Universidad Nacional de Colombia—CES.

Jobson, Ryan Cecil. 2020. "The Case for Letting Anthropology Burn: Sociocultural Anthropology in 2019." *American Anthropologist* 122 (2): 259–71.

Jusionyte, Ieva. 2015. *Savage Frontier: Making News and Security on the Argentine Border*. University of California Press.

Juzgado Tercero Penal del Circuito Especializado de Bogotá. 2010. "El caso del Palacio de Justicia: Delito de desaparición forzada; delitos de lesa humanidad; imprescriptibilidad; retroactividad; y aparatos organizados de poder." *Cuadernos de Derecho Penal* 4:57–108.

Kagan, Richard. 2000. *Urban Images of the Hispanic World, 1493–1793*. Yale University Press.

Karl, Robert A. 2017. *Forgotten Peace: Reform, Violence, and the Making of Contemporary Colombia*. University of California Press.

Kelty, Christopher. 2005. "Geeks, Social Imaginaries, and Recursive Publics." *Cultural Anthropology* 20 (2): 185–214.

Kockelman, Paul. 2016a. *The Chicken and the Quetzal: Incommensurate Ontologies and Portable Values in Guatemala's Cloud Forest*. Duke University Press.

Kockelman, Paul. 2016b. "Grading, Gradients, Degradation, Grace: Part 1; Intensity and Causality." *HAU: Journal of Ethnographic Theory* 6 (2): 389–423.

Kockelman, Paul. 2016c. "Grading, Gradients, Degradation, Grace: Part 2; Phenomenology, Materiality, and Cosmology." *HAU: Journal of Ethnographic Theory* 6 (3): 337–65.

Kornberger, Martin. 2012. "Governing the City: From Planning to Urban Strategy." *Theory, Culture & Society* 29 (2): 84–106.

Lakoff, Andrew, and Stephen J. Collier, eds. 2008. *Biosecurity Interventions: Global Health and Security in Question*. Columbia University Press.

Larkins, Erika Robb. 2015. *The Spectacular Favela: Violence in Modern Brazil*. University of California Press.

Leach, Neil. 1998. "The Dark Side of the Domus." *Journal of Architecture* 3 (1): 31–42.

Leal Martínez, Alejandra. 2016. "'You Cannot Be Here': The Urban Poor and the Specter of the Indian in Neoliberal Mexico City." *Journal of Latin American and Caribbean Anthropology* 21 (3): 539–59.

Lefebvre, Henri. 1991. *The Production of Space*. Translated by Donaldson Nicholson-Smith. Blackwell.

LeGrand, Catherine. 1986. *Frontier Expansion and Peasant Protest in Colombia, 1850–1936*. University of New Mexico Press.

León, Juanita, and Natalia Arenas. 2016. "'El Bronx es una señal porque no hemos acabado con todo el crimen organizado': Daniel Mejía." *La Silla Vacía*, June 6.

León Palacios, Paulo César. 2008. "El M-19 y la subversión cultural bogotana en los setenta: El caso de la revista Alternativa." *Anuario Colombiano de Historia Social y de la Cultura* 35:189–211.

Li, Tania M. 2005. "Beyond 'the State' and Failed Schemes." *American Anthropologist* 107 (3): 383–94.

Li, Tania M. 2007. *The Will to Improve: Governmentality, Development, and the Practice of Politics.* Duke University Press.

Li, Tania M. 2014. *Land's End: Capitalist Relations on an Indigenous Frontier.* Duke University Press.

López-Pedreros, A. Ricardo. 2019. *Makers of Democracy: A Transnational History of the Middle Classes in Colombia.* Duke University Press.

Low, Setha. 2003. *Behind the Gates: Life, Security, and the Pursuit of Happiness in Fortress America.* Routledge.

Low, Setha, and Mark Maguire, eds. 2019. *Spaces of Security: Ethnographies of Securityscapes, Surveillance, and Control.* New York University Press.

Lyons, Kristina. 2020. *Vital Decomposition: Soil Practitioners and Life Politics.* Duke University Press.

Magic Markers. 2015. "El lado oscuro de los rascacielos en Bogotá." YouTube video, 8:24, June 22. https://www.youtube.com/watch?v=9jhgp4TOgWU.

Makaremi, Chowra. 2010. "The Utopias of Power: From Human Security to the Responsibility to Protect." In *Contemporary States of Emergency: The Politics of Military and Humanitarian Interventions*, edited by Didier Fassin and Mariella Pandolfi. Zone Books.

Maldonado Copello, María Mercedes. 2003. "Los principios éticos y jurídicos en materia de ordenamiento territorial y gestión del suelo en Colombia." In *Reforma urbana y desarrollo territorial: Experiencias y perspectivas de aplicación de las leyes 9a de 1989 y 388 de 1997*, edited by María Mercedes Maldonado Copello. Alcaldía Mayor de Bogotá, Lincoln Institute of Land Policy, Universidad de los Andes-CIDER, and Fedevivienda.

Marín Correa, Alexánder, and Jaime Flórez Suárez. 2016. "Arquitectura criminal del Bronx: Torturaban hasta en edificios del Distrito." *El Espectador*, June 4.

Márquez, Francisca, and Andrés Góngora. 2023. "Ruinas urbanas: Topofilias y narrativas del despojo en Santiago y en Bogotá." *Revista EURE—Revista de Estudios Urbano Regionales* 49 (147): 1–24.

Marx, Karl. 1977. *Capital: A Critique of Political Economy.* Vintage Books.

Masco, Joseph. 2014. *The Theater of Operations: National Security Affect from the Cold War to the War on Terror.* Duke University Press.

Massey, Doreen. 2005. *For Space.* Sage.

Mathur, Nayanika. 2016. *Paper Tiger: Law, Bureaucracy, and the Developmental State in Himalayan India.* Cambridge University Press.

Mattern, Shannon. 2013. "Methodolatry and the Art of Measure: The New Wave of Urban Data Science." *Places Journal*, November 2013. https://placesjournal.org/article/methodolatry-and-the-art-of-measure/.

Mawdsley, Emma. 2012. "The Changing Geographies of Foreign Aid and Development Cooperation: Contributions from Gift Theory." *Transactions of the Institute of British Geographers* 37 (2): 256–72.

Maya Sierra, Maureén. 2005. "La toma del Palacio de Justicia: Una fractura en la historia Nacional." *Corte Suprema de Justicia—Revista* 20 (8): 28–45.

Maya Sierra, Tania. 2007. "Nuevo palacio de justicia de Bogotá: La arquitectura como máscara." *Ensayos: Historia y Teoría del Arte* 13:6–43.

Mbembe, Achille. 2002. "The Power of the Archive and Its Limits." In *Refiguring the Archive*, edited by Carolyn Hamilton, Veme Harris, Jane Taylor, Michele Pickover, Graeme Reici, and Razia Saleh. David Philip.

McCann, Eugene. 2011 "Urban Policy Mobilities and Global Circuits of Knowledge: Toward a Research Agenda." *Annals of the Association of American Geographers* 101 (1): 107–30.

McFarlane, Colin. 2011. *Learning the City: Knowledge and Translocal Assemblage.* Wiley-Blackwell.

McFarlane, Colin. 2016. "The Geographies of Urban Density: Topology, Politics and the City." *Progress in Human Geography* 40 (5): 629–48.

McFarlane, Colin. 2021. *Fragments of the City: Making and Remaking Urban Worlds.* University of California Press.

Medellín Pérez, Iris Alejandra. 2024. "Los fuegos que alimentaba el Cocinol: Combustibles domésticos, modernización, energía y política en Bogotá, 1970–1989." *Anuario Colombiano de Historia Social y de la Cultura* 51 (2): 119–48.

Medina, Medófilo. 1984. *La protesta urbana en Colombia en el siglo XX.* Ediciones Aurora.

Mejía Pavony, Germán. 1999. *Los años del cambio: Historia urbana de Bogotá, 1820–1910.* CEJA.

Merry, Sally Engle. 2009. *Human Rights and Gender Violence: Translating International Law into Local Justice.* University of Chicago Press.

Millar, Kathleen. 2018. *Reclaiming the Discarded: Life and Labor on Rio's Garbage Dump.* Duke University Press.

Miraftab, Faranak. 2004. "Public-Private Partnerships: The Trojan Horse of Neoliberal Development?" *Journal of Planning Education and Research* 24 (1): 89–101.

Miraftab, Faranak. 2009. "Insurgent Planning: Situating Radical Planning in the Global South." *Planning Theory* 8 (1): 32–50.

Mitchell, Timothy. 1988. *Colonizing Egypt.* Cambridge University Press.

Mitchell, Timothy. 1999. "Society, Economy, and the State Effect." In *State/Culture: State-Formation After the Cultural Turn*, edited by George Steinmetz. Cornell University Press.

Mitchell, Timothy. 2002. *Rule of Experts: Egypt, Techno-Politics, Modernity.* University of California Press.

Molano Camargo, Frank. 2010. "El Paro Cívico Nacional del 14 de septiembre de 1977 en Bogotá: Las clases subalternas contra el modelo hegemónico de ciudad." *Ciudad Paz-ando* 3 (2): 111–42.

Moncada, Eduardo. 2016. *Cities, Business, and the Politics of Urban Violence in Latin America.* Stanford University Press.

Monroe, Kristin V. 2016. *The Insecure City: Space, Power, and Mobility in Beirut.* Rutgers University Press.

Montero, Sergio, and Isabel Peñaranda. 2020. "An Urban Perspective on the Colombian 'Paro Nacional'—Spotlight on Urban Revolts." *International Journal of Urban and Regional Research.* https://www.ijurr.org/spotlight-on/urban-revolts/an-urban-perspective-on-the-colombian-paro-nacional/.

Moore, Donald. 2005. *Suffering for Territory: Race, Place, and Power in Zimbabwe.* Duke University Press.

Moore, Sally Falk. 2001. "Certainties Undone: Fifty Turbulent Years of Legal Anthropology, 1949–1999." *Journal of the Royal Anthropological Institute* 7 (1): 95–116.

Morris, Meghan L. 2017. "La cuestión de la tierra: El despojo y la posesión en el trabajo etnográfico." *Revista Colombiana de Antropología* 53 (1): 27–57.

Morris, Meghan L. 2019. "Speculative Fields: Property in the Shadow of Post-Conflict Colombia." *Cultural Anthropology* 34 (4): 580–606.

Morris Rincón, Ingrid. 2011. *En un lugar llamado El Cartucho: Crónica.* Instituto Distrital de Patrimonio Cultural.

Mumford, Lewis. 1961. *The City in History: Its Origins, Its Transformations, and Its Prospects.* Harcourt.

Munn, Nancy. 1992. *The Fame of Gawa: A Symbolic Study of Value Transformation in a Massim Society.* Duke University Press.

Muñoz, Catalina, and Friederike Fleischer. 2022. "Contentious Memories: History and Urban Redevelopment in Bogotá, Colombia." *Journal of Urban Affairs* 44 (1): 38–56.

Murphy, Keith. 2015. *Swedish Design: An Ethnography.* Cornell University Press.

Murphy, Keith. 2016. "Design and Anthropology." *Annual Review of Anthropology* 45:433–49.

Myers, Fred. 2000. "Ways of Place-Making." In *Culture, Landscape and the Environment: The Linare Lectures, 1997,* edited by Kate Flint and Howard Morphy. Oxford University Press.

Nader, Laura. 1969. "Up the Anthropologist: Perspectives Gained from Studying Up." In *Reinventing Anthropology,* edited by Dell Hymes. Pantheon Books.

Nader, Laura. 1997. "Controlling Processes: Tracing the Dynamic Components of Power." *Current Anthropology* 38 (5): 711–38.

Nakassis, Constantine V. 2013. "Materiality, Materialization." *HAU: Journal of Ethnographic Theory* 3 (3): 399–406.

Navaro, Yael, Zerrin Özlem Biner, Alice von Bieberstein, and Seda Altuğ. 2021. "Introduction: Reverberations of Violence Across Time and Space." In *Reverberations: Violence Across Time and Space,* edited by Yael Navaro, Zerrin Özlem Biner, Alice von Bieberstein, and Seda Altuğ. University of Pennsylvania Press.

Navaro-Yashin, Yael. 2007. "Make-Believe Papers, Legal Forms and the Counterfeit: Affective Interactions Between Documents and People in Britain and Cyprus." *Anthropological Theory* 7 (1): 79–98.

Navaro-Yashin, Yael. 2009. "Affective Spaces, Melancholic Objects: Ruination and the Production of Anthropological Knowledge." *Journal of the Royal Anthropological Institute* 15 (1): 1–18.

Navaro-Yashin, Yael. 2012. *The Make-Believe Space: Affective Geography in a Postwar Polity.* Duke University Press.

Ng'weno, Bettina. 2007. *Turf Wars: Territory and Citizenship in the Contemporary State.* Stanford University Press.

Niño Murcia, Carlos, and Sandra Reina Mendoza. 2010. *Carrera de la modernidad: Construcción de la carrera décima, Bogotá (1945–1960).* Instituto Distrital de Patrimonio Cultural.

Nordstrom, Carolyn. 1997. *A Different Kind of War Story.* University of Pennsylvania Press.

Oelze, Micah. 2017. "Demolishing Legitimacy: Bogotá's Urban Reforms for the 1948 Pan-American Conference." *Journal of Latin American Studies* 49 (1): 83–113.

Offner, Amy. 2019. *Sorting Out the Mixed Economy: The Rise and Fall of Welfare and Developmental States in the Americas.* Princeton University Press.

Ojeda, Diana. 2012. "Green Pretexts: Ecotourism, Neoliberal Conservation and Land Grabbing in Tayrona National Natural Park, Colombia." *Journal of Peasant Studies* 39 (2): 357–75.

Ojeda, Diana. 2016. "Los paisajes del despojo: Propuestas para un análisis desde las reconfiguraciones socioespaciales." *Revista Colombiana de Antropología* 52 (2): 19–43.

Ojeda, Diana, and María Camila González. 2018. "Elusive Space: Peasants and Resource Politics in the Colombian Caribbean." In *Land Rights, Biodiversity Conservation and Justice: Rethinking Parks and People*, edited by Sharlene Mollet and Thembela Kepe. Routledge.

Ojeda, Diana, and Lina Pinto García. 2020. "The Militarization of Life Under War, 'Post-Conflict,' and the COVID-19 Crisis." *Platypus: The CASTAC Blog*, April 6. https://blog.castac.org/2020/04/the-militarization-of-life-under-war-post-conflict-and-the-covid-19-crisis/.

O'Neill, Kevin, and Benjamin Fogarty-Valenzuela. 2013. "Verticality." *Journal of the Royal Anthropological Institute* 19 (2): 378–89.

O'Neill, Kevin, and Kedron Thomas, eds. 2011. *Securing the City: Neoliberalism, Space, and Insecurity in Postwar Guatemala*. Duke University Press.

Ong, Aihwa. 2005. "Ecologies of Expertise: Assembling Flows, Managing Citizenship." In *Global Assemblages: Technology, Politics, and Ethics as Anthropological Problems*, edited by Aihwa Ong and Stephen J. Collier. Blackwell.

Orozco, Armando. 1988. "Festival Iberoamericano de Teatro Bogotá-88." *Voz*, April 7.

Palacios, Marco. 1979. *El café en Colombia (1870–1970): Una historia económica, social y política*. Editorial Presencia Ltda.

Palacios, Marco. 2006. *Between Legitimacy and Violence: A History of Colombia, 1875–2002*. Duke University Press.

Peattie, Lisa. 1987. *Planning: Rethinking Ciudad Guayana*. University of Michigan Press.

Peck, Jamie. 2016. "Economic Rationality Meets Celebrity Urbanology: Exploring Edward Glaeser's City." *International Journal of Urban and Regional Research* 40 (1): 1–30.

Peña Ardila, Nicolás. 2012. "Colombia audiovisual, años 80." PhD diss., Pontificia Universidad Javeriana.

Peñaranda, Isabel, and Julián Gómez-Delgado. 2019. "Colombia's New Awakening." *Jacobin*, December 8.

Pérez, Federico. 2016. "Excavating Legal Landscapes: Juridical Archaeology and the Politics of Bureaucratic Materiality in Bogotá, Colombia." *Cultural Anthropology* 31 (2): 215–43.

Pérez, Federico. 2020. "Materializing (In)securities: Urban Terrain, Paperwork, and Housing in Downtown Bogotá." *Anthropological Quarterly* 93 (1): 1491–522.

Pérez Ballén, Henry. 2015. *Historia de una pasión: La telenovela colombiana según nueve libretistas nacionales*. Universidad Jorge Tadeo Lozano.

Pérez Fernández, Federico. 2010. "Laboratorios de reconstrucción urbana: Hacia una antropología de la política urbana en Colombia." *Antípoda* 10:51–84.

Pergolis, Juan Carlos. 1998. *Bogotá fragmentada: Cultura y espacio urbano a fines del siglo XX*. Tercer Mundo Editores-Universidad Piloto de Colombia.

Perry, Keisha-Khan Y. 2013. *Black Women Against the Land Grab: The Fight for Racial Justice in Brazil*. University of Minnesota Press.

Pinilla, Gabriel. 2014. *Policarpo: Historias del barrio Poilcarpa contadas por Luis Hernando Forero*. Alcaldía Mayor de Bogotá.

Pinilla, Juan Felipe, and Martín Arteaga. 2021. "Governance Through Conflict: Consensus Building in the Fenicia Urban Renewal Project in Bogotá, Colombia." *Built Environment* 47 (1): 31–55.

Pinilla Pineda, Juan Felipe. 2010. "Los avances del proceso de implementación de los instrumentos de la Ley 388 de 1997 en Bogotá." In *Bogotá en el cambio de siglo: Promesas y realidades*, edited by Samuel Jaramillo. OLACCHI.

Porter, Libby, Ananya Roy, and Crystal Legacy. 2021. "Planning Solidarity? From Silence to Refusal." *Planning Theory & Practice* 22 (1): 111–38.

Proa. 1947. "La ciudad del empleado en Bogotá." *Proa* 7:7–11.

Puentes, Ana. 2021. "Grafiti y protesta social en Bogotá: Los muros que no callan en el paro." *El Tiempo*, October 26.

Quijano, Aníbal. 2000. "Colonialidad del poder, Eurocentrismo y América Latina." In *Colonialidad del saber, Eurocentrismo y ciencias sociales*, edited by Edgardo Lander. CLACSO-UNESCO.

Rabie, Kareem. 2021. *Palestine Is Throwing a Party and Everyone Is Invited: Capital and State Building in the West Bank*. Duke University Press.

Rabinow, Paul. (1989) 1995. *French Modern: Norms and Forms of the Social Environment*. University of Chicago Press.

Rama, Angel. (1984) 1996. *The Lettered City*. Translated and edited by John Charles Chasteen. Duke University Press.

Ramírez, María Clemencia. 1997. "Hacia una nueva comprensión de la violencia en Colombia: Concepciones teóricas y metodológicas sobre violencia y cultura." In *Nuevas visiones sobre la violencia en Colombia,* edited by Alvaro Camacho, Alvaro Guzmán, María Clemencia Ramírez, and Fernando Gaitán. IEPRI/FESCOL.

Ramírez, María Clemencia. 2011. *Between the Guerrillas and the State: The Cocalero Movement, Citizenship, and Identity in the Colombian Amazon*. Duke University Press.

Ramírez, María Clemencia. 2019. "Militarism on the Colombian Periphery in the Context of Illegality, Counterinsurgency, and the Postconflict." *Current Anthropology* 60 (S19): S134–47.

Rancière, Jacques. 2006. *The Politics of Aesthetics: The Distribution of the Sensible*. Translated by Gabriel Rockhill. Continuum.

Ranganathan, Malini, David L. Pike, and Sapana Doshi. 2023. *Corruption Plots: Stories, Ethics, and Publics of the Late Capitalist City*. Cornell University Press.

Rao, Vyjayanthi. 2006. "Slum as Theory: The South/Asian City and Globalization." *International Journal of Urban and Regional Research* 30 (1): 225–32.

Rao, Vyjayanthi. 2007. "Proximate Distances: The Phenomenology of Density in Mumbai." *Built Environment* 33 (2): 227–48.

Rao, Vyjayanthi. 2009. "Embracing Urbanism: The City as Archive." *New Literary History* 40 (2): 371–83.

Rao, Vyjayanthi. 2015a. "Infra-City: Speculations on Flux and History in Infrastructure-Making." In *Infrastructural Lives: Urban Infrastructure in Context*, edited by Stephen Graham and Colin McFarlane. Routledge.

Rao, Vyjayanthi. 2015b. "Speculation, Now." In *Speculation, Now: Essays and Artwork*, edited by Vyjayanthi Rao, Prem Krishnamurthy, and Carin Kuoni. Duke University Press.

Restrepo Jaramillo, Juan Esteban. 2016. "Actores sociales durante el gobierno de Alfonso López Michelsen, Colombia (1974–1978)." *Revista Forum*, no. 8/9: 9–29.

Revista Arcadia. 2019. "La molestia de Peñalosa con la decisión de declarar patrimonio cultural los columbarios del Cementerio Central." October 11.

Riaño Alcalá, Pilar, and María Victoria Uribe. 2016. "Constructing Memory Amidst War: The Historical Memory Group of Colombia." *International Journal of Transitional Justice* 10 (1): 6–24.

Ricoeur, Paul. 1984. *Time and Narrative*. Vol. 1. University of Chicago Press.

Riles, Annelise. 2006. Introduction to *Documents: Artifacts of Modern Knowledge*, edited by Annelise Riles. University of Michigan Press.

Ritterbusch, Amy. 2016. "Mobilities at Gunpoint: The Geographies of (Im)mobility of Transgender Sex Workers in Colombia." *Annals of American Association of Geographers* 106 (2): 422–33.

Ritterbusch, Amy, and El Cilencio. 2020. "'We Will Always Be Street.'" *City* 24 (1–2): 210–19.

Rivera Cusicanqui, Silvia. 2012. "Ch'ixinakax utxiwa: A Reflection on the Practices and Discourses of Decolonization." *South Atlantic Quarterly* 111 (1): 95–109.

Robledo Gómez, Ángela María, and Patricia Rodríguez Santana. 2008. *Emergencia del sujeto excluido: Aproximación genealógica a la no-ciudad en Bogotá*. Editorial Pontificia Universidad Javeriana.

Roca, Juan Manuel. 2012. "La memoria, un mapa por armar." In *Bogotá, ciudad memoria*, by Centro de Memoria, Paz y Reconciliación. Alcaldía Mayor de Bogotá.

Rodgers, Dennis, and Bruce O'Neill. 2012. "Infrastructural Violence: Introduction to the Special Issue." *Ethnography* 13 (4): 401–12.

Rodríguez Silva, Roberto, Jean-François Jolly, and Alexander Niño Soto. 2004. *Algunos apuntes sobre causas e indicadores del deterioro urbano: Contribuciones a un debate sobre vitalidad urbana*. Pontificia Universidad Javeriana.

Roitman, Janet. 2014. *Anti-Crisis*. Duke University Press.

Rojas, Cristina. 2002. *Civilization and Violence: Regimes of Representation in Nineteenth-Century Colombia*. University of Minnesota Press.

Roldán, Mary. 2003. "Wounded Medellín: Narcotics Traffic Against a Background of Industrial Decline." In *Wounded Cities: Destruction and Reconstruction in a Globalized World*, edited by Ida Susser and Jane Schneider. Berg.

Rolnik, Raquel. 2019. *Urban Warfare: Housing Under the Empire of Finance*. Translated by Felipe Hirschhorn. Verso.

Roseberry, William. 1994. "Hegemony and the Language of Contention." In *Everyday Forms of State Formation: Revolution and the Negotiation of Rule in Modern Mexico*, edited by Gilbert M. Joseph and Daniel Nugent. Duke University Press.

Roy, Ananya. 2005. "Urban Informality: Toward an Epistemology of Planning." *Journal of the American Planning Association* 71 (2): 147–58.

Roy, Ananya. 2009. "Civic Governmentality: The Politics of Inclusion in Beirut and Mumbai." *Antipode* 41 (1): 159–79.

Roy, Ananya. 2011. "Slumdog Cities: Rethinking Subaltern Urbanism." *International Journal of Urban and Regional Research* 35 (2): 223–38.

Roy, Ananya. 2016. "Who's Afraid of Postcolonial Theory?" *International Journal of Urban and Regional Research* 40 (1): 200–209.

Rutas del Conflicto. 2019. "Masacre de Honduras y La Negra." October 16. https://rutasdelconflicto.com/masacres/honduras-la-negra.

Saénz Rovner, Eduardo. 1992. *La ofensiva empresarial: Industriales, políticos y violencia en los años 40 en Colombia*. Tercer Mundo.

Safford, Frank, and Marco Palacios. 2002. *Colombia: Fragmented Land, Divided Society*. Oxford University Press.

Said, Edward. 1979. *Orientalism*. Vintage.

Salazar Ferro, José. 2018. *Construir la ciudad moderna: Superar el subdesarrollo; Enfoques de la planeación urbana en Bogota (1950–2010)*. Universidad Nacional de Colombia.

Salcedo Fidalgo, Andrés. 2015. *Víctimas y trasegares: Forjadores de ciudad en Colombia, 2002–2005*. Universidad Nacional de Colombia.

Salcedo Fidalgo, Andrés, Carlos José Suárez, and Elkin Vallejo. 2010. "Faces da ilegalidade em Bogotá." *Tempo Social* 22 (2): 123–42.

Saldarriaga Roa, Alberto. 2000. *Bogotá siglo XX: Urbanismo, arquitectura y vida urbana.* Alcaldía Mayor de Bogotá, D.C.

Salge Ferro, Manuel, and Luis Gonzalo Jarmillo E. 2021. "El Monumento a los Héroes es una metáfora ciudadana." *Cerosetenta*, September 27. https://cerosetenta. uniandes.edu.co/monumento-heroes-metafora-ciudadana/.

Samara, Tony Roshan. 2010. "Policing Development: Urban Renewal as Neo-Liberal Security Strategy." *Urban Studies* 47 (1): 197–214.

Sanabria Ortiz, Lizbeth Katherine. 2021. "Antimonumento a los Héroes: El aporte del arte juvenil a la construcción de un sentido común crítico en Bogotá en el marco del Estallido Social." Specialization thesis, Universidad Nacional de Colombia.

Sanchez-Beltran, Maria del Pilar. 2022. "Welfare as Warfare: The Role of Modern Architecture During the Colombian Dictatorship." *Architecture and Culture* 10 (1): 96–116.

Sandilands, Roger. 1990. *The Life and Political Economy of Lauchlin Currie: New Dealer, Presidential Advisor, and Development Economist.* Duke University Press.

Sarmiento Rojas, Stephanie Carolina. 2017. *Santa Bárbara, el barrio que no soportó las tempestades: Recuperación de una historia disidente en el proceso de construcción del relato histórico de Bogotá entre 1980 y 1983.* Editorial Universidad del Rosario.

Scheper-Hughes, Nancy, and Philippe Bourgois. 2004. "Introduction: Making Sense of Violence." In *Violence in War and Peace: An Anthology*, edited by Nancy Scheper-Hughes and Philippe Bourgois. Blackwell.

Schön, David. 1983. *The Reflective Practitioner: How Professionals Think in Action.* Basic Books.

Schwenkel, Christina. 2020. *Building Socialism: The Afterlife of East German Architecture in Urban Vietnam.* Duke University Press.

Scott, Felicity D. 2016. *Outlaw Territories: Environments of Insecurity/Architectures of Counterinsurgency.* Zone Books.

Scott, James C. 1998. *Seeing like a State: How Certain Schemes to Improve the Human Condition Have Failed.* Yale University Press.

Sekula, Allan. 2014. "Photography and the Limits of National Identity." *Grey Room* 55:28–33.

Semana. 1983a. "'Don Chinche': Nuevo fenómeno de la T.V." May 16.

Semana. 1983b. "Un Robin Hood paisa." April 19.

Serje, Margarita. 2005. *El revés de la nación: Territorios salvajes, fronteras y tierras de nadie.* Ediciones Uniandes.

Shange, Savannah. 2019. *Progressive Dystopia: Abolition, Antiblackness, and Schooling in San Francisco.* Duke University Press.

Shaw, Rosalind, and Lars Waldorf, with Pierre Hazan, eds. 2010. *Localizing Transitional Justice: Interventions and Priorities After Mass Violence.* Stanford University Press.

Simmel, Georg. (1903) 1995. "The Metropolis and Mental Life." In *Metropolis: Center and Symbol of Our Times*, edited by Philip Kasinitz. New York University Press.

Simone, AbdouMaliq. 2004. "People as Infrastructure: Intersecting Fragments in Johannesburg." *Public Culture* 16 (3): 407–29.

Simone, AbdouMaliq. 2010. *City Life from Jakarta to Dakar: Movements at the Crossroads.* Routledge.

Simone, AbdouMaliq, and Edgar Pieterse. 2017. *New Urban Worlds: Inhabiting Dissonant Times*. Polity.

Smith, Neil. 1996. *The New Urban Frontier: Gentrification and the Revanchist City*. Routledge.

Smolka, Martim. 2013. *Implementing Value Capture in Latin America: Policies and Tools for Urban Development*. Lincoln Institute of Land Policy.

Sopranzetti, Claudio. 2017. "Framed by Freedom: Emancipation and Opression in Post-Fordist Thailand." *Cultural Anthropology* 32 (1): 68–92.

Stewart, Kathleen. 2007. *Ordinary Affects*. Duke University Press.

Stewart, Kathleen. 2011. "Atmopheric Attunements." *Environment and Planning D: Society and Space* 29:445–53.

Stoetzer, Bettina. 2018. "Ruderal Ecologies: Rethinking Nature, Migration, and the Urban Landscape in Berlin." *Cultural Anthropology* 33 (2): 295–323.

Stoler, Ann Laura. 2009. *Along the Archival Grain: Epistemic Anxieties and Colonial Common Sense*. Princeton University Press.

Stoler, Ann Laura. 2013a. "Introduction: 'The Rot Remains'; From Ruins to Ruination." In *Imperial Debris: On Ruins and Ruination*, edited by Ann Laura Stoler. Duke University Press.

Stoler, Ann Laura. 2013b. Preface to *Imperial Debris: On Ruins and Ruination*, edited by Ann Laura Stoler. Duke University Press.

Stoler, Ann Laura. 2016. *Duress: Imperial Durabilities in Our Time*. Duke University Press.

Subramanian, Ajantha. 2009. *Shorelines: Space and Rights in South India*. Stanford University Press.

Suchman, Lucy. 1987. *Plans and Situated Actions: The Problem of Human-Machine Communication*. Cambridge University Press.

Suchman, Lucy. 2011. "Anthropological Relocations and the Limits of Design." *Annual Review of Anthropology* 40 (1): 1–18.

Suchman, Lucy. 2021. "Border Thinking About Anthropologies/Designs." In *Designs and Anthropologies: Frictions and Affinities*, edited by Keith Murphy and Eitan Wilf. University of New Mexico Press.

Suchman, Lucy, Karolina Follis, and Jutta Weber. 2017. "Tracking and Targeting: Sociotechnologies of (In)security." *Science, Technology, and Human Values* 42 (6): 983–1002.

Tamayo Arboleda, Fernando, and Mariana Valverde. 2021. "The Travels of a Set of Numbers: The Multiple Networks Enabled by the Colombian 'Estrato' System." *Social and Legal Studies* 30 (5): 685–703.

Tarchópulos, Doris. 2022. *Le Corbusier, Sert y Wiener: Las huellas del plan para Bogotá*. Editorial Pontificia Universidad Javeriana.

Tate, Winifred. 2007. *Counting the Dead: The Culture and Politics of Human Rights Activism in Colombia*. University of California Press.

Tate, Winifred. 2015. "The Aspirational State: State Effects in Putumayo." In *State Theory and Andean Politics: New Approaches to the Study of Rule*, edited by Christopher Krupa and David Nugent. University of Pennsylvania Press.

Taussig, Michael. 1999. *Defacement: Public Secrecy and the Labor of the Negative*. Stanford University Press.

Taussig, Michael. 2003. *Law in a Lawless Land: Diary of a Limpieza in Colombia*. University of Chicago Press.

Taylor, Diana. 2009. "Performing Ruins." In *Telling Ruins in Latin America*, edited by Michael J. Lazzara and Vicky Unruh. Palgrave Macmillan.

Theidon, Kimberly. 2010. "Histories of Innocence: Postwar Stories in Peru." In *Localizing Transitional Justice: Interventions and Priorities After Mass Violence*, edited by Rosalind Shaw and Lars Waldorf with Pierre Hazan. Stanford University Press.

Theidon, Kimberly. 2012. *Intimate Enemies: Violence and Reconciliation in Peru.* University of Pennsylvania Press.

Theidon, Kimberly. 2015. "Pasts Imperfect: Talking About Justice with Former Combatants in Colombia." In *Genocide and Mass Violence: Memory, Symptom, and Recovery*, edited by Devon E. Hinton and Alexander L. Hinton. Cambridge University Press.

Till, Karen E. 2012. "Wounded Cities: Memory-Work and a Place-Based Ethics of Care." *Political Geography* 31 (1): 3–14.

Torres Carrillo, Alfonso. (1993) 2013. *La ciudad en la sombra: Barrios y luchas populares en Bogotá, 1950–1977.* Universidad Piloto de Colombia.

Trouillot, Michel-Rolph. 1995. *Silencing the Past: Power and the Production of History.* Beacon.

Tsing, Anna. 2015. *The Mushroom at the End of the World: On the Possibility of Life in Capitalist Ruins.* Princeton University Press.

Ugarte, Magdalena. 2014. "Ethics, Discourse, or Rights? A Discussion About a Decolonizing Project in Planning." *Journal of Planning Literature* 29 (4): 403–14.

Urbina Vanegas, Diana Carolina. 2015. "Antes y después del centro cultural: Renovación urbana y desplazamiento en Bogotá." *Revista Colombiana de Antropología* 51 (1): 217–44.

Uribe, Simón. 2017. *Frontier Road: Power, History, and the Everyday State in the Colombian Amazon.* John Wiley & Sons.

Uribe Mallarino, Consuelo. 2008. "Estratifcación social en Bogotá: De la política pública a la dinámica de la segregación social." *Universitas Humanística* 65:139–71.

Uribe Tobón, Carlos Alberto. 1990. "Cultura, cultura de la violencia, y violentología." *Revista de Antropología y Arqueología* 6 (2): 83–100.

United Nations Conference on Human Settlements. 1976a. *Background to Habitat.* Canadian Habitat Secretariat.

United Nations Conference on Human Settlements. 1976b. *Vancouver Declaration on Human Settlements.* UN Doc A/CONF.70/15.

Universidad de los Andes. 1972. "Centro de Planeación y Urbanismo C.P.U." *Boletín Informativo* 23–24, January–February.

UNOSAT (United Nations Satellite Centre). 2024. *Gaza Strip Comprehensive Damage Assessment.* September 26. https://unosat.org/products/3984.

Valencia Tovar, Álvaro. 1969. "Estructura y filosofía de un plan de erradicación de tugurios urbanos." In *Urbanización y marginalidad.* Asociación Colombiana de Facultades de Medicina.

Valverde, Mariana. 2014. "'Time Thickens, Takes On Flesh': Spatiotemporal Dynamics in Law." In *The Expanding Spaces of Law: A Timely Legal Geography*, edited by Irus Braverman, Nicholas Blomley, David Delaney, and Alexandre (Sandy) Kedar. Stanford University Press.

Vargas, Jenniffer, and Sonia Uribe. 2017. "State, War, and Land Dispossession: The Multiple Paths to Land Concentration." *Journal of Agrarian Change* 17 (4): 749–58.

Vega Cantor, Renán. 2016. "La masacre del Palacio de Justicia: Ejemplo emblemático del terrorismo de estado en Colombia (6–7 de noviembre de 1985)." *El Ágora U.S.B.* 16 (1): 107–33.

Verdery, Katherine. 2003. *The Vanishing Hectare: Property and Value in Postsocialist Transylvania.* Cornell University Press.

Vignolo, Paolo. 2013. "¿Quién gobierna la ciudad de los muertos?: Políticas de la memoria y desarrollo urbano en Bogotá." *Memoria y Sociedad* 17 (35): 125–42.

Villaveces-Izquierdo, Santiago. 1998. "Violentologists and Magistrates: Questions of Justice and Responses to Violence in Contemporary Colombia." PhD diss., Rice University.

Virilio, Paul. 1994. *Bunker Archaeology*. Translated by George Collins. Princeton Architectural Press.

Virilio, Paul, and Sylvère Lotringer. 1983. *Pure War*. Semiotext(e).

Voz. 1983. "¡Cocinol! ¡cocinol! ¡cocinol!" September 15.

Wade, Peter. 1993. *Blackness and Race Mixture: The Dynamics of Racial Identity in Colombia*. Johns Hopkins University Press.

Waterhouse, Amy C. 2019. "Colombia's National Protests Show That Infrastructure, Too, Is Politics." *NACLA Report on the Americas*, December 3. https://nacla.org/news/2019/12/03/colombia-national-protests-infrastructure-politics-dilan-cruz.

Weber, Max. 1978. *Economy and Society: An Outline of Interpretive Sociology*. University of California Press.

Weinstein, Liza. 2017. "Insecurity as Confinement: The Entrenched Politics of Staying Put in Delhi and Mumbai." *International Sociology* 32 (4): 512–31.

Weizman, Eyal. 2007. *Hollow Land: Israel's Architecture of Occupation*. Verso.

Weizman, Eyal. 2017. *Forensic Architecture: Violence at the Threshold of Detectability*. MIT Press.

Weld, Kirsten. 2014. *Paper Cadavers: The Archives of Dictatorship in Guatemala*. Duke University Press.

West, Harry G., and Todd Sanders, eds. 2003. *Transparency and Conspiracy: Ethnographies of Suspicion in the New World Order*. Duke University Press.

Williams, Raymond. 1975. *The City and the Country*. Oxford University Press.

Williams, Raymond. 1977. *Marxism and Literature*. Oxford University Press.

Wilmott, Clancy. 2020. "Surface: Seeing, Solidifying, and Scaling Urban Space in Hong Kong." In *Voluminous States: Sovereignty, Materiality, and the Territorial Imagination*, edited by Franck Billé. Duke University Press.

Wittgenstein, Ludwig. 1953. *Philosophical Investigations*. Translated by G. E. M. Anscombe. Macmillan.

Wright, Gwendolyn. 1991. *The Politics of Design in French Colonial Urbanism*. University of Chicago Press.

Yiftachel, Oren. 2006. *Ethnocracy: Land and Identity Politics in Israel/Palestine*. University of Pennsylvania Press.

Zeiderman, Austin. 2016. *Endangered City: The Politics of Security and Risk in Bogotá*. Duke University Press.

Zhang, Li. 2010. *Strangers in Paradise: Middle-Class Living in a Chinese Metropolis*. Cornell University Press.

Zorro, Carlos, and Edgar Reveiz. 1974. *Primera etapa de estudios sobre los inquilinatos (vivienda compartida en arrendamientos)*. CEDE (Centro de Estudios Sobre Desarrollo Económico), Universidad de los Andes.

Index

Alcaldía, 64, 114, 116, 155, 222
Arango, Andrés Pastrana, 59
Andrés, 157, 161, 164, 169–70, 172–74
Avenida de los Cerros, 42–43

Bogotá, 51–52, 59, 62, 67, 73, 75, 81,
    111, 180–81, 235; and activists, 233;
    administration of, 1, 12; and affluent
    neighborhoods, 15–16; and Alcaldía Mayor
    de Bogotá, 114; and beautification projects,
    34; and Carrera Décima, 36; and Centro
    de Memoria Paz y Reconciliación, 25; and
    city center, 1–2, 4, 14–15, 19, 28, 31–32,
    34–39, 40–41, 58, 63, 73, 92–94, 110, 112,
    124–25, 128–29, 132–33, 138, 142, 151,
    155–56, 167–68, 177, 193, 200, 210, 217, 219,
    221–22, 233; and *ciudad memoria*, 49; and
    Ciudad Memoria, 27; and criminal violence,
    31; and cultural center, 103–4; culture of,
    70; and decay, 129–30; and densification,
    38, 158, 183; and development, 47; and El
    Cartucho, 61; and elite, 146; and Empresa
    de Renovación Urbana de Bogotá D.C., 102;
    and historical memory, 26; and insecurity,
    10; and Instituto de Crédito Territorial (ICT),
    39–40; and main plaza, 1; and MEPOT, 179;
    north, 131, 185; and political violence, 30,
    35, 156; and renewal plans, 17–19, 30, 44,
    193, 203; and Sabana de Bogotá, 184; and
    Secretaría Distrital de Planeación, 13–14;
    and security, 253n76; and terrorism, 4; and
    theater festival, 250n113; uprising, 219; and
    urban governance, 12; and urban planning,
    28–30, 33, 41, 55, 124, 160–61, 163–64, 166,
    185, 188–89, 192, 237–38; and urbanization,
    19; and urban mafias, 2; and urban protest,
    42; and urban warfare, 228; west, 140; and
    western periphery, 39
Bogotá Humana, 2
Bronx, 52
bureaucracy, 10, 14, 94, 120–21, 161; aesthetics
    of, 90, 107; forms of, 90; landscapes of, 101;
    materialities of, 91, 106; practices of, 89;
    state, 71; urban, 17, 90, 116, 150; violence
    of, 266n32

bureaucratic activism, 116
bureaucratic artifacts, 89–91, 106–7, 119,
    254n6
bureaucratic force, 4, 15–16
bureaucratic infrastructure, 37
bureaucratic insecurity, 93, 96, 98
bureaucratic knowledge, 105, 107
bureaucratic logics, 3
bureaucratic management, 161
bureaucratic power, 120
bureaucratic routines, 14
bureaucratic socialización, 203
bureaucratic violence, 3, 15, 89, 92, 115,
    117–18, 120

Calle Real, 1
capitalism, 6, 8, 29, 95, 98, 127, 149, 201,
    257n84, 263n45; and "creative destruction",
    54; and expansion, 53, 100; and exploitation,
    45; global, 65; neoliberal, 260n3; and
    productivity, 211; racial, 128; and
    urbanization, 127
capitalist colonial modernity, 187–88, 209
capitalist development, 38, 42, 48, 94, 128, 226,
    255n41
Cementerio de los Pobres, 25, 29
Center for Planning and Urbanism (CPU),
    198–200
citizenship, 5, 10, 189, 196, 200, 203, 219,
    228, 237–38; contradictions of, 120; and
    governance, 129, 151; infrastructure, 116;
    and law, 128; liberal, 92; middle-class, 39;
    modalities of, 116; and nation building,
    14; practices of, 109; propertied, 99, 101,
    119, 128, 141, 226; and property, 92, 95, 99,
    110, 150, 196; regimes of, 120; spaces of,
    13; traumatic, 115; urban, 12; and urban
    governance, 29; and urbanity, 122
cocinol, 220–22
Consejo Territorial de Planeación Distrital
    (CTPD), 169
Consuelo, 75–78
Cortés, Jorge Gaitán, 38, 64–65
counterinsurgency, 2, 7, 19, 31, 35, 38, 41, 75,
    197, 229, 243n8, 249n73, 253n74

www.ingramcontent.com/pod-product-compliance
Lightning Source LLC
Chambersburg PA
CBHW022303280326
41932CB00010B/958